Advance Praise for *Multifractal Volatility*

"Calvet and Fisher provide a valuable and thorough development of a novel class of models of financial market volatility. The methods and models exposited so nicely in their book should be part of the toolkit of researchers interested in understanding and characterizing the stochastic nature of volatility fluctuations. Their book is simultaneously accessible and complete. It shows how to use these models in practice, and it provides a rigorous foundation for their application."
—**Lars Hansen,** *Livingston Distinguished Service Professor, University of Chicago, IL*

"Volatility is a central concern of modern financial econometrics, challenging econometricians to build plausible models and practical methods of inference. Calvet and Fisher draw together the ingredients of a promising new research agenda, integrating a decade of work on multifractal modeling into a masterful overview of the field of volatility, demonstrating the advantages of Markov switching multifractals in aggregating components of differing persistence and showing us how rare events need not be studied in isolation as curiosa. A compelling read for financial theorists and practitioners."
—**Peter C. B. Philips,** *Sterling Professor of Economics & Statistics, Yale University, CT*

"To accommodate the high persistence and variability of volatility in financial time series, Calvet and Fisher developed the class of Markov-Switching Multifractal models. This book, which summarizes ten years of their research, is of great interest to researchers in asset pricing and essential reading for practitioners working on risk management or volatility forecasting."
—**Jose Scheinkman,** *Theodore Wells '29 Professor of Economics, Princeton University, NJ*

MULTIFRACTAL VOLATILITY
Theory, Forecasting, and Pricing

Laurent E. Calvet

Tanaka Business School, Imperial College
HEC Paris, France

Adlai J. Fisher

Sauder School of Business,
University of British Columbia

AMSTERDAM • BOSTON • HEIDELBERG • LONDON
NEW YORK • OXFORD • PARIS • SAN DIEGO
SAN FRANCISCO • SINGAPORE • SYDNEY • TOKYO

Academic Press is an imprint of Elsevier

Academic Press is an imprint of Elsevier
30 Corporate Drive, Suite 400, Burlington, MA 01803, USA
525 B Street, Suite 1900, San Diego, California 92101-4495, USA
84 Theobald's Road, London WC1X 8RR, UK

Library of Congress Cataloging-in-Publication Data
Application submitted

British Library Cataloguing-in-Publication Data
A catalogue record for this book is available from the British Library.

ISBN: 978-0-12-150013-9

For information on all Academic Press publications
visit our website at *www.elsevierdirect.com*

Printed in the United States of America
08 09 10   9 8 7 6 5 4 3 2 1

Working together to grow
libraries in developing countries

www.elsevier.com | www.bookaid.org | www.sabre.org

ELSEVIER   BOOK AID
              International   Sabre Foundation

Contents

Acknowledgments

Our interest in fractal modeling was spurred during our graduate years at Yale by conversations with Benoît Mandelbrot, the father of fractal geometry. This interaction evolved into the collaborative development of the Multifractal Model of Asset Returns (MMAR), which was originally circulated in three Cowles Foundation Discussion Papers (Calvet, Fisher, and Mandelbrot, 1997). The core of this work was eventually published in the *Review of Economics and Statistics* in 2002.

In order to develop practical applications such as volatility forecasting and pricing, we then independently developed a Markov model with multifrequency characteristics, which we called the Markov-switching multifractal (MSM). We first presented MSM, both in discrete and continuous time, at the 1999 National Bureau of Economic Research Summer Institute organized by Francis Diebold and Kenneth West, and published this work in the corresponding special issue of *Journal of Econometrics*. MSM stimulated a flow of subsequent research on the econometric and pricing applications of multifrequency volatility risk, which we are now presenting in this book.

Many of the chapters draw heavily from earlier publications in academic journals. The presentation of discrete-time MSM in Chapter 3 follows "How to Forecast Long-Run Volatility: Regime-Switching and the Estimation of Multifractal Processes," presented in 2002 at the CIRANO Conference on Extremal Events in Finance, organized by René Garcia and Eric Renault, and published in the *Journal of Financial Econometrics*. Multivariate MSM in Chapter 4 was presented in September 2003 at the Penn-IGIER conference organized by Francis Diebold and Carlo Favero, and appeared in the *Journal of Econometrics* under the title "Volatility Comovement: A Multifrequency Approach." This article is joint with Samuel Thompson, a former Harvard colleague now at Arrowstreet Capital, L.P.

Chapters 6 and 8 follow the *Review of Economics and Statistics* article "Multifractality in Asset Returns: Theory and Evidence." The discussion of continuous-time MSM in Chapter 7 is a thoroughly revised version of the *Journal of Econometrics* publication "Forecasting Multifractal Volatility." Chapter 9 is based on "Multifrequency News and Stock Returns," which was first presented at Wharton in March 2003 and appeared in the *Journal of Financial Economics*. Chapter 10 borrows from "Multifrequency Jump-Diffusions: An Equilibrium Approach," which was prepared for the 2005 NSF/CEME Conference in Honor of Gérard Debreu organized by Chris Shannon at UC Berkeley and was published in *Journal of Mathematical Economics*. We have liberally added and subtracted from these earlier papers in order to produce a coherent book.

We would like to thank many colleagues and friends who have contributed to the development of the multifrequency research presented in this book. We are especially grateful to John Campbell and Francis Diebold for their continued support over the past decade. During our graduate years, the faculty of Yale University gave us insightful feedback, and John Geanakoplos, Peter Phillips, Robert Shiller and Christopher Sims in particular provided us with invaluable help. We thank Samuel B. Thompson for the fruitful collaboration on which Chapter 4 is based. We also acknowledge the generous help of Karim Abadir, Andrew Abel, Torben Andersen, Donald Andrews, Tim Bollerslev, Michael Brandt, Andrea Buraschi, Bernard Cornet, Walter Distaso, Darrell Duffie, Robert Engle, Francesco Franzoni, René Garcia, William Goetzmann, James Hamilton, Lars Hansen, Oliver Hart, Jean Jacod, Guido Kuersteiner, Guy Laroque, Oliver Linton, Eric Maskin, Nour Meddahi, Andrew Metrick, Marcelo Moreira, Jacques Olivier, Jack Porter, Stephen Ross, Jose Scheinkman, Neil Shephard, Bruno Solnik, Robert Stambaugh, Jeremy Stein, James Stock, Jessica Wachter, Kenneth West, Amir Yaron, Paolo Zaffaroni, Stanley Zin, and our current and former colleagues at Harvard, HEC Paris, Imperial College London, New York University, and the University of British Columbia.

We thank Karen Maloney, our editor at Elsevier, who encouraged us to write this book and displayed considerable enthusiasm throughout the duration of this project. We are also grateful to Roxana Boboc and Melinda Ritchie for their patient assistance.

Last but not least, we thank our families for their love and kind support while this work was under way. This book is dedicated to them.

Foreword

The study of financial markets has become one of the most active and productive empirical endeavors in the social sciences. A cynic, or a trained economist, might say that the volume of financial research reflects the high price that market participants are willing to pay for it, but there are also deep intellectual reasons for the interest in financial market data.

First, these data are abundant at all frequencies from tick-by-tick data at one extreme, to century-by-century data at the other, and across multiple correlated assets. Such data abundance is atypical in the social sciences, and it compensates to some degree for the fact that the data are generated by the interactions of investors rather than by controlled experiments.

Second, the uncertainty that financial econometricians face when estimating their models is the same uncertainty that investors face when they trade in asset markets and determine market prices. As Campbell, Lo, and MacKinlay (1997) express it, "The random fluctuations that require the use of statistical theory to estimate and test financial models are intimately related to the uncertainty on which those models are based." This gives financial modelling a special relevance to market participants. Intellectually, it poses the challenge of building stochastic equilibrium models in which the second and higher moments of random shocks determine the first moments of asset returns.

As financial econometricians have explored the properties of asset return data over the past 30 years, they have uncovered some fascinating regularities. First, measured at high frequencies, the distribution of asset returns is very far from normal; there is excess kurtosis, a strong tendency for returns to stay either very close to the mean or far from it. Investors were forcefully reminded of the non-normality of stock returns when stock prices crashed in October 1987, although the basic facts were already well established in the academic literature.[1] This non-normality diminishes when returns are measured over longer time intervals.

Second, conditioning information can be used to predict both first and second moments of asset returns. The predictability in first moments is subtle, as one would expect given the fundamental insight of the efficient markets hypothesis, that competition among investors ensures modest trading profits so that most price variation is driven by the arrival of news. The predictability in second moments, on the other hand, is obvious even to a

---

[1] I vividly remember delivering a technical lecture on excess kurtosis at Princeton during the morning of October 19, 1987. A student at the back of the room put up his hand and said "Professor Campbell, are you aware that the Dow is down 200 points?" I was not.

casual observer. A vast literature on this phenomenon has documented that conditional volatility can move suddenly but also varies persistently, so that time-varying volatility is apparent both within the trading day and across decades. Movements in conditional volatility often appear to be correlated with asset returns themselves.

A direct way to model changing second moments is to write down a process for the volatility of returns, conditional on past returns and possibly other information available to an econometrician. In the early 1980's Robert Engle followed this direct approach when he proposed the ARCH model. This seminal contribution was recognized in 2003 by the award to Engle of the Nobel Memorial Prize in Economic Sciences.

While the ARCH framework is a natural way to model changing volatility, it does not offer an integrated explanation of return phenomena at different frequencies. It explains high-frequency non-normality by exogenous non-normal shocks, and persistence of volatility using a slowly decaying (fractionally integrated) volatility process. Each of these features must be chosen separately to match different aspects of financial market data.

An alternative approach, which has attracted interest in recent years, is to write down a process for a latent state variable that is not observable to the econometrician.[2] The simplest version of this "stochastic volatility" approach assumes that, conditional on the state variable, returns are normally distributed with a volatility governed by the state variable, and that the state variable follows a smooth autoregressive process. Since the state variable is unobserved, returns are not in general normal conditional on observed information, so in principle a smoothly evolving stochastic volatility model can explain a wide variety of asset pricing phenomena. In practice, however, empirical analyses of stochastic volatility models find that additional jumps are needed to fit the data: jumps in volatility, to accommodate sudden changes in volatility, and jumps in prices, to generate the extreme non-normality observed in high-frequency return data. Correlation between these jumps causes sudden movements in asset prices to predict subsequent volatility (Duffie, Pan, and Singleton, 2000, Eraker; Johannes, and Polson, 2003).

Once stochastic volatility is allowed to jump, it becomes natural to consider a discrete-state regime-switching model of the sort introduced to the economics literature by Hamilton (1988, 1989). Regime-switching models are particularly appealing because they are tractable both for econometricians and for financial economists solving asset pricing models.[3] Given

---

[2] For surveys, see Ghysels, Harvey, and Renault (1996) or Andersen and Benzoni (2008).

[3] Mehra and Prescott (1985) used a regime-switching model in their seminal paper on the equity premium puzzle. Garcia, Meddahi, and Tédongap (2008) use a regime-switching model to analyze several models that have been popular in the recent literature on consumption-based asset pricing.

the richness of financial data, however, one would like to allow for many possible states in volatility. Until recently, this requirement has barred the use of regime-switching models in volatility modelling, because the number of parameters in regime-switching models increases with the square of the number of states, so the models become unusable very quickly as new states are added.

The research that Laurent Calvet and Adlai Fisher present in this volume is exciting because it breaks this barrier, and does so in a way that provides a unified explanation of many of the stylized facts of asset pricing. The Markov-Switching Multifractal (MSM) model assumes that volatility is the product of a large number of discrete variables, each of which can randomly switch to a new value drawn from a common distribution. The variables are ordered by their switching probability, which increases smoothly from low-frequency to high-frequency volatility components. Volatility jumps when a regime switch occurs, and the change in volatility can be extremely persistent if the switch affects a low-frequency component of volatility. The model has only four parameters even if it has many more volatility components and an enormous number of states. This parsimony makes the model a strong performer in forecasting volatility out of sample.

Because the MSM is easy to embed in a general equilibrium asset pricing framework, Calvet and Fisher are able to calculate the effects on prices of jumps in the volatility of fundamentals when investors are risk-averse. They find that exogenous jumps in fundamental volatility cause endogenous jumps in asset prices, providing an attractive economic explanation of the jump correlations documented by Eraker, Johannes, and Polson (2003) among others.

The appeal of the multifractal approach becomes clear when one considers its various applications together. Calvet, Fisher, and their coauthors have published a series of papers on multifractal volatility, but the importance of the work is much easier to see when it is presented in a unified manner in this volume. Multifractal volatility modelling is a major advance, and this book is a milestone in the modern literature on financial econometrics.

John Y. Campbell
Harvard University
June 2008

Credits and Copyright Exceptions

1
Introduction

Financial markets are uniquely complicated systems, combining the interactions of thousands of individuals and institutions and generating at every instant the prices to buy and sell claims to future uncertain cash flows. The timing of dividends, coupons, and other payoffs varies widely across assets, and valuations are correspondingly driven by news as diverse as short-run weather forecasts (Roll, 1984a) or technological breakthroughs that may take decades to come to fruition (Greenwood and Jovanovic, 1999; Pastor and Veronesi, 2008). Market participants adopt a variety of trading strategies and investment horizons. High-frequency speculators, arbitrageurs, and day traders attempt to exploit opportunities over the very short run, while insurance companies, pension funds and 401(k) participants have investment objectives spanning several decades. Furthermore, the recent diffusion of algorithmic trading techniques implies that even long-run investors now routinely engage in sophisticated high-frequency transactions.

The complexity of asset markets is matched by the rich dynamic properties of the return data that they produce, and quantifying risk has been for over a century one of the leading topics of investigation in finance. For some researchers, the pure scientific challenge of understanding this intricate environment is sufficient motivation. At the same time, the potential pecuniary rewards to improved modeling of financial data are substantial. The fields of portfolio management and asset pricing require an accurate view of the statistical properties of asset returns. Risk managers must quantify the exposure of trading positions and portfolios of contingent claims. Option values are largely determined by market forecasts of future volatility. The models we develop in this book capture empirically relevant and seemingly disparate features of financial returns in a single, parsimonious framework.

1.1 Empirical Properties of Financial Returns

One well-known property of financial volatility is its persistence. When returns are substantially positive or negative on a given day, further large movements are likely to follow.[1] In 1982, Robert Engle concisely modeled time-varying volatility in his seminal publication on autoregressive conditional heteroskedasticity (ARCH), which laid the foundation for his 2003 Nobel Memorial Prize in Economic Sciences.[2] Subsequent research showed that volatility clustering can remain substantial over very long horizons (Ding, Granger, and Engle, 1993), and that an accurate representation may require the possibility of extreme changes, or jumps, in volatility (e.g., Duffie, Pan, and Singleton, 2000). Under conditions where volatility is both highly persistent and highly variable, we should expect volatility fluctuations to have substantial valuation and risk management implications.

Asset prices themselves can change by large amounts in short periods of time, a phenomenon often described as tail risk. In continuous-time settings, such extreme events can be modeled as jumps (Press, 1967; Merton, 1976), or as sudden bursts of volatility (Mandelbrot and Taylor, 1967; Rosenberg, 1972; Clark, 1973). In discrete time, postulating a thick-tailed conditional distribution of returns can achieve a similar effect (Bollerslev, 1987). Extreme returns have been a pervasive feature of financial markets throughout their history, and recent turbulence (e.g., Greenspan, 2007) suggests that tail risk will continue to be important in the new century.

A deeper understanding of financial returns can be obtained by investigating their characteristics at various frequencies. For instance, the persistence and variability of financial volatility can be apparent whether one observes returns at intradaily, daily, weekly, monthly, yearly, or decennial intervals. That is, as casual observation suggests, there are volatile decades and quiet decades, volatile years and quiet years, and so on. Intuition suggests that these features are important for volatility forecasting, and that improved filtering can be used to distinguish between cycles of different durations.

The multifrequency nature of volatility is consistent with the intuition that economic shocks have highly heterogeneous degrees of persistence. For example, liquidity shocks tend to be sudden and transitory, but their duration is quite random. The liquidity crisis that started in the fall of 2007 is still in progress as we are writing these lines in April 2008. Volatility also

---

[1]Early suggestions of volatility persistence and corroborative empirical evidence for various financial series appear in Osborne (1962), Mandelbrot (1963), Fama (1965, 1970), Beaver (1968), Kassouf (1969), Praetz (1969), Fisher and Lorie (1970), Fielitz (1971), Black and Scholes (1972), Rosenberg (1972), Officer (1973), Hsu, Miller, and Wichern (1974), Black (1976), Latane and Rendleman (1976), and Schmalensee and Trippi (1978). Additional evidence is provided by, among others, Akgiray (1989), Baillie and Bollerslev (1989), Bollerslev (1987), Chou (1988), Diebold and Nerlove (1989), French, Schwert, and Stambaugh (1987), McCurdy and Morgan (1987), Milhoj (1987), Poterba and Summers (1986), Schwert (1989), and Taylor (1982).

[2]See Diebold (2004) for a discussion of Engle's contributions.

varies over horizons of a few years, for instance in conjunction with earnings and business cycles (e.g., Schwert, 1989; Hamilton and Lin, 1996). At longer horizons, slow variations in macroeconomic volatility, or uncertainty about oil reserves, technology, and global security can affect volatility over a generation or longer (e.g., Bansal and Yaron, 2004; Lettau, Ludvigson, and Wachter, 2004).

This heterogeneity is accompanied by important nonlinearities. For instance, the unconditional distribution of returns varies nonlinearly as the frequency of observation changes (e.g., Campbell, Lo, and MacKinlay, 1997, Chapter 1). At short horizons, returns tend to be either close to the mean or to take large values. By contrast, for longer horizons the bell and the tails of the return distribution become thinner, while the intermediate regions gain mass. These nonlinearities are also apparent in the behavior of return moments, as documented by the expanding literature on power variation. In many financial series, the moments of the absolute value of returns vary as a power function of the frequency of observation. Additionally, the growth rate of the qth moment is a nonlinear and strictly concave function of q, a feature consistent with the nonlinear variations of the return distribution with the sampling horizon (e.g., Andersen *et al.*, 2001; Barndorff-Nielsen and Shephard, 2003; Calvet and Fisher, 2002*a*; Calvet, Fisher, and Mandelbrot, 1997; Galluccio *et al.*, 1997; Ghashghaie *et al.*, 1996; Pasquini and Serva, 1999, 2000; Richards, 2000; Vandewalle and Ausloos, 1998; Vassilicos, Demos, and Tata, 1993).

In equity markets, the unconditional distribution of returns is negatively skewed, since large negative returns are more frequently observed than large positive returns. Moreover, as pointed out by Fischer Black (1976), volatility is typically higher after a stock market fall than after a stock market rise, so stock returns are negatively correlated with future volatility. Black hypothesized that this effect could be caused by financial leverage, which rises after the market value of a firm declines thereby tending to exacerbate risk in the residual equity claim. The financial leverage channel is generally regarded as too small, however, to fully account for the skewness of equity index returns (e.g., Schwert, 1989; Aydemir, Gallmeyer, and Hollifield, 2006). An alternative explanation focuses on feedback between news about future volatility and current prices (Abel, 1988; Barsky, 1989; French, Schwert, and Stambaugh, 1987; Pindyck, 1984). When market participants revise upward their forecasts of future dividend volatility, they tend to price down the stock, creating a negative correlation between current returns and future volatility. Intuition suggests that heterogeneous horizons can play an important role in this context. High-frequency volatility shocks can capture the dynamics of typical variations, while lower-frequency movements can generate extreme returns through the feedback channel. Multifrequency shocks may therefore be helpful to understanding the skewness and kurtosis of asset returns.

1.2   Modeling Multifrequency Volatility

The theme of this book is that a simple class of models provides a parsimonious description of the seemingly disparate aspects of financial market returns discussed above. We have developed this approach in a series of scientific articles written over the past ten years. The motivation for this book is to provide a unified treatment that makes it accessible to a wider audience of practitioners and academics.

The model we describe is based on regime-switching, which was advanced in economics and finance by the seminal work of James Hamilton (1988, 1989). While the theoretical formulation of regime-switching is very general, researchers typically employ only a small number of discrete states in empirical applications. This partly stems from the common view that regimes change infrequently. In a general formulation, a more practical limitation is that the transition matrix, and therefore the number of parameters, grows quadratically with the cardinality of the state space. Restrictions on switching probabilities offer a natural solution, as pursued, for example, by Bollen, Gray, and Whaley (2000) in a four-regime model. We extend this approach by considering a tight set of restrictions inspired by the multifractal literature.

We start with the assumption that volatility is determined by components that have different degrees of persistence. These components randomly switch over time, generating a volatility process that can be both highly persistent and highly variable. The transition probabilities are heterogeneous across components and follow a tight geometric specification. We obtain additional parsimony by assuming that when a component switches, its new value is drawn from a fixed distribution that does not depend on the frequency. Our model therefore assumes that volatility shocks have the same magnitude at all time scales. These restrictions, which are inspired by earlier research on multifractals in the natural sciences, provide parsimony and appear broadly consistent with financial data at standard confidence levels.

This specification, which we call the Markov-Switching Multifractal (MSM), offers a number of appealing features to the practitioner and applied researcher. Because it is based on a Markov chain, MSM is a highly tractable multifrequency stochastic volatility model. The empiricist can apply Bayesian updating to compute the conditional distribution of the latent state and thus disentangle volatility components of different durations. Multistep forecasting is convenient, and estimation can be efficiently conducted by maximizing the likelihood function, which is available in closed form. In empirical applications, we routinely estimate the 4 parameters of MSM for specifications with ten frequencies and over a thousand states.

Our research shows that MSM can outperform some of the most reliable forecasting models currently in use, including Generalized ARCH ("GARCH," Bollerslev, 1986) and related models, both in- and out-of-sample. These improvements are especially pronounced in the medium and long run, and have been confirmed and extended in a variety of financial series (e.g., Bacry, Kozhemyak, and Muzy, 2008; Lux, 2008). MSM also captures well the power variation or "moment-scaling" of returns, works equally well in discrete time and in continuous time, and generalizes to multivariate settings.

To demonstrate some of the properties of the basic MSM approach and how these are consistent with financial returns, Figure 1.1 shows a simulation from a simple MSM process estimated later in this book (Chapter 3) alongside a time series of British pound/U.S. dollar daily returns. One can see in both figures the long volatility cycles, thick tails, and presence of multiple frequencies that characterize financial data.

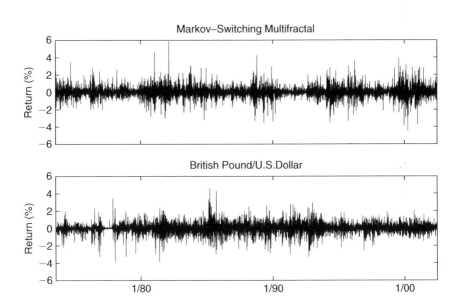

FIGURE 1.1. **Simulated Multifractal Process and British Pound/U.S. Dollar Exchange Rate.** This figure illustrates daily returns from a simulated Markov-switching multifractal process (top panel) and historical daily returns from the British pound/U.S. dollar series (bottom panel). The construction of MSM is described in Chapter 3. The simulation in the top panel is based on eight volatility components and the maximum likelihood parameter estimates reported in Chapter 3 for the pound series. The exchange rate data in the second panel spans from June 1, 1973 to June 28, 2002. Both panels have 7,298 returns.

1.3   Pricing Multifrequency Risk

We explore the pricing implications of multifrequency risk by embedding MSM within an economic equilibrium framework. We assume that fundamentals, such as dividend news, are subject to multifrequency volatility risk, and we value the resulting cash flow stream in a standard consumption-based model, as developed in Lucas (1978) and surveyed in Campbell (2003). The assumption that fundamentals are exposed to multifrequency risk seems reasonable given the heterogeneity of the news that drive financial returns, and the pervasive evidence of multifractality in weather patterns and other natural phenomena affecting the economy. Because MSM has a Markov structure, the resulting equilibrium is tractable and can be estimated by maximizing the likelihood of the excess return series, which is again available in closed form.

The MSM equilibrium model can capture the extreme realizations of actual equity returns. In examples calibrated to U.S. aggregate equity, small but persistent changes in dividend news volatility generate substantial price movements, which are comparable in size to the most extreme historical returns. Multifrequency risk also helps to explain the large difference between dividend and stock volatility that has long presented a puzzle to researchers (Shiller, 1981). For instance, in a classic paper John Campbell and Ludger Hentschel (1992) use a quadratic GARCH specification to fit dividend news, and show that the variance of returns exceeds the variance of dividends by about 1 to 2%. They attribute this modest amplification to the property of GARCH-type specifications that the volatility of volatility can only be large if volatility itself is large. In our multifrequency environment, the variance of returns exceeds the variance of dividends by about 20 to 40%, which brings us substantially closer to the amplification levels observed in practice.

Multifrequency risk is easily incorporated into the drift of fundamentals, such as aggregate consumption and dividend news. As in the work of Ravi Bansal and Amir Yaron (2004), we can use a reasonable level of risk aversion to match the equity premium and still generate a substantial contribution of equilibrium feedback to dividend volatility. The extension also offers a pure regime-switching formulation of long-run risks in a multifrequency environment.

In order to match the skewness of equity returns, we consider economies in which the volatility state is not directly observable by market participants. We derive the novel theoretical result that investors should learn abruptly about volatility increases (bad news) but slowly about volatility decreases (good news). Learning about a volatility increase should be abrupt because outliers are highly improbable if in fact volatility remains low. By contrast, realizations near the mean are a likely outcome under any volatility scenario, and hence investors should learn slowly about a volatility decrease. This learning asymmetry is a powerful source of negative skewness in returns.

Our learning results complement earlier research by Pietro Veronesi on how information quality affects stock returns. Whereas Veronesi (2000) considers learning about the latent drift in a two-state Lucas economy, our investors receive signals about an arbitrary number of dividend volatility components. By incorporating multiple shocks of heterogeneous durations, we obtain a structural learning model that can be applied to higher-frequency stock returns, in contrast to the lower-frequency calibrations typically considered in the learning literature. More broadly, multifrequency equilibrium modeling can be viewed as a first step toward bringing together the lower-frequency macro-finance and higher-frequency financial econometrics literatures.

Examining the equilibrium implications of multifrequency risk in continuous time provides additional insights. We consider an economy in which consumption and dividends follow continuous Itô diffusions. Markov switches in the drift or volatility of fundamentals induce endogenous jumps in equilibrium prices, in contrast to the exogenous price discontinuities typically postulated in the literature. The multifrequency specification further generates many small jumps, a few moderate jumps, and rare large jumps, while also producing additional features such as correlation between jumps in volatility and prices. Previous literature also emphasizes the empirical appeal of these properties, but generally assumes that they are exogenous features of the price process (e.g., Bakshi, Cao, and Chen, 1997; Bates, 2000; Duffie, Pan, and Singleton, 2000; Eraker, 2004; Eraker, Johannes, and Polson, 2003; Madan, Carr, and Chang, 1998). In our equilibrium, when the number of volatility components goes to infinity, the stock price weakly converges to the sum of a continuous multifractal diffusion and an infinite intensity pure jump process, producing a new stochastic process that we call a multifractal jump-diffusion.

1.4 Contributions to Multifractal Literature

The research described in this book makes several contributions to the extensive literature on fractals and multifractals. Earlier work in the natural sciences had focused on developing multifractal measures to represent the distribution of physical quantities, such as the distribution of minerals in the Earth's crust or the distribution of energy in turbulent dissipation. New frontiers of research were opened by the development of multifractal diffusions. Specifically, the Multifractal Model of Asset Returns ("MMAR," Calvet, Fisher, and Mandelbrot, 1997) proposed the first martingale multifractal diffusion in order to capture the dynamics of financial prices. The Markov-Switching Multifractal (Calvet and Fisher, 1999, 2001) improves on the MMAR's combinatorial (also called grid-bound or cartoon) construction by randomizing news arrival times, guaranteeing a strictly stationary stochastic process. MSM readily permits estimation and forecasting through standard econometric techniques, and subsequent research continues to build on these innovations (Calvet and Fisher, 2004, 2007; Calvet, Fisher, and Thompson 2006; Bacry, Kozhemyak, and Muzy, 2008; Lux, 2008).

MSM establishes a mutually beneficial bridge between multifractality and general Markov-switching models. Early research on multifractals is limited to informal visual tests based on moment scaling and power variation. In contrast, the MSM construction shows that a large class of multifractal processes can be obtained as high-dimensional cases of general regime-switching models. As a result, MSM can be estimated by maximum likelihood, standard errors and hypothesis tests are available, the conditional distribution of the latent state can be inferred at any instant, and multistep forecasting is convenient. Thus, the development of MSM made available to the multifractal literature the rigorous statistical foundations of general Markov-switching processes. Conversely, our research suggests that the regime-switching literature can benefit from fractal insights. Our four-parameter Markov specification accommodates arbitrarily many states, has a dense transition matrix, and works as well or better than models based on smooth autoregressive transitions. As noted by Hamilton (2006), specifying high-dimensional Markov-switching models with tight restrictions on parameters offers a promising new approach to financial econometrics.

Prior fractal literature emphasizes that the presence of crashes and outliers should be taken as evidence of a system out of equilibrium (e.g., Mandelbrot and Hudson, 2004). We suggest in this book that equilibrium theory and fractal modeling may be complementary in many instances, and can in fact be fruitfully combined. For instance, incorporating multifrequency risk in standard asset pricing models provides new insights into the potential magnitude of the volatility feedback effect, the skewness of equity returns, and the possibility of large outliers in equilibrium. Conversely, equilibrium pricing helps to endogenously generate the multifractal jump-diffusion, which is an entirely novel class of fractal model.

1.5   Organization of the Book

Part I of the book is devoted to discrete-time models. In Chapter 2, we review ARCH-type and Markov-switching processes. ARCH and its numerous variants, which are now essential to financial market practitioners, are based on smooth linear variations in volatility and a single decay rate in basic formulations. Markov-switching models have become increasingly useful in financial econometrics and represent one of the foundations of our approach. Chapter 3 introduces the workhorse of the book, the Markov-Switching Multifractal (MSM), which permits a rich diversity of volatility shocks. MSM produces good volatility forecasts, especially at longer horizons, and outperforms standard processes in- and out-of-sample. Chapter 4 establishes that the approach easily generalizes to several assets. In an empirical application, multivariate MSM provides reasonable estimates of the value-at-risk inherent in a single currency or a portfolio of currencies.

Part II shows that multifrequency modeling works equally well in continuous time. Chapter 5 provides background material on self-similar processes and multifractal measures. Self-similar processes, such as Brownian motion and Lévy stable processes, assume that the unconditional distribution of returns is identical across all time horizons, and do not adequately control for time-varying volatility. These models do, however, foreshadow certain aspects of the multifrequency approach that we develop in subsequent chapters. Multifractal measures were first applied in the natural sciences, and provide another building block of the MSM approach. Chapter 6 presents the earliest multifractal diffusion, the MMAR, defined as a Brownian motion in trading time, where trading time is the cumulative distribution function of a multifractal measure obtained by recursively reallocating mass within a finite time interval.

Chapter 7 shows that the discrete-time MSM approach developed in Chapter 3 easily extends to continuous time and solves the nonstationarity problems inherent in the MMAR. We demonstrate weak convergence of the discrete-time construction to the continuous-time process, and the connection between the parameters is available in closed form. The limit MSM process contains an infinite number of frequencies and its sample paths are characterized by a continuum of local scales. Chapter 8 presents empirical evidence on the power variation of returns at various frequencies and demonstrates its consistency with the multifractal model.

Part III of the book derives equilibrium implications of multifrequency volatility. In the discrete-time approach of Chapter 9, we assume that the volatility of dividend news follows an MSM process and we derive the endogenous stock return process. We find that variations in multifrequency volatility shocks can have substantial feedback effects on overall financial volatility. We also show that learning about volatility is a powerful source of endogenous skewness in returns, and develop a multifrequency version of long-run risk. Chapter 10 considers equilibrium stock returns in continuous time, focusing on endogenous jump-diffusions and convergence to a multifractal jump-diffusion. Unless stated otherwise, all proofs are in the Appendix.

The book should be accessible to practitioners working on risk management and volatility forecasting applications. It is also suited for researchers in economics, finance, econometrics, and statistics, or natural scientists and general readers interested in fractal modeling. Graduate students in economics and finance, as well as advanced undergraduates with solid foundations in econometrics, may find useful ideas and inspiration for future research.

Part I

Discrete Time

2

Background: Discrete-Time Volatility Modeling

In this chapter, we briefly discuss several common approaches to modeling financial volatility, including GARCH, stochastic volatility, and Markov-switching formulations. Our goal is not to provide a complete survey, but to briefly introduce key models that facilitate the development of MSM and provide comparisons. Excellent surveys of the literature can be found in Bollerslev, Engle, and Nelson (1994), Engle (2004), Ghysels, Harvey, and Renault (1996), Hamilton (2006), Hamilton and Raj (2002), and Shephard (2005).

2.1   Autoregressive Volatility Modeling

The most common approach to volatility modeling builds on the generalized autoregressive conditional heteroskedasticity (GARCH) class (Engle, 1982; Bollerslev, 1986), in which volatility follows a smooth autoregressive transition. Let r_t denote the log return of a financial asset, such as an exchange rate, between dates $t - 1$ and t. Under GARCH(p, q), the return is specified as

$$r_t = h_t^{1/2} \varepsilon_t,$$

where h_t denotes the conditional variance of r_t at date $t - 1$, and ε_t is an independently and identically distributed (i.i.d.) random variable with zero mean and unit variance. The conditional variance h_t follows the autoregressive process:

$$h_t = \omega + \sum_{i=1}^{p} \beta_i h_{t-i} + \sum_{j=1}^{q} \alpha_j r_{t-j}^2,$$

and is therefore a smooth deterministic function of past squared returns. The noise ε_t can be a standard normal (Engle, 1982; Bollerslev, 1986). In order to better capture the outliers of financial series, researchers have considered numerous extensions where ε_t has a distribution with thicker tails than the Gaussian, such as the Student-t (Bollerslev, 1987), the generalized error distribution (Nelson, 1991), or nonparametric specifications (Engle and Gonzalez-Rivera, 1991).[1]

The GARCH conditional variance h_t is known to the econometrician at date $t - 1$, and the conditional distribution of the period-t return, $r_t = h_t^{1/2} \varepsilon_t$, is a rescaled version of the noise ε_t. When the specification for ε_t has a closed-form density, the conditional distribution of r_t and more generally the likelihood of the return series $r_1, \ldots, r_T$ are available in closed form, which facilitates maximum likelihood estimation.

Because GARCH variance follows a smooth autoregressive transition, standard specifications have difficulty capturing the sudden changes in volatility exhibited by many financial series. For this reason, econometricians have considered extensions, called stochastic volatility models,[2] in which volatility is hit by separate shocks:

$$\ln(h_t) = \omega + \sum_{i=1}^{p} \beta_i \ln(h_{t-i}) + \sum_{j=1}^{q} \alpha_j r_{t-j}^2 + \eta_t.$$

The noise η_t is realized at date t jointly with the return r_t. If the econometrician has access only to returns, the volatility state is not directly observable and must be imputed. Consequently, the density of $r_t = h_t^{1/2} \varepsilon_t$ is unavailable in closed form and estimation proceeds by moment-based inference or simulation. As will be discussed in Chapter 3, the multifrequency approach also incorporates volatility-specific shocks. In contrast to standard stochastic volatility models, however, our model generates a closed-form likelihood, which permits convenient and efficient likelihood-based estimation.

---

[1] Extensions and applications of GARCH in finance and economics have been the object of a vast literature, which includes, among many other contributions, Baillie and Bollerslev (1989), Barone-Adesi, Engle, and Mancini (2008), Bera and Lee (1992), Bollerslev, Chou, and Kroner (1992), Bollerslev, Engle, and Nelson (1994), Campbell and Hentschel (1992), Chou, Engle, and Kane (1992), Diebold (1988), Drost and Nijman (1993), Engle (2002a, 2004), Engle and Rangel (2008), Engle and Ng (1993), Engle, Lilien, and Robins (1987), French, Schwert, and Stambaugh (1987), Gallant and Tauchen (1989), Gallant, Hsieh, and Tauchen (1991), Gallant, Rossi, and Tauchen (1992, 1993), Geweke (1989), Glosten, Jagannathan, and Runkle (1993), Gouriéroux and Montfort (1992), Nelson (1989, 1990, 1991), Nijman and Palm (1993), Pagan and Hong (1991), Pagan and Schwert (1990), Rossi (1996), Schwert (1989), Sentana (1995), and Zakoian (1994).

[2] Contributions to the stochastic volatility literature include Andersen (1994, 1996), Andersen and Sørensen (1996), Andersen, Benzoni, and Lund (2002), Bakshi, Cao, and Chen (1997), Barndorff-Nielsen and Shephard (2001, 2003), Bates (1996), Chernov, Gallant, Ghysels, and Tauchen (2003), Clark (1973), Eraker (2001), Eraker, Johannes and Polson (2003), Gallant, Hsieh, and Tauchen (1997), Ghysels, Harvey, and Renault (1996), Harvey, Ruiz, and Shephard (1994), Heston (1993), Hull and White (1987), Jacquier, Polson, and Rossi (1994, 2004), Johannes, Polson, and Stroud (2002), Jones (2003), Kim, Shephard, and Chib (1998), Melino and Turnbull (1990), Renault and Touzi (1996), Rosenberg (1972), Shephard (2005), Stein and Stein (1991), Taylor (1982, 1986), and Wiggins (1987).

Standard GARCH models provide good forecasts of short-run volatility dynamics, but often have difficulties capturing lower-frequency cycles. Consider, for instance, GARCH$(1,1)$, which is one of the best performing models in the GARCH literature (e.g., Akgiray, 1989; Andersen and Bollerslev, 1998a; Hansen and Lunde, 2005; Pagan and Schwert, 1990; West and Cho, 1995). Volatility follows

$$h_t = \omega + \beta h_{t-1} + \alpha r_{t-1}^2,$$

and forward iteration implies

$$h_t = \omega + \alpha r_{t-1}^2 + \beta(\omega + \alpha r_{t-2}^2 + \beta h_{t-2})$$

$$= \frac{\omega}{1-\beta} + \alpha \sum_{i=1}^{\infty} \beta^{i-1} r_{t-i}^2.$$

A volatility shock declines at a single exponential rate β. In practice, this implies that GARCH$(1,1)$ picks up the short-run autocorrelation in volatility but cannot easily capture longer cycles. More generally, stationarity places practical limits on the type of lower-frequency cycles that can be captured by a GARCH(p,q) model.

For this reason, econometricians have considered volatility models that incorporate stronger persistence in squared returns. Specifically, while typical ARCH/GARCH processes have weak persistence, long memory in squared returns is a characteristic feature of fractionally integrated GARCH (Baillie, Bollerslev, and Mikkelsen, 1996)[3] and long-memory stochastic volatility (Breidt, Crato, and de Lima, 1998; Comte and Renault, 1998; Harvey, 1998; Robinson and Zaffaroni, 1998).[4] Long-memory processes capture very low-frequency cycles in financial or other data by permitting slowly declining autocorrelations of a hyperbolic form at long horizons. By contrast, short-memory processes are characterized by the fast exponential declines of autocorrelations. Long memory was first analyzed in the context of fractional integration of Brownian motion by Mandelbrot (1965a) and Mandelbrot and van Ness (1968).[5] It has been documented in squared and absolute returns for many financial data sets (Dacorogna $et\ al.$, 1993; Ding, Granger, and Engle, 1993; Taylor, 1986). We refer the reader to Baillie (1996), Beran (1994), and Robinson (2003) for excellent surveys of long memory in econometrics and statistics.

---

[3] Ding and Granger (1996) develop the related Long Memory ARCH process.

[4] Additional contributions include Deo and Hurvich (2001), Deo, Hurvich, and Lu (2006), Gonçalves da Silva and Robinson (2007), Hurvich, Moulines, and Soulier (2005), Hurvich and Ray (2003), Robinson (2001), and Zaffaroni (2007).

[5] Granger and Joyeux (1980) and Hosking (1981) advanced the use of long memory in economics by introducing a discrete-time counterpart of fractional Brownian motion, the autoregressive fractionally integrated moving average (ARFIMA) process.

Another important strand of the ARCH literature attempts to jointly capture volatility dynamics in several financial markets. Multivariate GARCH, pioneered by Kraft and Engle (1982) and Bollerslev, Engle, and Wooldridge (1988), is perhaps the most commonly used class of models, and has been extended in many directions.[6] In Chapter 4 we show how to model multifrequency shocks in a multi-asset environment.

2.2   Markov-Switching Models

In contrast to the GARCH volatility models discussed earlier, stochastic regime-switching models permit the conditional mean and variance of financial returns to depend on an unobserved latent "state" that may change unpredictably. The application of regime-switching models in economics and finance was pioneered by Hamilton (1988, 1989, 1990), and a rich literature has emerged.[7]

The general approach considers a latent state $M_t \in \{m^1, ..., m^d\}$, where the positive integer d describes the number of possible states. Returns are given by

$$r_t = \mu(M_t) + \sigma(M_t)\, \varepsilon_t,$$

where $\mu(M_t)$ and $\sigma(M_t)$ are, respectively, the state-dependent conditional mean and variance of returns. The dynamics of the Markov chain M_t are fully characterized by the transition matrix $A = (a_{i,j})_{1 \le i,j \le d}$ with components $a_{ij} = \mathbb{P}(M_{t+1} = m^j | M_t = m^i)$.

Estimation and forecasting methods for regime-switching models are now standard. We provide details specific to our setting in the individual chapters, and the interested reader may refer to Hamilton (1994, Chapter 22) for further discussion of the general approach.

---

[6]Examples include Bollerslev (1990), Diebold and Nerlove (1989), Engle (1987, 2002b), Engle and Kroner (1995), Engle and Mezrich (1996), Engle, Ng, and Rothschild (1990), Kraft and Engle (1982), and Ledoit, Santa-Clara, and Wolf (2003).

[7]The likelihood-based estimation of Markov-switching processes was developed by Lindgren (1978) and Baum et al. (1980) in the statistics literature. Hamilton (1988, 1989, 1990) introduced these processes to the economics literature and spurred the development of a large body of research. Contributions to the original version of the model advance estimation and testing (Albert and Chib, 1993; Garcia, 1998; Hansen, 1992; Shephard, 1994), and investigate a wide range of empirical applications (e.g., Hamilton, 1988; Garcia and Perron, 1996). The approach has been extended to incorporate GARCH transitions (Cai, 1994; Gray, 1996; Hamilton and Susmel, 1994; Kim, 1994; Kim and Nelson, 1999; Klaassen, 2002), vector processes (Hamilton and Lin, 1996; Hamilton and Pérez-Quirós, 1996), and time-varying transition probabilities (Diebold, Lee, and Weinbach, 1994; Durland and McCurdy, 1994; Filardo, 1994; Maheu and McCurdy, 2000; Pérez-Quirós and Timmermann, 2000). See Hamilton and Raj (2002) and Hamilton (2006) for a survey.

In typical applications, researchers use Markov switching to model low-frequency variations and rely on other techniques for shorter-run dynamics. For example, Markov-switching ARCH and GARCH processes separately specify regime shifts at low frequencies, smooth autoregressive volatility transitions at midrange frequencies, and a thick-tailed conditional distribution of returns at high-frequency (Cai, 1994; Hamilton and Susmel, 1994; Gray, 1996; Klaassen, 2002). In Chapter 3, we develop the Markov-Switching Multifractal approach based on pure regime-switching at all frequencies, and we compare this model with earlier Markov-switching formulations.

3

The Markov-Switching Multifractal (MSM) in Discrete Time

In this chapter, we present the discrete-time version of the main model in this book, the Markov-Switching Multifractal (MSM). MSM closely matches the intuition that a range of economic uncertainties with varying degrees of persistence impact financial markets. Using a tight set of restrictions inspired by the multifractal literature, we define a pure regime-switching specification with multiple frequencies, arbitrarily many states, and a dense transition matrix. The MSM construction is strikingly parsimonious as it requires only four parameters.

MSM volatility is derived by multiplying together a finite number of random first-order Markov components. We assume for parsimony that the volatility components are identical except for differences in their switching probabilities, which follow an approximately geometric progression. The construction delivers a multifrequency stochastic volatility model with a closed-form likelihood, enabling us for the first time to apply a standard econometric toolkit to estimating and forecasting using a multifractal model.

An empirical investigation of four daily currency series shows that MSM performs well in comparison with leading forecasting models, including GARCH(1,1), both in- and out-of-sample. In the data, MSM has a higher likelihood than GARCH for all currencies, and the improvement is statistically significant. Since both models have the same number of parameters, the multifractal is also preferred by standard selection criteria. Out-of-sample, MSM matches the accuracy of GARCH forecasts at very short horizons such as one day, and provides substantially better forecasts at longer horizons, such as 20 to 50 business days. We also demonstrate that the multifractal model improves on Markov-switching GARCH (MS-GARCH) and fractionally integrated GARCH (FIGARCH) out of sample.

Traditional Markov-switching approaches such as MS-GARCH use regime-switching only for low-frequency events, while also using linear autoregressive transitions at medium frequencies and a thick-tailed conditional distribution of returns. By contrast, MSM captures long-memory features, intermediate frequency volatility dynamics, and thick tails in returns all with a single regime-switching approach. It is noteworthy that

This chapter is based on an earlier paper: "How to Forecast Long-Run Volatility: Regime-Switching and the Estimation of Multifractal Processes" (with A. Fisher), *Econometrics*, 2: 49–83, Spring 2004.

a single mechanism can play all three of these roles so effectively, and the innovation that achieves this surprising economy of modeling technique is based on scale-invariance.

3.1   The MSM Model of Stochastic Volatility

3.1.1   Definition

We consider a financial series P_t defined in discrete time on the regular grid $t = 0, 1, 2, \ldots, \infty$. In applications, P_t will be the price of a financial asset or exchange rate. Let $r_t \equiv \ln(P_t/P_{t-1})$ denote the log-return. The economy is driven by a first-order Markov state vector with $\bar{k}$ components:

$$M_t = \left(M_{1,t}; M_{2,t}; \ldots; M_{\bar{k},t} \right) \in \mathbb{R}_+^{\bar{k}}.$$

The components of M_t have the same marginal distribution but evolve at different frequencies, as we now explain.

Assume that the volatility state vector has been constructed up to date $t-1$. For each $k \in \{1, \ldots, \bar{k}\}$, the next period multiplier $M_{k,t}$ is drawn from a fixed distribution M with probability γ_k, and is otherwise equal to its previous value: $M_{k,t} = M_{k,t-1}$. The dynamics of $M_{k,t}$ can be summarized as

$M_{k,t}$ drawn from distribution M with probability γ_k
$M_{k,t} = M_{k,t-1}$ with probability $1 - \gamma_k$,

where the switching events and new draws from M are assumed to be independent across k and t. We require that the distribution of M has a positive support and unit mean: $M \geq 0$ and $\mathbb{E}(M) = 1$.

Under these assumptions, the random multipliers $M_{k,t}$ are persistent and nonnegative, and satisfy $\mathbb{E}(M_{k,t}) = 1$. The multipliers differ in their transition probabilities γ_k but not in their marginal distribution M. Components of different frequencies are mutually independent; that is, the variables $M_{k,t}$ and $M_{k',t'}$ are independent if k differs from k'. These features greatly contribute to the parsimony of the model.

We model stochastic volatility by

$$\sigma(M_t) \equiv \bar{\sigma} \left(\prod_{i=1}^{\bar{k}} M_{k,t} \right)^{1/2},$$

where $\bar{\sigma}$ is a positive constant. Returns r_t are then

$$r_t = \sigma(M_t)\varepsilon_t, \tag{3.1}$$

where the random variables $\{\varepsilon_t\}$ are i.i.d. standard Gaussians $\mathcal{N}(0,1)$. Since the multipliers are statistically independent, the parameter $\bar{\sigma}$ coincides with the unconditional standard deviation of the innovation r_t.

The transition probabilities $\gamma \equiv (\gamma_1, \gamma_2, \ldots, \gamma_{\bar{k}})$ are specified as

$$\gamma_k = 1 - (1 - \gamma_1)^{\left(b^{k-1}\right)}, \tag{3.2}$$

where $\gamma_1 \in (0,1)$ and $b \in (1, \infty)$. This specification was initially introduced in connection with the discretization of Poisson arrivals with exponentially increasing intensities, as will be explained Chapter 7.[1] Consider a process with very persistent components and thus a very small parameter γ_1. For small values of k, the quantity $\gamma_1 b^{k-1}$ remains small, and the transition probability satisfies

$$\gamma_k \approx \gamma_1 b^{k-1}.$$

The transition probabilities of low-frequency components grow approximately at geometric rate b. At higher frequencies, the rate of increase slows down, and condition (3.2) guarantees that the parameter γ_k remains lower than 1. In empirical applications, it is numerically convenient to estimate parameters of the same magnitude. Since $\gamma_1 < \ldots < \gamma_{\bar{k}} < 1 < b$, we choose $(\gamma_{\bar{k}}, b)$ to specify the set of transition probabilities.

We call this construct the Markov-Switching Multifractal (or Markov-Switching Multifrequency) process. The notation $\text{MSM}(\bar{k})$ refers to versions of the model with $\bar{k}$ frequencies, and we view the choice of $\bar{k}$ as a model selection problem. Economic intuition suggests that the multiplicative structure (3.1) is appealing to model the high variability and high volatility persistence exhibited by financial time series. When a low-level multiplier changes, volatility varies discontinuously and has strong persistence. In addition, high-frequency multipliers produce substantial outliers.

MSM imposes only minimal restrictions on the marginal distribution of the multipliers: $M \geq 0$ and $\mathbb{E}(M) = 1$, allowing flexible parametric or nonparametric specifications of M. A simple example is *binomial MSM*, in which the random variable M takes only two values, m_0 or m_1. For simplicity, we often assume that these two outcomes occur with equal probability, which implies that $m_1 = 2 - m_0$. The full parameter vector is then

$$\psi \equiv (m_0, \bar{\sigma}, b, \gamma_{\bar{k}}) \in \mathbb{R}_+^4,$$

where m_0 characterizes the distribution of the multipliers, $\bar{\sigma}$ is the unconditional standard deviation of returns, and b and $\gamma_{\bar{k}}$ define the set of switching probabilities.

---

[1] In continuous time, we will consider Poisson arrivals of intensity $\lambda_1 b^{k-1}$, $k \in \{1, \ldots, \bar{k}\}$. Correspondingly, the discretized process on a grid of step size Δt has transition probabilities $\gamma_k = 1 - \exp(-\lambda_1 b^{k-1} \Delta t)$, which satisfies (3.2).

We can naturally consider other parametric specifications for the distribution M. For example, *multinomial MSM* extends binomial MSM by allowing any discrete distribution satisfying the positivity and unit mean requirements. Continuous densities can also be useful. In Chapters 7 and 8 we assume that the distribution of M is lognormal, which defines *lognormal MSM*. In the remainder of Chapter 3 and in Chapter 4, we will see that even the simplest version of binomial MSM with equal probabilities is sufficient to produce good results in- and out-of-sample.

3.1.2   Basic Properties

$MSM(\bar{k})$ permits the parsimonious specification of a high-dimensional state space. Assume, for instance, that the distribution M is a binomial. Each volatility component $M_{k,t}$ is either high or low, and the state vector M_t can take $2^{\bar{k}}$ possible values. We will routinely work with models that have 10 components, or $2^{10} = 1,024$ states. MSM is also remarkably parsimonious. In a general Markov chain, the size of the transition matrix is equal to the square of the number of states. For instance, a Markov chain with 2^{10} states generally needs to be parametrized by $2^{10} \times 2^{10}$ or more than a million elements. In contrast, binomial MSM only requires four parameters.

Because binomial MSM is a pure regime-switching model, we can use all the tools that commonly apply to this class of processes. In the next section, we will review Bayesian updating and write the closed-form likelihood function. This book therefore brings to the literature a class of stochastic volatility models that have multiple degrees of persistence and can be estimated by maximum likelihood. The approach also creates a bridge between Markov-switching and multifractals, and permits the application of standard inference techniques to multifractal processes. The connection between fractal modeling and MSM will become more apparent in Part II.

A representative return series is illustrated in Figure 3.1. The graph reveals large heterogeneity in volatility levels and substantial outliers. This is notable since the return process has by construction finite moments of every order. It would be easy to obtain thick tails by considering i.i.d. shocks ε_t with Paretian distributions. In this chapter, however, we focus on the Gaussian case for several reasons. First, the likelihood is then available in closed form. Second, we will show that even when ε_t is Gaussian, high-frequency regime switches are sufficient to mimic in finite samples the heavy tails exhibited by financial data. Finally, the basic specification performs well relative to existing competitors and provides a useful benchmark for future refinements.

3.1.3   Low-Frequency Components and Long Memory

The MSM construction permits low-frequency regime shifts and long volatility cycles in sample paths. We will see that in exchange rate series,

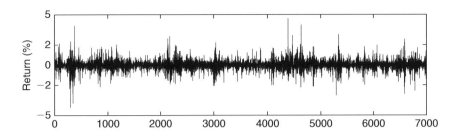

FIGURE 3.1. **Simulated MSM Process.** This figure illustrates the simulated log-returns of a binomial Markov-switching multifractal. The process has $\bar{k} = 8$ frequencies and parameter values $m_0 = 1.4$, $\bar{\sigma} = 0.5$, $\gamma_{\bar{k}} = 0.95$, and $b = 3$. These parameter values are roughly consistent with estimates reported in later sections of the chapter.

the duration of the most persistent component, $1/\gamma_1$, is typically of the same order as the length of the data. Estimated processes thus tend to generate volatility cycles with periods proportional to the sample size, a property also apparent in the sample paths of long-memory processes. As seen in Chapter 2, long memory is often defined by a hyperbolic decline in the autocovariance function as the lag goes to infinity. Fractionally integrated processes generate such patterns by assuming that an innovation linearly affects future periods at a hyperbolically declining weight. We now show that over a large range of intermediate lags, MSM similarly provides a slow decline in autocovariances, and hence mimics a defining characteristic of long memory with a Markov regime-switching mechanism that also gives abrupt volatility changes.

Consider a fixed parameter vector ψ, and for every moment $q \geq 0$ and every integer n, define the autocorrelation in levels:

$$\rho_q(n) = Corr(|r_t|^q, |r_{t+n}|^q).$$

Let $\alpha_1 < \alpha_2$ denote two arbitrary numbers in the open interval $(0, 1)$. The set of integers

$$I_{\bar{k}} = \{n : \alpha_1 \log_b(b^{\bar{k}}) \leq \log_b n \leq \alpha_2 \log_b(b^{\bar{k}})\}$$

contains a broad collection of lags. In the Appendix, we show the following:

Proposition 1 (Long-memory feature) *The autocorrelation in levels satisfies*

$$\sup_{n \in I_{\bar{k}}} \left| \frac{\ln \rho_q(n)}{\ln n^{-\delta(q)}} - 1 \right| \to 0 \ \ as \ \bar{k} \to +\infty,$$

where $\delta(q) = \log_b \mathbb{E}(M^q) - \log_b \left\{ [\mathbb{E}(M^{q/2})]^2 \right\}$.

Multifrequency volatility is therefore consistent over a large range of lags with the hyperbolic autocorrelation exhibited by many financial series.[2]

The proof of this result builds on the decomposition of log autocorrelation:

$$\ln \rho_q(n) \approx \sum_{k=1}^{\bar{k}} \ln \frac{\mathbb{E}(M_{k,t}^{q/2} M_{k,t+n}^{q/2})}{\mathbb{E}(M^q)},$$

and the mean-reversion property:

$$\mathbb{E}(M_{k,t}^{q/2} M_{k,t+n}^{q/2}) = \mathbb{E}(M^q)(1 - \gamma_k)^n + [\mathbb{E}(M^{q/2})]^2 [1 - (1 - \gamma_k)^n].$$

We infer:

$$\ln \rho_q(n) \approx \sum_{k=1}^{\bar{k}} \ln \frac{1 + (b^{\delta(q)} - 1)(1 - \gamma^*)^{nb^{k-\bar{k}}}}{b^{\delta(q)}}, \tag{3.3}$$

where the transition probability $\gamma^* = \gamma_{\bar{k}}$ is a fixed parameter. For any $n \in I_{\bar{k}}$, consider $k(n)$ such that $nb^{k(n)-\bar{k}} \approx 1$, or equivalently $k(n) \approx \bar{k} - \log_b(n)$. The kth addend in (3.3) is negligible if $k < k(n)$, and close to $-\delta(q) \ln b$ if $k > k(n)$, implying

$$\ln \rho_q(n) \approx -\delta(q)[\bar{k} - k(n)] \ln b,$$

or $\ln[\rho_q(n)] \approx -\delta(q) \ln n$. We also note that for n sufficiently large, the autocorrelation transitions smoothly from a hyperbolic to an exponential rate of decline.

The proof of Proposition 1 is reminiscent of Granger (1980) and Robinson (1978), who generate long memory by aggregating first-order autoregressive processes with heterogeneous coefficients.[3] MSM components are similarly mean-reverting with diverse decay rates, and their product correspondingly exhibits hyperbolic decay. The result also complements earlier research that has emphasized the difficulty of distinguishing between long memory and structural change in finite samples (e.g., Bhattacharya, Gupta, and Waymire, 1983; Diebold and Inoue, 2001; Granger and Hyung, 1999; Hidalgo and Robinson, 1996; Klemeš, 1974; Künsch, 1986; Lobato and Savin, 1997). The structure provided by MSM permits direct analysis of the approximate shape of the autocorrelation function, and allows us to identify the region of lags in which long memory-like behavior holds.

---

[2] See, for instance, Dacorogna *et al.* (1993), Ding, Granger, and Engle (1993), Baillie, Bollerslev, and Mikkelsen (1996), and Gouriéroux and Jasiak (2002).

[3] Ding and Granger (1996) use similar aggregation insights to specify a model of long-memory volatility.

MSM thus illustrates that a Markov chain can imitate one of the defining features of long memory, a hyperbolic decline of the autocovariogram.[4] The combination of long-memory behavior with sudden volatility movements in MSM has a natural appeal for financial econometrics.

3.2   Maximum Likelihood Estimation

When the multiplier M has a discrete distribution, there exist a finite number of volatility states. Standard filtering methods then provide the likelihood function in closed form.

3.2.1   Updating the State Vector

We assume in this section and the rest of the chapter that the distribution M is discrete. The Markov state vector M_t then takes finitely many values $m^1, \ldots, m^d \in \mathbb{R}_+^{\bar{k}}$, and its dynamics are characterized by the transition matrix $A = (a_{i,j})_{1 \leq i,j \leq d}$ with components $a_{ij} = \mathbb{P}(M_{t+1} = m^j \mid M_t = m^i)$.

Conditional on the volatility state, the return r_t has Gaussian density $f_{r_t}\left(r \mid M_t = m^i\right) = n\left[r; \sigma^2\left(m^i\right)\right]$, where $n\left(.; \sigma^2\right)$ denotes the density of a centered normal with variance σ^2. The econometrician does not directly observe M_t but can compute the conditional probabilities

$$\Pi_t^j \equiv \mathbb{P}\left(M_t = m^j \mid r_1, \ldots, r_t\right). \tag{3.4}$$

We can stack these probabilities in the row vector $\Pi_t = \left(\Pi_t^1, \ldots, \Pi_t^d\right) \in \mathbb{R}_+^d$.

The conditional probability vector is computed recursively. By Bayes' rule, Π_t can be expressed as a function of the previous belief Π_{t-1} and the innovation r_t:

$$\Pi_t = \frac{\omega(r_t) * (\Pi_{t-1} A)}{[\omega(r_t) * (\Pi_{t-1} A)] \mathbf{1}'}, \tag{3.5}$$

where $\mathbf{1} = (1, \ldots, 1) \in \mathbb{R}^d$, $x * y$ denotes the Hadamard product $(x_1 y_1, \ldots, x_d y_d)$ for any $x, y \in \mathbb{R}^d$, and

$$\omega(r_t) = \left(n\left[r_t; \sigma^2\left(m^1\right)\right], \ldots, n\left[r_t; \sigma^2\left(m^d\right)\right]\right).$$

These results are familiar in regime-switching models. In empirical applications, the initial vector Π_0 is chosen to be the ergodic distribution of

---

[4] Liu (2000) provides an example of long memory in a non-Markovian regime-switching environment. The model assumes independently drawn regimes with inter-arrival times drawn from a thick-tailed infinite variance distribution, which requires history dependence in transition probabilities.

the Markov process. Since the multipliers are mutually independent, the ergodic distribution is given by $\Pi_0^j = \prod_{l=1}^{\bar{k}} \mathbb{P}(M = m_l^j)$ for all j.

The multifrequency model can generate rich forecast dynamics. Consider the vector of past and current returns

$$\mathcal{R}_t = \{r_1, \ldots, r_t\}.$$

For each k, the n-step component forecast $\mathbb{E}(M_{k,t+n}|\mathcal{R}_t)$ monotonically reverts to $\mathbb{E}(M) = 1$ as the time horizon n increases, but the volatility forecasts $\mathbb{E}\left(\sigma^2\left(M_{t+n}\right)|\mathcal{R}_t\right)$ need not be monotonic in n. Consider, for instance, a state M_t with a low value of the transitory component $M_{\bar{k},t}$, and high values of $M_{1,t}, \ldots, M_{\bar{k}-1,t}$. In such a state, current volatility $\sigma^2\left(M_t\right)$ is high, but the volatility forecast $\mathbb{E}(\sigma^2\left(M_{t+n}\right)|M_t)$ can *increase* with n in the short run before decreasing toward the long-run mean $\bar{\sigma}^2$ at longer horizons. This suggests that MSM can provide finer filtering and forecasts than a unifrequency model.

3.2.2   Closed-Form Likelihood

Having solved the conditioning problem, we easily check that the log-likelihood function is

$$\ln L\left(r_1, \ldots, r_T; \psi\right) = \sum_{t=1}^{T} \ln[\omega(r_t) \cdot (\Pi_{t-1}A)],$$

where $x \cdot y$ denotes the inner product $x_1 y_1 + \cdots + x_d y_d$ for any $x, y \in \mathbb{R}^d$.

For a fixed $\bar{k}$, we know that the maximum likelihood (ML) estimator is consistent and asymptotically efficient as $T \to \infty$. The parsimonious parameterization of the transition matrix represents an important difference between MSM and standard Markov-switching models. This allows us to estimate MSM with reasonable precision even under a very large state space. While the Expectation Maximization (EM) algorithm (Hamilton, 1990) is not directly applicable to constrained transition probabilities, we have shown in Calvet and Fisher (2004) that numerical optimization of the likelihood function produces good results. Specifically, ML estimation of the parameters $m_0, \bar{\sigma}, b$, and $\gamma_{\bar{k}}$ of binomial MSM and model selection for the number of frequency components $\bar{k}$ produce reliable results in finite samples of the size considered in this book.

3.3   Empirical Results

Using a binomial specification for the multiplier M, we apply ML estimation to four exchange rate series and obtain preferred specifications with a large number of volatility frequencies.

3.3.1 Currency Data

The empirical analysis uses daily exchange rate data for the Deutsche mark (DM), Japanese yen (JA), British pound (UK), and Canadian dollar (CA), all against the U.S. dollar. The data consists of daily prices reported at noon by the Federal Reserve Bank of New York. The fixed exchange rate system broke down in early 1973, and the DM, JA, and UK series accordingly begin on 1 June 1973. The CA series starts a year later (1 June 1974) because the Canadian currency was held essentially at parity with the U.S. dollar for several months after the demise of Bretton Woods. The Deutsche mark was replaced by the euro at the beginning of 1999. The DM data thus ends on 31 December 1998, while the other three series run until 30 June 2002. Overall, the series contains 6,420 observations for the Deutsche mark, 7,049 observations for the Canadian dollar, and 7,299 observations for the yen and the pound.

Figure 3.2 illustrates the daily returns of each series and shows apparent volatility clustering at a range of frequencies. For each series, we compute in Table 3.1 the standard deviation of returns over the entire sample and over four subsamples of equal length. The sample standard deviation varies substantially across subperiods, consistent with the low-frequency regime shifts in MSM.

3.3.2 ML Estimation Results

Table 3.2 reports ML estimation results for all four currencies. The columns of the table correspond to the number of frequencies $\bar{k}$ varying from 1 to 10. The first column is a standard Markov-switching model with only two possible values for volatility. As $\bar{k}$ increases, the number of states increases at the rate $2^{\bar{k}}$. There are thus over one thousand states when $\bar{k} = 10$.

TABLE 3.1. Currency Volatility

	Standard Deviations of Daily Returns (%)				
	Entire Sample	By Subperiod			
		1	2	3	4
DM	0.664	0.587	0.716	0.708	0.635
JA	0.657	0.545	0.640	0.646	0.775
UK	0.607	0.486	0.724	0.699	0.473
CA	0.274	0.220	0.255	0.284	0.327

Notes: For each currency, this table reports the standard deviation of daily returns in percent over the entire subsample and over four evenly spaced subsamples. The Deutsche mark (DM) series begins on 1 June 1973 and ends on 31 December 1998. The Japanese yen (JA) and British pound (UK) samples span 1 June 1973 to 31 December 2002. The Canadian dollar (CA) series begins 1 June 1974 and ends 31 December 2002. The results show that the variability of return variance is substantial even at very low frequencies.

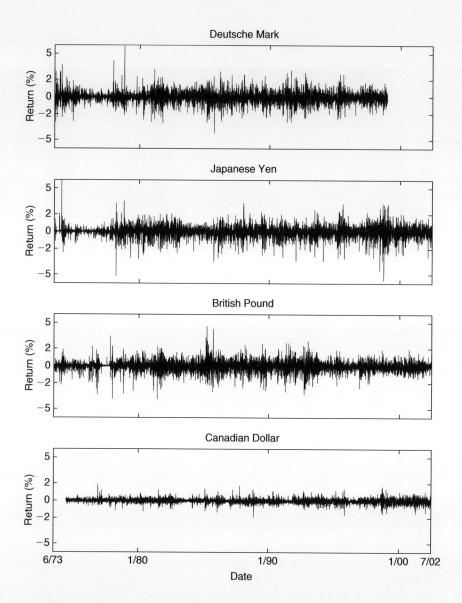

FIGURE 3.2. **Daily Currency Returns.** This figure illustrates the daily log-returns, in percent, of four exchange rate series. The Japanese yen and British pound run from 1 June 1973 to 31 December 2002. The Canadian dollar was held essentially at parity with the U.S. dollar shortly after the demise of the Bretton Woods system, and our sample therefore starts on 1 June 1974. The Deutsche mark was replaced by the euro at the beginning of 1999, and the series ends on 31 December 1998.

TABLE 3.2. Maximum Likelihood Results

	$\bar{k}=1$	2	3	4	5	6	7	8	9	10
					Deutsche Mark/U.S. Dollar					
$\hat{m}_0$	1.654	1.590	1.555	1.492	1.462	1.413	1.380	1.353	1.351	1.326
	(0.013)	(0.012)	(0.013)	(0.013)	(0.012)	(0.013)	(0.012)	(0.011)	(0.013)	(0.015)
$\hat{\sigma}$	0.682	0.651	0.600	0.572	0.512	0.538	0.547	0.550	0.674	0.643
	(0.012)	(0.018)	(0.014)	(0.016)	(0.018)	(0.026)	(0.021)	(0.025)	(0.035)	(0.073)
$\hat{\gamma}_{\bar{k}}$	0.075	0.107	0.672	0.714	0.751	0.858	0.932	0.974	0.966	0.959
	(0.011)	(0.022)	(0.151)	(0.096)	(0.106)	(0.128)	(0.071)	(0.042)	(0.065)	(0.066)
$\hat{b}$	—	8.01	21.91	10.42	7.89	5.16	4.12	3.38	3.29	2.70
		(2.58)	(7.30)	(1.92)	(1.31)	(0.76)	(0.48)	(0.36)	(0.47)	(0.36)
$\ln L$	−5920.86	−5782.96	−5731.78	−5715.31	−5708.25	−5706.91	−5704.48	−5704.77	−5704.86	−5705.09
					Japanese Yen/U.S. Dollar					
$\hat{m}_0$	1.797	1.782	1.693	1.654	1.640	1.573	1.565	1.513	1.475	1.448
	(0.011)	(0.009)	(0.010)	(0.010)	(0.010)	(0.010)	(0.010)	(0.010)	(0.010)	(0.011)
$\hat{\sigma}$	0.630	0.538	0.566	0.462	0.709	0.642	0.518	0.514	0.486	0.461
	(0.011)	(0.009)	(0.017)	(0.013)	(0.023)	(0.023)	(0.018)	(0.020)	(0.026)	(0.036)
$\hat{\gamma}_{\bar{k}}$	0.199	0.345	0.312	0.697	0.778	0.899	0.897	0.975	0.995	0.998
	(0.019)	(0.033)	(0.054)	(0.080)	(0.076)	(0.060)	(0.057)	(0.034)	(0.010)	(0.006)
$\hat{b}$	—	134.20	12.46	15.58	16.03	8.07	7.46	5.65	4.43	3.76
		(48.27)	(2.18)	(2.67)	(2.67)	(1.03)	(0.89)	(0.78)	(0.53)	(0.45)
$\ln L$	−6451.80	−6102.18	−5959.72	−5900.67	−5882.93	−5871.35	−5867.88	−5863.20	−5863.01	−5862.68

British Pound/U.S. Dollar

	$k=1$	$k=2$	$k=3$	$k=4$	$k=5$	$k=6$	$k=7$	$k=8$	$k=9$	$k=10$
$\hat{m}_0$	1.716	1.671	1.648	1.609	1.579	1.534	1.503	1.461	1.428	1.403
	(0.012)	(0.011)	(0.011)	(0.011)	(0.011)	(0.012)	(0.012)	(0.011)	(0.011)	(0.009)
$\hat{\sigma}$	0.609	0.590	0.513	0.467	0.421	0.468	0.389	0.384	0.374	0.370
	(0.009)	(0.011)	(0.016)	(0.016)	(0.017)	(0.019)	(0.014)	(0.015)	(0.022)	(0.022)
$\hat{\gamma}_{\bar{k}}$	0.110	0.222	0.278	0.645	0.637	0.784	0.811	0.958	0.964	0.982
	(0.017)	(0.034)	(0.052)	(0.080)	(0.075)	(0.078)	(0.083)	(0.052)	(0.043)	(0.031)
$\hat{b}$	—	19.90	14.29	12.51	11.02	8.32	6.72	5.23	4.08	3.45
		(5.19)	(2.58)	(2.00)	(1.74)	(1.15)	(0.91)	(0.69)	(0.41)	(0.32)
$\ln L$	−5960.18	−5724.37	−5622.73	−5570.02	−5537.80	−5523.64	−5516.89	−5515.37	−5515.28	−5514.94

Canadian Dollar/U.S. Dollar

	$k=1$	$k=2$	$k=3$	$k=4$	$k=5$	$k=6$	$k=7$	$k=8$	$k=9$	$k=10$
$\hat{m}_0$	1.646	1.556	1.474	1.435	1.386	1.374	1.338	1.319	1.296	1.278
	(0.012)	(0.012)	(0.014)	(0.015)	(0.012)	(0.013)	(0.012)	(0.016)	(0.013)	(0.012)
$\hat{\sigma}$	0.280	0.278	0.293	0.263	0.251	0.295	0.282	0.262	0.259	0.262
	(0.005)	(0.006)	(0.014)	(0.009)	(0.010)	(0.011)	(0.013)	(0.017)	(0.015)	(0.021)
$\hat{\gamma}_{\bar{k}}$	0.064	0.109	0.129	0.171	0.441	0.524	0.593	0.594	0.631	0.644
	(0.009)	(0.016)	(0.040)	(0.062)	(0.153)	(0.128)	(0.145)	(0.151)	(0.155)	(0.158)
$\hat{b}$	—	10.92	4.76	3.95	4.02	4.08	3.11	2.72	2.35	2.11
		(3.12)	(1.15)	(0.83)	(0.76)	(0.58)	(0.39)	(0.39)	(0.25)	(0.18)
$\ln L$	−271.01	−129.80	−105.16	−91.32	−88.41	−84.73	−84.03	−83.40	−83.06	−83.00

Notes: This table reports maximum likelihood estimates of binomial MSM for the four exchange rate series. The estimates are based on daily log returns in percent. Each column corresponds to a given number of components k in the MSM specification. The likelihood function increases monotonically in the number of volatility components for all currencies except the Deutsche mark, which peaks at $\bar{k} = 7$. Asymptotic standard errors are in parentheses.

We begin by examining the DM data. The multiplier parameter $\hat{m}_0$ tends to decline with $\bar{k}$ because with a larger number of components, less variability is required in each $M_{k,t}$ to match the fluctuations in volatility exhibited by the data. The estimates of $\hat{\sigma}$ vary across $\bar{k}$ with no particular pattern. Standard errors of $\hat{\sigma}$ increase with $\bar{k}$, consistent with the idea that long-run averages are difficult to identify in models permitting long volatility cycles. We next examine the frequency parameters $\hat{\gamma}_{\bar{k}}$ and $\hat{b}$. When $\bar{k} = 1$, the single multiplier has a duration slightly lower than two weeks. As $\bar{k}$ increases, the switching probability of the highest frequency multiplier increases until a switch occurs about once a day for large $\bar{k}$. At the same time, the estimate $\hat{b}$ decreases steadily with $\bar{k}$. When $\bar{k} = 10$, we infer from (3.2) that the lowest frequency multiplier has a duration approximately equal to ten years, or about one-third the sample size. Thus, as $\bar{k}$ increases, the range of frequencies spreads out, while the spacing between frequencies becomes tighter.

The other currencies generate parameter estimates with similar properties. In all cases, $\hat{m}_0$ tends to decrease with $\bar{k}$. The values of $\hat{m}_0$, and thus the importance of stochastic volatility, are largest for JA and UK and smallest for CA. Variability across $\bar{k}$ in the estimates of $\hat{\sigma}$ is also greatest for JA and UK and least for CA. As $\bar{k}$ increases, the most transitory multiplier switches more often and the spacing between frequencies becomes tighter for all currencies. The most persistent multiplier has the longest duration for the yen at approximately three times the sample size and the smallest for the Canadian dollar at approximately one-tenth the sample size.

For large $\bar{k}$, the estimated $\text{MSM}(\bar{k})$ processes generate substantial outliers despite having finite moments of every order. For each currency, we use the estimated process with $\bar{k} = 10$ frequencies to generate ten thousand paths of the same length as the data, and we compute a Hill (1975) tail index α for each simulated path.[5] Basing the index on 100 order statistics, the empirical tail index and the average α in the simulated samples are, respectively, equal to 4.74 and 4.34 (DM), 3.91 and 3.75 (JA), 4.59 and 4.03

---

[5] The tail index measures the rate of decline in the extremes of a distribution. For example, given a Paretian tail satisfying $\mathbb{P}\left(X > x\right) \sim kx^{-\alpha}$ for large x, the characteristic exponent, or tail index, is α, and only moments of order up to α are finite. If $X_{n1} \leq X_{n2} \leq \ldots \leq X_{nn}$ are the order statistics of $\{X_t\}_{t=1}^{n}$ in ascending order, then Hill's (1975) tail estimator is

$$\hat{\alpha}_s = \left(\frac{1}{s} \sum_{j=1}^{s} \ln X_{n,n-j+1} - \ln X_{n,n-s} \right)^{-1}.$$

This estimator is consistent and asympotically normal (Hall, 1982). Related estimators of the tail index are proposed by Pickands (1975) and de Haan and Resnick (1980). Applications in finance and extensions include Gabaix *et al.* (2003, 2006), Hols and de Vries (1991), Jansen and de Vries (1991), Kearns and Pagan (1997), Loretan and Phillips (1994), Quintos, Fan, and Phillips (2001), and Wagner and Marsh (2005).

(UK), and 4.40 and 4.79 (CA). Furthermore, for all currencies we cannot at the 10% level reject equality of the simulated and empirical tail statistics. This result is caused by the variations in volatility in the estimated models. The distribution of returns in MSM is a mixture of Gaussians, which has finite moments of every order. With the highest frequency multipliers taking new values almost daily, this mixture appears to be more than sufficient to capture the tail characteristics of the data, even in a sample containing thirty years of daily observations.[6]

We finally examine the behavior of the log-likelihood function as the number of frequencies $\bar{k}$ increases from 1 to 10. For each currency, the likelihood goes up substantially at low $\bar{k}$ and in most cases continues to increase at a decreasing rate. The only exception to the monotonic increase in likelihood occurs in the DM series, for which the likelihood reaches a peak at $\bar{k} = 7$. In all other cases, the likelihood reaches a maximum at $\bar{k} = 10$. This behavior of the likelihood confirms that fluctuations in volatility occur with heterogeneous degrees of persistence, and explicitly incorporating a larger number of frequencies results in a better fit.

3.3.3 Model Selection

We now examine the statistical significance of the differences in likelihoods across estimated MSM($\bar{k}$) processes. Consider two models MSM($\bar{k}$) and MSM($\bar{k}'$), $\bar{k} \neq \bar{k}'$, with respective densities f and g. The processes are nonnested and have log-likelihood difference:

$$\sqrt{T}(\ln L_T^f - \ln L_T^g) = \frac{1}{\sqrt{T}} \sum_{t=1}^{T} \ln \frac{f(r_t \,|\, r_1, \ldots, r_{t-1})}{g(r_t \,|\, r_1, \ldots, r_{t-1})}.$$

Consider the null hypothesis that the models have identical unconditional expected log-likelihoods. When the observations $\{r_t\}$ are i.i.d., Vuong (1989) shows that the difference $\ln L_T^f - \ln L_T^g$ is asymptotically normal under the null. In addition, the variance of this difference is consistently estimated by the sample variance of the addends $\ln[f(r_t \,|\, r_1, \ldots, r_{t-1})/g(r_t \,|\, r_1, \ldots, r_{t-1})]$. Since the observations $\{r_t\}$ are typically not i.i.d. in financial applications, in the Appendix we construct a heteroskedasticity and autocorrelation consistent (HAC) version of the Vuong test. Our discussion is a simplified version of the broader approach proposed by Rivers and Vuong (2002).

For each $\bar{k} \in \{1, \ldots, 9\}$, we test in Table 3.3 the null hypothesis that MSM($\bar{k}$) and MSM(10) fit the data equally well. Since HAC-adjusted

---

[6] An extensive literature investigates the close connection between mixtures and fat tails. For instance, Student and Cauchy distributions can be represented as mixtures of normals (e.g., Andrews and Mallows, 1974; Blattberg and Gonedes, 1974; Praetz, 1972), and the distinction between mixtures and Paretian distributions is therefore difficult to make in practice (e.g., Kon, 1984). Furthermore, MSM mimics long-memory behavior, which impacts tail index estimation (e.g., Kearns and Pagan, 1997).

TABLE 3.3. MSM Model Selection

	$\bar{k}=1$	2	3	4	5	6	7	8	9
A. Vuong (1989) Test									
DM	-8.655	-5.523	-2.972	-1.858	-0.688	-0.733	0.341	0.204	0.337
	(0.000)	(0.000)	(0.001)	(0.032)	(0.246)	(0.232)	(0.633)	(0.581)	(0.632)
JA	-13.067	-8.406	-5.342	-3.154	-2.156	-1.192	-1.108	-0.180	-0.162
	(0.000)	(0.000)	(0.000)	(0.001)	(0.016)	(0.117)	(0.134)	(0.429)	(0.436)
UK	-11.810	-8.337	-6.267	-4.360	-2.984	-1.334	-0.408	-0.149	-0.236
	(0.000)	(0.000)	(0.000)	(0.000)	(0.001)	(0.089)	(0.342)	(0.441)	(0.407)
CA	-8.475	-4.421	-3.289	-1.795	-2.108	-0.862	-0.825	-0.472	-0.158
	(0.000)	(0.000)	(0.000)	(0.036)	(0.017)	(0.194)	(0.205)	(0.318)	(0.437)
B. HAC-Adjusted Vuong Test									
DM	-4.285	-3.033	-1.683	-1.101	-0.402	-0.424	0.197	0.120	0.194
	(0.000)	(0.001)	(0.046)	(0.135)	(0.344)	(0.336)	(0.578)	(0.548)	(0.577)
JA	-5.219	-4.262	-2.865	-1.645	-1.224	-0.648	-0.663	-0.105	-0.098
	(0.000)	(0.000)	(0.002)	(0.050)	(0.111)	(0.259)	(0.254)	(0.458)	(0.461)
UK	-3.788	-2.804	-2.803	-2.195	-1.759	-0.779	-0.242	-0.088	-0.137
	(0.000)	(0.003)	(0.003)	(0.014)	(0.039)	(0.218)	(0.404)	(0.465)	(0.446)
CA	-4.237	-2.383	-1.789	-1.019	-1.150	-0.480	-0.445	-0.276	-0.091
	(0.000)	(0.009)	(0.037)	(0.154)	(0.125)	(0.316)	(0.328)	(0.391)	(0.464)

Notes: This table reports *t*-ratios and one-sided *p*-values for the log-likelihood difference of the model in each column against MSM with 10 frequencies. Panel A uses the Vuong (1989) methodology, and Panel B adjusts for heteroskedasticity and autocorrelation using Newey and West (1987, 1994). A low *p*-value indicates that the corresponding model would be rejected in favor of MSM with 10 frequencies.

tests tend to perform poorly in small samples,[7] we compute t-ratios and one-sided p-values using both the original and the HAC-adjusted methods. For $\bar{k} \in \{1, 2, 3\}$, the log-likelihood difference is significant at the 1% level in the nonadjusted case (Table 3.3A) and at the 5% level in the HAC case (Table 3.3B). This represents strong evidence that MSM(10) significantly outperforms models with one to three frequencies. For $\bar{k} \in \{4, 5\}$, we reject the null at the 5% (nonadjusted) and 20% (HAC-adjusted) levels in almost all cases. These results provide substantial evidence that MSM(10) outperforms models with four or five frequencies. Lower significance levels are obtained for larger values of $\bar{k}$, and the overall conclusion is that MSM works better for larger numbers of frequencies. For this reason and for consistency in the remaining analysis, we henceforth focus on the MSM($\bar{k} = 10$) process for all currencies.

3.4   Comparison with Alternative Models

We now compare the multifractal model with GARCH(1,1) and Markov-switching GARCH, which are among the best traditional models for volatility forecasting. The multifractal is then compared with fractionally integrated GARCH in order to assess the connection between long memory and forecasting performance.

The alternative processes have the form $r_t = h_t^{1/2} \varepsilon_t$, where h_t is the conditional variance of r_t at date $t - 1$, and $\{\varepsilon_t\}$ are i.i.d. Student innovations with unit variance and ν degrees of freedom. GARCH(1,1) assumes the recursion $h_{t+1} = \omega + \alpha r_t^2 + \beta h_t$, as described in Chapter 2. MS-GARCH combines short-run autoregressive dynamics with low-frequency regime shifts. A latent state $s_t \in \{1, 2\}$ follows a first-order Markov process with transition probabilities

$$p_{ij} = \mathbb{P}\left(s_{t+1} = j \,\middle|\, s_t = i\right).$$

In every period, the econometrician observes the return r_t but not the latent s_t. For $i = \{1, 2\}$, let $h_{t+1}(i) = Var_t(r_{t+1}|s_{t+1} = i)$ be the variance of r_{t+1} conditional on $s_{t+1} = i$ and past returns $\{r_s\}_{s=1}^t$. The quantity h_t is latent in every period, and the econometrician can similarly define $\mathbb{E}_t\left[h_t(s_t)\,|s_{t+1} = i\right]$, the expectation of h_t conditional on $s_{t+1} = i$ and past returns. Klaassen (2002) assumes the conditional dynamics:

$$h_{t+1}(i) = \omega_i + \alpha_i r_t^2 + \beta_i \mathbb{E}_t\left[h_t(s_t)\,|s_{t+1} = i\right]. \tag{3.6}$$

Klaassen shows that this model provides better forecasts for three of the exchange rates considered in this chapter (DM, JA, and UK) than the

---

[7] See, for example, Andrews (1991), Andrews and Monahan (1992), and den Haan and Levin (1997).

earlier Markov-Switching GARCH formulation of Gray (1996), and also permits analytical multistep forecasting.

3.4.1 In-Sample Comparison

Table 3.4 presents the ML estimates of GARCH and MS-GARCH. The coefficient $1/\nu$ is the inverse of the degrees of freedom in the Student distribution. Each coefficient σ_i, $i = 1, 2$, represents the standard deviation of returns conditional on the volatility state: $\sigma_i^2 = \omega_i/(1 - \alpha_i - \beta_i)$.

Table 3.5 shows that MSM has a higher likelihood than GARCH for all exchange rates, even though both processes have the same number of parameters. MS-GARCH uses nine parameters as compared to four with either GARCH or MSM. Using the Schwarz BIC criterion to adjust for this difference, the multifractal model is indistinguishable from MS-GARCH in the UK data and is preferred for DM and CA.

As suggested by Vuong (1989), we evaluate the statistical significance of BIC differences. The last two columns of Table 3.5 test the alternative models against MSM under this metric.[8] We again give p-values for both the original version of the test and a HAC-adjusted variant. For the standard test, the in-sample performance of MSM over GARCH is highly significant for the mark, the yen, and the pound, and somewhat significant for the Canadian dollar. The HAC adjustments produce analogous but slightly weaker results. Overall, the in-sample analysis suggests that the multifractal matches the performance MS-GARCH and significantly outperforms GARCH(1,1).

3.4.2 Out-of-Sample Forecasts

We now investigate the out-of-sample performance of the competing models over forecasting horizons ranging from 1 to 50 days. For each currency, we estimate the three processes on the beginning of the series, and we use the last 12 years of data (or approximately half the sample) for out-of-sample comparison.

In Table 3.6, we report the results for one-day forecasts. The first two columns correspond to the Mincer–Zarnowitz regressions of squared returns on their forecasts[9]:

$$r_t^2 = \gamma_0 + \gamma_1 \mathbb{E}_{t-1}(r_t^2) + u_t.$$

---

[8] A BIC test of GARCH against the multifractal model is identical to a likelihood test since both have the same number of parameters.

[9] The forecasting regressions used by Mincer and Zarnowitz (1969) are common in the financial econometrics literature. See, for instance, Andersen and Bollerslev (1998a), Andersen, Bollerslev, Diebold, and Labys (2003), Andersen, Bollerslev, and Meddahi (2005), Pagan and Schwert (1990), and West and Cho (1995).

TABLE 3.4. Alternative Processes

		Regime 1				Regime 2				
	$1/\nu$	σ_1	α_1	β_1	p_{11}	σ_2	α_2	β_2	p_{22}	$\ln L$
Deutsche Mark/U.S. Dollar										
GARCH	0.1929 (0.011)	1.5539 (0.405)	0.0879 (0.009)	0.9108 (0.009)						−5730.52
MS-GARCH	0.2041 (0.011)	1.0749 (0.288)	0.2048 (0.023)	0.7896 (0.024)	0.9998 (0.0003)	1.3145 (0.282)	0.0718 (0.010)	0.9241 (0.011)	0.9999 (0.0002)	−5694.78
Japanese Yen/U.S. Dollar										
GARCH	0.2290 (0.0002)	0.1638 (0.059)	0.0652 (0.006)	0.9348 (0.006)						−5965.07
MS-GARCH	0.2632 (0.012)	0.4443 (0.137)	0.3420 (0.040)	0.6500 (0.040)	0.9999 (0.0002)	0.9639 (0.121)	0.0650 (0.010)	0.9227 (0.013)	0.9999 (0.0002)	−5833.59

British Pound/U.S. Dollar

GARCH	0.2007 (0.008)	0.2365 (0.070)	0.0681 (0.005)	0.9319 (0.005)						−5562.00
MS-GARCH	0.2202 (0.009)	0.8423 (0.013)	0.3653 (0.053)	0.6051 (0.056)	0.9860 (0.005)	0.9343 (0.012)	0.0587 (0.008)	0.9365 (0.008)	0.9986 (0.0003)	−5492.44

Canadian Dollar/U.S. Dollar

GARCH	0.1528 (0.037)	0.3108 (0.008)	0.0810 (0.008)	0.9108 (0.010)						−96.03
MS-GARCH	0.1385 (0.011)	0.2046 (0.035)	0.0584 (0.009)	0.9361 (0.010)	0.9896 (0.004)	0.2972 (0.025)	0.2587 (0.074)	0.2925 (0.215)	0.9415 (0.023)	−73.51

Notes: This table shows maximum likelihood estimation results for alternative processes for the four exchange rate series. Asymptotic standard errors are in parentheses. For the GARCH(1,1) model, the parameter estimates for the Japanese yen and British pound are on the boundary of the restriction $\alpha + \beta \leq 1 - \epsilon$, where $\epsilon = 10^{-5}$.

TABLE 3.5. In-Sample Model Comparison

	No. of Parameters	ln L	BIC	BIC p-value vs. MSM	
				Vuong (1989)	HAC Adj
Deutsche Mark/U.S. Dollar					
Binomial MSM	4	−5705.09	1.7830		
GARCH	4	−5730.52	1.7910	0.005	0.071
MS-GARCH	9	−5694.78	1.7866	0.140	0.248
Japanese Yen/U.S. Dollar					
Binomial MSM	4	−5862.68	1.6115		
GARCH	4	−5965.07	1.6396	0.000	0.008
MS-GARCH	9	−5833.59	1.6097	0.619	0.572
British Pound/U.S. Dollar					
Binomial MSM	4	−5514.94	1.5162		
GARCH	4	−5562.00	1.5291	0.004	0.070
MS-GARCH	9	−5492.44	1.5162	0.505	0.503
Canadian Dollar/U.S. Dollar					
Binomial MSM	4	−83.00	0.0286		
GARCH	4	−96.03	0.0323	0.072	0.200
MS-GARCH	9	−73.51	0.0322	0.092	0.235

Notes: This table summarizes information about in-sample goodness of fit for the three models. The Bayesian Information Criterion is given by BIC $= T^{-1}(-2\ln L + NP\ln T)$, where NP is the number of free parameters in the specification. The sample lengths T are 6,419 for the Deutsche mark, 7,298 for the Japanese yen and British pound, and 7,048 for the Canadian dollar. The last two columns give p-values from a test that the corresponding model dominates MSM by the BIC criterion. The first value uses the Vuong (1989) methodology, and the second value adjusts the test for heteroskedasticity and autocorrelation. A low p-value indicates that the corresponding model would be rejected in favor of MSM.

Unbiased forecasts would imply $\gamma_0 = 0$ and $\gamma_1 = 1$. We adjust standard errors for parameter uncertainty as in West and McCracken (1998), and for HAC effects using the weighting and lag selection methodology of Newey and West (1987, 1994).

With the multifractal process, the estimated intercept $\hat{\gamma}_0$ is slightly positive and the slope $\hat{\gamma}_1$ is slightly lower than unity for all currencies. These differences, however, are not statistically significant. In particular, the hypothesis $\gamma_0 = 0$ is accepted at the 5% confidence level for all currencies, and $\gamma_1 = 1$ is accepted at the 5% level for the yen and the Canadian dollar,

TABLE 3.6. One-Day Forecasts

	Mincer–Zarnowitz		Restricted $\gamma_0 = 0, \gamma_1 = 1$	
	γ_0	γ_1	MSE	R^2
Deutsche Mark/U.S. Dollar				
Binomial MSM	0.098	0.703	0.7263	0.041
	(0.072)	(0.126)		
GARCH	0.153	0.622	0.7304	0.035
	(0.061)	(0.105)		
MS-GARCH	0.042	0.740	0.7296	0.037
	(0.080)	(0.130)		
Japanese Yen/U.S. Dollar				
Binomial MSM	0.028	0.772	1.6053	0.053
	(0.090)	(0.117)		
GARCH	0.172	0.668	1.6137	0.048
	(0.075)	(0.105)		
MS-GARCH	0.080	0.709	1.6141	0.048
	(0.084)	(0.109)		
British Pound/U.S. Dollar				
Binomial MSM	0.053	0.715	0.5081	0.057
	(0.049)	(0.100)		
GARCH	0.085	0.751	0.4980	0.076
	(0.044)	(0.098)		
MS-GARCH	0.017	0.814	0.4997	0.072
	(0.051)	(0.108)		
Canadian Dollar/U.S. Dollar				
Binomial MSM	0.015	0.905	0.0345	0.051
	(0.016)	(0.156)		
GARCH	0.033	0.679	0.0348	0.042
	(0.012)	(0.111)		
MS-GARCH	0.025	0.785	0.0344	0.055
	(0.013)	(0.124)		

Notes: This table gives out-of-sample forecasting results for the three models at a one-day horizon. The first two columns correspond to parameter estimates from the Mincer-Zarnowitz OLS regression $r_t^2 = \gamma_0 + \gamma_1 \mathbb{E}_{t-1}(r_t^2) + u_t$. Asymptotic standard errors in parentheses are corrected for heteroskedasticity and autocorrelation using the method of Newey and West (1987, 1994) and for parameter uncertainty using the method of West and McCracken (1998). MSE is the mean squared forecast error, and R^2 is one less the MSE divided by the sum of squared demeaned squared returns in the out-of-sample period.

and at the 1% level for the mark and the pound. The Mincer–Zarnowitz regressions show little evidence of bias in MSM forecasts.

The regression coefficients are slightly worse with GARCH(1,1). Intercepts are further away from zero for all currencies, and slopes are further away from unity for three currencies. These biases are statistically significant. The hypotheses $\gamma_0 = 0$ and $\gamma_1 = 1$ are rejected at the 5% level in seven out of eight cases. Since $0 < \hat{\gamma}_1 < 1$, these results suggest that GARCH forecasts are too variable and can be improved by the linear smoothing rule $\hat{\gamma}_0 + \hat{\gamma}_1 \mathbb{E}_{t-1}(r_t^2)$.

Markov-switching GARCH improves on the out-of-sample performance of GARCH(1,1). We accept that $\gamma_0 = 0$ at the 5% confidence level for all currencies and that $\gamma_1 = 1$ at the 1% level for DM, UK, and CA. Furthermore, the regression estimates are best with MS-GARCH for two currencies (DM and UK) and with the multifractal for the other two. We also report in Table 3.6 two standard measures of goodness of fit: the mean squared error (MSE) and the restricted R^2 coefficient.[10] The multifractal produces the best forecasting R^2 for the mark and the yen. On the other hand, GARCH produces better results for the pound and MS-GARCH for the Canadian dollar. To summarize the one-day forecast results, binomial MSM appears to slightly dominate GARCH(1,1) and to produce results comparable to MS-GARCH.

Multistep forecasts provide stronger empirical differences between the three models. Following Andersen and Bollerslev (1998a), the dependent variable is the sum of squared daily returns over n days, $RV_{t,n} = \sum_{s=t-n+1}^{t} r_s^2$. In Table 3.7, we report the results of the Mincer–Zarnowitz regression:

$$RV_{t,n} = \gamma_0 + \gamma_1 \mathbb{E}_{t-n}(RV_{t,n}) + u_t$$

for $n = 20$ days. Because the average size of returns increases with the sampling interval, the estimated intercepts $\hat{\gamma}_0$ are larger in Table 3.7 than in Table 3.6. For each currency, the multifractal produces point estimates of γ_0 and γ_1 that are closest to their preferred values. We also accept the hypotheses $\gamma_0 = 0$ and $\gamma_1 = 1$ in all cases at the 5% confidence level. In contrast, for the other models each currency leads to a strong rejection of either one hypothesis (MS-GARCH) or both (GARCH) at the 5% confidence level. The reported MSE and R^2 further confirm that the multifractal provides the best 20-day forecasts for all currencies. The difference is particularly large in the case of the DM and JA. The R^2 coefficient is

---

[10] The mean squared error (MSE) quantifies the forecast errors in the out-of-sample period: $MSE = K^{-1} \sum_{t=T-K+1}^{T} (r_t^2 - \mathbb{E}_{t-1} r_t^2)^2$, where K is the number of days in the out-of-sample period. The out-of-sample coefficient of determination is $R^2 = 1 - MSE/TSS$, where TSS is the out-of-sample variance of squared returns: $TSS = K^{-1} \sum_{t=T-K+1}^{T} \left(r_t^2 - \sum_{t=T-K+1}^{T} r_t^2/K \right)^2$.

TABLE 3.7. Twenty-Day Forecasts

	Mincer–Zarnowitz		Restricted $\gamma_0 = 0, \gamma_1 = 1$	
	γ_0	γ_1	MSE	R^2
Deutsche Mark/U.S. Dollar				
Binomial MSM	1.749	0.706	37.12	0.135
	(1.649)	(0.150)		
GARCH	4.474	0.443	49.24	−0.147
	(1.108)	(0.092)		
MS-GARCH	1.934	0.568	50.66	−0.180
	(1.577)	(0.118)		
Japanese Yen/U.S. Dollar				
Binomial MSM	−1.248	0.909	76.95	0.205
	(2.160)	(0.155)		
GARCH	5.311	0.488	99.15	−0.024
	(1.233)	(0.086)		
MS-GARCH	2.148	0.573	103.29	−0.067
	(1.776)	(0.108)		
British Pound/U.S. Dollar				
Binomial MSM	0.330	0.792	27.35	0.250
	(1.114)	(0.120)		
GARCH	2.702	0.606	29.61	0.188
	(0.760)	(0.085)		
MS-GARCH	0.641	0.730	29.08	0.203
	(1.021)	(0.105)		
Canadian Dollar/U.S. Dollar				
Binomial MSM	−0.038	1.179	1.6339	0.217
	(0.385)	(0.221)		
GARCH	0.676	0.707	1.6615	0.204
	(0.243)	(0.121)		
MS-GARCH	0.630	0.754	1.6719	0.199
	(0.270)	(0.140)		

Notes: This table gives out-of-sample forecasting results for the three models at a twenty-day horizon. The first two columns correspond to parameter estimates from the Mincer-Zarnowitz OLS regression $RV_{t,20} = \gamma_0 + \gamma_1 \mathbb{E}_{t-20}(RV_{t,20}) + u_t$, where $RV_{t,n} = \sum_{s=t-n+1}^{t} r_s^2$. Asymptotic standard errors in parentheses are corrected for heteroskedasticity and autocorrelation using the method of Newey and West (1987, 1994) and for parameter uncertainty using the method of West and McCracken (1998). MSE is the mean squared forecast error, and R^2 is one less the MSE divided by the sum of squared demeaned squared returns in the out-of-sample period.

13.5% and 20.5% respectively for DM and JA with the multifractal, while GARCH and MS-GARCH produce negative values.[11]

Table 3.8 reports summary forecasting results and significance tests for horizons of 1, 5, 10, 20, and 50 days. Panel A shows the forecasting R^2 for each model. For the mark and the yen, binomial MSM dominates at the five-day horizon and increasingly outperforms the other models at longer horizons. For the pound and the Canadian dollar, binomial MSM is more accurate at horizons of 20 days and higher. Panel B analyzes the statistical significance of these results. At horizons of 50 days, the multifractal model outperforms the other models very significantly for the mark, the pound, and the yen, and with marginal significance for the Canadian dollar. The superior forecasts of the multifractal are also highly significant at horizons of 10 and 20 days for DM, and somewhat strong at the 20-day horizons for the yen and the pound.

These results show the power of the multifractal model. GARCH(1,1) is often viewed as a standard benchmark that is very difficult to outperform in forecasting exercises. Our results show that MSM matches or slightly improves on GARCH and MS-GARCH at short horizons, and substantially dominates these models at longer horizons.

3.4.3 Comparison with FIGARCH

The out-of-sample results suggest that MSM accurately captures the dependence structure of volatility at long horizons. It is natural to next investigate whether a fractionally integrated GARCH (FIGARCH) volatility process also provides good long-range forecasts. We consider the FIGARCH$(1, d, 0)$ specification of Baillie, Bollerslev, and Mikkelsen (1996).[12] The return process is given by $r_t = h_t^{1/2}\varepsilon_t$, where $\{\varepsilon_t\}$ are i.i.d. Student innovations with unit variance and ν degrees of freedom. The conditional variance h_t satisfies

$$h_{t+1} = \omega + \beta(h_t - r_t^2) + [1 - (1 - L)^d]r_t^2,$$

where L denotes the lag operator and $d \in [0, 1]$ the long-memory parameter. FIGARCH is well-defined, strictly stationary, and ergodic when $\omega \geq 0$ and $|\beta| < 1$. For every $d > 0$, the process is not covariance stationary because

---

[11] Binomial MSM produces a higher R^2 for 20-day returns than for daily returns. This stems from the fact that our measure of 20-day volatility is a sum of daily squared returns. As in Andersen and Bollerslev (1998a), reduced noise in the volatility measure leads to an increase in explanatory power.

[12] In unreported work, FIGARCH$(1, d, 0)$ was not rejected in favor of more general FIGARCH(p, d, q) specifications for any of the exchange rate series.

TABLE 3.8. Forecast Summary, Multiple Horizons

	Horizon (Days)				
	1	5	10	20	50

A. Restricted R^2

Deutsche Mark/U.S. Dollar

Binomial MSM	0.041	0.124	0.160	0.135	0.038
GARCH	0.035	0.069	0.033	−0.147	−0.761
MS-GARCH	0.039	0.072	0.030	−0.180	−1.137

Japanese Yen/U.S. Dollar

Binomial MSM	0.053	0.113	0.142	0.205	0.213
GARCH	0.048	0.054	0.011	−0.024	−0.358
MS-GARCH	0.048	0.044	−0.009	−0.067	−0.569

British Pound/U.S. Dollar

Binomial MSM	0.057	0.165	0.235	0.250	0.273
GARCH	0.076	0.191	0.244	0.188	−0.026
MS-GARCH	0.072	0.165	0.238	0.203	0.038

Canadian Dollar/U.S. Dollar

Binomial MSM	0.051	0.172	0.221	0.217	0.111
GARCH	0.042	0.154	0.205	0.204	0.070
MS-GARCH	0.055	0.181	0.229	0.199	0.036

B. Mean Squared Error Test vs. MSM (p-value)

Deutsche Mark/U.S. Dollar

GARCH	0.307	0.040	0.009	0.001	0.000
MS-GARCH	0.314	0.004	0.000	0.000	0.000

Japanese Yen/U.S. Dollar

GARCH	0.426	0.208	0.144	0.117	0.063
MS-GARCH	0.415	0.143	0.071	0.021	0.000

British Pound/U.S. Dollar

GARCH	0.906	0.824	0.606	0.156	0.016
MS-GARCH	0.857	0.499	0.547	0.108	0.000

(continued)

TABLE 3.8. *(continued)*

	Horizon (Days)				
	1	5	10	20	50
Canadian Dollar/U.S. Dollar					
GARCH	0.294	0.3590	0.410	0.447	0.292
MS-GARCH	0.597	0.603	0.565	0.380	0.065

Notes: This table summarizes out-of-sample forecasting results across multiple horizons. Panel A gives the restricted forecasting R^2 for each model and horizon. Panel B gives p-values from testing that the corresponding model has a lower out-of-sample forecasting mean squared error than binomial MSM. The tests are corrected for autocorrelation and heteroskedasticity using Newey and West (1987, 1994). A low p-value indicates that forecasts from the corresponding model would be rejected in favor of binomial MSM forecasts.

the unconditional variance is infinite, as discussed in Baillie, Bollerslev, and Mikkelsen (1996).

We estimate FIGARCH by maximum likelihood and report the corresponding results in Table 3.9A.[13] For every currency, FIGARCH has the lowest in-sample likelihood of all estimated models. In particular, the reported p-values indicate a difference in likelihood relative to MSM that is statistically significant at the 1% level for JA and at the 10% level for the other currencies. MSM thus outperforms FIGARCH in-sample.

Table 3.9B shows that out-of-sample forecasts also favor the multifractal model at all horizons. Binomial MSM dominates at short horizons (1 and 5 days) for DM, JA, and CA, and at long horizons (10, 20, and 50 days) for DM, JA, and UK. Despite its long memory, FIGARCH performs especially poorly at 50-day horizons. The corresponding R^2 are negative for DM, JA, and UK. The p-values of the MSEs confirm the statistical significance of these results. At the 10% confidence level, nine of the sixteen MSM forecasts significantly outperform FIGARCH, while none of the FIGARCH forecasts significantly improves on MSM.

We check the robustness of these results to inference methods that account for potential long memory. For each series of log-likelihood

---

[13] For JA, the estimated value of $\omega = 0$ is on the boundary. Under standard GARCH, this parameter determines the unconditional volatility, but in FIGARCH unconditional volatility is infinite and hence interpretation of this result is more problematic. We can view the reported estimates for JA as corresponding to an earlier specification with $\omega = 0$ introduced by Robinson (1991).

TABLE 3.9. Comparison with FIGARCH

A. In-Sample

	Parameter Estimates					p-val
	ω	β	d	$1/\nu$	$\ln L$	vs. MSM
DM	0.003	0.906	0.994	0.195	-5731.93	0.056
	(0.001)	(0.028)	(0.045)	(0.011)		
JA	0	0.930	1.000	0.228	-5974.64	0.006
	$(-)$	(0.006)	$(-)$	(0.008)		
UK	0.000	0.931	1.000	0.202	-5567.80	0.053
	(0.000)	(0.005)	$(-)$	(0.008)		
CA	0.005	0.236	0.347	0.148	-105.96	0.062
	(0.001)	(0.034)	(0.028)	(0.011)		

B. Out-of-Sample

	Horizon (Days)				
	1	5	10	20	50

Restricted R^2

DM	0.022	0.065	0.080	0.028	-0.167
JA	0.042	0.009	-0.076	-0.153	-0.588
UK	0.074	0.183	0.231	0.167	-0.071
CA	0.030	0.152	0.232	0.246	0.142

MSE Test vs. Multifractal (p-value)

DM	0.125	0.050	0.056	0.046	0.014
JA	0.350	0.127	0.087	0.073	0.044
UK	0.882	0.716	0.462	0.102	0.011
CA	0.047	0.275	0.609	0.703	0.738

Notes: This table reports FIGARCH estimation results and compares in- and out-of-sample results with MSM. In Panel A, the first four columns give parameter estimates for FIGARCH(1, d, 0). In all cases, this specification could not be rejected in favor of more general FIGARCH(p, d, q). Asymptotic standard errors are in parentheses. For both the Japanese yen and British pound, the estimated value of d is on the boundary of $1 - \epsilon$ where $\epsilon = 10^{-5}$. For the yen, the estimated value of ω is on the boundary $\omega = 0$, corresponding to a long-memory volatility process suggested by Robinson (1991). We also report the value of the log-likelihood and a p-value from a test of whether the FIGARCH likelihood dominates MSM. The test corresponds to Vuong (1989) adjusted for heteroskedasticity and autocorrelation. In Panel B, we report out-of-sample forecasting R^2 statistics and their associated p-values, HAC adjusted. For all tests, a low p-value indicates that FIGARCH would be rejected in favor of MSM.

differences, we calculate local Whittle estimates[14] of d and obtain values of approximately -0.08 for DM, 0.08 for JA, -0.05 for UK and 0.09 for CA.[15] These statistics are insignificant or marginally significant. We then use the memory autocorrelation consistent (MAC) estimation method developed by Peter Robinson (2005) to calculate alternative variance estimates for the log-likelihood differences and assess statistical significance.[16] These p-values are respectively equal to 0.0001 (DM), 0.015 (JA), 0.01 (UK) and 0.077 (CA), again suggesting that the MSM outperforms FIGARCH in-sample. We similarly check robustness of the MSE difference tests reported in Panel B to MAC adjustment, and find moderate attenuation of t-statistics and movement of p-values toward 0.5 for long horizons. Overall, the results reported in this section support the good performance of MSM relative to FIGARCH both in- and out-of-sample.

3.5   Discussion

This chapter presents the Markov-Switching Multifractal, which suggests an expanded role for regime-switching in volatility modeling. Traditional regime-switching approaches such as MS-GARCH augment low-frequency switches with midrange GARCH transitions and a thick-tailed conditional distribution of returns. By contrast, MSM effectively captures the relevant empirical features of financial data at all horizons with the single mechanism of multifrequency regime-switching.

The original research on which this chapter is based showed for the first time how to use standard econometric tools to estimate multifractal processes with confidence intervals on parameters, test hypotheses, and conduct multistep volatility forecasting. We compare the performance of the multifractal model with leading volatility models such as GARCH, MS-GARCH, and FIGARCH. Like MSM, these models conveniently permit maximum likelihood estimation and analytical forecasting. In-sample, binomial MSM has significantly higher likelihood than either GARCH or FIGARCH even though these processes have the same number of parameters. Out-of-sample, MSM matches or outperforms all three comparison

---

[14] The local Whittle estimator of d was proposed and developed by Künsch (1987) and Robinson (1995b). Additional contributions on the asymptotic properties of the estimator, modifications, and discussions of robustness under alternative specifications of long memory include Hurvich and Chen (2000), Phillips (1999), Phillips and Shimotsu (2004), Shimotsu and Phillips (2005, 2006), and Velasco (1999). The long-memory parameter d may also be estimated by log periodogram regression (Geweke and Porter-Hudak, 1983; Robinson, 1995a; Hurvich, Deo, and Brodsky, 1998; Andrews and Guggenberger, 2003).

[15] We use a bandwidth equal to $T^{0.6}$ in all of our estimates.

[16] Abadir, Distaso, and Giraitis (2008) provide a detailed assessment of the asymptotic properties and robustness of the MAC estimator.

models at short horizons and substantially dominates at 20- to 50-day horizons. The recent study by Lux (2008) confirms many of these findings.

Researchers often focus on applications of immediate practical value when assessing statistical models. Correspondingly, this chapter has shown that MSM performs well by several standard metrics. In the remainder of this book, we show that MSM extends easily to multivariate applications, generalizes naturally to continuous time while capturing the power variations exhibited by many financial series, and incorporates productively into existing asset pricing frameworks in both discrete and continuous time.

4
Multivariate MSM

Joint movements in volatility across asset markets influence the distribution of returns at the portfolio level and therefore play an important role in risk management, portfolio selection, and derivative pricing. Comovements in volatility also help our understanding of financial markets and shed light on issues such as contagion and the transmission of shocks through the financial system (e.g., Engle, Ito, and Lin, 1990).

This chapter begins by investigating possible linkages between the MSM volatility components of three currencies and several macroeconomic and financial indicators over the 1973–2003 period. We find no robust pattern between MSM components and variables such as inflation, money supply, interest rates, industrial production, and stock market volatility. On the other hand, oil and gold prices both correlate positively with currency volatility over the past three decades, consistent with the view that these commodities may act as proxies for global economic and political risk.

Across currency pairs, volatility components from different series with similar frequencies tend to move together, while components with very different frequencies display less correlation. These findings motivate the construction of a bivariate model of volatility. This specification, called bivariate MSM, is parsimonious as the number of parameters is independent of $\bar{k}$. Positive semidefiniteness of the covariance matrix is guaranteed by construction. Furthermore, the likelihood function can be written in closed form, and maximum likelihood estimation can be implemented for relatively small state spaces. To accommodate a large number of frequencies, we develop a particle filter that permits convenient inference and forecasting using simulations. Monte Carlo experiments confirm the good performance of this approach, which broadens the range of computationally tractable MSM specifications.

We estimate the bivariate model by maximum likelihood, and we verify that the goodness of fit increases with the number of volatility components. Likelihood ratio tests also confirm that the main assumptions of the model are empirically valid. Bivariate MSM compares favorably to constant correlation GARCH (CC-GARCH) in-sample. Out-of-sample, bivariate MSM captures well the conditional distribution of a variety of currency portfolios and provides reasonable measures of value-at-risk.

This chapter is based on an earlier paper: "Volatility Comovement: A Multifrequency Approach" (with A. Fisher and S. Thompson), *Journal of Econometrics*, 131: 179–215, March 2006.

4.1   Comovement of Univariate Volatility Components

4.1.1   Comovement of Exchange Rate Volatility

The empirical analysis investigates daily returns on the Deutsche mark (DM), Japanese yen (JA), and British pound (UK), all against the U.S. dollar. As in Chapter 3, the returns are imputed from noon daily prices reported by the Federal Reserve Bank of New York. The Deutsche mark is spliced with the euro at the beginning of 1999. Each series runs between 1 June 1973 and 30 October 2003, and contains 7,635 observations.

For each currency, we estimate MSM by maximum likelihood on the entire sample, and we report the results in Table 4.1. These univariate results are similar to those reported in Chapter 3 even though the sample used for ML estimation is slightly longer.

Using the ML estimates, we compute for each currency the smoothed state probabilities $\mathbb{P}(M_t = m^j | r_1, \ldots, r_T)$ as in Kim (1994).[1] We also calculate the expectation of the individual multipliers conditional on the entire sample:

$$\hat{M}_{k,t} = \mathbb{E}(M_{k,t} | r_1, \ldots, r_T) \qquad (4.1)$$

and report in Table 4.2 the correlations of the smoothed components $\hat{M}_{k,t}$. The first panel shows that different components of the DM series are moderately correlated, and correlation decreases in the distance between frequencies.[2] Untabulated results for the pound and yen series are similar. The second and third panels of Table 4.2 show comovement of the mark components with the yen and the pound. Correlation between the smoothed beliefs $\hat{M}_{k,t}^{\alpha}$ and $\hat{M}_{k',t}^{\beta}$ of two currencies tends to be high when k and k' are close, and low otherwise. This suggests that the volatility components of two exchange rates are most correlated when their frequencies are similar.

The interpretation is slightly complicated by the fact that the set of volatility frequencies is not identical across currencies. To address this issue, we introduce a simple bivariate model in which currencies are statistically independent but have identical frequency parameters b and $\gamma_{\bar{k}}$. The log-likelihood of the two series is

$$L(r_t^{\alpha}; m_0^{\alpha}, \bar{\sigma}_{\alpha}, b, \gamma_{\bar{k}}) + L(r_t^{\beta}; m_0^{\beta}, \bar{\sigma}_{\beta}, b, \gamma_{\bar{k}}), \qquad (4.2)$$

---

[1] The smoothed state probabilities (4.1) are conditioned on all available data, while the filtered probabilities given in equation (3.4) are based only on information available up to date t. See Hamilton (1994) for further discussion.

[2] Since the econometrician does not directly observe the multipliers, correlation in smoothed beliefs is not inconsistent with the assumed independence of the unobserved components $M_{k,t}$ and $M_{k',t}$, $k \neq k'$.

TABLE 4.1. Univariate ML Estimation

	$k=1$	2	3	4	5	6	7	8
				Deutsche Mark				
$\hat{m}_0$	1.617	1.556	1.535	1.472	1.445	1.396	1.365	1.338
	(0.019)	(0.015)	(0.012)	(0.012)	(0.013)	(0.012)	(0.011)	(0.011)
$\hat{\sigma}$	0.672	0.649	0.594	0.567	0.504	0.537	0.549	0.552
	(0.012)	(0.017)	(0.013)	(0.015)	(0.016)	(0.027)	(0.020)	(0.021)
$\hat{\gamma}_{\bar{k}}$	0.074	0.086	0.841	0.779	0.812	0.909	0.979	0.998
	(0.002)	(0.018)	(0.096)	(0.082)	(0.083)	(0.103)	(0.036)	(0.008)
$\hat{b}$	—	6.85	34.31	11.86	9.02	5.83	4.67	3.82
		(2.44)	(10.55)	(1.99)	(1.24)	(0.82)	(0.60)	(0.49)
$\ln L$	-7121.92	-6975.92	-6916.81	-6900.06	-6891.67	-6888.91	-6885.60	-6885.90
				Japanese Yen				
$\hat{m}_0$	1.783	1.774	1.688	1.644	1.579	1.567	1.559	1.508
	(0.011)	(0.009)	(0.011)	(0.011)	(0.010)	(0.010)	(0.010)	(0.010)
$\hat{\sigma}$	0.632	0.537	0.568	0.473	0.473	0.634	0.514	0.508
	(0.011)	(0.009)	(0.019)	(0.017)	(0.023)	(0.023)	(0.019)	(0.017)
$\hat{\gamma}_{\bar{k}}$	0.208	0.358	0.276	0.713	0.861	0.894	0.894	0.977
	(0.022)	(0.038)	(0.048)	(0.082)	(0.053)	(0.060)	(0.058)	(0.030)
$\hat{b}$	—	147.47	11.76	15.73	9.13	8.22	7.60	5.88
		(59.61)	(2.02)	(2.67)	(1.18)	(0.99)	(0.87)	(0.74)
$\ln L$	-6776.19	-6421.01	-6279.02	-6216.85	-6196.55	-6184.90	-6181.29	-6174.96

(continued)

TABLE 4.1. (continued)

British Pound

	$k=1$	2	3	4	5	6	7	8
$\hat{m}_0$	1.708	1.666	1.640	1.612	1.574	1.529	1.498	1.457
	(0.013)	(0.013)	(0.011)	(0.014)	(0.011)	(0.012)	(0.011)	(0.010)
$\hat{\sigma}$	0.606	0.580	0.523	0.516	0.431	0.455	0.385	0.380
	(0.009)	(0.018)	(0.018)	(0.016)	(0.015)	(0.017)	(0.013)	(0.014)
$\hat{\gamma}_{\overline{k}}$	0.113	0.213	0.271	0.549	0.617	0.782	0.817	0.959
	(0.016)	(0.036)	(0.065)	(0.086)	(0.074)	(0.078)	(0.083)	(0.001)
$\hat{b}$	—	18.69	13.92	14.39	11.59	8.49	6.83	5.33
		(4.84)	(2.68)	(2.67)	(1.84)	(1.16)	(0.87)	(0.04)
$\ln L$	−6220.55	−5987.37	−5882.60	−5826.92	−5792.97	−5778.58	−5771.92	−5770.20

Notes: This table shows maximum likelihood estimation results for binomial MSM on three currencies. The estimates are based on daily log returns in percent for data spanning 1 June 1973 to 30 October 2003. Each column corresponds to a given number of components k in the MSM specification. Asymptotic standard errors are in parentheses.

TABLE 4.2. Correlation of Smoothed Univariate MSM Volatility Components

	DM1	DM2	DM3	DM4	DM5	DM6	DM7	DM8	$|r_{\mathrm{DM}}|$	r^2_{DM}
DM1	1.000	0.762	0.377	0.174	0.099	0.066	0.031	0.020	0.189	0.115
DM2	0.762	1.000	0.600	0.328	0.151	0.093	0.043	0.028	0.255	0.174
DM3	0.377	0.600	1.000	0.603	0.307	0.168	0.077	0.052	0.312	0.245
DM4	0.174	0.328	0.603	1.000	0.738	0.432	0.201	0.137	0.374	0.295
DM5	0.099	0.151	0.307	0.738	1.000	0.792	0.420	0.297	0.463	0.373
DM6	0.066	0.093	0.168	0.432	0.792	1.000	0.770	0.610	0.667	0.539
DM7	0.031	0.043	0.077	0.201	0.420	0.770	1.000	0.961	0.887	0.713
DM8	0.020	0.028	0.052	0.137	0.297	0.610	0.961	1.000	0.894	0.716
$|r_{\mathrm{DM}}|$	0.189	0.255	0.312	0.374	0.463	0.667	0.887	0.894	1.000	0.872
r^2_{DM}	0.115	0.174	0.245	0.295	0.373	0.539	0.713	0.716	0.872	1.000
JA1	0.590	0.287	0.036	0.020	0.036	0.032	0.012	0.007	0.051	0.002
JA2	0.611	0.302	0.048	0.023	0.038	0.034	0.013	0.008	0.056	0.006
JA3	0.788	0.440	0.172	0.063	0.065	0.048	0.021	0.013	0.104	0.048
JA4	0.368	0.185	0.162	0.064	0.030	0.036	0.020	0.013	0.073	0.062
JA5	0.157	0.177	0.150	0.231	0.169	0.109	0.053	0.036	0.103	0.084
JA6	0.058	0.062	0.127	0.279	0.349	0.284	0.155	0.111	0.192	0.174
JA7	0.029	0.023	0.032	0.106	0.206	0.321	0.312	0.267	0.284	0.258
JA8	0.012	0.008	0.011	0.043	0.095	0.209	0.339	0.353	0.333	0.303
$|r_{\mathrm{JA}}|$	0.187	0.108	0.092	0.134	0.177	0.256	0.328	0.327	0.363	0.346
r^2_{JA}	0.091	0.048	0.065	0.101	0.142	0.209	0.261	0.256	0.297	0.344

(continued)

TABLE 4.2. (continued)

	DM1	DM2	DM3	DM4	DM5	DM6	DM7	DM8	$|r_{\mathrm{DM}}|$	r^2_{DM}
UK1	0.819	0.525	0.170	0.081	0.052	0.042	0.018	0.011	0.114	0.054
UK2	0.730	0.558	0.246	0.165	0.094	0.062	0.028	0.018	0.134	0.073
UK3	0.464	0.526	0.254	0.163	0.072	0.050	0.023	0.015	0.128	0.086
UK4	0.251	0.505	0.308	0.195	0.075	0.049	0.021	0.014	0.143	0.111
UK5	0.070	0.131	0.516	0.571	0.365	0.200	0.091	0.062	0.213	0.169
UK6	0.149	0.162	0.239	0.440	0.536	0.423	0.228	0.162	0.291	0.242
UK7	0.082	0.079	0.092	0.185	0.319	0.463	0.431	0.362	0.407	0.354
UK8	0.030	0.030	0.035	0.074	0.145	0.301	0.473	0.488	0.471	0.409
$|r_{\mathrm{UK}}|$	0.168	0.213	0.221	0.254	0.273	0.360	0.462	0.462	0.564	
r^2_{UK}	0.081	0.135	0.178	0.213	0.234	0.305	0.390	0.391	0.508	0.571

Notes: This table shows correlations from a frequency decomposition of binomial MSM with $\bar{k} = 8$ components for the univariate DM series with itself, JA, and UK. The sample consists of daily log returns from 1 June 1973 to 30 October 2003. For each series, the smoothed components $\hat{M}_{k,t} = \mathbb{E}(M_{k,t}|r_1,\ldots,r_T)$ of different volatility states are calculated. We denote these probabilities by DM1,…,DM8, JA1,…,JA8, UK1,…,UK8. The table then shows correlations of the DM decomposition with decompositions from all three series. Correlations are generally strongest near the diagonal.

where L denotes the log-likelihood of univariate MSM. This specification, called the *combined univariate*, is an important building block of the bivariate model introduced in the next section.

In Table 4.3, we report empirical results for the combined univariate. Panel A shows ML estimates for the mark and yen series. Some parameter estimates differ noticeably from the unrestricted univariate results in Table 4.1, but substantial discrepancies only seem to occur for low values of $\bar{k}$. For instance, with $\bar{k} = 8$, we compare the likelihood of -13063.11 with the sum of unrestricted likelihoods, that is, $-6885.90 - 6174.96 = -13060.86$, finding a difference of 2.25. Under the combined univariate, the likelihood ratio (LR) statistic, 2×2.25, is asymptotically distributed as a chi-squared with two degrees of freedom. This test statistic is not significant at conventional levels, confirming that the frequency restrictions are reasonable. The second part of Panel A reports more generally the p-values of the LR tests corresponding to each frequency and currency combination. When $\bar{k} = 8$, the frequency restrictions are not rejected for any currency combination.

Panel B of Table 4.3 shows correlations between smoothed volatility components for the mark and yen series under the combined univariate model. With frequencies identical across currencies, we expect results to be stronger than in Table 4.2, and this is confirmed. Results for other currency pairs are similar. We conclude that (i) restricting frequencies to be identical across currencies is reasonable, and (ii) components of similar frequencies tend to move together while components with very different frequencies do not. These findings are helpful to develop a bivariate MSM specification.

4.1.2   Currency Volatility and Macroeconomic Indicators

We now investigate whether currency volatility comovement relates to other macroeconomic and financial variables. Earlier research leads us to be relatively pessimistic. For instance, the first moments of exchange rates are weakly linked to fundamentals (e.g., Meese and Rogoff, 1983; Andersen and Bollerslev, 1998b; Rogoff, 1999; Sarno and Taylor, 2002).[3] Variances are also difficult to explain, at least in stock market data (e.g., Schwert, 1989). We examine whether the new MSM multifrequency decomposition confirms these negative results.

We consider monthly macroeconomic data from the International Monetary Fund for the 1973–2000 period, including monetary aggregates (M1, M2 and M3), short and long interest rates, producer price index, consumer price index, wages, and growth rate of industrial production. We compute

---

[3] See also Lyons (2001) for evidence at higher-frequency.

TABLE 4.3. Combined Univariate MSM Results

A. MLE Estimation

DM–JA Parameter Estimates

	$k = 1$	2	3	4	5	6	7	8
$\hat{m}_0^{DM}$	1.643	1.618	1.515	1.474	1.445	1.405	1.397	1.367
	(0.013)	(0.014)	(0.013)	(0.013)	(0.011)	(0.013)	(0.012)	(0.011)
$\hat{m}_0^{JA}$	1.775	1.757	1.687	1.638	1.578	1.565	1.522	1.488
	(0.018)	(0.010)	(0.010)	(0.011)	(0.010)	(0.010)	(0.010)	(0.014)
$\hat{\sigma}_{DM}$	0.669	0.577	0.597	0.569	0.504	0.565	0.449	0.472
	(0.010)	(0.011)	(0.015)	(0.018)	(0.015)	(0.021)	(0.018)	(0.018)
$\hat{\sigma}_{JA}$	0.613	0.544	0.565	0.487	0.476	0.632	0.384	0.532
	(0.016)	(0.010)	(0.018)	(0.018)	(0.023)	(0.024)	(0.016)	(0.027)
$\hat{\gamma}_{\bar{1}k}$	0.129	0.257	0.301	0.756	0.844	0.872	0.959	0.982
	(0.013)	(0.026)	(0.068)	(0.057)	(0.055)	(0.054)	(0.036)	(0.022)
$\hat{b}$	—	69.57	11.97	13.21	9.14	7.16	6.16	4.93
		(21.57)	(2.04)	(1.61)	(0.95)	(0.65)	(0.57)	(0.45)
ln L	−13913.86	−13424.24	−13203.13	−13119.07	−13088.39	−13077.02	−13072.22	−13063.11

LR Tests Against Unrestricted Univariate

DM–JA	0.000	0.000	0.001	0.116	0.849	0.040	0.005	0.106
DM–UK	0.136	0.002	0.000	0.037	0.004	0.004	0.004	0.111
JA–UK	0.004	0.000	0.701	0.361	0.017	0.237	0.754	0.863

B. Correlation of Smoothed Volatility Component Beliefs

	DM1	DM2	DM3	DM4	DM5	DM6	DM7	DM8	$|r_{DM}|$	r^2_{DM}
JA1	0.628	0.714	0.349	0.072	0.009	0.038	0.020	0.007	0.081	0.028
JA2	0.690	0.774	0.405	0.135	0.016	0.048	0.027	0.011	0.101	0.043
JA3	0.595	0.686	0.228	0.140	0.018	0.049	0.028	0.012	0.078	0.033
JA4	0.306	0.234	0.147	0.114	0.036	0.022	0.027	0.013	0.065	0.065
JA5	−0.019	−0.034	0.052	0.113	0.302	0.227	0.116	0.056	0.117	0.102
JA6	0.028	0.023	0.040	0.084	0.255	0.352	0.258	0.145	0.206	0.186
JA7	0.008	0.009	0.007	0.021	0.103	0.224	0.342	0.294	0.299	0.274
JA8	0.004	0.004	0.002	0.009	0.048	0.123	0.287	0.353	0.333	0.304
$|r_{JA}|$	0.177	0.191	0.093	0.088	0.128	0.193	0.301	0.326	0.363	0.346
r^2_{JA}	0.087	0.094	0.039	0.066	0.100	0.156	0.243	0.254	0.297	0.344

Notes: Panel A shows maximum likelihood estimation results for the combined univariate MSM specification, which for two series α and β has likelihood $L(r^\alpha_t; m^\alpha_0, \bar{\sigma}_\alpha, b, \gamma_{\bar{k}}) + L(r^\beta_t; m^\beta_0, \bar{\sigma}_\beta, b, \gamma_{\bar{k}})$. This corresponds to the likelihood of two statistically independent univariate MSM processes constrained to have the same frequency parameters b and $\gamma_{\bar{k}}$. The sample consists of daily log returns from 1 June 1973 to 30 October 2003. Columns of the table correspond to the number of frequencies $\bar{k}$ in the estimated model. Estimation results with asymptotic standard errors in parentheses are presented for the DM-JA currency pair only. The second part of Panel A shows p-values from a likelihood ratio test of combined univariate MSM against two unrestricted MSM processes. A low p-value indicates rejection of the restriction that frequency parameters are identical across currencies. Panel B then shows correlations from a frequency decomposition of the DM-JA combined univariate model with eight components. For each series, the smoothed components $\hat{M}_{k,t} = \mathbb{E}(M_{k,t}|r_1,\ldots,r_T)$ of volatility states are calculated. For convenience, we denote these probabilities by DM1,...,DM8, JA1,...,JA8.

57

the correlation between monthly volatility and the macroeconomic variables of each country, their difference and the absolute value of their difference. We use several measures of volatility, such as the absolute value of the monthly return, realized monthly volatility, and MSM volatility components. In untabulated results using a variety of lag structures, we find no robust link between currency volatility and these variables. These findings are consistent with results in Andersen and Bollerslev (1998b), who show that macroeconomic announcements induce volatility shocks that are of comparable magnitude to daily volatility. It is thus not surprising that little impact is found at the monthly frequency.

Economic theory suggests that exchange rates might be more strongly linked to equity markets, since both classes of instruments incorporate forward-looking information about rates of return, national economic conditions and corporate profits. In Table 4.4, we investigate the comovement of each currency with volatility in local and U.S. stock markets. Daily returns are imputed from the Center for Research in Security Prices (CRSP) value-weighted index of U.S. stocks, the German composite DAX index, the UK Financial Times-Actuaries All Share index and the Japanese Nikkei 225 stock average. Realized monthly stock volatility (RV) is computed as the sum of squared daily returns. We compare it with the currency return, absolute return, realized volatility and MSM frequency-specific components. We obtain no robust link between currency and equity volatility.

Oil prices are often viewed as proxies for global economic and political uncertainty (e.g., Hamilton, 2003). As seen in Table 4.4, the dollar price of oil correlates positively with the realized volatility of the mark and the pound exchange rates,[4] and the MSM decomposition further reveals that this is primarily a low-frequency phenomenon. The results become more intriguing for the yen. While the raw oil price shows little correlation with the RV of the yen, it is again strongly correlated with low-frequency MSM components. The MSM decomposition thus finds evidence of a regularity that direct analysis of realized volatility would not uncover. Similar results are obtained with gold, further suggesting that currency volatility and certain commodity prices may be linked at low frequencies through an unidentified global risk factor.

The link between exchange rates and fundamentals remains an open area of research (e.g., Engel and West, 2005). The finding that volatility components of similar frequencies are strongly correlated across currencies motivates the development of multivariate MSM.

---

[4]We use the domestic first purchase price of crude oil expressed in dollars per barrel provided by Global Insight/Data Resources Inc.

TABLE 4.4. Correlation of Exchange Rates with Other Financial Prices

	r_t	$|r_t|$	RV	MSM Volatility Component Beliefs							
				$k=1$	2	3	4	5	6	7	8
Deutsche Mark											
CRSP RV	−0.0849	0.1712	0.0904	0.0930	0.0360	0.0316	0.1964	0.1421	0.0678	−0.0056	−0.0479
DAX RV	−0.1515	0.0916	0.1205	0.2087	0.1296	0.1086	0.1541	0.1041	0.0111	−0.0363	−0.0395
Oil	0.1142	0.0235	0.2138	0.5254	0.4859	0.2685	0.1649	0.0241	−0.0178	−0.1062	−0.1137
Gold	0.0774	0.0652	0.1642	0.7378	0.4979	0.1334	0.0571	−0.0104	−0.0613	−0.0755	−0.0497
Japanese Yen											
CRSP RV	−0.0969	0.1696	0.2097	−0.1841	−0.1924	−0.2137	−0.1439	−0.0920	0.0011	−0.0136	0.0221
NIKKEI RV	−0.0280	0.1155	0.2291	0.3069	0.3013	0.2764	−0.3071	−0.0965	−0.0526	−0.0781	−0.0400
Oil	0.0465	0.0429	0.0046	0.2803	0.2858	0.2838	0.1306	−0.1608	0.0335	−0.0422	0.0052
Gold	−0.0135	0.1323	0.1444	0.5233	0.5306	0.5332	0.2071	0.0586	0.0417	−0.0633	−0.1053
British Pound											
US CRSP RV	0.0480	0.0590	−0.0746	−0.0299	0.0907	0.0496	−0.0597	0.0291	0.0570	−0.0342	−0.0405
FTSE RV	0.0113	0.0390	−0.0986	−0.4642	−0.2036	−0.0865	−0.1638	0.1450	0.0405	−0.0329	−0.0518
Oil	−0.0900	0.0864	0.2583	0.5495	0.3972	0.2652	0.2846	0.2087	0.0766	−0.0175	−0.0455
Gold	0.0396	0.0837	0.1466	0.6963	0.5087	0.4084	0.2824	−0.1019	0.0658	0.0083	−0.0243

Notes: This table investigates for each country the comovement between exchange rates and four financial variables: the monthly realized volatility (RV) on the U.S. and local stock market, the oil price (in U.S. dollars per barrel), and the gold price (in U.S. dollars per ounce). Monthly realized volatilities are imputed as the sum of squared daily returns. Correlation between currency and equity RV is positive for the mark and the yen, but negative for the pound. Oil and gold prices are positively correlated to exchange rate volatility for all countries, and the MSM decomposition reveals that this result is primarily a low-frequency phenomenon.

4.2   A Bivariate Multifrequency Model

4.2.1   The Stochastic Volatility Specification

We consider two financial series α and β defined on the regular grid $t = 0, 1, 2, \ldots, \infty$. Their log-returns r_t^α and r_t^β in period t are stacked into the column vector

$$r_t = \begin{bmatrix} r_t^\alpha \\ r_t^\beta \end{bmatrix} \in \mathbb{R}^2.$$

As in univariate MSM, volatility is stochastic and is hit by shocks of heterogeneous frequencies indexed by $k \in \{1, \ldots, \bar{k}\}$. For every frequency k, the currencies have volatility components $M_{k,t}^\alpha$ and $M_{k,t}^\beta$. Consider

$$M_{k,t} = \begin{bmatrix} M_{k,t}^\alpha \\ M_{k,t}^\beta \end{bmatrix} \in \mathbb{R}_+^2.$$

The period-t volatility column vectors $M_{k,t}$ are stacked into the $2 \times \bar{k}$ matrix

$$M_t = (M_{1,t}; M_{2,t}; \ldots; M_{\bar{k},t}).$$

Each row of the matrix M_t contains the volatility components of a particular currency, while each column corresponds to a particular frequency. As in univariate MSM, we assume that $M_{1,t}, M_{2,t} \ldots M_{\bar{k},t}$ at a given time t are statistically independent. The main task is to choose appropriate dynamics for each vector $M_{k,t}$.

Economic intuition suggests that volatility arrivals are correlated but not necessarily simultaneous across currency markets. For this reason, we allow arrivals across series to be characterized by a correlation coefficient λ. Assume that the volatility vector associated with the kth frequency has been constructed up to date $t - 1$. In period t, each series $c \in \{\alpha, \beta\}$ is hit by an arrival with probability γ_k. Let $1_{k,t}^c$ denote the indicator function equal to 1 if there is an arrival on $M_{k,t}^c$, and equal to 0 otherwise. The arrival vector $1_{k,t} = (1_{k,t}^\alpha, 1_{k,t}^\beta)$ is specified to be i.i.d., and its unconditional distribution is defined by three conditions. First, the arrival vector is symmetrically distributed: $(1_{k,t}^\beta, 1_{k,t}^\alpha) \overset{d}{=} (1_{k,t}^\alpha, 1_{k,t}^\beta)$. Second, the switching probability of a series is equal to an exogenous constant:

$$\mathbb{P}(1_{k,t}^\alpha = 1) = \gamma_k.$$

Third, there exists $\lambda \in [0, 1]$ such that

$$\mathbb{P}(1_{k,t}^{\beta} = 1 | 1_{k,t}^{\alpha} = 1) = (1 - \lambda)\gamma_k + \lambda.$$

As shown in the Appendix, these three conditions define a unique distribution for $1_{k,t}$. Arrivals are independent if $\lambda = 0$ and simultaneous if $\lambda = 1$. More generally, λ is the unconditional correlation between $1_{k,t}^{\alpha}$ and $1_{k,t}^{\beta}$.

Given the realization of the arrival vector $1_{k,t}$, the construction of the volatility component is based on a bivariate distribution $M = (M^{\alpha}, M^{\beta}) \in \mathbb{R}_{+}^{2}$. We assume for now that M is defined by two parameters m_{0}^{α} and m_{0}^{β}, and that each of its components has a unit mean: $\mathbb{E}(M) = \mathbf{1}$. If arrivals hit both series ($1_{k,t}^{\alpha} = 1_{k,t}^{\beta} = 1$), the state vector $M_{k,t}$ is drawn from M. If only series $c \in \{\alpha, \beta\}$ receives an arrival, the new component $M_{k,t}^{c}$ is sampled from the marginal M^{c} of the bivariate distribution M. Finally, $M_{k,t} = M_{k,t-1}$ if there is no arrival.

Consistent with previous notation, let

$$\sigma_{\alpha}(M_t) \equiv \bar{\sigma}_{\alpha}(M_{1,t}^{\alpha} M_{2,t}^{\alpha} \dots M_{\bar{k},t}^{\alpha})^{1/2},$$

$$\sigma_{\beta}(M_t) \equiv \bar{\sigma}_{\beta}(M_{1,t}^{\beta} M_{2,t}^{\beta} \dots M_{\bar{k},t}^{\beta})^{1/2},$$

where $\bar{\sigma}_{\alpha}, \bar{\sigma}_{\beta} > 0$. Individual returns satisfy

$$r_t^{\alpha} = \sigma_{\alpha}(M_t)\varepsilon_t^{\alpha},$$

$$r_t^{\beta} = \sigma_{\beta}(M_t)\varepsilon_t^{\beta}.$$

The vector $\varepsilon_t \equiv (\varepsilon_t^{\alpha}, \varepsilon_t^{\beta}) \in \mathbb{R}^2$ is i.i.d. Gaussian $\mathcal{N}(0, \Sigma)$, where

$$\Sigma = \begin{bmatrix} 1 & \rho_{\varepsilon} \\ \rho_{\varepsilon} & 1 \end{bmatrix}.$$

The construction permits correlation in volatility through the bivariate distribution M and correlation in returns through the Gaussian vector ε_t. As in the univariate case, the transition probabilities are defined by

$$\gamma_k = 1 - (1 - \gamma_{\bar{k}})^{(b^{k - \bar{k}})}, \qquad (4.3)$$

where $\gamma_{\bar{k}} \in (0, 1)$ and $b \in (1, \infty)$. This completes the specification of *bivariate MSM*.

Under bivariate MSM, univariate dynamics coincide with the univariate model presented in Chapter 3. The parameter $\bar{\sigma}_c$ is again the unconditional standard deviation of each univariate series $c \in \{\alpha, \beta\}$, and other univariate parameters have similar equivalents. The complete specification of bivariate MSM is given by eight parameters:

$$\psi \equiv (\bar{\sigma}_\alpha, \bar{\sigma}_\beta, m_0^\alpha, m_0^\beta, b, \gamma_{\bar{k}}, \rho_\varepsilon, \lambda).$$

Focusing on the simple specification where each $M_{k,t}$ is drawn from a bivariate binomial distribution $M = (M^\alpha, M^\beta)'$, the first element M^α takes values $m_0^\alpha \in [1, 2]$ and $m_1^\alpha = 2 - m_0^\alpha \in [0, 1]$ with equal probability. Similarly, M^β is a binomial taking values $m_0^\beta \in [1, 2]$ and $m_1^\beta = 2 - m_0^\beta$ with equal probability. Consequently, the random vector M has four possible values, whose unconditional probabilities are given by the matrix $(p_{i,j}) = (\mathbb{P}\{M = (m_i^\alpha, m_j^\beta)\})_{0 \le i,j \le 1}$. The conditions $\mathbb{P}(M^\alpha = m_0^\alpha) = 1/2$ and $\mathbb{P}(M^\beta = m_0^\beta) = 1/2$ impose that

$$\begin{bmatrix} p_{00} & p_{01} \\ p_{10} & p_{11} \end{bmatrix} = \frac{1}{4} \begin{bmatrix} 1 + \rho_m^* & 1 - \rho_m^* \\ 1 - \rho_m^* & 1 + \rho_m^* \end{bmatrix}$$

for some $\rho_m^* \in [-1, 1]$, where ρ_m^* is the correlation between components M^α and M^β under the distribution M.

4.2.2   Properties

Each component $M_{k,t}$ has a unique ergodic distribution $\bar{\Pi}_k$, as shown in the Appendix. Since different components are statistically independent, the ergodic distribution of the volatility state M_t is the product measure $\bar{\Pi} = \bar{\Pi}_1 \otimes \ldots \otimes \bar{\Pi}_{\bar{k}}$.

The return series have correlation coefficient

$$Corr(r_t^\alpha; r_t^\beta) = \rho_\varepsilon \prod_{k=1}^{\bar{k}} \mathbb{E}[(M_{k,t}^\alpha M_{k,t}^\beta)^{1/2}], \tag{4.4}$$

which is lower than ρ_ε by the Cauchy-Schwarz inequality. Uncorrelated changes in volatility represent additional sources of noise that reduce the correlation of asset returns.

The econometrician observes the set of past returns $\mathcal{R}_t \equiv \{r_s\}_{s=1}^t$. Returns are unpredictable under this information set: $\mathbb{E}(r_t | \mathcal{R}_{t-1}) = 0$, and bivariate MSM is thus consistent with some standard forms of market efficiency.[5] Comovement is quantified by the conditional correlation

$$Corr_t(r_{t+n}^\alpha; r_{t+n}^\beta) = \rho_\varepsilon \prod_{k=1}^{\bar{k}} \frac{\mathbb{E}_t[(M_{k,t+n}^\alpha M_{k,t+n}^\beta)^{1/2}]}{[(\mathbb{E}_t M_{k,t+n}^\alpha)(\mathbb{E}_t M_{k,t+n}^\beta)]^{1/2}} \le \rho_\varepsilon, \tag{4.5}$$

---

[5] See Campbell, Lo, and MacKinlay (1997, Chapter 2) for a discussion.

which is large when the volatility components of the currencies are high. Similarly, provided $\rho_m^* > 0$ the correlation between absolute returns is high in periods of high volatility.[6]

4.3   Inference

Bayesian updating and the likelihood function are available in closed form, and ML estimation is practical with a moderate number of volatility components. Alternative computational methods are designed for high-dimensional state spaces.

4.3.1   Closed-Form Likelihood

Since each frequency vector $M_{k,t}$ is drawn from a bivariate binomial, the volatility state M_t takes $d = 4^{\bar{k}}$ possible values $m^1, \ldots, m^d \in \mathbb{R}_+^{\bar{k}}$. Its dynamics are characterized by the transition matrix $A = (a_{i,j})_{1 \leq i,j \leq d}$ with components $a_{ij} = \mathbb{P}(M_{t+1} = m^j \,|\, M_t = m^i)$.

The econometrician observes the set of past returns $\mathcal{R}_t \equiv \{r_s\}_{s=1}^t$. As in Chapter 3, the conditional probabilities $\Pi_t^j = \mathbb{P}(M_t = m^j \,|\, \mathcal{R}_t)$ are computed recursively by Bayesian updating. Let $\Pi_t = (\Pi_t^1, \ldots, \Pi_t^d) \in \mathbb{R}_+^d$. In the next period, state M_{t+1} is drawn, and the econometrician observes the return vector r_{t+1}. By Bayes' rule, the updated probability is

$$\Pi_{t+1} \propto f(r_{t+1}) * \Pi_t A, \tag{4.6}$$

where $f(r)$ is the vector of conditional densities $(f_{r_{t+1}}(r_{t+1}|M_{t+1} = m^i))_i$. In empirical applications, the initial vector Π_0 is chosen equal to the ergodic distribution $\bar{\Pi}$ of the Markov chain. The log-likelihood has the closed-form expression:

$$\ln L(r_1, \ldots, r_T; \psi) = \sum_{t=1}^T \ln[f(r_t) \cdot (\Pi_{t-1} A)].$$

4.3.2   Particle Filter

The transition matrix contains $4^{\bar{k}} \times 4^{\bar{k}}$ elements and thus grows quickly with $\bar{k}$. For instance, with eight frequencies, the transition matrix has cardinality $2^{32} \approx 4 \times 10^9$, and is computationally expensive to use.

---

[6]When $\bar{k}$ is large, the formula is:

$$Corr_t(|r_{t+n}^\alpha|; |r_{t+n}^\beta|) \sim C_\varepsilon \prod_{k=1}^{\bar{k}} \frac{\mathbb{E}_t[(M_{k,t+n}^\alpha M_{k,t+n}^\beta)^{1/2}]}{[(\mathbb{E}_t M_{k,t+n}^\alpha)(\mathbb{E}_t M_{k,t+n}^\beta)]^{1/2}},$$

where $C_\varepsilon = \mathbb{E}(|\varepsilon_1^\alpha \varepsilon_1^\beta|)$.

Following the literature on Markov chains,[7] we now propose a simulation-based inference methodology based on a particle filter, a recursive algorithm that generates independent draws

$$M_t^{(1)}, \ldots, M_t^{(B)}$$

from the conditional distribution Π_t.

We begin at $t = 0$ by drawing B states from the ergodic distribution $\bar{\Pi}$. For any $t \geq 0$, assume that $M_t^{(1)}, \ldots, M_t^{(B)}$ have been independently sampled from Π_t. Given a new return r_{t+1}, we rewrite the updating formula (4.6) as

$$\Pi_{t+1}^j \propto f_{r_{t+1}} \left(r_{t+1} | M_{t+1} = m^j \right) \sum_{i=1}^{d} \mathbb{P} \left(M_{t+1} = m^j | M_t = m^i \right) \Pi_t^i.$$

We obtain $M_{t+1}^{(1)}, \ldots, M_{t+1}^{(B)}$ by simulating each $M_t^{(b)}$ one-step forward and reweighting using an importance sampler. Specifically:

    1.   Simulate the Markov chain one-step ahead to obtain $\hat{M}_{t+1}^{(1)}$ given $M_t^{(1)}$. Repeat B times to generate B draws $\hat{M}_{t+1}^{(1)}, \ldots, \hat{M}_{t+1}^{(B)}$. This preliminary step only uses information available at date t and must therefore be adjusted to account for the new return.

    2.   Draw a random number q from 1 to B with probability

$$\mathbb{P}(q = b) \equiv \frac{f_{r_{t+1}}(r_{t+1} | M_{t+1} = \hat{M}_{t+1}^{(b)})}{\sum_{b'=1}^{B} f_{r_{t+1}}(r_{t+1} | M_{t+1} = \hat{M}_{t+1}^{(b')})}.$$

The vector $M_{t+1}^{(1)} = \hat{M}_{t+1}^{(q)}$ is a draw from Π_{t+1}. Repeat B times to obtain B draws $M_{t+1}^{(1)}, \ldots, M_{t+1}^{(B)}$.

This recursive procedure provides a discrete approximation to Bayesian updating, which is computationally convenient in large state spaces.

4.3.3   Simulated Likelihood

We can use the particle filter to compute the likelihood function. Each one-step ahead density satisfies $f(r_t | \mathcal{R}_{t-1}) = \sum_{i=1}^{d} f(r_t | M_t = m^i)$

---

[7]See, for instance, Chib, Nardari, and Shephard (2002), Jacquier, Polson, and Rossi (1994), and Pitt and Shephard (1999).

$\mathbb{P}(M_t = m^i | \mathcal{R}_{t-1})$. Given simulated draws $\hat{M}_t^{(b)}$ from $M_t | \mathcal{R}_{t-1}$, the Monte Carlo estimate of the conditional density is defined as

$$\widehat{f}(r_t | \mathcal{R}_{t-1}) \equiv \frac{1}{B} \sum_{b=1}^{B} f(r_t | M_t = \hat{M}_t^{(b)}),$$

and the log-likelihood is approximated by $\sum_{t=1}^{T} \ln \hat{f}(r_t | \mathcal{R}_{t-1})$. We can use these calculations to carry out simulated likelihood estimation. In practice, an arbitrarily close approximation can be achieved by increasing B. Larger state spaces require more draws to achieve the same degree of precision.

Table 4.5 presents a Monte Carlo assessment of this method. We focus on the univariate specification with $\bar{k} = 8$ components. Using the particle filter, we generate 500 approximations of the log-likelihood of the univariate DM series at the optimized ML estimates from Table 4.1. Each calculation uses independent sets of Monte Carlo draws. We then compare the mean, standard deviation, and quantiles of the estimates with the exact value obtained in Table 4.1 by analytical Bayesian updating. All particle filter evaluations use $B = 10,000$ random draws. The particle filter estimate of the log-likelihood has a relatively small standard deviation, and the average across simulations, -6887.3, is close to the true value of -6885.9. The quantiles are tightly clustered as well. The table also shows particle filter estimates of the forecast variance, which are accurate and approximately

TABLE 4.5. Evaluation of Particle Filter

		$\mathbb{E}_t \sum_{j=1}^{n} r_{t+j}^2$				
	$\ln L$	$n = 1$	5	10	20	50
True value	-6885.9	0.432	2.194	4.442	8.991	22.66
Simulation average	-6887.3	0.431	2.187	4.426	8.953	22.54
Standard deviation	1.851	0.012	0.064	0.142	0.325	0.983
1% quantile	-6892.1	0.405	2.036	4.076	8.103	19.79
25% quantile	-6888.4	0.423	2.147	4.338	8.747	21.97
50% quantile	-6887.3	0.431	2.191	4.435	8.957	22.66
75% quantile	-6886.2	0.439	2.231	4.525	9.179	23.23
99% quantile	-6883.3	0.458	2.330	4.739	9.633	24.42

Notes: This table compares values generated by the particle filter with their true values generated by exact Bayesian updating. $\ln L$ is the value of the log-likelihood function for the Deutsche mark series with $\bar{k} = 8$ evaluated at the maximum likelihood estimates in Table 4.1. The forecasted variance of the series is denoted $\mathbb{E}_t \sum_{j=1}^{n} r_{t+j}^2$. For each quantity, the table provides the true value along with the average, standard deviation, and quantiles over 500 particle filter approximations using independent sets of random draws. Each approximation uses $B = 10,000$ random draws.

unbiased. These results confirm that the particle filter produces reasonable estimates of the likelihood and moments of the series for problems of reasonable size.

The particle filter extends the range of computationally feasible multifractal specifications. In Chapter 3, we have used ten binomial components, or 2^{10} states. While this gives good results in the univariate case, multivariate models require a correspondingly larger number of state variables. We show in the empirical section that the particle filter produces good results in a bivariate model with $\bar{k} = 8$ components, or 2^{16} states.

4.3.4   Two-Step Estimation

Two-step estimation offers additional computational benefits, permitting the econometrician to decompose inference into a sequence of lower-dimensional optimization problems. In the bivariate multifractal, each series $c \in \{\alpha, \beta\}$ follows a univariate MSM with parameters $m_0^c, \bar{\sigma}_c, b$ and $\gamma_{\bar{k}}$. This implies that we can estimate six of the eight parameters using the likelihood and smaller state space of the univariate model. This motivates us to develop the two-step method described below. The Appendix shows that this procedure is a special case of generalized method of moments (GMM), implying consistency and asymptotic normality of the estimator.

In the first stage, we obtain the parameters $(m_0^\alpha, m_0^\beta, \bar{\sigma}_\alpha, \bar{\sigma}_\beta, b, \gamma_{\bar{k}})$ by optimizing the sum of the two univariate log-likelihoods, as in (4.2). Intuitively, this gives consistent estimates for all parameters since the gradient of this sum with respect to the true parameters is zero. Because this objective function coincides with the likelihood of the combined univariate, the first step has already been completed in Section 4.1.

The second stage gives estimates for the remaining three parameters, $(\rho_\varepsilon, \rho_m^*, \lambda)$, which are unique to the bivariate model. Our empirical work focuses on the specification $\rho_m^* = 1$, which in untabulated results is never rejected in the currency data. When the state space is not too large ($\bar{k} \leq 5$), we maximize the analytical bivariate likelihood conditional on the first-stage estimates. For higher-dimensional specifications, ($\bar{k} = 6, 7, 8$), we instead use the particle filter to optimize the simulated likelihood.[8]

---

[8]Simulated likelihood is appealing for intermediate values of $\bar{k}$ because it potentially entails a small loss in efficiency. As discussed in Chapter 8, moment-based estimation can further reduce computational requirements, which is especially helpful for large problems.

4.4 Empirical Results

4.4.1 Bivariate MSM Estimates

Table 4.6 reports ML results for $\bar{k} \leq 5$ and exchange rate pairs (DM,JA), (DM,UK) and (JA,UK). The estimates are obtained by maximizing the full likelihood of bivariate MSM, as described in Section 4.3. As in univariate MSM, $\widehat{m}_0$ declines with $\bar{k}$, while the standard deviations $\widehat{\sigma}_\alpha$ and $\widehat{\sigma}_\beta$ tend to vary with $\bar{k}$, with no apparent trend. The correlation between Gaussian innovations $\widehat{\rho}_\varepsilon$ is positive and roughly constant across $\bar{k}$. The arrival correlation $\widehat{\lambda}$ is also large and approximately invariant to the number of volatility components. The two parameters specific to the bivariate specification, $\widehat{\rho}_\varepsilon$ and $\widehat{\lambda}$, thus seem precisely estimated. Finally, the estimated $\widehat{\lambda}$ is highest when $\widehat{\rho}_\varepsilon$ is highest and lowest when $\widehat{\rho}_\varepsilon$ is lowest. We infer that correlation in volatility is higher for currencies with more correlated returns.

The likelihood functions sharply increase with the number of frequencies. For instance, with the mark and the yen series, the log-likelihood increases by more than 800 when $\bar{k}$ goes from 1 to 5. Since the models are nonnested and specified by the same number of parameters, this is a substantial increase of fit in-sample. We also compare the goodness of fit to the independent case in Table 4.3, and we find that for the mark and the yen with $\bar{k} = 5$, the gain in likelihood is over 1300 points. Results are similar

TABLE 4.6. Bivariate MSM: Maximum Likelihood Estimation

	$k = 1$	2	3	4	5
			DM and JA		
$\widehat{m}_0^{DM}$	1.637	1.589	1.543	1.484	1.447
	(0.011)	(0.013)	(0.013)	(0.013)	(0.011)
$\widehat{m}_0^{JA}$	1.718	1.701	1.667	1.621	1.573
	(0.011)	(0.009)	(0.010)	(0.010)	(0.010)
$\widehat{\sigma}_{DM}$	0.679	0.621	0.575	0.559	0.524
	(0.009)	(0.011)	(0.014)	(0.017)	(0.015)
$\widehat{\sigma}_{JA}$	0.683	0.649	0.577	0.573	0.509
	(0.011)	(0.014)	(0.017)	(0.018)	(0.024)
$\widehat{\gamma}_{\bar{k}}$	0.122	0.217	0.732	0.828	0.905
	(0.013)	(0.022)	(0.066)	(0.049)	(0.038)
$\widehat{b}$	—	16.23	23.71	13.60	8.70
		(3.09)	(4.54)	(1.48)	(0.83)
$\widehat{\rho}_\varepsilon$	0.580	0.589	0.576	0.580	0.580
	(0.008)	(0.009)	(0.010)	(0.009)	(0.009)
$\widehat{\lambda}$	0.647	0.641	0.589	0.634	0.637
	(0.041)	(0.039)	(0.056)	(0.048)	(0.049)
$\ln L$	-12519.99	-12001.70	-11797.05	-11688.44	-11655.80

(continued)

TABLE 4.6. *(continued)*

	$k = 1$	2	3	4	5
			DM and UK		
$\hat{m}_0^{DM}$	1.651	1.570	1.522	1.492	1.484
	(0.012)	(0.010)	(0.012)	(0.012)	(0.011)
$\hat{m}_0^{JA}$	1.731	1.656	1.624	1.588	1.564
	(0.010)	(0.010)	(0.009)	(0.017)	(0.010)
$\hat{\sigma}_{DM}$	0.681	0.706	0.626	0.560	0.498
	(0.009)	(0.014)	(0.011)	(0.031)	(0.012)
$\hat{\sigma}_{JA}$	0.629	0.658	0.573	0.506	0.458
	(0.009)	(0.015)	(0.012)	(0.042)	(0.015)
$\hat{\gamma}_{\bar{k}}$	0.227	0.422	0.746	0.791	0.864
	(0.021)	(0.052)	(0.057)	(0.067)	(0.040)
$\hat{b}$	—	13.29	15.24	11.71	10.83
		(2.28)	(2.26)	(1.68)	(1.35)
$\hat{\rho}_\epsilon$	0.707	0.714	0.707	0.708	0.710
	(0.007)	(0.007)	(0.007)	(0.007)	(0.007)
$\hat{\lambda}$	0.837	0.852	0.833	0.822	0.827
	(0.023)	(0.023)	(0.026)	(0.027)	(0.025)
$\ln L$	-10894.41	-10513.18	-10335.82	-10270.90	-10240.51
			JA and UK		
$\hat{m}_0^{DM}$	1.764	1.718	1.693	1.629	1.608
	(0.014)	(0.008)	(0.009)	(0.010)	(0.010)
$\hat{m}_0^{UK}$	1.729	1.661	1.633	1.595	1.571
	(0.005)	(0.012)	(0.012)	(0.011)	(0.010)
$\hat{\sigma}_{DM}$	0.655	0.619	0.531	0.489	0.709
	(0.008)	(0.014)	(0.015)	(0.014)	(0.021)
$\hat{\sigma}_{UK}$	0.603	0.578	0.514	0.474	0.385
	(0.006)	(0.012)	(0.018)	(0.011)	(0.009)
$\hat{\gamma}_{\bar{k}}$	0.219	0.304	0.449	0.748	0.791
	(0.011)	(0.027)	(0.054)	(0.046)	(0.043)
$\hat{b}$	—	21.50	15.08	13.21	11.91
		(4.32)	(2.08)	(1.43)	(1.40)
$\hat{\rho}_\epsilon$	0.447	0.453	0.449	0.438	0.440
	(0.007)	(0.004)	(0.011)	(0.012)	(0.011)
$\hat{\lambda}$	0.499	0.565	0.560	0.544	0.535
	(0.048)	(0.047)	(0.054)	(0.056)	(0.059)
$\ln L$	-12247.45	-11647.36	-11404.09	-11266.91	-11211.52

Notes: This table shows maximum likelihood estimation results for bivariate MSM. The results reported are based on daily log returns in percent over the sample period 1 June 1973 to 30 October 2003. Each column corresponds to a given number of components $\bar{k}$ in the MSM model. Asymptotic standard errors are in parentheses.

for other currencies, demonstrating that the bivariate model improves over independent univariate models.

In Table 4.7, we reestimate bivariate MSM with the two-step procedure of Subsection 4.3. The second stage uses the analytical bivariate likelihood for $\bar{k} \leq 5$ and the particle filter for $\bar{k} \in \{6, 7, 8\}$. When $\bar{k} \leq 5$, the two-step parameter estimates are comparable to the full ML results, demonstrating that the two-step procedure works well. For $\bar{k} \in \{6, 7, 8\}$, the results appear consistent with the univariate ML estimates of Table 4.1 as well as the estimates of the lower dimensional bivariate models. The particle filter is effective in extending the range of tractable models.

We compare bivariate MSM with the constant correlation GARCH (CC-GARCH) of Bollerslev (1990), which is a standard benchmark in the multivariate volatility literature. CC-GARCH returns are specified as

$$r_t^\alpha = \sqrt{h_t^\alpha} \varepsilon_t^\alpha \text{ and } r_t^\beta = \sqrt{h_t^\beta} \varepsilon_t^\beta,$$

where ε_t^α and ε_t^β are two standard normals with correlation ρ_ε. The conditional variances h_t^α and h_t^β satisfy the familiar GARCH recursions: $h_{t+1}^c = \omega_c + a_c(\varepsilon_t^c)^2 + b_c h_t^c$ for each $c \in \{\alpha, \beta\}$. CC-GARCH is thus specified by seven parameters as compared to eight with bivariate MSM.

TABLE 4.7. Bivariate MSM: Two-Step Estimation

	$k = 1$	2	3	4	5	6	7	8
				DM and JA				
$\widehat{m}_0^{DM}$	1.643	1.618	1.515	1.474	1.445	1.405	1.397	1.367
	(0.020)	(0.019)	(0.022)	(0.023)	(0.022)	(0.022)	(0.022)	(0.022)
$\widehat{m}_0^{JA}$	1.775	1.757	1.687	1.638	1.578	1.565	1.522	1.488
	(0.013)	(0.012)	(0.016)	(0.017)	(0.020)	(0.018)	(0.019)	(0.021)
$\widehat{\sigma}_{DM}$	0.669	0.577	0.597	0.569	0.504	0.565	0.449	0.472
	(0.014)	(0.011)	(0.019)	(0.020)	(0.021)	(0.018)	(0.027)	(0.035)
$\widehat{\sigma}_{JA}$	0.613	0.544	0.565	0.487	0.476	0.632	0.384	0.532
	(0.010)	(0.010)	(0.018)	(0.016)	(0.021)	(0.017)	(0.022)	(0.041)
$\widehat{\gamma}_{\bar{k}}$	0.129	0.257	0.301	0.756	0.844	0.872	0.959	0.982
	(0.014)	(0.024)	(0.037)	(0.072)	(0.075)	(0.081)	(0.047)	(0.027)
$\widehat{b}$	—	69.57	11.97	13.21	9.14	7.16	6.16	4.93
		(21.80)	(2.20)	(2.11)	(1.32)	(1.29)	(0.86)	(0.56)
$\widehat{\rho}_\epsilon$	0.566	0.570	0.581	0.574	0.578	0.581	0.581	0.618
	(0.013)	(0.014)	(0.016)	(0.017)	(0.017)	(0.049)	(0.009)	(0.010)
$\widehat{\lambda}$	0.587	0.544	0.646	0.585	0.624	0.633	0.659	0.633
	(0.065)	(0.067)	(0.064)	(0.082)	(0.080)	(0.032)	(0.038)	(0.023)

(continued)

TABLE 4.7. *(continued)*

	$k=1$	2	3	4	5	6	7	8
				DM and UK				
$\widehat{m}_0^{DM}$	1.626	1.565	1.519	1.473	1.452	1.406	1.401	1.370
	(0.020)	(0.021)	(0.022)	(0.023)	(0.022)	(0.022)	(0.023)	(0.022)
$\widehat{m}_0^{UK}$	1.697	1.657	1.641	1.602	1.573	1.521	1.492	1.454
	(0.016)	(0.017)	(0.019)	(0.021)	(0.022)	(0.022)	(0.022)	(0.022)
$\widehat{\sigma}_{DM}$	0.671	0.645	0.599	0.568	0.493	0.563	0.471	0.474
	(0.013)	(0.017)	(0.018)	(0.021)	(0.018)	(0.018)	(0.028)	(0.033)
$\widehat{\sigma}_{UK}$	0.605	0.588	0.515	0.468	0.422	0.457	0.391	0.385
	(0.011)	(0.015)	(0.015)	(0.016)	(0.017)	(0.020)	(0.019)	(0.026)
$\widehat{\gamma}_{\bar{k}}$	0.090	0.151	0.388	0.683	0.672	0.798	0.844	0.969
	(0.011)	(0.019)	(0.052)	(0.082)	(0.087)	(0.093)	(0.092)	(0.043)
$\widehat{b}$	—	12.33	15.25	11.97	10.09	6.97	6.23	5.02
		(3.38)	(3.02)	(2.07)	(1.68)	(1.48)	(0.88)	(0.65)
$\widehat{\rho}_\epsilon$	0.697	0.703	0.704	0.709	0.711	0.700	0.689	0.704
	(0.010)	(0.011)	(0.012)	(0.013)	(0.012)	(0.011)	(0.012)	(0.010)
$\widehat{\lambda}$	0.814	0.818	0.826	0.802	0.820	0.790	0.844	0.800
	(0.041)	(0.037)	(0.042)	(0.048)	(0.045)	(0.050)	(0.022)	(0.027)
				JA and UK				
$\widehat{m}_0^{JA}$	1.776	1.762	1.688	1.645	1.631	1.568	1.558	1.507
	(0.062)	(0.031)	(0.032)	(0.025)	(0.024)	(0.024)	(0.021)	(0.023)
$\widehat{m}_0^{UK}$	1.728	1.680	1.640	1.607	1.575	1.525	1.499	1.458
	(0.016)	(0.016)	(0.019)	(0.020)	(0.021)	(0.022)	(0.021)	(0.021)
$\widehat{\sigma}_{JA}$	0.624	0.546	0.569	0.471	0.702	0.631	0.514	0.509
	(0.011)	(0.011)	(0.017)	(0.014)	(0.028)	(0.030)	(0.025)	(0.031)
$\widehat{\sigma}_{UK}$	0.606	0.561	0.522	0.508	0.432	0.457	0.384	0.379
	(0.012)	(0.012)	(0.015)	(0.015)	(0.016)	(0.021)	(0.018)	(0.023)
$\widehat{\gamma}_{\bar{k}}$	0.161	0.303	0.275	0.635	0.697	0.847	0.864	0.970
	(0.015)	(0.027)	(0.030)	(0.062)	(0.068)	(0.064)	(0.067)	(0.034)
$\widehat{b}$	—	43.46	12.73	14.55	13.60	8.22	7.24	5.60
		(10.62)	(2.27)	(2.14)	(2.08)	(1.04)	(0.91)	(0.70)
$\widehat{\rho}_\epsilon$	0.439	0.439	0.448	0.439	0.439	0.436	0.414	0.436
	(0.017)	(0.018)	(0.019)	(0.021)	(0.021)	(0.010)	(0.018)	(0.017)
$\widehat{\lambda}$	0.494	0.519	0.570	0.549	0.524	0.575	0.625	0.561
	(0.068)	(0.071)	(0.063)	(0.076)	(0.080)	(0.049)	(0.027)	(0.015)

Notes: This table shows two-step estimates for bivariate MSM. The results are based on daily log returns in percent over the sample period 1 June 1973 to 30 October 2003. Each column corresponds to a given number of components $\bar{k}$ in the MSM model. First-stage estimates are obtained by optimizing the combined univariate likelihood as in Panel A of Table 4.3. As described in the Appendix, this provides consistent estimates for the parameters $(m_0^\alpha, m_0^\beta, \bar{\sigma}_\alpha, \bar{\sigma}_\beta, b, \gamma_{\bar{k}})$. For $\bar{k} \leq 5$, the second stage optimizes the analytically calculated bivariate MSM likelihood conditional on the first-stage estimates. For $\bar{k} = 6, 7, 8$, the optimization of the likelihood is numerically implemented using the particle filter approximation. Standard errors in parentheses are calculated by recasting the optimization in a GMM context, as described in the Appendix, and are HAC-adjusted using Newey and West (1987).

Table 4.8 reports an in-sample comparison of CC-GARCH against bivariate MSM with $\bar{k} = 5$ components. It is immediately clear that MSM gives much higher likelihoods, although it has only one additional parameter. For all three pairs of exchange rates, the difference in log-likelihood exceeds 1000 points. The same results hold whether comparing full ML results from the two models, or the likelihoods obtained under two-step estimation. To account for the difference in the number of parameters, we compute the BIC statistic for each model, and test the significance of the difference using the original method suggested by Vuong (1989) and the HAC-adjusted version explained in Chapter 3. In all cases, the p-value from the test that CC-GARCH has a superior BIC statistic to multivariate MSM is substantially less than 1%. In-sample evidence thus strongly favors bivariate MSM.

4.4.2   Specification Tests

In-sample comparisons have shown that bivariate MSM performs well relative to CC-GARCH. It is now natural to investigate whether, in an absolute sense, the restrictions imposed by the model are supported by the data. We weaken one assumption at a time, and we assess improvement in fit by likelihood ratio (LR) tests. When a restriction applies equally to the univariate and bivariate models, we choose to test on the univariate series. This allows us to distinguish between misspecifications originating in univariate MSM and those unique to the bivariate approach.

Heterogeneity in volatility persistence is made parsimonious by the frequency parameterization (4.3). We focus on univariate models with $\bar{k} = 8$ components. For each currency, we consider the *restricted* univariate ML estimates in Table 4.1 and denote by L_r the corresponding likelihood. In contrast, we call *unrestricted* model $k \in \{1, \ldots, \bar{k}\}$ the extension in which frequency parameter γ_k is free and all other frequencies satisfy (4.3). We estimate the kth unrestricted model and denote by $L_u(k)$ the corresponding likelihood. Under the restricted model, $2[L_u(k) - L_r]$ converges to $\chi^2(1)$ as $T \to \infty$. This methodology generates eight LR statistics for each of the three currencies. We report salient features of the analysis in the text. For DM, none of the tests provides evidence against the MSM frequency restrictions at the 1% level. One statistic ($k = 6$) is significant for JA, and two tests ($k = 6, 7$) are significant for UK. Evidence against the frequency specification is thus limited to 3 of the 24 tests.

We similarly assess on univariate series whether volatility components have identical distributions across frequencies. Unrestricted specification k permits component $M_{k,t}$ to have its own distribution parameter $m_0(k)$. Results are mixed. For DM, only two of the eight tests ($k = 1, 6$) are significant at the 1% level. For JA, the first five tests suggest a value of $m_0(k)$ larger than for the other components. Similarly for the UK series, LR tests of the first 4 components suggest stronger shocks at low than at high-frequency. Overall, the DM data seems to match the MSM model

TABLE 4.8. In-Sample Bivariate Model Comparison

	No. of Parameters	ln L	BIC	BIC p-value vs. Multifractral	
				Vuong (1989)	HAC Adj
A. Maximum Likelihood Estimates					
DM and JA					
Bivariate MSM	8	−11655.80	3.0626		
CC GARCH	7	−12825.63	3.3679	< 0.001	< 0.001
DM and UK					
Bivariate MSM	8	−10240.51	2.6919		
CC GARCH	7	−11331.00	2.9764	< 0.001	< 0.001
JA and UK					
Bivariate MSM	8	−11211.52	2.9462		
CC GARCH	7	−12550.49	3.2958	< 0.001	< 0.001
B. Two-Step Estimates					
DM and JA					
Bivariate MSM	8	−11658.89	3.0634		
CC GARCH	7	−12830.98	3.3693	< 0.001	< 0.001
DM and UK					
Bivariate MSM	8	−10262.05	2.6975		
CC GARCH	7	−11434.17	3.0034	< 0.001	< 0.001
JA and UK					
Bivariate MSM	8	−11233.59	2.9521		
CC GARCH	7	−12559.72	3.2982	< 0.001	< 0.001

Notes: This table summarizes information about in-sample goodness of fit. The Bayesian Information Criterion is given by $BIC = T^{-1}(-2\ln L + NP \ln T)$, where NP is the number of free parameters in the specification. The last two columns give p-values from a test that the corresponding model dominates bivariate MSM by the BIC criterion. The first value uses the Vuong (1989) methodology, and the second value adjusts the test for heteroskedasticity and autocorrelation as described in the Appendix to Chapter 3. A low p-value indicates that the CC GARCH model would be rejected in favor of the multifractal model. Panel A presents the results when both models have been estimated by Full MLE. Panel B presents results where both models are estimated by two-step procedures.

remarkably well, while JA and UK appear to prefer stronger low-frequency variation.

We finally test the restrictions imposed by bivariate MSM on volatility comovement. For each currency pair, the restricted model is given by the full ML estimates with $\bar{k} = 5$ in Table 4.6. Unrestricted model k permits that component k may have its own unique arrival correlation λ_k. We report no rejections at the 1% level for JA-UK, one significant test ($k = 5$) for the DM-UK pair, and two significant statistics ($k = 2, 5$) for the DM-JA pair. Overall, MSM incorporates empirically reasonable restrictions that permit parsimonious specification of bivariate multifrequency volatility.

4.4.3   Out-of-Sample Diagnostics

We now perform out-of-sample diagnostics with probability integral transforms, as suggested by Rosenblatt (1952) and implemented in a financial econometrics context by Diebold, Gunther, and Tay (1998) and Elerian, Chib, and Shephard (2001). In all remaining empirical work, we consider bivariate MSM with $\bar{k} = 5$ components. We first estimate MSM and CC-GARCH on the 1973–1989 subsample. The out-of-sample evaluations are based on the 3473 daily observations from 1990 to 2003. Let $y_{t,n} \equiv \sum_{i=1}^{n} r_{t+i}$ denote the forward-looking n-period return at time t. MSM and CC-GARCH each generate a conditional forecast distribution

$$F_{t,n}(y) \equiv \mathbb{P}(y_{t,n} \leq y | r_1, \ldots, r_t).$$

Under correct specification, the random variables $U_{t,n} = F_{t,n}(y_{t,n})$ are uniformly distributed on $[0, 1]$; they are also independent if $n = 1$.

In Figure 4.1, we compare histograms of selected integral transforms $\{U_{t,n}\}$ for the two models. Histograms are shown for $n = 1$ and $n = 5$ days using the following portfolios: DM, JA, an equal-weighted position in the two currencies, and a hedge portfolio with weights $(1, -1)$.[9] We see that MSM provides approximately uniform histograms. In contrast, CC-GARCH generates tent-shaped plots, with a large concentration of values around 0 and 1. These feature are symptomatic of tails that are too thin in the estimated CC-GARCH process. Similar results are obtained with other currencies.

---

[9] The random variables U_t are constructed as follows. In every period, we use the particle filter to draw B values $y_{t,n}^{(1)}, \ldots, y_{t,n}^{(B)}$ from the conditional distribution of $y_{t,n}$ given $r_1, \ldots, r_t$. We then approximate $F_{t,n}(y)$ by the empirical c.d.f. $\hat{F}_{t,n}(y) = \frac{1}{B} \sum_{b=1}^{B} 1\{y_{t,n}^{(b)} \leq y\}$. Sensitivity tests indicate that $B = 10,000$ draws are more than sufficient to provide a good approximation.

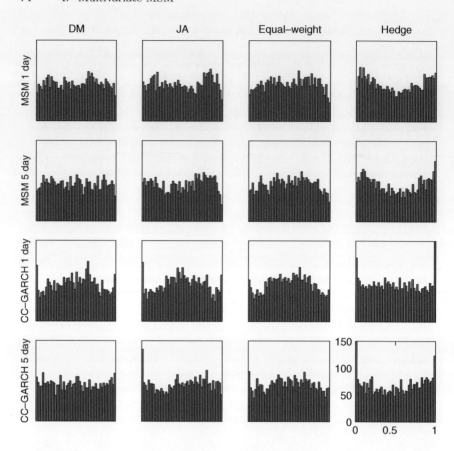

FIGURE 4.1. **Probability Integral Transforms.** These figures show histograms of the probability integral transforms $\{U_{t,n}\}$ for horizons (in rows) of $n = 1$ and $n = 5$ days and portfolios (in columns) of DM, JA, an equal-weighted portfolio of the two currencies, and a hedge portfolio with weights $(1, -1)$. The models considered are bivariate MSM with $\bar{k} = 5$ components and CC-GARCH. Under correct specification, the integral transforms are uniformly distributed.

The Cramér-von Mises criterion, which measures the goodness of fit of a probability distribution, confirms these graphical results.[10] We report the criterion in Table 4.9 for all currencies and portfolios. At the 1% level, we

---

[10] Let T^* denote the number of out-of-sample periods, and $\hat{F}_U$ the empirical distribution of the transforms $U_{t,1}$. As $T^* \to \infty$, the Cramér-von Mises criterion $T^* \int_0^1 [y - \hat{F}_U(y)]^2 dy$ weakly converges to a weighted series of independent χ^2 random variables:

$$T^* \int_0^1 [y - \hat{F}_U(y)]^2 dx \Rightarrow \sum_{j=1}^{\infty} \left(\frac{z_j}{j\pi}\right)^2$$

where the $\{z_j\}$ are IID $\mathcal{N}(0,1)$. See Shorack and Wellner (1986) for further details.

TABLE 4.9. Goodness of Fit One-Day Forecasts

	Bivariate MSM			CC GARCH		
	DM, JA	DM, UK	JA, UK	DM, JA	DM, UK	JA, UK
Currency α	0.22	0.16	0.54	**1.07**	**1.07**	**1.70**
Currency β	0.47	0.51	0.29	**1.70**	**2.57**	**2.56**
Equal-weight	0.67	0.05	0.23	**2.48**	**1.06**	**2.51**
Hedge	**2.27**	0.59	**1.06**	0.56	**5.93**	0.52

Notes: This table shows the Cramer-von Mises distance between a uniform distribution and the empirical distribution of the probability integral transform of the corresponding model forecast. The bivariate MSM specification uses $\bar{k} = 5$ components. Currency α and β correspond, respectively, to the first and second currency in each pair. Equal-weight is an equal-weighted portfolio, in which a U.S. investor allocates 50% of the fund's dollar value to currency α and 50% to currency β. Hedge is a portfolio consisting of a long position in α and a short position in β with an initial net investment of zero. Under correct specification, the reported statistics are greater than 0.73 in about 1% of samples. A high value of the statistic thus indicates rejection of the corresponding model. Rejections at the 1% level are indicated by boldface.

reject MSM in only 2 out of 12 cases, while CC-GARCH is rejected in 10 out of 12 cases.[11] The Cramér-von Mises statistics thus confirm that the conditional density forecasts of MSM are broadly consistent with exchange rate data.

4.4.4   Value-at-Risk

The tail properties of financial series are of direct interest for risk management and financial regulation. Value-at-risk (VaR) is a particularly widespread method that summarizes the expected maximum loss over a target horizon within a given confidence interval. Given a confidence level p, we define the value-at-risk of a portfolio to be the $1 - p^{th}$ quantile of the conditional return distribution:

$$VaR_{t,n}(p) \equiv F_{t,n}^{-1}(1 - p).$$

With probability p, we expect to lose no more than $VaR_{t,n}(p)$ over the next n days.

The accuracy of a value-at-risk model is most easily verified by recording the failure rate, that is, the number of times VaR is exceeded in a given sample (e.g., Kupiec, 1995; Jorion, 1997).[12] Table 4.10 reports the failure

---

[11] We do not adjust the critical values for estimation error. Earlier work (e.g., Thompson, 2000) suggests that such adjustments would only have small effects.

[12] The failure rate is thus the proportion of out-of-sample days in which $r_{t+1} + \cdots + r_{t+n} < VaR_{t,n}(p)$.

rates of MSM and CC-GARCH for portfolios held for $n = 1$ and 5 days and confidence levels of 1%, 5%, and 10%. As described in the Appendix, we forecast for each bivariate process the value-at-risk of individual currencies, equal-weighted portfolios, and hedge portfolios.

The results in Table 4.10 show that MSM is more conservative in estimating value-at-risk than CC-GARCH. For example, under a one-day predicted failure rate of 1%, actual portfolio losses exceed the MSM VaR forecast more than 1% of the time for 3 out of 12 portfolios, whereas actual losses exceed the 1% CC-GARCH quantile more than 1% of the time in 11 out of 12 portfolios.

Of course, an excessively conservative model does not necessarily lead to superior risk management. Statistical tests suggest that MSM is not overly conservative. For each portfolio and VaR quantile we test the null hypothesis that the empirical failure rate is equal to the expected failure

TABLE 4.10. Failure Rates of Value-at-Risk Forecasts

	Bivariate MSM			CC GARCH		
	1%	5%	10%	1%	5%	10%
A. One-Day Horizon						
DM and JA						
Currency α	0.69	4.35	9.10	**1.81**	5.13	9.01
Currency β	0.95	4.81	9.56	**2.30**	5.38	9.10
Equal-Weight	0.86	**3.92**	**8.32**	1.30	4.66	8.21
Hedge	0.69	5.64	**12.21**	**2.25**	**6.68**	**11.81**
DM and UK						
Currency α	0.92	4.92	10.14	**1.81**	5.13	9.01
Currency β	0.72	5.27	10.68	**1.44**	**4.61**	**8.29**
Equal-Weight	1.07	4.69	10.28	**1.87**	5.18	8.98
Hedge	**0.55**	4.72	9.13	0.92	**4.00**	**7.00**
JA and UK						
Currency α	1.01	5.04	9.88	**2.30**	5.38	9.10
Currency β	0.60	4.41	9.70	**1.44**	4.61	**8.29**
Equal-Weight	0.84	4.55	8.78	**1.64**	4.69	**8.03**
Hedge	1.15	5.64	**11.37**	**2.25**	**6.25**	10.34
B. Five-Day Horizon						
DM and JA						
Currency α	0.78	4.21	9.57	1.61	5.48	10.72
Currency β	1.07	5.30	10.55	**2.31**	**7.06**	11.62
Equal-Weight	0.72	4.44	8.50	1.64	5.25	9.14
Hedge	0.92	5.42	12.16	**3.29**	**8.39**	**13.46**

(continued)

TABLE 4.10. *(continued)*

	Bivariate MSM			CC GARCH		
	1%	5%	10%	1%	5%	10%
DM and UK						
Currency α	0.95	5.13	10.35	1.64	5.51	10.72
Currency β	0.75	5.28	11.01	0.98	4.79	9.77
Equal-Weight	0.84	5.07	10.93	1.27	5.94	10.61
Hedge	0.69	4.01	8.76	0.86	3.86	8.48
JA and UK						
Currency α	1.21	5.53	10.75	**2.36**	6.86	11.70
Currency β	**0.46**	4.67	9.02	1.53	4.93	9.57
Equal-Weight	0.84	4.12	9.02	1.53	4.93	9.57
Hedge	1.73	6.40	11.24	1.76	6.34	11.53

Notes: This table displays the frequency of returns that exceed the value-at-risk forecasted by the model. The bivariate MSM specification uses $\bar{k} = 5$ components. For quantile p the number reported is the frequency of portfolio returns below quantile p predicted by the model. If the VaR forecast is correct, the observed failure rate should be close to the prediction. Boldface numbers are statistically different from α at the 1% level. Panel A shows results for a one-day horizon, while Panel B shows a five-day horizon. Currency α and β refer to the first currency and second currency in each pair. Equal-Weight is an equal-weighted portfolio, in which a U.S. investor allocates 50% of the fund's dollar value to currency α and 50% to currency β. Hedge is a portfolio consisting of a long position in α and a short position in β with an initial net investment of zero. Standard errors in Panel A are computed by $p(1-p)/3473$, where 3473 is the number of out-of-sample observations. Standard errors in Panel B are computed using Newey and West (1987).

rate. For the MSM model, the failure rates are statistically different from the 1% prediction for only 1 out of 12 portfolios. The CC-GARCH failure rates are statistically different from 1% in 11 out of 12 portfolios. MSM thus provides more accurate quantile forecasts than CC-GARCH.

4.5 Discussion

This chapter uses MSM to implement a univariate frequency decomposition of volatility in several exchange rate series. We find that the estimated components are generally difficult to relate to standard macroeconomic variables. Low-frequency volatility components from all currencies covary positively with oil and gold prices, suggesting that these commodities may act as proxies for global economic risk.

Across exchange rate pairs, volatility components tend to have high correlation when their durations are similar and low correlations otherwise.

This finding motivates the development of bivariate MSM, a multifrequency model of comovement in stochastic volatility and covariation in financial prices. The model permits a parsimonious specification of bivariate shocks with heterogeneous durations, capturing the economic intuition that shared fundamentals may have different innovation frequencies. Bayesian updating and the likelihood function are always available in closed form, but are practical only when the state space is of moderate size. We develop a particle filter suitable for larger state spaces, and demonstrate its good performance in inference and forecasting. Bivariate MSM performs well in- and out-of-sample relative to a standard benchmark, CC-GARCH. Likelihood ratio tests also confirm some of the principal restrictions of the model. The bivariate MSM framework permits us to conduct inference and forecasting for good-performing pure regime-switching models with 2^{16} states and only eight parameters.

The bivariate MSM model investigated in this Chapter generalizes to the multivariate case with many assets, as is discussed in the Appendix. We can consider either an arbitrary arrival correlation matrix across asset markets, which might be useful for applications with a relatively small number of assets. Alternatively, we propose a factor model of multifrequency stochastic volatility, which is specified by a number of volatility parameters that grows linearly in the number of assets. Estimation can be conducted by maximizing the closed-form likelihood or by implementing the particle filter methodology.

Part II

Continuous Time

5

Background: Continuous-Time Volatility Modeling, Fractal Processes, and Multifractal Measures

This chapter provides background material for the continuous-time multifractal volatility models that are fully developed in the remainder of Part II (Chapters 6–8), and in Chapter 10 of Part III. Our goal is not to survey the literature in any area, but to provide a brief introduction to the continuous-time concepts employed in the rest of the book.

Much of the background information given here is directly useful to understanding the first multifractal diffusion, the MMAR. Specifically, *time deformation* and *multifractal measures* are critical building blocks for the MMAR. The less directly related but nonetheless important *self-similar processes*, which have a long history in finance, are cousins of the multifractal diffusions considered in the remainder of Part II. The MMAR is discussed in Chapter 6.

Chapter 7 takes an alternative path to generating a multifractal diffusion by following continuous-time versions of the MSM processes developed in Chapter 3 to their weak limit. This approach bypasses the need to work with combinatorial multifractal measures constructed on a fixed grid. Continuous-time MSM has the same moment-scaling properties as the MMAR, and Chapter 8 confirms these predictions in currency and equity data.

In this background review, we also briefly discuss jump-diffusion models of financial prices. Jump-diffusions are particularly relevant in Chapter 10, where we obtain endogenous discontinuities in prices and other appealing features by using equilibrium valuation.

5.1   Continuous-Time Models of Asset Prices

5.1.1   Brownian Motion, Time Deformation, and Jump-Diffusions

The Brownian motion (Bachelier, 1900) is the workhorse of continuous-time finance theory.[1] Among many examples, Black and Scholes (1973) and Merton (1973) specify the log-price of a financial asset as a Brownian motion with constant drift and volatility. While highly tractable in theoretical applications, the Brownian motion representation assumes independent Gaussian increments and thus cannot capture the outliers and volatility cycles exhibited by typical financial returns.

The Brownian motion is conveniently extended by considering deformations of clock time, as suggested by Bochner (1949):

Definition 5.1 (Time deformation and compound process) *Let* $\{B(t)\}$ *be a stochastic process, and* $\theta(t)$ *an increasing function of clock time* t. *We call*

$$X(t) \equiv B[\theta(t)]$$

a compound process, and $\theta(t)$ *the trading time or time-deformation process.*

When the process B is a martingale, innovations in trading time may speed up or slow down the process $X(t)$ without influencing its direction. Compounding can thus separate the direction and the size of price movements, and has been used to model the unobserved natural time scale of economic series (Clark, 1973; Mandelbrot and Taylor, 1967; Stock, 1987, 1988). In Chapters 6 and 7, we show how compounding can be used to define multifractal diffusions.

To account for thick tails in asset returns and the corresponding implied volatility smiles in near-maturity options, another approach used in continuous time is to incorporate jumps in financial prices.[2] For example, Merton (1976) assumes that the stock price follows an exogenous

---

[1] We refer the reader to Baxter and Rennie (1996), Bjork (2004), Cochrane (2005), Cont and Tankov (2003), Dana and Jeanblanc (2007), Dothan (1990), Duffie (1988, 2001), Hunt and Kennedy (2004), Ingersoll (1987), Karatzas and Shreve (2001), Merton (1990), Musiela and Rutkowski (2007), Neftci (2000), Nielsen (1999), Shreve (2005), and Wilmott (2006), among others, for excellent book length treatments of the continuous-time finance literature.

[2] Numerous studies provide evidence for jumps in the valuation of stocks and other financial securities, based on the series of either the assets themselves or their derivative claims, against increasingly broad diffusion alternatives. See, for example, Ait-Sahalia (2002), Ait-Sahalia and Jacod (2008), Andersen, Benzoni, and Lund (2002), Andersen,

jump-diffusion with constant volatility. Subsequent research considers econometric refinements such as stochastic volatility, priced jumps, jumps in volatility, correlation between jumps in returns and volatility, and infinite activity.[3] Among numerous contributions, Bakshi, Cao, and Chen (1997) and Bates (2000) investigate price processes with exogenous jumps and stochastic volatility, and conclude that additional discontinuities in volatility are necessary to match option valuations. Duffie, Pan, and Singleton (2000) analyze an extension with discrete volatility changes while exogenously specifying the relation between volatility and returns. A related line of research (e.g., Madan, Carr, and Chang, 1998) considers pure jump processes characterized by infinite activity with many small events and fewer large discontinuities. In all of this literature, jumps in valuations and their relation to volatility are exogenously specified.[4] In Chapter 10, we use equilibrium valuation to generate price jumps linked endogenously to volatility changes, and derive an inverse relation between the size and frequency of price discontinuities in a multifrequency environment.

5.1.2   Self-Similar (Fractal) Processes

The French mathematician Benoît Mandelbrot has long recommended departing from Itô diffusions in favor of adopting fat-tailed "fractal" processes. This alternative modeling approach builds on the concept of scale invariance. In a 1963 publication, Mandelbrot suggested that the shape of the distribution of returns should be invariant when the time scale is changed:

Definition 5.2 (Self-similar process) *A random process* $\{X(t)\}$ *that satisfies*

$$\{X(ct_1), \ldots, X(ct_k)\} \stackrel{d}{=} \{c^H X(t_1), \ldots, c^H X(t_k)\}$$

for some $H > 0$ *and all* $c, k, t_1, \ldots, t_k \geq 0$, *is called self-similar or self-affine. The number* H *is the self-similarity index, or scaling exponent, of the process* $\{X(t)\}$.

Bollerslev, and Diebold (2007), Ball and Torous (1985), Barndorff-Nielsen and Shephard (2004, 2006), Bates (1996, 2000), Carr, Geman, Madan, and Yor (2002), Carr and Wu (2003), Eraker (2004), Eraker, Johannes, and Polson (2003), Huang and Tauchen (2005), Jarrow and Rosenfeld (1984), Jorion (1988), Maheu and McCurdy (2004), and Press (1967).

[3] Jump processes are classified as having finite or infinite activity depending on whether the number of jumps in a bounded time interval is finite or infinite.

[4] Other applications of jump processes in finance include Barndorff-Nielsen (1998), Eberlein, Keller, and Prause (1998), Liu, Pan, and Wang (2005), Naik and Lee (1990), and Pan (2002).

The Brownian motion is self-similar with $H = 1/2$. Besides the Brownian motion, the Lévy-stable process and the fractional Brownian motion are the main examples of self-similar processes in finance. Embrechts and Maejima (2002), Mandelbrot (1997), and Samorodnitsky and Taqqu (1994) provide thorough discussions of self-similar processes in finance and the natural sciences, and we briefly review two important examples.

The stable processes of Paul Lévy (1924) are characterized by fat tails in the unconditional distribution of returns. They have been widely applied in financial econometrics to model a variety of commodity, equity and currency prices (e.g., Blattberg and Gonedes, 1974; Fama, 1963, 1965; Fama and Roll, 1971; Fielitz, 1976; Granger and Morgenstern, 1970; Koedijk and Kool, 1992; Mandelbrot, 1963, 1967; Officer, 1972; Phillips, McFarland, and McMahon, 1996; Samuelson, 1967, 1976). A problem with Lévy-stable processes in financial applications is that they imply infinite variance, which appears to be empirically inaccurate in typical financial data. Moreover, the Lévy-stable model assumes that increments are independent through time, which is at odds with substantial empirical evidence of time-varying volatility.

The fractional Brownian motion (FBM), introduced by Kolmogorov (1940) and Mandelbrot (1965a), has continuous sample paths as well as Gaussian and possibly dependent increments. A fractional Brownian motion $B_H(t)$ is an ordinary Brownian motion for $H = 1/2$, is antipersistent when $0 < H < 1/2$, and persistent with long memory in returns when $1/2 < H < 1$. The FBM has been widely used in hydrology and climatology, as reviewed in Samorodnitsky and Taqqu (1994). Applications in finance are limited by the fact that the FBM does not disentangle long memory in volatility from long memory in returns. Chapters 6 and 7 show that multifractal volatility modeling resolves this difficulty.

Empirical evidence suggests that many financial series are not self-similar, but instead have thinner tails and become less peaked in the bells when the sampling interval increases (e.g., Campbell, Lo, and MacKinlay, 1996, Chapter 1). The volatility models in Chapters 6 and 7 capture this nonlinearity, as well as thick tails and long-memory volatility persistence, by building on a generalized form of scaling that has been developed in the multifractal literature.

5.2   Multifractal Measures

The history of multifractals begins in the natural sciences, where multifractal measures have proven useful in numerous applications.[5] We

---

[5]The literature on applications of multifractals includes wide-ranging contributions across many areas of study. A survey is beyond the scope of this book, but examples include agronomy (Kravchenko, Bullock, and Boast, 2000; Zeleke and Si, 2004), astronomy

now review the simplest multifractal, the binomial measure on a compact interval, which generalizes to random multiplicative measures.

5.2.1   The Binomial Measure

Fractals are sets that can be constructed by iterating a simple transformation. Well-known examples include the Cantor set, which is constructed by recursively eliminating the middle third of intervals, or the Koch flake, which is obtained by recursively transforming segments into tent-shaped curves. Mandelbrot (1982) provides a classic exposition of fractals and their applications in the natural sciences.

Analogous to fractal sets, multifractal measures are built by iterating a simple transformation. The binomial measure[6] on $[0, 1]$ provides a simple example, and is easily derived as the limit of a *multiplicative cascade*. Consider the uniform probability measure μ_0 on the unit interval and two positive numbers m_0 and m_1 adding up to 1. In the first step of the cascade, we define a measure μ_1 by uniformly spreading the mass m_0 on the *left* subinterval $[0, 1/2]$, and the mass m_1 on the *right* subinterval $[1/2, 1]$. The density of μ_1 is a step function, as illustrated in Figure 5.1a.

In the second stage of the cascade, we split the interval $[0, 1/2]$ into two subintervals of equal length. The left subinterval $[0, 1/4]$ is allocated a fraction m_0 of $\mu_1[0, 1/2]$, while the right subinterval $[1/4, 1/2]$ receives a fraction m_1. Applying a similar procedure to $[1/2, 1]$, we obtain a measure

(Borgani, 1995; Jones *et al.*, 1988, 2004; Martinez, 1999; Pietronero, 1987; Valdarnini, Borgani, and Provenzale, 1992), ecology (Borda-de-Agua, Hubbell, and MacAllister, 2002; Drake and Weishampel, 2001; Kirkpatrick and Weishampel, 2005), geology and geochemistry (Agterberg, 2007; Cheng, 1999; Cheng and Agterberg, 1995; de Wijs, 1951; Goncalves, 2001; Paredes and Elorza, 1999; Xie and Bao, 2004), genetics (Gutierrez, Rodriguez, and Abramson, 2001; Tino, 2002; Yu, Anh, and Lao, 2003), hydrology (Boufadel *et al.*, 2000; Koscielny-Bunde *et al.*, 2006; Labat, Mangin, and Ababou, 2002; Liu and Moltz, 1997; Pandey, Lovejoy, and Schertzer, 1998), meteorology (Carvalho, Lavallee, and Jones, 2002; Deidda, 2000; Lilley *et al.*, 2006; Lovejoy and Schertzer, 2006; Olsson and Niemczynowicz, 1996; Schertzer and Lovejoy, 1987; Tessier, Lovejoy, and Schertzer, 1994), biology and medicine (Cornforth and Jelinek, 2008; Fernandez *et al.*, 1999; Oprisan, Ardelean, and Frangopol, 2000; Smith, Lange, and Marks, 1996; Stojic, Reljin, and Reljin, 2006; Takahashi *et al.*, 2004), network traffic modeling (Atzori, Aste, and Isola, 2006; Gilbert, Willinger, and Feldmann, 1999; Krishna, Gadre, and Desai, 2003; Riedi *et al.*, 1999), seismology (Geilikman, Golubeva, and Pisarenko, 1990; Godano and Caruso, 1995; Nakaya and Hashimoto, 2002; Molchan and Kronrod, 2007; Sornette and Ouillon, 2005), soil science (Dathe, Tarquis, and Perrier, 2006; Folorunso *et al.*, 1994; Grout, Tarquis, and Wiesner, 1998; Martin and Montero, 2002; Posadas *et al.*, 2003), and turbulence (Frisch and Parisi, 1985; Kolmogorov, 1962; Mandelbrot 1972, 1974; Meneveau and Sreenivasan, 1987, 1991; Muzy, Bacry, and Arneodo, 1991; Yaglom, 1966). For further discussion of some of these areas, see Davis *et al.* (1994), Mandelbrot (1989, 1999), Sornette (2004), and Stanley and Meakin (1988).

[6]The binomial is sometimes called the Bernoulli or Besicovitch measure.

μ_2 such that:

$$\mu_2[0, 1/4] = m_0 m_0, \qquad \mu_2[1/4, 1/2] = m_0 m_1,$$
$$\mu_2[1/2, 3/4] = m_1 m_0, \qquad \mu_2[3/4, 1] = m_1 m_1.$$

Iteration of this procedure generates an infinite sequence of measures (μ_k) that weakly converges to the binomial measure μ. Figure 5.1b illustrates the density of the measure μ_4 obtained after $k = 4$ steps of the recursion.

Since $m_0 + m_1 = 1$, each stage of the construction preserves the mass of split dyadic intervals.[7] Consider the interval $[t, t + 2^{-k}]$, where $t = \sum_{i=1}^{k} \eta_i 2^{-i}$ and $\eta_1, \ldots, \eta_k \in \{0, 1\}$, and let φ_0 and φ_1 denote the relative frequencies of 0s and 1s in $(\eta_1, \ldots, \eta_k)$. The measure of the dyadic interval is then

$$\mu[t, t + 2^{-k}] = m_0^{k\varphi_0} m_1^{k\varphi_1}.$$

Its values range between m_1^k and m_0^k, which illustrates that the construction creates large and increasing heterogeneity in the allocation of mass. As a result, the binomial is a continuous but singular probability measure that has no density and no point mass.

5.2.2   Random Multiplicative Cascades

The binomial construction is easily generalized. First, we can uniformly split intervals into an arbitrary number $b \geq 2$ of cells at each stage of the cascade. The corresponding subintervals are indexed from left to right by $\beta \in \{0, \ldots, b - 1\}$. Second, and more importantly, we can randomize the allocation of mass between subintervals. The multiplier of each cell is specified by a random variable M_β. Assume for parsimony that the multipliers have identical marginal distributions ($M_\beta \overset{d}{=} M \quad \forall \beta$) and that multipliers defined at different stages of the construction are independent. Under general assumptions, the recursion converges to a limit random multiplicative measure μ (Mandelbrot, 1974, 1989).

The construction can accommodate various hypotheses about the joint distribution of the multipliers $(M_0, \ldots, M_{b-1})$ at each stage. When mass is conserved exactly: $\sum M_\beta \equiv 1$, the limit measure is called *conservative* and the limit mass of the unit interval is equal to unity. The limit measure μ is instead called *canonical* when mass is preserved only on average: $\mathbb{E}(\sum M_\beta) = 1$ or equivalently $\mathbb{E}(M) = 1/b$. A canonical measure can for instance be constructed by using independent multipliers $M_0, \ldots, M_{b-1}$.

Figure 5.1c shows the conservative random density obtained after $k = 10$ iterations of the random binomial measure with parameters $b = 2$ and

---

[7]A number $t \in [0, 1]$ is called *dyadic* if $t = 1$ or $t = \eta_1 2^{-1} + \cdots + \eta_k 2^{-k}$ for a finite k and $\eta_1, \ldots, \eta_k \in \{0, 1\}$. A dyadic interval has dyadic endpoints.

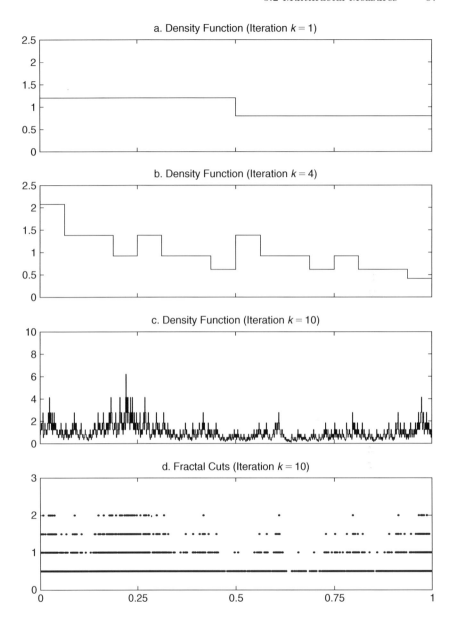

FIGURE 5.1. **Construction of the Binomial Measure.** In Panels (a) and (b), the construction is deterministic with the fraction $m_0 = 0.6$ of the mass always allocated to the left and fraction $m_1 = 0.4$ always allocated to the right. Panel (c) shows a randomized binomial measure after $k = 10$ stages. The masses m_0 and m_1 each have equal probabilities of going to the left or right. The final panel shows the fractal character of "cuts" of various sizes. Each cut shows the set of instants at which the random measure in Panel (c) exceeds a given level. The clustering of these sets has a self-similar structure, and the extreme bursts of volatility are intermittent, as discussed in the Appendix.

$m_0 = 0.6$. This density begins to show the properties we desire in modeling financial volatility. Larger allocations of density correspond to occasional bursts of volatility, which can generate thick tails. Because the reshuffling of mass follows the same rule at each stage of the cascade, volatility clustering is present at all time scales.

Multiplicative measures exhibit distinctive moment-scaling properties. Consider, for instance, the generating cascade of a *conservative* measure μ. The measure of a cell with starting point $t = \sum_{i=1}^{k} \eta_i b^{-i}$ and length $\Delta t = b^{-k}$ is the product $\mu(\Delta t) = M_{\eta_1} M_{\eta_1, \eta_2} \ldots M_{\eta_1, \ldots, \eta_k}$. Since multipliers defined at different stages of the cascade are independent, we infer that $\mathbb{E}\left[\mu(\Delta t)^q\right] = \left[\mathbb{E}(M^q)\right]^k$, or equivalently

$$\mathbb{E}\left[\mu(\Delta t)^q\right] = (\Delta t)^{\tau(q)+1}, \tag{5.1}$$

where

$$\tau(q) = -\log_b \mathbb{E}(M^q) - 1. \tag{5.2}$$

The moment of an interval's measure is thus a power functions of its length.

The scaling relation (5.1) easily generalizes to a *canonical* measure μ. The mass of the unit interval is then a random variable

$$\Omega = \mu[0, 1] \geq 0.$$

More generally, the measure of a b-adic cell[8] satisfies

$$\mu(\Delta t) = M_{\eta_1} M_{\eta_1, \eta_2} \ldots M_{\eta_1, \ldots, \eta_k} \Omega_{\eta_1, \ldots, \eta_k}, \tag{5.3}$$

where $\Omega_{\eta_1, \ldots, \eta_k}$ has the same distribution as Ω. This directly implies the scaling relationship

$$\mathbb{E}\left[\mu(\Delta t)^q\right] = \mathbb{E}(\Omega^q) (\Delta t)^{\tau(q)+1}, \tag{5.4}$$

which generalizes (5.1).

The right tail of the measure $\mu(\Delta t)$ is determined by the way mass is preserved at each stage of the construction. When μ is conservative, the cell's mass is bounded above by the mass of the unit interval: $0 \leq \mu(\Delta t) \leq \mu[0, 1] = 1$, and therefore has finite moments of every order. Consider now a canonical measure generated by independent multipliers M_β. Guivarc'h (1987) assumes multipliers with finite moments of every order, $\mathbb{E}(M^q) < \infty$ for every $q \geq 0$, and shows that if the multipliers take values greater than

---

[8]A b-adic interval has endpoints of the form $t = 1$ or $t = \eta_1 b^{-1} + \cdots + \eta_k b^{-k}$ for a finite k and $\eta_1, \ldots, \eta_k \in \{0, 1\}$.

unity with positive probability, then the mass of the unit interval has a Paretian right tail:

$$\mathbb{P}\{\Omega > \omega\} \sim C\ \omega^{-q_{crit}} \text{ as } \omega \to +\infty,$$

where C is a positive constant, and the critical moment q_{crit} is finite and larger than unity:

$$1 < q_{crit} < \infty.$$

In the above equation and throughout the rest of the book, we write $f(\omega) \sim g(\omega)$ to designate that two functions f and g satisfy $f(\omega)/g(\omega) \to 1$. The condition $q_{crit} > 1$ guarantees that the mass of a cell has a well-defined mean, and that $\mathbb{E}\left[\mu(\Delta t)\right] = \Delta t$. By (5.3), the mass of every cell has the same critical moment as the random variable Ω, and the critical moment q_{crit} is therefore independent of Δt.[9]

The multiplicative measures constructed so far are *grid-bound*, in the sense that the scaling rule (5.4) holds only on b-adic intervals. Let $\mathcal{D}$ denote the set of instants and increments $(t, \Delta t)$ satisfying scaling rule (5.4). As is shown in the Appendix, the closure of $\mathcal{D}$ contains $[0, 1] \times \{0\}$. That is, the scaling relation holds "in the neighborhood of any instant." Alternatively, we can consider *grid-free* random measures that are fully stationary and satisfy scaling rule (5.4) asymptotically as Δt converges to zero. This leads to the following:

Definition 5.3 (Multifractal measure) *A random measure μ defined on $[0, 1]$ is called multifractal if it satisfies for all $q \in \mathcal{Q}$:*

$$\mathbb{E}\left(\mu[t, t + \Delta t]^q\right) \sim c\left(q\right)(\Delta t)^{\tau(q)+1} \qquad \text{as } \Delta t \to 0,$$

where $\mathcal{Q}$ is an interval containing $[0, 1]$, and $\tau(q)$ and $c\left(q\right)$ are deterministic functions defined on $\mathcal{Q}$.

Initial studies of multifractal diffusions focus on grid-bound constructions (Chapter 6), while subsequent developments have led to grid-free models (Chapter 7).

5.2.3   Local Scales and the Multifractal Spectrum

Multifractal measures are characterized by rich local properties that are described by the local Hölder exponent, a concept borrowed from real analysis.

---

[9]The cascade construction also implies that Ω satisfies the invariance relation $\sum_{i=1}^{b} M_i \Omega_i \overset{d}{=} \Omega$, where $M_1, \ldots, M_b, \Omega_1, \ldots, \Omega_b$ are independent copies of the random variables M and Ω.

Definition 5.4 (Local Hölder exponent) *Let g be a function defined on the neighborhood of a given date t. The number*

$$\alpha(t) = Sup\ \{\beta \geq 0 : |g(t + \triangle t) - g(t)| = O(|\triangle t|^{\beta})\ as\ \triangle t \to 0\}$$

is called the local Hölder exponent or local scale of g at t.

The Hölder exponent describes the local variability of the function at a point in time. Heuristically, we can express the infinitesimal variations of the function as being of order $|dg| \approx (dt)^{\alpha(t)}$ around instant t. Lower values of $\alpha(t)$ correspond to more abrupt variations. The exponent $\alpha(t)$ is nonnegative when the function g is bounded around t, as is always the case in this book. The definition readily extends to measures on the real line. At a given date t, a measure simply has the local exponent of its cumulative distribution function.

We can compute Hölder exponents for many functions and processes. For instance, the local scale of a function is 0 at points of discontinuity and 1 at (nonsingular) differentiable points. On the other hand, the unique scale $\alpha(t) = 1/2$ is observed on the jagged sample paths of a Brownian motion or of a continuous Itô diffusion.[10] Similarly, a fractional Brownian $B_H(t)$ is characterized by a unique exponent $\alpha(t) = H$. Thus, the continuous processes typically used in finance each have a unique Hölder exponent. In contrast, multifractal measures contain a continuum of local scales.

The mathematics literature has developed a convenient representation for the distribution of Hölder exponents in a multifractal. From Definition 5.4, the Hölder exponent $\alpha(t)$ is the limit inferior of the ratio

$$\ln |g(t, \triangle t)| / \ln(\triangle t)\ as\ \triangle t \to 0,$$

where $g(t, \triangle t) \equiv g(t + \triangle t) - g(t)$. This suggests estimating the distribution of the local scale $\alpha(t)$ at a random instant. For increasing $k \geq 1$, we partition the unit interval into b^k subintervals $[t_i, t_i + \triangle t]$ of length $\triangle t = b^{-k}$, and calculate for each subinterval the *coarse Hölder exponent*

$$\alpha_k(t_i) \equiv \ln |g(t_i, \triangle t)| / \ln \triangle t.$$

This operation generates a set $\{\alpha_k(t_i)\}$ of b^k observations.

We divide the range of α's into small intervals of length $\triangle \alpha$, and denote by $N_k(\alpha)$ the number of coarse exponents contained between α and $\alpha + \triangle \alpha$. It would then seem natural to calculate a histogram with the relative frequencies $N_k(\alpha)/b^k$, which converge as $k \to \infty$ to the probability that a

---

[10]More precisely, the set $\{t : \alpha(t) \neq 1/2\}$ of instants with a local scale different from 1/2 has a Hausdorff-Besicovitch measure (and therefore a Lebesgue measure) equal to zero. This set can thus be neglected in our analysis. See Kahane (1997) for a survey of this topic.

random instant t has Hölder exponent α. Using this method, the histogram would degenerate into a spike because multifractals typically have a dominant exponent α_0, in the sense that $\alpha(t) = \alpha_0$ at almost every instant. Mandelbrot (1974, 1989) instead suggested

Definition 5.5 (Multifractal spectrum) *The limit*

$$f(\alpha) \equiv \lim \left(\frac{\ln N_k(\alpha)}{\ln b^k} \right) \quad as \ k \to \infty \qquad (5.5)$$

represents a renormalized probability distribution of local Hölder exponents, and is called the multifractal spectrum.

For instance if $b = 3$ and $N_k(\alpha) = 2^k$, the frequency $N_k(\alpha)/b^k = (2/3)^k$ converges to zero as $k \to \infty$, while the ratio $\ln N_k(\alpha)/\ln b^k = \ln 2/\ln 3$ is a positive constant. The multifractal spectrum helps to identify events that happen many times in the construction but at a vanishing frequency.

The quantity $f(\alpha)$ coincides with the fractal (or Hausdorff-Besicovitch) dimension of the set of instants having local Hölder exponent α, $T(\alpha) = \{t : \alpha(t) = \alpha\}$, as was shown by Frisch and Parisi (1985) and Halsey *et al.* (1986). For various levels of α, Figure 5.1d illustrates the subintervals with coarse exponent $\alpha_k(t_i) < \alpha$. When the number of iterations k is sufficiently large, these "cuts" display a self-similar structure. The Appendix provides a more detailed discussion of this interpretation.

5.2.4   The Spectrum of Multiplicative Measures

Large Deviation Theory can be used to derive closed-form expressions for the multifractal spectrum of multiplicative measures. Let μ denote a conservative measure on the unit interval. The mass of a b-adic subinterval of length $\Delta t = b^{-k}$ is the product $\mu[t, t + \Delta t] = M_{\eta_1} M_{\eta_1, \eta_2} \cdots M_{\eta_1, \dots, \eta_k}$. The coarse exponent $\alpha_k(t) = \ln \mu[t, t + \Delta t]/\ln \Delta t$ can therefore be written as the equal-weighted average

$$\alpha_k = \frac{1}{k} \sum_{i=1}^{k} V_i, \qquad (5.6)$$

where $V_i \equiv -\log_b M_{\eta_1, \dots, \eta_i}$. We interpret coarse Hölder exponents as draws of the random variable α_k.

By the Strong Law of Large Numbers, α_k converges almost surely to[11]

$$\alpha_0 = \mathbb{E}(V_1) = -\mathbb{E}(\log_b M) > 1. \qquad (5.7)$$

---

[11]The relation $-\mathbb{E}(\log_b M) > 1$ follows from Jensen's inequality and $\mathbb{E}(M) = 1/b$.

As $k \to \infty$, almost all coarse exponents are contained in a small neighborhood of α_0. Although the standard histogram $N_k(\alpha)/b^k$ collapses to a spike at α_0, the other coarse exponents are nonetheless important. In fact, most of the mass concentrates on intervals with Hölder exponents that are bounded away from α_0.[12] Information on these "rare events" is contained in the tail of the random variable α_k.

Tail behavior is the object of Large Deviation Theory. In 1938, Harald Cramér established the following theorem under conditions that were gradually weakened.

Proposition 2 (Cramér's theorem) *Let $\{V_k\}$ denote a sequence of i.i.d. random variables. Then as $k \to \infty$,*

$$\frac{1}{k} \ln \mathbb{P} \left\{ \frac{1}{k} \sum_{i=1}^{k} V_i > \alpha \right\} \to \inf_q \left(\ln \left[\mathbb{E} \, e^{q(\alpha - V_1)} \right] \right), \qquad (5.8)$$

for any $\alpha > \mathbb{E}(V_1)$.

Proofs can be found in Billingsley (1979), Dembo and Zeitouni (1998), and van der Vaart (1998).

Cramér's theorem provides information about the tail behavior of coarse Hölder exponents. We can apply (5.8) to (5.6), and infer that the tail distribution satisfies

$$\frac{1}{k} \log_b \mathbb{P}\left(\alpha_k > \alpha\right) \to \inf_q \left[\alpha q + \log_b \mathbb{E}(M^q)\right].$$

As discussed in the Appendix, this limiting result implies:

Proposition 3 (Multifractal spectrum and scaling function) *The multifractal spectrum $f(\alpha)$ is the Legendre transform*

$$f(\alpha) = \inf_q \left[\alpha q - \tau(q)\right] \qquad (5.9)$$

of the scaling function $\tau(q)$.

This result holds for both conservative and canonical measures.

The proposition leads immediately to explicit formulas for the spectrum. For instance, assume the multiplier distribution M is lognormal

---

[12]Let T_k denote the set of b-adic cells with local exponents greater than $(1 + \alpha_0)/2$. When k is large, T_k contains "almost all" cells, but its mass:

$$\sum_{t \in T_k} (\Delta t)^{\alpha_k(t)} \leq b^k (\Delta t)^{(\alpha_0 + 1)/2} = b^{-k(\alpha_0 - 1)/2}$$

converges to zero as k goes to infinity.

TABLE 5.1. Examples of Multifractal Spectra

Distribution of V	Multifractal Spectrum $f_\theta(\alpha)$
Normal(λ, σ^2)	$1 - (\alpha - \lambda)^2/[4(\lambda - 1)]$
Binomial	$1 - \log_b(2) - \frac{\alpha_{\max} - \alpha}{\alpha_{\max} - \alpha_{\min}} \log_b\left(\frac{\alpha_{\max} - \alpha}{\alpha_{\max} - \alpha_{\min}}\right) - \frac{\alpha - \alpha_{\min}}{\alpha_{\max} - \alpha_{\min}}$ $\log_b\left(\frac{\alpha - \alpha_{\min}}{\alpha_{\max} - \alpha_{\min}}\right)$
Poisson(γ)	$1 - \gamma/\ln b + \alpha \log_b(\gamma e/\alpha)$
Gamma(β, γ)	$1 + \gamma \log_b(\alpha\beta/\gamma) + (\gamma - \alpha\beta)/\ln b$

Notes: This table shows the multifractal spectrum of a multiplicative measure and its corresponding trading time when the random variable $V = -\log_b M$ is, respectively, (1) a Gaussian density of mean λ and variance σ^2, (2) a binomial distribution taking discrete values $\alpha_{\min} = -\log_b(m_0)$ and $\alpha_{\max} = -\log_b(m_1)$ with equal probability, (3) a discrete Poisson distribution $p(x) = e^{-\gamma}\gamma^x/x!$, and (4) a Gamma distribution with density $p(x) = \beta^\gamma x^{\gamma-1} e^{-\beta x}/\Gamma(\gamma)$.

$-\log_b M \sim \mathcal{N}(\lambda, \sigma^2)$, and let the multiplicative cascade structure described above generate the random measure μ and its cumulative distribution function θ. Following the requirements outlined previously, we impose conservation of mass at each step of the cascade, which requires $\mathbb{E}(M) = 1/b$ or, equivalently $\sigma^2 = 2(\lambda - 1)/(\ln b)$. Straightforward calculations show that the scaling function (5.2) has the closed-form expression $\tau(q) = \lambda q - 1 - q^2\sigma^2(\ln b)/2$. Applying Proposition 3 then gives the multifractal spectrum as the quadratic function

$$f_\theta(\alpha) = 1 - (\alpha - \lambda)^2/[4(\lambda - 1)], \qquad (5.10)$$

parameterized by the unique real number $\lambda > 1$. Table 5.1 provides additional examples where the random variable $V = -\log_b M$ is binomial, Poisson, or Gamma. These results provide a foundation for the empirical work developed in Chapter 8, where an estimation procedure for the scaling function $\tau(q)$ is obtained and the Legendre transform yields an estimate of the multifractal spectrum $f(\alpha)$.

6
Multifractal Diffusions Through Time Deformation and the MMAR

This chapter shows that multifractal diffusions can be created by compounding a standard Brownian motion with a multifractal time deformation. The resulting price process is a semimartingale with a finite variance, which precludes investors from making arbitrage profits in the sense of Harrison and Kreps (1979). The multifractal time deformation also implies that the moments of returns scale as a power function of the frequency of observation, a property that has been extensively documented in many financial time series. The time deformation approach was used to define the first multifractal diffusion with uncorrelated increments, the Multifractal Model of Asset Returns ("MMAR," Calvet, Fisher, and Mandelbrot, 1997), which is also reviewed in this chapter. We will discuss in Chapter 7 another leading example, continuous-time MSM.

In the MMAR, the multifractal time deformation is the cumulative distribution function (c.d.f.) of a random multiplicative cascade. The construction produces the moment-scaling, thick tails, and long-memory volatility persistence exhibited by many financial time series. The MMAR substantially improves on traditional fractal specifications. In addition to the semimartingale property, the MMAR accommodates flexible tail behaviors with the highest finite moment taking any value greater than two. The model also captures the nonlinear changes in the unconditional distribution of returns at various sampling frequencies, while retaining the parsimony and tractability of fractal approaches.

The MMAR provides a fundamentally new class of stochastic processes for financial applications. In particular, the multifractal model is a diffusion that lies outside the class of Itô processes. While the sample paths of Itô diffusions vary locally as $(dt)^{1/2}$, the MMAR generates the richer class $(dt)^{\alpha(t)}$ with the local scale $\alpha(t)$ taking a continuum of values in any finite interval.

6.1 Multifractal Processes

Consistent with the definition of multifractal measures, we can define a multifractal process by its moment-scaling properties:

This chapter is based on an earlier paper: "Multifractality in Asset Returns: Theory and Evidence" (with A. Fisher), *Review of Economics and Statistics*, 84: 381–406, August 2002.

Definition 6.1 (Multifractal process) *A stochastic process $\{X(t)\}$ is called multifractal if it has stationary increments and satisfies the moment scaling rule*

$$\mathbb{E}\left(|X(t + \Delta t) - X(t)|^q\right) \sim c_X(q)\,(\Delta t)^{\tau_X(q)+1} \qquad (6.1)$$

as Δt converges to zero.

The function $\tau_X(q)$ is called the scaling function. Setting $q = 0$ in condition (6.1), we see that all scaling functions have the same intercept $\tau_X(0) = -1$. We verify in the Appendix that the scaling function $\tau_X(q)$ is weakly concave, a direct implication of Hölder's inequality.

A self-similar process has a linear scaling function $\tau_X(q)$. The invariance condition $X(t) \overset{d}{=} t^H X(1)$ implies $\mathbb{E}\left(|X(t)|^q\right) = t^{Hq}\mathbb{E}\left(|X(1)|^q\right)$, and the scaling rule (6.1) therefore holds with

$$\tau_X(q) = Hq - 1.$$

Since the intercept $\tau_X(0) = -1$ is fixed, a linear scaling function is fully determined by its slope H. For this reason, self-similar processes are often called *uniscaling* or *unifractal*. As discussed in Chapter 5, self-similar processes do not capture the changing distribution of returns at different horizons that is typical of most financial data. In this book, we focus on *multiscaling* processes, which have a nonlinear and therefore strictly concave scaling function $\tau_X(q)$.

6.2   Multifractal Time Deformation

We now show how multiscaling multifractal processes can be obtained through time deformation. Consider the price of a financial asset $P(t)$ on a bounded interval $[0, T]$, and define the *log-price* process

$$X(t) \equiv \ln P(t) - \ln P(0).$$

We model $X(t)$ by compounding a Brownian motion with a multifractal trading time:

Condition 1 *$X(t)$ is a compound process*

$$X(t) \equiv B[\theta(t)],$$

where $B(t)$ is a Brownian motion, and $\theta(t)$ is a stochastic time deformation.

Condition 2 *The time deformation $\theta(t)$ is the cumulative distribution function (c.d.f.) of a multifractal measure μ defined on $[0, T]$.*

Condition 3 *The processes $\{B(t)\}$ and $\{\theta(t)\}$ are independent.*

Condition 1 can be easily generalized to permit time deformation of the fractional Brownian motion $B_H(t)$, as we show in Section 6.4. Condition 2 specifies trading time $\theta(t) = \mu[0, t]$ as the c.d.f. of a multifractal measure. This is a general condition that nests a variety of specifications including the MMAR (Section 6.3) and continuous-time MSM (Chapter 7). By definition of a multifractal measure (see Chapter 5), the critical moment of trading time $q_{crit}(\theta)$ is greater than unity:

$$q_{crit}(\theta) > 1.$$

Condition 3 ensures that the unconditional distribution of returns is symmetric. Weakening this assumption could allow correlation between volatility and returns, as in EGARCH (Nelson, 1991) and Glosten, Jagannathan, and Runkle (1993). In Part III, we pursue an alternative approach to generating a link between volatility and prices by using equilibrium valuation.

Under Conditions 1–3, the moments of the compound process are given by:

$$\mathbb{E}\left[|X(t)|^q\right] = \mathbb{E}[\theta(t)^{q/2}]\mathbb{E}\left[|B(1)|^q\right]. \tag{6.2}$$

By Definition 5.3, the trading time θ satisfies the relation $\mathbb{E}[\theta(t)^q] \sim c_\theta(q)$ $t^{\tau_\theta(q)+1}$. Return moments therefore scale as a power function of the frequency of observation:

$$\mathbb{E}\left[|X(t)|^q\right] \sim c_X(q)t^{\tau_X(q)+1} \qquad \text{as } t \to 0, \tag{6.3}$$

where $\tau_X(q) = \tau_\theta(q/2)$ and $c_X(q) = c_\theta(q/2)\mathbb{E}\left[|B(1)|^q\right]$. These results are summarized by:

Proposition 4 (Multifractality of price process) *The time-deformed log-price $X(t)$ is a multifractal process with scaling function $\tau_X(q) \equiv \tau_\theta(q/2)$.*

We note that the multifractal trading time θ controls the tails of the price and return processes. By (6.2), the q-th moment of the log-price exists if and only if the time deformation has a moment of order $q/2$, implying that

$$q_{crit}(X) = 2q_{crit}(\theta) > 2.$$

Multifractal diffusions obtained as time-deformed Brownian motions thus have finite variance, but are otherwise consistent with a wide range of potential tail behaviors as we will observe in the examples below.

A multifractal diffusion resulting from Conditions 1–3 also has an appealing autocorrelation structure:

Proposition 5 (Martingale property) *The price $\{P(t)\}$ is a semi-martingale with respect to its natural filtration, and the process $\{X(t)\}$ is a martingale with finite variance and uncorrelated increments.*

The assumptions thus imply that asset returns have a white spectrum, a property that has been extensively discussed in the market efficiency literature.[1]

Since the price $P(t)$ is a semimartingale, stochastic integration can be used to calculate the gains from trading multifractal assets. Consider, for instance, the *two-asset economy* consisting of the multifractal security with price $P(t)$, and a riskless bond with constant rate of return r. Following Harrison and Kreps (1979), we can analyze if arbitrage profits can be made by frequently rebalancing a portfolio of these two securities. The semimartingale property of Proposition 5 directly implies

Proposition 6 (No arbitrage) *There are no arbitrage opportunities in the two-asset economy.*

Thus, multifractal diffusions can be embedded in standard economies and are consistent with the basic requirements of equilibrium valuation. Part III of this book considers equilibrium valuation in greater detail.

6.3   The Multifractal Model of Asset Returns

The Multifractal Model of Asset Returns (MMAR) is obtained as a special case of the time-deformation conditions above. Specifically, we narrow the second condition:

Condition 2' (The MMAR) *The trading time $\theta(t)$ is the cumulative distribution function of a random multiplicative cascade μ.*

The MMAR specification was developed and empirically investigated in Calvet, Fisher, and Mandelbrot (1997) and Calvet and Fisher (2002a). We now discuss some of its additional properties.

6.3.1   Unconditional Distribution of Returns

Tail behavior is controlled by the multiplicative cascade. If μ is conservative, trading time is bounded and the log-price has finite moments of every

---

[1] See Campbell, Lo, and MacKinlay (1997) for a discussion of these concepts.

order: $q_{crit}(X) = +\infty$. If instead the measure is canonical, the total mass $\theta(T) \equiv \mu[0,T]$ has a Paretian right tail and a finite critical moment larger than unity under the conditions mentioned in Chapter 5. The log-price and returns then have a finite critical moment, $2 < q_{crit}(X) < +\infty$, which is appealing for some financial applications.

We next analyze how the unconditional distribution of returns varies with the time horizon. For instance, when the measure is conservative, trading time at the final instant T is deterministic, and the random variable $X(T) = B[\theta(T)]$ is normally distributed. As we move to smaller horizons, the allocation of mass becomes increasingly heterogeneous and tails become thicker. If μ is a binomial, the mass of a dyadic cell can be written as $m_0^{k\varphi_0} m_1^{k(1-\varphi_0)}$, which can take very extreme values. At the same time, the law of large numbers implies that draws of φ_0 concentrate increasingly in the neighborhood of $1/2$, implying that the bell of the distribution becomes thicker as well. The distribution of $X(t)$ accumulates more mass in the tails and in the bell as the time horizon decreases, while the middle of the distribution becomes thinner. These features of the MMAR are qualitatively consistent with the properties of financial data. Lux (2001) confirms that the MMAR does indeed capture the nonlinear deformation of the unconditional return distribution in a variety of equity, commodity, and currency series.

6.3.2   Long Memory in Volatility

We now consider persistence in the size of price changes. The concept of long memory is often defined by a hyperbolic decline in the autocovariance of a process as the lag between observations goes to infinity. However since the MMAR is defined only on a bounded time range, asymptotic dependence needs to be defined slightly differently. For any stochastic process Z with stationary increments $Z(a, \Delta t) \equiv Z(a + \Delta t) - Z(t)$, the *autocovariance in levels*

$$\delta_Z(t, q) = Cov(|Z(a, \Delta t)|^q, \ |Z(a + t, \Delta t)|^q)$$

quantifies the dependence in the size of the process's increments. It is well defined when $\mathbb{E}\left(|Z(a, \Delta t)|^{2q}\right)$ is finite. For a fixed $q > 0$, we say that the process has *long memory in the size of increments* if the autocovariance in levels is hyperbolic in t when $t/\Delta t \to \infty$. That is, we can define long memory by letting the step size Δt go to zero. We show in the Appendix:

Proposition 7 (Long memory) *When μ is a multiplicative measure, trading time $\theta(t)$ and log-price $X(t)$ have long memory in the size of increments for $0 < q < q_{crit}(X)/2$.*

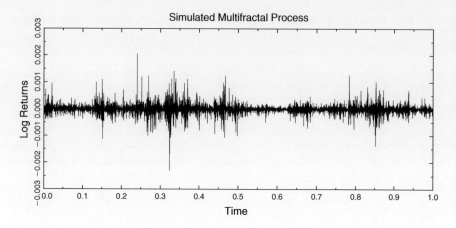

FIGURE 6.1. **MMAR Simulation.** This figure shows the log returns of an MMAR simulation obtained by compounding a standard Brownian motion with a binomial trading time. The simulation displays volatility clustering at all time scales and intermittent large fluctuations.

This result can be illustrated graphically. Figure 6.1 shows simulated first differences of the multifractal model when $\theta(t)$ is the c.d.f. of a randomized binomial measure with multiplier $m_0 = 0.6$. The simulated returns display marked temporal heterogeneity at all time scales and intermittent large fluctuations. The MMAR is thus a flexible continuous-time framework that accommodates long memory in volatility, a variety of tail behaviors, unpredictability in returns, and volatility persistence at all frequencies.

6.3.3 Sample Paths

We next examine the geometric properties of MMAR sample paths. The infinitesimal variation in price around a date t is heuristically of the form

$$|\ln P(t + dt) - \ln P(t)| \approx C_t(dt)^{\alpha(t)}.$$

The MMAR contains a *continuum* of local scales $\alpha(t)$ within any finite time interval. Denoting by $f_Z(\alpha)$ the spectrum of a process $Z(t)$, we show:

Proposition 8 (Multifractal spectrum of price process) *The price $P(t)$ and the log-price $X(t)$ have identical multifractal spectra:* $f_P(\alpha) \equiv f_X(\alpha) \equiv f_\theta(2\alpha).$

Thus, multifractal processes are *not* continuous Itô diffusions and cannot be generated by standard techniques. Fractal geometry imposes that in the MMAR, the instants $\{t : \alpha(t) < \alpha\}$ with local scale less than α cluster in clock time, which accounts for the concentration of outliers in the model.

Let $\alpha_0(Z)$ denote the most probable exponent of a process Z. Since $\alpha_0(\theta) > 1$, the log-price has a local scale $\alpha_0(X) \equiv \alpha_0(\theta)/2$ larger than $1/2$ at almost every instant. Despite their apparent irregularity, the MMAR's sample paths are almost everywhere *smoother* than the paths of a Brownian motion.

The standard deviation of returns is of order $(\Delta t)^{1/2}$:

$$\sqrt{\mathbb{E}\left\{[X(t + \Delta t) - X(t)]^2\right\}} = c_X(2)^{1/2}\sqrt{\Delta t}. \tag{6.4}$$

This property is a direct consequence of Proposition 4 and the fact that $\tau_X(2) = \tau_\theta(1) = 1$. The rare exponents $\alpha < \alpha_0(X)$ appear frequently enough to alter the scaling properties of the variance. This contrasts with the common view that a standard deviation in $(\Delta t)^{1/2}$ implies that most shocks are of the same order. While jump-diffusions permit negligible sets to contribute to the total variation, multifractal processes are notable for combining *continuous* paths with variations dominated by rare events.

6.4 An Extension with Autocorrelated Returns

The multifractal model presented in the previous section is characterized by long memory in volatility, but the absence of correlation in returns. While there is little evidence of fractional integration in stock returns (Lo, 1991), long memory has been identified in the first differences of many economic series,[2] including aggregate output (Adelman, 1965; Diebold and Rudebusch, 1989; Sowell, 1992), the Beveridge (1925) Wheat Price Index, the U.S. Consumer Price Index (Baillie, Chung, and Tieslau, 1996), and interest rates (Backus and Zin, 1993). This has led authors to model these series with the fractional Brownian motion or discrete-time autoregressive fractionally integrated specifications.

The volatility patterns of these economic series may be closer to the multifractal model than to the fractional Brownian motion. This suggests modeling a fractional Brownian motion in multifractal time:

$$X(t) \equiv B_H[\theta(t)],$$

maintaining the multifractality of trading time (Condition 2) and the independence of the processes $B_H(t)$ and $\theta(t)$ (Condition 3). The generalization coincides with the martingale specification in Section 6.2 if $H = 1/2$. For other values of H, the increments of $X(t)$ are antipersistent ($H < 1/2$) or have positive autocorrelations and long memory ($H > 1/2$).

---

[2] Maheswaran and Sims (1993) suggest potential applications in finance for processes lying outside the class of semimartingales.

The self-similarity of $B_H(t)$ implies that the process $X(t)$ is multifractal and has scaling function $\tau_X(q) = \tau_\theta(Hq)$. We observe that

$$\tau_X(1/H) = \tau_\theta(1) = 0,$$

which allows the estimation of the index H in empirical work. We easily check that the multifractal spectrum of the compound process is $f_X(\alpha) = f_\theta(\alpha/H)$. The self-similarity parameter H thus renormalizes the scaling function and multifractal spectrum.

6.5   Connection with Related Work

The MMAR implies that the return moments $\mathbb{E}(|X(\Delta t)|^q)$ vary as power functions of the horizon Δt. Scaling of the second moment $(q = 2)$ with the time horizon Δt has been studied extensively in the variance ratio literature (e.g., Campbell and Mankiw, 1987; Lo and MacKinlay, 1988). Müller *et al.* (1990) also report scaling of absolute returns $(q = 1)$ for four exchange rates. For higher moments, early visual evidence of multiscaling in financial data was reported in Vassilicos, Demos, and Tata (1993), Ghashghaie *et al.* (1996), and Galluccio *et al.* (1997). The study by Ghashghaie *et al.* investigated the unconditional distribution of exchange rate differences[3] $P(t + \Delta t) - P(t)$ at different timescales, but did not attempt to derive a complete dynamic specification for financial prices or returns. This study suggested an analogy between exchange rate differences and the velocity differences of two points in a turbulent flow. Arneodo *et al.* (1996) and Mantegna and Stanley (1996) criticized the proposed analogy, pointing out that financial returns are approximately uncorrelated over the relevant range of intermediate horizons larger than a few minutes, whereas velocities in a turbulent field show strong correlations over many orders of magnitude. Arneodo *et al.* (1996) correctly pointed out that such strong correlations, if present in financial markets, would imply easy profit opportunities.[4]

The development of the MMAR in 1997 resolved the apparent tension in choosing between multifractal moment-scaling and uncorrelated returns. In particular, the complete dynamic specification of a Brownian motion in a multifractal trading time produced martingale log-price dynamics with long-memory features in volatility, thick tails in returns, and the

---

[3] The properties of price differences $P(t + \Delta t) - P(t)$ are not commonly the object of direct empirical investigation. Attention more often focuses on relative price changes (returns) or log price differences (continuously compounded returns).

[4] Arneodo *et al.* (1996) and Mantegna and Stanley (1996) both advocate the use of a truncated Lévy law. This alternative approach permits uncorrelated increments and flexible modeling of the unconditional distribution of returns, but does not capture volatility clustering and other higher order dependencies.

moment-scaling properties that characterize multifractals. Furthermore, this definition of a multifractal price process permitted the recovery of a realistic stochastic generating mechanism that was simulated and compared with other competing models of returns. These informal Monte Carlo tests were made rigorous in Calvet and Fisher (2002a) by using a global test statistic based on simulated moments, as will be discussed in Chapter 8.

6.6 Discussion

Time deformation provides a powerful tool to construct multifractal processes out of general multifractal measures. The first example of this technique in the literature is the Multifractal Model of Asset Returns, which incorporates the outliers and volatility persistence exhibited by many financial time series, as well as a rich pattern of local variations and moment-scaling properties.

The MMAR provides a fundamentally new class of diffusions to both finance and mathematics. These diffusions have potentially uncorrelated increments and continuous sample paths but lie outside the Itô class. Whereas standard processes can be characterized by a single local scale that describes the local growth rate of variation, sample paths of multifractal processes contain a *continuum* of local Hölder exponents within any time interval.

The main drawback of the MMAR is that the construction of trading time on a grid results in a nonstationary model, which creates an obstacle for typical financial applications such as volatility forecasting. The next chapter corrects this difficulty by randomizing the instants at which volatility components change.

7
Continuous-Time MSM

This chapter develops the Markov-Switching Multifractal in continuous time. Consistent with the discrete-time construction in Chapter 3, we specify volatility at a given instant t as the multiplicative product of a finite number of random components. A Poisson process of fixed intensity γ_k can trigger switches in a given volatility component k, and heterogeneous frequencies are parsimoniously incorporated into the construction by assuming that the arrival intensities γ_k follow a tight geometric progression. Continuous-time MSM is naturally defined on an unbounded time domain, which is a substantial improvement over the MMAR. It also generates volatility clustering on a wide frequency range, corresponding to the intuition that economic factors such as technology shocks, business and earnings cycles, and liquidity shocks have different time scales.

When the number of components goes to infinity, the limiting price process displays complex features. Local volatility becomes degenerate, but the time-deformation process is a positive martingale that has a nondegenerate quadratic variation over finite intervals. As in the MMAR, the limit multifractal time deformation generates continuous sample paths with clustering and long memory in volatility. Furthermore, continuous-time MSM improves on the MMAR by producing strictly stationary increments, which is crucial to facilitate estimation and forecasting in common financial applications.

We complete the link with the discrete-time MSM processes developed in Chapter 3 by showing that an appropriately chosen sequence of discrete processes weakly converges to continuous-time MSM as the grid step size goes to zero. This ensures that the discrete model provides a consistent set of filters for continuous-time MSM. The chapter thus demonstrates that the Markov-switching approach works equally well in discrete time and in continuous time, and that it is straightforward to go back and forth between the two formulations.

We close the chapter by discussing the link between MSM and recent related stochastic volatility approaches that have been developed in the physics, mathematics, and econometrics literatures.

This chapter is based on an earlier paper: "Forecasting Multifractal Volatility" (with A. Fisher), *Econometrics*, 105: 27–58, November 2006.

7.1   MSM with Finitely Many Components

This section introduces a grid-free multifrequency diffusion. Analogous to the approach discussed in Chapter 3, the continuous-time construction is based on the Markov state vector

$$M_t = (M_{1,t}; M_{2,t}; \ldots; M_{\bar{k},t}) \in \mathbb{R}_+^{\bar{k}}, \qquad t \in [0, +\infty).$$

Given the Markov state M_t at date t, the dynamics over an infinitesimal interval are defined as follows. For each $k \in \{1, \ldots, \bar{k}\}$, a change in $M_{k,t}$ may be triggered by a *Poisson arrival* with intensity γ_k:

$M_{k,t+dt}$ drawn from distribution M with probability $\gamma_k dt$
$M_{k,t+dt} = M_{k,t}$ with probability $1 - \gamma_k dt$.

The Poisson arrivals and new draws from M are independent across k and t. As with any process driven by Poisson arrivals, the sample paths of a component $M_{k,t}$ are cadlag, that is, are right-continuous and have a limit point to the left of any instant.[1] The construction can accommodate any distribution M with unit mean and positive support.

The arrival intensities follow the geometric progression:

$$\gamma_k = \gamma_1 b^{k-1}, \qquad k \in \{1, \ldots, \bar{k}\}. \tag{7.1}$$

The parameter γ_1 determines the persistence of the lowest frequency component, and $b > 1$ the spacing between component frequencies. The intensity sequence is thus exactly geometric in continuous time, and in the Appendix we show that its discretization on a time grid leads to the discrete-time definition (3.2).

The log-price $X(t) = \ln P(t) - \ln P(0)$ has a constant drift $\bar{g}$ and stochastic volatility

$$\sigma(M_t) \equiv \bar{\sigma} \left(\prod_{k=1}^{\bar{k}} M_{k,t} \right)^{1/2}, \tag{7.2}$$

where $\bar{\sigma}$ is a positive constant. The process $X(t)$ is formally defined as

$$X_t \equiv \bar{g}t + \int_0^t \sigma(M_s) dZ(s),$$

where Z is a standard Brownian. The stochastic integral exists since $\mathbb{E}\left[\int_0^t \sigma^2(M_s) ds \right] = \bar{\sigma}^2 t < \infty$. Equivalently, the log-price satisfies the

---

[1] Cadlag is a French acronym for *continue à droite, limites à gauche*. We refer the reader to Billingsley (1999) for further details.

stochastic differential equation

$$dX_t \equiv \bar{g}dt + \sigma(M_t)dZ(t). \tag{7.3}$$

Continuous-time MSM is fully specified by the distribution M and the parameters $(\bar{g}, \bar{\sigma}, \gamma_1, b)$. It has strictly stationary increments, and thus resolves the grid-bound nonstationarity of the MMAR. Continuous-time MSM can be easily integrated into an equilibrium framework, as will be shown in Chapter 10.

Figure 7.1 illustrates the construction when the distribution M is a binomial. The top panel shows the lowest frequency component $M_{1,t}$, the second panel shows the product $M_{1,t}M_{2,t}$, and the third panel, $\sigma^2(M_t) \equiv \bar{\sigma}^2 M_{1,t}M_{2,t}\ldots M_{\bar{k},t}$, where $\bar{\sigma} = 1$ and $\bar{k} = 12$. The fourth and fifth panels display the corresponding returns and prices. The returns show pronounced peaks and intermittent bursts of volatility, accommodating a broad range of long-run, medium-run, and short-run dynamics.

Continuous-time MSM provides a parsimonious diffusion with Markov-switching volatility and multiple frequencies. The model fits naturally within the finance literature on Itô diffusions and regime-switching when the number of frequencies is finite. In particular, we can then apply to MSM all the tools that have been developed for general Markov processes (e.g., Ethier and Kurtz, 1986; Rogers and Williams, 2000). The model also easily extends to the multivariate case, as is discussed in the Appendix.

7.2 MSM with Countably Many Components

In this section, we investigate how the price diffusion evolves as $\bar{k} \to \infty$ and components of increasingly high frequency are added into the state vector. Two apparently contradictory observations can be made. On the one hand, Figure 7.1 suggests that the volatility process $\sigma(M_t)$ exhibits increasingly extreme behavior as $\bar{k}$ increases. On the other hand, the price process appears relatively insensitive to higher-frequency components. We now show how these two observations can be reconciled by deriving the limit behavior of the price dynamics.

7.2.1 Limiting Time Deformation

Let $M_t = (M_{k,t})_{k=1}^{\infty} \in \mathbb{R}_+^{\infty}$ be an MSM state process with countably many frequencies, parameters $(\bar{g}, \bar{\sigma}, \gamma_1, b)$, and fixed multiplier distribution M. The process M_t is defined for $t \in [0, \infty)$, and has mutually independent components. Each component $M_{k,t}$ is characterized by the arrival intensity $\gamma_k = \gamma_1 b^{k-1}$. For a finite $\bar{k}$, stochastic volatility is the product of the first $\bar{k}$ components of the state vector: $\sigma_{\bar{k}}(M_t) \equiv \bar{\sigma}(M_{1,t}M_{2,t}\ldots M_{\bar{k},t})^{1/2}$.

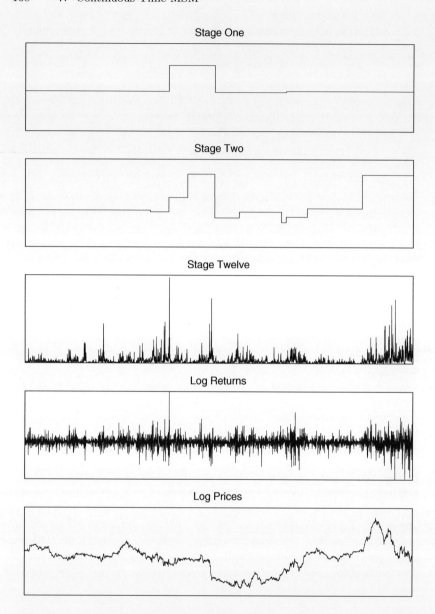

FIGURE 7.1. **Construction of Continuous-Time MSM.** The top three panels illustrate the construction of a continuous-time MSM process. Multipliers are drawn from a lognormal distribution $-\log_b M \sim \mathcal{N}(\lambda - 1, 2(\lambda - 1)/\ln b)$ with parameters $\lambda = 1.09$ and $b = 2$. The bottom two panels illustrate the corresponding log returns and log prices. The return series shows long-memory volatility clustering and outliers that are produced by intermittent bursts of extreme volatility. The construction fully randomizes the timing of volatility innovations, and the resulting return process is strictly stationary.

Since instantaneous volatility $\sigma_{\bar{k}}(M_t)$ depends on an increasing number of components, the differential representation (7.3) becomes unwieldy as $\bar{k} \rightarrow \infty$. We instead characterize dividend dynamics by the time deformation

$$\theta_{\bar{k}}(t) \equiv \int_0^t \sigma_{\bar{k}}^2(M_s)ds. \qquad (7.4)$$

Given a fixed instant t, the sequence $\{\theta_{\bar{k}}(t)\}_{\bar{k}=1}^{\infty}$ is a positive martingale with bounded expectation. By the martingale convergence theorem, the random variable $\theta_{\bar{k}}(t)$ converges to a limit distribution when $\bar{k} \rightarrow \infty$. A similar argument applies to any vector sequence $\{\theta_{\bar{k}}(t_1); \ldots; \theta_{\bar{k}}(t_d)\}$, guaranteeing that the stochastic process $\theta_{\bar{k}}$ has at most one limit point.

We verify that a limit process does indeed exist by checking that the sequence $(\theta_{\bar{k}})_{\bar{k}}$ is tight[2] on any bounded time interval $[0, T]$. Intuitively, tightness prevents the process from oscillating too wildly as $\bar{k} \rightarrow \infty$. We assume

Condition 4 $\mathbb{E}(M^2) < b$.

which restricts fluctuations in the time deformation by requiring that volatility shocks be sufficiently small or have durations decreasing sufficiently fast. In the Appendix we prove:

Proposition 9 (Time deformation with countably many frequencies) *Under Condition 4, the sequence $(\theta_{\bar{k}})_{\bar{k}}$ weakly converges to a process θ_∞ in the space of continuous functions on $[0, T]$. Furthermore, $\sup_k \mathbb{E}\left[\theta_{\bar{k}}^2(t)\right] < \infty$ for every fixed t.*

Additional intuition is gained by considering why we work with the time-deformation process θ_∞ rather than attempt to take the pointwise limit of the integrand $\sigma_{\bar{k}}^2(M_t)$ in Equation (7.4). By the Law of Large Numbers, $\sigma_{\bar{k}}^2(M_s) = \exp\left(\sum_k \ln M_{k,s}\right)$ converges almost surely to zero as $\bar{k} \rightarrow \infty$, which might suggest that the limit trading time θ_∞ degenerates to zero. In fact, the limit trading time θ_∞ is not zero, which can be confirmed by noting that for every fixed $t > 0$, $\mathbb{E}\left[\theta_{\bar{k}}(t)\right] = \bar{\sigma}^2 t$, $\sup_{\bar{k}} \mathbb{E}\left[\theta_{\bar{k}}^2(t)\right] < \infty$, and therefore

$$\mathbb{E}\left[\theta_\infty(t)\right] = \bar{\sigma}^2 t > 0.$$

To understand why the trading time θ_∞ remains positive even though volatility $\sigma_{\bar{k}}(M_t)$ goes to zero almost surely as $\bar{k} \rightarrow \infty$, consider the importance of rare events. On any finite interval, large realizations of

---

[2] We refer the reader to Billingsley (1999), Pollard (1984), and Davidson (1994) for book-length treatments of the weak convergence of stochatic processes.

volatility $\sigma_{\bar{k}}(M_t)$ appear sufficiently frequently to guarantee that the integral (7.4) does not vanish. The trading time of continuous-time MSM thus provides an example in which the Lebesgue dominated convergence theorem does not apply. The importance of rare events for the trading time θ_∞ will have natural consequences for the local variations of MSM sample paths, as we will discuss in the next subsection.

Trading time $\theta_\infty(t)$ exhibits moment-scaling for small values of t. We prove in the Appendix:

Proposition 10 (Moment scaling) *The qth moment of trading time satisfies*

$$\mathbb{E}\left\{[\theta_\infty(t)^q]\right\} \sim c_q t^{\tau_\theta(q)+1} \quad as \quad t \to 0$$

where $\tau_\theta(q) = -\log_b\left[\mathbb{E}(M^q)\right] + q - 1$ and c_q is a positive constant.

The scaling function $\tau_\theta(q)$ is concave by Hölder's inequality.[3]

Trading time is easily extended to the infinite time domain $[0, \infty)$. Consider the space $D[0, \infty)$ of cadlag functions defined on $[0, \infty)$, and let d_∞° denote the Skorohod distance. Proposition 9 then directly leads to:

Corollary 1 (Unbounded time domain) *If $\mathbb{E}(M^2) < b$, the sequence $(\theta_{\bar{k}})_{\bar{k}}$ weakly converges as $\bar{k} \to \infty$ to a measure θ_∞ defined on the metric space $(D[0, \infty), d_\infty^\circ)$. The sample paths of θ_∞ are continuous almost surely.*

The ability to define trading time over an unbounded interval is a substantial advantage of the Markov construction over the MMAR.

7.2.2 Multifractal Price Diffusion

As components of increasingly high frequencies are added into the state vector, the MSM diffusions considered in Section 7.1 converge to a weak limit, which can be represented by $X(t) \equiv \bar{g}t + B[\theta_\infty(t)]$. The processes $\{B(t)\}$ and $\{\theta_\infty(t)\}$ are again independent, and:

Condition 2" (Continuous-time MSM) *The trading time θ_∞ is an MSM time deformation with countably many frequencies.*

The limiting MSM diffusion $X(t)$ improves on the MMAR in two related ways. First, the new model is a grid-free process in which volatility components switch at random instants and not at predetermined points of time. Second, $X(t)$ can be interpreted as a stochastic volatility model with a Markov latent state defined on an unbounded time domain.

---

[3] The multiplier satisfies the normalization conditions $\mathbb{E}(M) = 1/b$ in the MMAR and $\mathbb{E}(M) = 1$ in MSM. This leads to slightly different relations between $\tau_\theta(q)$ and $\mathbb{E}(M^q)$.

In addition to these improvements, the limiting MSM diffusion shares many of the appealing properties of the MMAR. The compound process $B[\theta_\infty(t)]$ is a martingale because the increments of the Brownian motion B have unpredictable signs. The price process $P(t) = \exp[X(t)]$ is then a semimartingale, which precludes arbitrage in the presence of a risk-free bond. The scaling properties of trading time given in Proposition 10 imply that returns satisfy asymptotic moment scaling:

$$\mathbb{E}\left[|X(t)|^q\right] \sim C_q t^{\tau_X(q)+1} \quad \text{as } t \to 0, \tag{7.5}$$

where $\tau_X(q) \equiv \tau_\theta(q/2)$.[4] Figure 7.2 uses Monte Carlo simulations to show that this property also holds remarkably well for finite time increments. In the next chapter, we show that many financial time series, including exchange rates and equities, exhibit moment-scaling.

Another important feature captured by MSM is long memory in volatility. In Chapter 6, we introduced a quantitative description of long memory for a continuous-time process defined on a bounded time interval. Consistent with this approach, we show in Figure 7.3 that autocovariances of squared returns decline hyperbolically in simulated MSM data.

Finally, following the discussion of the importance of rare events to trading time in the previous subsection, the local variations of MSM are almost everywhere smoother than the $(dt)^{1/2}$ variations of an Itô process. Furthermore, despite continuity of the sample paths most of the variation within any finite interval occurs on a set of instants with Lebesgue measure zero. Thus, analogous to the quadratic variations (6.4) of the MMAR discussed previously, "rare events" are important to understanding the variations of continuous-time MSM.

7.2.3   Connection between Discrete-Time and Continuous-Time Versions of MSM

We now analyze how continuous-time MSM relates to the discrete-time model presented in Chapter 3. Specifically, we establish that a rescaled version of discrete-time MSM converges to continuous-time MSM when the number of frequencies goes to infinity.

Consider the following definitions:

Continuous-Time Construction. We continue to denote by θ_∞ an MSM trading time defined on a bounded interval $[0, T]$. It is specified by $(\bar{\sigma}, \gamma_1, b)$ and a fixed distribution M. We also assume that there exists $q > 0$ such that $\tau_\theta(q) > 0$.[5]

---

[4] If the drift $\bar{g}$ differs from zero, the scaling rule holds if $\tau(q) + 1 < q$. Violations of this inequality occur on an interval $[0, \bar{q}]$, $\bar{q} < 2$, when the distribution M satisfies $\mathbb{E}(\log_b M) < -1$.

[5] This property holds under Condition 4 because one can easily check that $\tau_\theta(q)$ is strictly positive for $q = 2$ if and only if $\mathbb{E}(M^2) < b$. More generally, since $\tau_\theta(1) = 0$, the

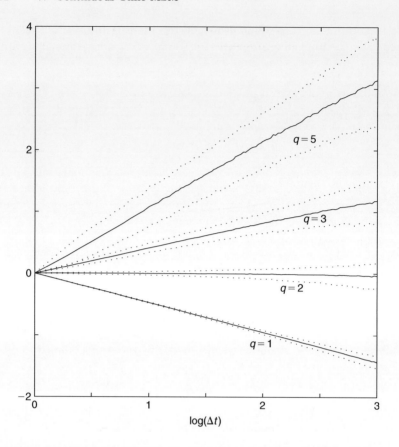

FIGURE 7.2. **Moment-Scaling in Continuous-Time MSM.** This figure illustrates the scaling of moments $q = 1, 2, 3, 5$ for a continuous-time MSM process. Multipliers are drawn from a lognormal distribution $-\log_b M \sim \mathcal{N}(\lambda - 1, 2(\lambda - 1)/\ln b)$ with parameters $\lambda = 1.09$ and $b = 2$. The vertical axis corresponds to the logarithm of the sample moment times the number of increments with size Δt in a sample of length 20,000. The solid line shows these moments averaged over 500 independent simulations of length 20,000. The twentieth and eightieth percentiles are plotted in dotted lines. For convenience, each line is vertically displaced to begin at zero. All of the moments demonstrate the predicted asymptotic scaling.

Discrete-Time Construction. Consider the regular grid $s = 0, 1, \ldots, c^{\bar{k}}$, where $c > 1$ is a fixed integer. The discrete-time MSM volatility $\theta_{\bar{k}}^{**}(s)$ is defined on the grid by M, $\bar{\sigma}$, and transition probabilities $\gamma_{k,\bar{k}} = 1 - \exp(-\gamma_1 b^{k-1} T / c^{\bar{k}})$. We then use linear interpolation to extend the domain of $\theta_{\bar{k}}^{**}(s)$ to the continuous interval $[0, c^{\bar{k}}]$.

---

scaling function takes strictly positive values on a neighborhood of $q = 1$ if $\tau_\theta'(1) > 0$, or equivalently $\mathbb{E}[M \ln(M)] < \ln(b)$.

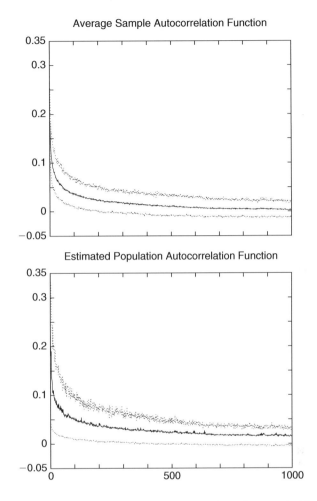

FIGURE 7.3. **Long-Memory Features in the Squared Returns of Continuous-Time MSM.** Each panel is based on 300 independent simulations of a continuous-time MSM process. Multipliers are drawn from a lognormal distribution $-\log_b M \sim \mathcal{N}(\lambda - 1, 2(\lambda - 1)/\ln b)$ with parameters $\lambda = 1.09$ and $b = 2$. Each simulation has a length of 10,000 increments. The average over all 300 simulations is shown in bold in each panel, and the tenth and ninetieth percentiles are shown as dotted lines. In the top panel, the autocorrelation functions were calculated after demeaning each simulated series by its sample mean. In the second panel, each series is demeaned by the estimated unconditional expectation, which was obtained by averaging the sample means across the 300 independent paths. The difference in the two panels is caused by low-frequency variations in multifractal volatility. The sample mean of squared returns slowly converges to its unconditional expectation. As a result, while both panels show hyperbolic decay, the second panel appears to show greater persistence at long lags. This is because low-frequency volatility components are partially filtered out when we demean the squared returns series by their sample means rather than the true population mean.

Rescaled Version. The discretized trading time $\theta_{\bar{k}}^*$ is defined on the time interval $[0, T]$ by

$$\theta_{\bar{k}}^*(t) = \theta_{\bar{k}}^{**}(tc^{\bar{k}}/T).$$

The process $\theta_{\bar{k}}^*$ is continuous and piecewise linear.

We provide two alternative conditions under which the sequence of trading times $\{\theta_{\bar{k}}^*\}_{\bar{k}=1}^\infty$ weakly converge to the process θ_∞.

Condition 5 $b < c$.

Condition 6 $\mathbb{E}(M^2)b < c^2$.

Condition 5 requires that the number of grid points grows faster than the volatility frequencies, whereas Condition 6 allows the grid size to grow at an identical or slower rate than the volatility frequencies. When $b = c$, this assumption reduces to $\mathbb{E}(M^2) < b$, which was used in the proof of Proposition 9. In the Appendix we show:

Proposition 11 (Weak convergence) *Under Condition 5 or Condition 6, the sequence $\{\theta_{\bar{k}}^*\}_{\bar{k}=1}^\infty$ of discretized trading times weakly converges to the continuous-time process θ_∞.*

The weak convergence of the discretized trading times to θ_∞ implies that discrete-time MSM can be used to forecast volatility, as in Chapter 3, and the forecast will be consistent for the continuous-time version of the model under an appropriate sequence of increasingly refined discretizations. This result is appealing as it implies that researchers may easily move back and forth between discrete time, where applied work is often more natural, and continuous time, where theory is sometimes more convenient.

7.3   MSM with Dependent Arrivals

The MSM formulations considered thus far assume that arrivals and multipliers are independent across frequencies. We have also used in Calvet and Fisher (1999, 2001) a related construction that permits dependence in the arrival times of different components. Specifically, we assumed that if an arrival occurs in component k at instant t, then arrivals are triggered in all higher-frequency components $k' > k$. Weak convergence of this "dependent" construction also holds under Conditions 5 and 6.

This variant might be useful in economic settings in which a lower-frequency arrival may impact higher-frequency components. For instance, a terrorist attack or unexpected military offensive may simultaneously trigger switches in volatility components of different durations. We further discuss this "dependent" construction in the Appendix.

7.4   Connection with Related Work

The development of the MMAR (Calvet, Fisher, and Mandelbrot, 1997) prompted researchers to construct multifractal processes that satisfy stationarity of increments, which is a useful property for financial applications. We correspondingly developed continuous-time MSM in Calvet and Fisher (1999), which was presented at the of National Bureau of Economic Research Summer Institute in 1999 and later appeared in the special issue of *Journal of Econometrics* from that conference. In this subsection we review alternative approaches that have been developed in the physics, mathematics and econometrics literatures.

Multifractal literature

Emmanuel Bacry, Jean Delour, and Jean-François Muzy introduced a model they label the "Multifractal Random Walk" (MRW) in a series of physics publications (e.g., Muzy, Delour, and Bacry, 2000; Bacry, Delour, and Muzy, 2001; Muzy and Bacry, 2002). Given a finite grid of instants with step size Δ, the MRW $X_\Delta(t)$ is the step-wise constant stochastic process:

$$X_\Delta(t) = \bar{\sigma}\sqrt{\Delta} \sum_{i=0}^{[t\Delta^{-1}]} e^{\omega_\Delta(i\Delta)} \varepsilon_i \qquad (7.6)$$

where $[x]$ denotes the greatest integer smaller than x, ε_i is a Gaussian white noise $\mathcal{N}(0,1)$, and $\omega_\Delta(t)$ is a Gaussian process. The random variables $\omega_\Delta(t)$ are identically distributed, with mean

$$\mathbb{E}\left(\omega_\Delta(t)\right) = -\lambda^2 \ln\left(\frac{T_1}{\Delta}\right), \qquad (7.7)$$

and covariance

$$Cov\left(\omega_\Delta(t); \omega_\Delta(t+\tau)\right) = \begin{cases} \lambda^2 \left(\ln\left(T_1/\Delta\right) + 1 - \tau/\Delta\right) & \text{if } \tau \leq \Delta, \\ \lambda^2 \ln\left(T_1/\tau\right) & \text{if } \Delta \leq \tau \leq T_1, \\ 0 & \text{if } \tau > T_1. \end{cases}$$

In MRW, log volatility is normal and decays at a logarithmic rate on a range of frequencies. A multifractal diffusion X is obtained by taking the limit of X_Δ as the step size goes to zero.

The MRW is intimately connected to MSM with lognormal multipliers. As in Section 7.2.3, consider a discrete-time MSM return process on a grid of step size $\Delta = b^{-\bar{k}}T_1$. Returns are specified by a fixed lognormal distribution: $\ln(M) \sim \mathcal{N}(-2\lambda^2; 4\lambda^2)$, the scale parameter $\bar{\sigma}$, and the transition probabilities $\gamma_{k,\Delta} = 1 - \exp(-b^{k-1}\Delta/T_1)$, $k \in \{1, \ldots, \bar{k}\}$. The MSM log-price can then be represented by (7.6), where log volatility is the Gaussian stationary process

$$\omega_\Delta(i\Delta) = \frac{1}{2} \sum_{k=1}^{\bar{k}} \ln(M_{k,i\Delta})$$

with mean $\mathbb{E}\left(\omega_\Delta(i\Delta)\right) = -\lambda^2 \log_b\left(T_1/\Delta\right)$, analogous to (7.7). The auto-covariogram of log volatility in MSM is

$$Cov\left(\omega_\Delta(t), \omega_\Delta(t+\tau)\right) = \lambda^2 \sum_{k=1}^{\bar{k}} e^{-b^{k-1}\tau/T_1}. \tag{7.8}$$

Let $k(\tau)$ denote the greatest integer smaller than $\log_b(T_1/\tau)$. The term $e^{-b^{k-1}\tau/T_1}$ is close to 1 if $k < k(\tau)$ and close to 0 otherwise, and the covariance of log volatility thus satisfies

$$Cov\left(\omega_\Delta(t); \omega_\Delta(t+\tau)\right) \approx \lambda^2 \log_b\left(\frac{T_1}{\tau}\right).$$

MSM and MRW both imply that log volatility $\omega_\Delta(t)$ decays at a logarithmic rate on a range of lags, which is a characteristic of $1/f$ noise (e.g., Mandelbrot, 1965b, 1999). In particular, $\omega_\Delta(t)$ decays more slowly in this range than a stationary fractionally integrated process.[6]

MSM and MRW both generate multifractal features in a parsimonious framework, implying moment-scaling for a range of frequencies and a logarithmic rate of decline in the autocovariogram of log volatility. A difference is that MRW has an abrupt low-frequency cutoff at which volatility auto-correlations switch from a hyperbolic decay to zero, while MSM mimics long-memory features on a range of intermediate lags before smoothly transitioning to an exponential decline at low frequencies (7.8).

MSM and MRW share common aspects in their development. Calvet and Fisher (1999) introduced MSM, demonstrated the weak convergence of the continuous-time process under Condition 4, and provided a sequence of discrete filters to use in empirical applications. Muzy, Delour, and Bacry

---

[6] An autoregressive fractionally integrated moving average process $ARFIMA(p,d,q)$ must have a long-memory parameter d strictly lower than one half in order to be stationary (e.g., Granger, 1980; Hosking, 1981). The asymptotic autocovariance of the process is then of order $\tau^{-(1-2d)}$, which decays faster than $\ln(T_1/\tau)$ when τ and T_1/τ are both large.

(2000) introduced MRW, and Bacry and Muzy (2003) used Condition 4 to demonstrate the existence of a weak limit for their process. Calvet and Fisher (2002b, 2004) and Calvet, Fisher, and Thompson (2006) demonstrated the use of econometric techniques such as maximum likelihood estimation, simulated method of moments estimation, particle filtering, and closed-form multistep forecasting. In a similar vein to Calvet and Fisher (2002b, 2004), Bacry, Kozhemyak, and Muzy (2008) show that MRW outperforms standard GARCH-type specifications out-of-sample, which confirms the findings of Chapter 3 and Lux (2008).

MRW and a related approach by Barral and Mandelbrot (2002) incorporate a continuum of time scales and do not require a "dilation parameter" b, which provides elegance to the mathematical construct. In these approaches, trading time can be represented as an integral over a cone in the space of scales and time.[7] It remains an open question whether these mathematical generalizations provide meaningful empirical differences compared to MSM.

By contrast, MSM is based on Markov-switching and offers the advantages of such models, including a closed-form likelihood function.[8] Chapters 3 and 4 showed that in typical applications the MSM likelihood function levels off in the range of eight to ten volatility components,[9] which suggests that improvements of the likelihood function are likely to be limited as $\bar{k}$ goes to infinity and the dilation parameter b correspondingly goes to unity. The tractable Markov-switching state space representation also aids the integration of MSM into asset pricing models, as will be seen in Part III.

The literature on multifractal volatility therefore continues to advance on a number of fronts. While the methodologies used by researchers may slightly differ, a salient common theme is that multifractal methods provide accurate forecasts of volatility and estimates of value-at-risk. We anticipate that these methods will continue to prove useful in financial applications in coming years.

Alternative stochastic volatility specifications

MSM and the multifractal processes discussed previously are stochastic volatility (SV) models that share certain moment-scaling properties.

---

[7] See the Appendix for further discussion.

[8] Calvet and Fisher (2002b) shows that the efficiency gains from ML estimation are substantial relative to a variety of simulated method of moments estimators, and the improvement in estimation efficiency confirmed by Lux (2008).

[9] Improvements in forecasting accuracy for MSM specifications with up to fifteen components are found in Lux (2008). These results are obtained in a restricted setting where the dilation parameter b and lowest volatility component frequency γ_1 are arbitrarily fixed, due to difficulty identifying these parameters with method of moments estimation. In Chapter 3, we are able to estimate these parameters with reasonable precision using the likelihood function.

Among the broader set of SV models, the long-memory stochastic volatility (LMSV) models mentioned in Chapter 2 (e.g., Breidt, Crato, and de Lima, 1998; Comte and Renault, 1998; Harvey, 1998; Robinson and Zaffaroni, 1998) have in common with multifractals slowly declining autocovariograms of squared returns.

Recent developments in the LMSV literature have confirmed that improvements in volatility prediction can be obtained by models with long-memory features. Rohit Deo, Clifford Hurvich, and Yi Lu (2006) consider a specification in which log volatility follows an autoregressive fractionally integrated moving average (ARFIMA) process:

$$\Phi(L)(1 - L)^d \sigma_t^2 = \Theta(L)\eta_t,$$

where L denotes the lag operator, η_t is IID $\mathcal{N}(0, \sigma_\eta^2)$, $0 < d < 0.5$, and Φ and Θ are polynomials with all roots outside the unit circle. The authors estimate the model by maximizing the frequency domain quasi maximum likelihood, derive an optimal multistep linear predictor, and show that this approach outperforms GARCH and component GARCH models[10] at horizons of up to 4 weeks. These results confirm the potential benefits of accounting for low-frequency volatility fluctuations.

A related approach by Ole Barndorff-Nielsen and Neil Shephard (2001) specifies volatility as a weighted sum of independent Ornstein-Uhlenbeck (O-U) processes with heterogeneous persistence rates

$$\sigma^2(t) = \sum_{k=1}^{\bar{k}} w_k \sigma_k^2(t), \tag{7.9}$$

where the weights w_k are positive and sum to unity. Each process $\sigma_k^2(t)$ follows

$$d\left[\sigma_k^2(t)\right] = -\lambda_k \sigma_k^2(t)dt + dz_k(\lambda_k t), \tag{7.10}$$

where the $\{z_k(t)\}$ are independent non-Gaussian subordinators (that is, have nonnegative, independent and stationary increments).[11] The components σ_k^2 therefore exhibit occasional upward jumps but otherwise revert

---

[10] Ding and Granger (1996) and Engle and Lee (1999) develop GARCH models with multiple components. Empirical applications typically focus on the case of two volatility factors, representing long- and short-run fluctuations. Stochastic volatility specifications with two components have also been shown to improve on single-factor specifications under a variety of in-sample diagnostics (Alizadeh, Brandt, and Diebold, 2002; Bates, 2000; Bollerslev and Zhou, 2002; Chacko and Viceira, 2003; Chernov et al., 2003; Gallant, Hsu, and Tauchen, 1999; Xu and Taylor, 1994). Out-of-sample, a two-component volatility model is useful for forecasting volatility at long horizons (Brandt and Jones, 2006), for option pricing (Christoffersen, Jacobs, and Wang, 2008), and for cross-sectional stock pricing (Adrian and Rosenberg, 2008).

[11] Bookstaber and Pomerantz (1989) consider a single-frequency version of the Barndorff-Nielsen and Shephard model.

toward zero at rate λ_k. An advantage of this approach is that closed-form expressions are available for option pricing, as pursued by Nicolato and Venardos (2003).

Some of the features of the Barndorff-Nielsen and Shephard approach are similar to MSM. Volatility is hit by shocks of multiple durations, and the autocorrelation function of returns is a sum of exponentials:

$$Corr(\sigma^2(t); \sigma^2(t+n)) = \sum_{k=1}^{\bar{k}} w_k e^{-\lambda_k n},$$

which can approximate a hyperbolic decay and mimic long memory, consistent with Proposition 1. Similar to MSM, the approach also has implications for the power variation of returns, as discussed in Barndorff-Nielsen and Shephard (2003).

The O-U specification (7.10) implies the asymmetry that volatility components occasionally jump upward and otherwise slowly decline toward zero. In MSM, components remain constant until an arrival triggers the draw of a new value, but as is the case with an O-U process, the conditional expectation of a future volatility state $\mathbb{E}_t(M_{k,t+n}) = 1 + (1-\gamma_k)^n (M_{k,t} - 1)$ converges to the long-run mean.

As in other component SV models, the Barndorff-Nielsen specification requires a potentially large number of parameters as the dimensionality of the state space grows. This contrasts with the small number of parameters in MSM, obtained by imposing empirically verifiable restrictions across different time scales. As is typical of other SV models, superposed Ornstein-Uhlenbeck volatility does not have a closed form likelihood, and inference is typically recommended to proceed by Monte Carlo Markov chain (MCMC) or other simulation-based methods. A unique characteristic of MSM among SV models is that a large number of volatility components may be specified with a small number of parameters, while also permitting a closed-form likelihood function and convenient multistep forecasting.

7.5   Discussion

Continuous-time MSM is a multifrequency diffusion with fully stationary increments and heterogeneous volatility components, which can be naturally defined on an unbounded time domain. The instants of changes in volatility components are randomly generated by a sequence of Poisson arrival processes with increasing frequencies. The model parsimoniously captures the volatility persistence, moment-scaling, and thick tails that characterize many financial time series, and is also consistent with the different time scales of economic variables such as technology shocks, business and earnings cycles, and liquidity shocks.

MSM implies semimartingale prices and precludes arbitrage in a standard two-asset setting. Squared returns have long memory, and the highest finite moment of returns may take any value greater than two. This wide range of tail behaviors is fully provided by intermittent bursts of volatility and does not require separate modeling of the tails. Forecasting is facilitated by discrete MSM which has a finite state space and a simple Markov structure. We show that the discretize model weakly converges to continuous-time MSM as the grid step size goes to zero, ensuring that the discrete filters are consistent in estimation and forecasting applications.

8

Power Variation

The multifractal diffusions considered in previous chapters imply that the moments of returns vary as a power law of the time horizon. In this chapter, we confirm the empirical validity of this property on currency and equity data. For Deutsche mark/U.S. dollar (DM/USD) exchange rates, we use a high-frequency data set of approximately 1.5 million quotes collected over one year, and a 24-year sample of daily prices. The exchange rate displays multifractal moment-scaling over a remarkable range of time horizons. We estimate the spectrum of local Hölder exponents and infer an MSM generating mechanism. Monte Carlo simulations show that GARCH and FIGARCH are less likely to reproduce these results than a multifractal model. In addition, we find evidence of scaling in a U.S. equity index and five individual stocks.

This chapter is largely based on results reported in Calvet, Fisher, and Mandelbrot (1997) and Calvet and Fisher (2002a), updated to reflect the strictly stationary MSM specification.[1] Numerous complementary studies confirm that multiscaling is a common feature of many financial time series (e.g., Gallucio *et al.*, 1997; Ghashghaie *et al.*, 1996; Pasquini and Serva, 1999, 2000; Richards, 2000; Vandewalle and Ausloos, 1998). Multifractal models such as MSM provide a parsimonious representation of these empirical features of financial data.

8.1 Power Variation in Currency Markets

8.1.1 Data

We first demonstrate multifractality of the DM/USD exchange rate. We use two data sets provided by Olsen and Associates, a currency research and trading firm based in Zürich. The first data set ("daily") contains

---

[1] The similarity between the results reported in this chapter and those originally published using the MMAR confirms that the two models generate very similar scaling in return moments.

This chapter is based on an earlier paper: "Multifractality in Asset Returns: Theory and Evidence" (with A. Fisher), *Review of Economics and Statistics*, 84: 381–406, August 2002.

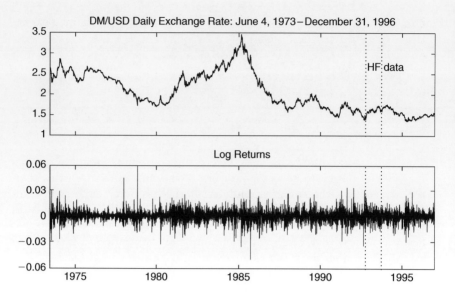

FIGURE 8.1. **DM/USD Daily Data.** The data is provided by Olsen and Associates and spans from 1 June 1973 to 31 December 1996. The outlined area labeled "HF data" shows the one-year period from 1 October 1992 to 30 September 1993 that corresponds to the span of the high-frequency data.

24 years of daily returns from June 1973 to December 1996.[2] Figure 8.1 shows the daily data, which exhibits volatility clustering at all time scales and intermittent large fluctuations.

The second data set ("high-frequency") contains all bid/ask quotes and transmittal times collected over the one-year period from 1 October 1992 to 30 September 1993. We convert quotes to price observations using the same methodology as Olsen, and we obtain a round-the-clock data set of 1,472,241 observations. The high-frequency data show strong patterns of daily seasonality. We correspondingly use a seasonally modified version of a multifractal diffusion:

$$\ln P(t) - \ln P(0) = B_H \left\{ \theta \left[SEAS(t) \right] \right\},$$

where the seasonal transformation $SEAS(t)$ smooths the variation in average absolute returns over 15-minute intervals of the week. The results reported here do not change significantly if we use other reasonable methods

---

[2] Olsen collects price quotes from banks and other institutions through several electronic networks. A price observation is obtained by taking the geometric mean of the concurrent bid and ask. The reported price in the daily data is then calculated by linear interpolation of the price observations closest to 16:00 UK on each side.

of deseasonalizing the high-frequency data. Combining the daily data and the high-frequency data allows us to examine moment scaling over three orders of magnitude for $\triangle t$.

8.1.2   Methodology

Consider the log-price series $X(t) \equiv \ln P(t) - \ln P(0)$ observed over the time interval $[0, T]$. Partitioning $[0, T]$ into integer N intervals of length $\triangle t$, we define the *partition function* or *realized power variation*

$$S_q(T, \triangle t) \equiv \sum_{i=0}^{N-1} |X(i\triangle t + \triangle t) - X(i\triangle t)|^q. \qquad (8.1)$$

When $X(t)$ is multifractal and has a finite q^{th} moment, the scaling law (6.1) yields $\mathbb{E}\left[|X(\triangle t)|^q\right] = c_X(q)(\triangle t)^{\tau_X(q)+1}$, or equivalently

$$\ln \mathbb{E}[S_q(T, \triangle t)] = \tau_X(q) \ln(\triangle t) + c^*(q) \qquad (8.2)$$

where $c^*(q) = \ln c_X(q) + \ln T$. Technically, the condition holds on a grid under the MMAR and asymptotically for small $\triangle t$ under continuous-time MSM. We will see, however, that these discrepancies play no material role in practice.

Given a set of positive moments q and time scales $\triangle t$, we calculate the realized power variations $S_q(T, \triangle t)$ of the data, and plot them against $\triangle t$ in logarithmic scales. By (8.2), these plots should be approximately linear, and regression estimates of the slopes provide the scaling exponents $\widehat{\tau}_X(q)$.

8.1.3   Main Empirical Results

Figures 8.2 and 8.3 illustrate the realized power variations of the two DM/USD data sets. Values of $\triangle t$ are chosen to increase multiplicatively by a factor of 1.1 from minimum to maximum. Since we focus on the slopes $\widehat{\tau}_X(q)$ but not the intercepts, plots for each q are renormalized to begin at zero for the lowest value of $\triangle t$ in each graph. The daily and high-frequency plots are also presented together to highlight the similarity in their slopes.[3]

Figure 8.2 shows the full range of calculated $\triangle t$, from 15 seconds to 6 months, and five values of q ranging from 1.75 to 2.25. We assume that the log-price follows $X(t) = B_H[\theta(t)]$, where θ is an MSM time deformation with countably many frequencies (as described in Chapter 7). Since $\tau_X(1/H) = 0$ and the standard Brownian specification $H = 1/2$ has previous empirical support, we expect to find $\tau_X(q) = 0$ for a value of q near two.

---

[3] We vertically displace the plot of the daily data to provide the best ordinary least squares fit, under the restriction that both lines have the same slope.

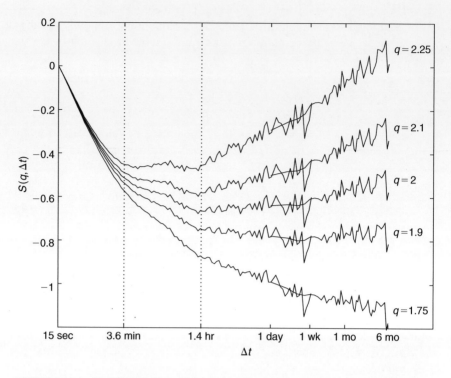

FIGURE 8.2. **DM/USD Realized Power Variations for the Full Set of Time Scales and Moments q near 2.** This figure identifies a scaling region from about 1.4 hours to at least 6 months, the largest horizon for which realized power variations are calculated. The change in scaling at high frequencies is consistent with market frictions such as bid-ask spread, discreteness of prices, and noncontinuous trade. Moments q near 2 are chosen to investigate the martingale hypothesis for returns by the equation $\tau(q = 1/H) = 0$. We find a flat slope near $q = 1.88$, implying $\widehat{H} = 0.53$, or slight persistence.

We first note the approximate linearity of the partition functions beginning at $\Delta t = 1.4$ hours and extending to the largest increment used, $\Delta t = 6$ months. In this range, the slope is zero for a value of q slightly smaller than two, and we report

$$\widehat{H} \approx 0.53,$$

which implies very slight persistence in the DM/USD series. It is not immediately clear whether this result is sufficiently close to $H = 1/2$ to be consistent with the martingale version of the multifractal model, and we return to this issue in the following section using simulation-based inference.

The realized power variation plots in Figure 8.2 also show breaks in linearity at high frequencies. These are consistent with microstructure effects

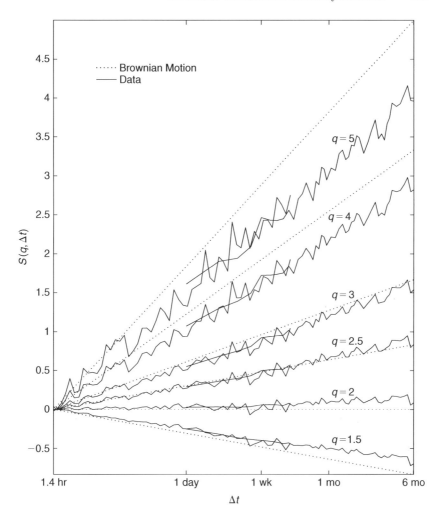

FIGURE 8.3. **DM/USD Realized Power Variations in the Scaling Region for Moments** $1.5 \leq q \leq 5$. For each moment, the first solid line plotted from 1.4 hours to two weeks corresponds to the high-frequency data. The second solid line ranges from $\Delta t = 1$ day to 6 months, and corresponds to the daily data. The lines are remarkably straight, as predicted by the model, and have nearly identical slopes. Also, their scaling is noticeably different from that of the Brownian motion, which is shown by the dotted lines in the figure.

such as bid-ask spreads, discreteness of quoting units, and discontinuous trading. In particular, such microstructure effects can be expected to induce a negative autocorrelation at high frequencies, as is well understood in the case of bid-ask bounce (Roll, 1984b). Negative autocorrelation tends to raise the empirical sum of squared returns, as previously discussed in

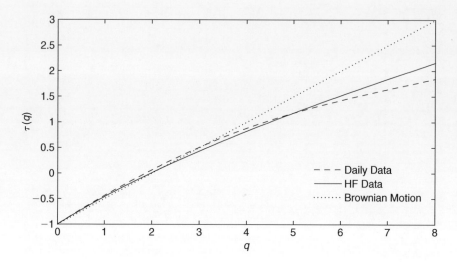

FIGURE 8.4. **Estimated DM/USD Scaling Functions.** For each partition function $S_q(T, \Delta t)$, we estimate the slope $\widehat{\tau}_X(q)$ by OLS. The estimated scaling functions for both data sets are concave and have a similar shape until high moments are reached. For comparison, the scaling function of Brownian motion is shown by the dotted line.

the variance ratio literature (e.g., Campbell and Mankiw, 1987; Lo and MacKinlay, 1988; Richardson and Stock, 1989; Faust, 1992). The results in Figure 8.2 are analogous to variance ratio tests, exactly so if we focus on the moment $q = 2$. As we move to the left on the graph and sampling frequency increases, microstructure-induced negative autocorrelation increases, and the plots bend upward corresponding to the increase in variability.

Descriptive statistics help to confirm that high-frequency breaks in linearity are related to microstructure effects. The departure from linearity begins at a frequency of approximately $\Delta t = 1.4$ hours, highlighted by the dotted lines in Figure 8.2. We calculate the average absolute change in the DM/USD rate over a time increment of 1.4 hours, and find that this equals approximately 0.0014 DM. Comparing this to the average spread of 0.0007 DM,[4] it appears reasonable that microstructure effects should be important at this horizon. For time scales between 3.6 minutes and 1.4 hours, the partition function has an approximate slope of zero for the moment $q = 2.25$, implying $H \approx 0.44 < 1/2$, consistent with negative autocorrelation induced by microstructure effects. In the remainder of the analysis we discard values of Δt less than 1.4 hours, leaving three orders of magnitude of sampling frequencies.

Figure 8.3 presents partition functions for a larger range of moments $1.5 \leq q \leq 5$ with Δt between 1.4 hours and 6 months. Higher moments

---

[4] The two most common spread sizes are 0.0005 DM (38.25%) and 0.0010 DM (52.55%), together comprising over 90% of all observed spreads.

capture information in the tails of the distribution of returns and are thus generally more sensitive to deviations from scaling. All of the plots are nonetheless remarkably linear, and the overlapping values from the two data sets appear to have almost the same slope. Thus despite the long 24-year series of daily data, multifractal scaling seems to hold over a broad range of sampling frequencies.

To obtain scaling functions $\hat{\tau}_X(q)$ for each data set, we estimate the slopes of the partition functions for a range of q, using ordinary least squares (OLS), and report the results in Figure 8.4.[5] The estimated functions are strictly concave, indicating multifractality, and the daily and high-frequency spectra are similar except for very large moments.

Chapter 5 suggests estimating the multifractal spectrum $f_X(\alpha)$ by taking the Legendre transform of $\hat{\tau}_X(q)$. Following this logic, Figure 8.5 shows the estimated multifractal spectrum of the daily data. The estimated spectrum is concave, in contrast to the degenerate spectra of Brownian motion and other unifractals.

The specific shape of the daily spectrum is very nearly quadratic, and Chapter 5 has shown that quadratic spectra are indicative of lognormally distributed multipliers M. To obtain an estimated MSM generating mechanism, we specify $-\log_b M \sim \mathcal{N}(\lambda - 1, \sigma^2)$, giving trading time $\theta(t)$ with multifractal spectrum $f_\theta(\alpha) = 1 - (\alpha - \lambda)^2/[4(\lambda - 1)]$.[6] The log-price process has the most probable exponent $\alpha_0 = \lambda H$ and spectrum

$$f_X(\alpha) = 1 - \frac{(\alpha - \alpha_0)^2}{4H(\alpha_0 - H)}.$$

Since $\hat{H} = 0.53$, the free parameter α_0 is used to fit the estimated spectrum. We report

$$\hat{\alpha}_0 = 0.589,$$

which produces the parabola shown in Figure 8.5. Choosing a generating construction with base $b = 2$,[7] this immediately implies $\hat{\lambda} = 1.11$ and

---

[5] The increasing variability of the partition function plots with the time scale Δt suggests a weighted least squares or generalized least squares approach. In practice, weighting the observations has little effect on the results because the plots are very nearly linear. Preferring simplicity, we report OLS regression results.

[6] A multiplier has a mean equal to unity in MSM and to $1/b$ in the MMAR. An MSM multiplier M must therefore be divided by b in order to be an admissible MMAR multiplier. The specification $-\log_b M \sim \mathcal{N}(\lambda - 1, \sigma^2)$ implies that $-\log_b(M/b) \sim \mathcal{N}(\lambda, \sigma^2)$, and the formula for the multifractal spectrum (5.10) can then be applied without modification.

[7] The base b of the multifractal generating process is not uniquely identified by the spectrum alone; hence we assume the commonly used value $b = 2$. Chapter 3 develops a likelihood based filter under which b can be estimated for the class of multinomial multifractals.

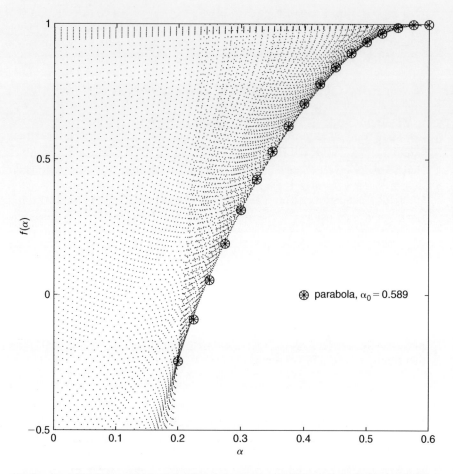

FIGURE 8.5. **Estimated Multifractal Spectrum of Daily DM/USD Data.** The estimated spectrum is obtained from the Legendre transform $\widehat{f}_X(\alpha) = \underset{q}{\mathrm{Inf}}[\alpha q - \widehat{\tau}(q)]$, shown in this graph by the lower envelope of the dotted lines. The shape is nearly quadratic, with a fitted parabola shown by marked symbols, suggesting a lognormal distribution for multipliers M.

$\widehat{\sigma}^2 = 0.32$.[8] It is also natural to consider the martingale version of the multifractal model with the restriction $H = 1/2$. For this case, we estimate the single parameter $\widehat{\alpha}_0 = 0.545$.

In both cases, the estimated value of the most probable local Hölder exponent α_0 is greater than $1/2$. On a set of Lebesgue measure 1, the estimated multifractal process is therefore more regular than a Brownian

---

[8] Mandelbrot (1989) shows that the partition function methodology provides reasonable estimates of $\tau_X(q)$ only for moments $q < 1/\sqrt{\alpha_0(X)/H - 1}$, which is approximately equal to 5.66 in our estimated process.

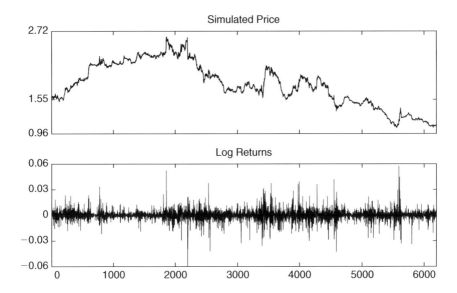

FIGURE 8.6. **Simulated MSM Generating Process for the DM/USD Data.** We use the estimated values of $\widehat{H} = 0.53$ and $\widehat{\alpha}_0 = 0.589$ with the lognormal specification of MSM. The plots show volatility clustering at all time scales and occasional large fluctuations.

motion. However, the concavity of the spectrum also implies the existence of lower Hölder exponents that correspond to more irregular instants of the price process. These contribute disproportionately to quadratic variations.

Figure 8.6 shows the levels and log-differences of a random price path generated by the estimated lognormal MSM. The simulation shows a variety of large price changes, apparent trends, persistent bursts of volatility, and other characteristics found in the DM/USD series.

8.1.4 Comparison of MSM vs. Alternative Specifications

To assess whether the estimated MSM process is able to replicate the scaling features of DM/USD data, we first simulate several long series from the extended MSM specification estimated above with $\widehat{H} = 0.53$ and $\widehat{\alpha}_0 = 0.589$. For each of four simulated series of 100,000 observations, we calculate partition functions and display these in Figure 8.7a. For comparison,[9] Figure 8.7b shows partition functions from simulated GARCH(1,1) series where parameter estimates are taken from Baillie and Bollerslev (1989). Figure 8.7c considers the FIGARCH$(1, d, 0)$ specification

---

[9] LeBaron (2001) suggests multiple component stochastic volatility alternatives. Mandelbrot (2001) and Stanley and Plerou (2001) provide discussions.

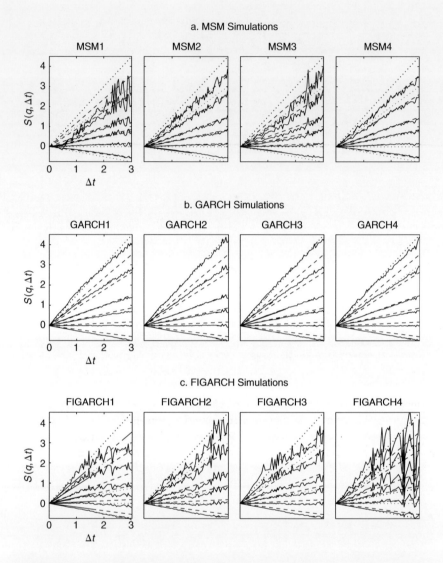

FIGURE 8.7. **Simulated Realized Power Variations.** Each panel shows realized power variations for a simulated sample of 100,000 observations. The data-generating process in (a) uses our estimates from the extended MSM. The data-generating processes in (b) and (c) use specifications from previously published research on daily DM/USD exchange rates. Large simulated samples are used to reduce noise. Dotted lines in each figure represent the scaling predicted for Brownian motion, and dashed lines represent the scaling found in the data. MSM appears most likely to capture scaling in the DM/USD data. The GARCH simulations tend to scale like Brownian motion. FIGARCH simulations occasionally show scaling that is similar to the data, but in general tend to be much more irregular.

of Baillie, Bollerslev, and Mikkelsen (1996). The figure shows that the MSM partition functions are approximately linear and close to the slopes of the DM/USD data. By contrast, the GARCH(1,1) partition functions are fairly linear, but their apparent slope is similar to the predicted slope of Brownian motion rather than the data. This is symptomatic of short memory in GARCH models. Over long time periods, temporal clustering disappears, and GARCH scales like a Brownian motion. The FIGARCH partition function plots appear more irregular than those of MSM and the data.

We now provide a more systematic assessment of ability to replicate the scaling features of DM/USD data. The analysis focuses on four processes: the extended MSM (with arbitrary H), the martingale MSM ($H = 1/2$), FIGARCH, and GARCH. These models are, respectively, indexed by $m \in \{1, \ldots, 4\}$. For each model m, we simulate $J = 10{,}000$ paths with the same length $T = 6{,}118$ as the DM/USD data. We denote each path by $Y_j^m = \{Y_{j,t}^m\}_{t=1}^T$, $(1 \leq j \leq J)$, and we focus the analysis on the moments $q \in Q = \{0.5, 1, 2, 3, 5\}$. For each path and each q, an OLS regression provides a slope estimate $\hat{\tau}(q, Y_j^m)$ and the corresponding sum of squared errors $SSE(q, Y_j^m)$. Tables 8.1 and 8.2 report the percentiles of these statistics for each model. The distributions of the reported statistics appear unimodal, with smoothly declining tails.

Table 8.1 shows that the extended MSM is very close to the data in both its theoretically predicted slopes τ_0 and the mean slopes $\bar{\tau}$. Furthermore, the estimated slopes from the DM/USD data are well within the central bells of the simulated slope distributions generated by the extended MSM. For the martingale version of MSM, the estimated slopes from the DM/USD data are generally close to the model slopes, but for low moments the statistics from the data are in the upper tail of the simulated distribution for the model.

Table 8.2 analyzes the variability of the simulated partition functions around their slopes. The extended and martingale versions of the MSM yield nearly identical results. For low moments, the data falls well within the likely range of the SSE statistic for both models. For high moments, the partition functions are typically more variable for the simulated MSM than for the data. Overall, MSM appears to successfully match the main scaling features of the data.

Comparing GARCH and FIGARCH to these results, Tables 8.1 and 8.2 confirm that the GARCH partition functions, while linear, have very different slopes than the DM/USD data. The simulated FIGARCH slopes improve over the GARCH slopes, but are not as close to the data as the multifractal model. The SSEs from the data, reported in Table 8.2, are also far in the tails of their distributions generated under FIGARCH. Thus, the two MSM specifications appear more likely to replicate the scaling features of the exchange rate data than alternative models.

TABLE 8.1. Realized Power Variation: Estimated Slopes

A. Predicted Slopes and Mean Slopes from Model Simulations and DM/USD Data

	DM/USD Data	i. MSM			ii. MSM $(H=1/2)$			iii. FIGARCH $(1,d,0)$		iv. GARCH $(1,1)$	
q	$\hat\tau$	τ_0	$\bar\tau_{sim}$	s.d.	τ_0	$\bar\tau_{sim}$	s.d.	$\bar\tau_{sim}$	s.d.	$\bar\tau_{sim}$	s.d.
0.5	−0.711	−0.71	−0.72	0.01	−0.73	−0.74	0.01	−0.74	0.01	−0.75	0.01
1.0	−0.440	−0.44	−0.45	0.02	−0.49	−0.48	0.02	−0.49	0.03	−0.50	0.02
2.0	0.058	0.06	0.05	0.06	0.00	−0.01	0.06	−0.01	0.08	−0.01	0.05
3.0	0.500	0.49	0.48	0.12	0.43	0.42	0.10	0.42	0.16	0.47	0.08
5.0	1.208	1.19	1.17	0.27	1.16	1.12	0.24	1.14	0.35	1.36	0.17

B. Probabilities that the Simulated Model Slopes are Less than the Slopes from DM/USD Data: $\mathbb{P}(\tau_{sim} < \hat\tau)$

q	i. MSM	ii. MSM	iii. FIGARCH	iv. GARCH
0.5	0.6356	0.9835	0.9969	0.9993
1.0	0.5732	0.9614	0.9787	0.9959
2.0	0.5568	0.8820	0.8363	0.9186
3.0	0.5851	0.7968	0.7209	0.6587
5.0	0.5572	0.6554	0.5656	0.1754

C. Percentiles of the Simulated Model Slopes

i. MSM

q	P0.5	P1	P2.5	P5	P10	P25	P50	P75	P90	P95	P97.5	P99	P99.5
0.5	−0.746	−0.743	−0.739	−0.735	−0.731	−0.723	−0.715	−0.707	−0.700	−0.695	−0.692	−0.687	−0.683
1.0	−0.508	−0.502	−0.493	−0.486	−0.477	−0.461	−0.445	−0.429	−0.413	−0.405	−0.396	−0.387	−0.381

2.0	−0.107	−0.093	−0.068	−0.050	−0.027	0.009	0.049	0.089	0.127	0.151	0.172	0.201	0.220
3.0	0.157	0.192	0.246	0.288	0.331	0.401	0.476	0.552	0.625	0.674	0.721	0.779	0.817
5.0	0.353	0.453	0.603	0.715	0.835	1.003	1.173	1.343	1.508	1.609	1.710	1.834	1.918

ii. MSM($H = 1/2$)

0.50	−0.767	−0.764	−0.759	−0.755	−0.751	−0.744	−0.735	−0.728	−0.721	−0.716	−0.713	−0.709	−0.707
1.00	−0.544	−0.539	−0.528	−0.521	−0.512	−0.497	−0.481	−0.466	−0.452	−0.443	−0.436	−0.427	−0.423
2.00	−0.152	−0.137	−0.116	−0.098	−0.078	−0.044	−0.007	0.030	0.063	0.086	0.103	0.123	0.144
3.00	0.142	0.174	0.213	0.249	0.286	0.347	0.415	0.483	0.550	0.589	0.629	0.677	0.708
5.00	0.445	0.529	0.643	0.735	0.822	0.960	1.119	1.274	1.423	1.508	1.603	1.715	1.783

iii. FIGARCH(1, d, 0)

0.5	−0.776	−0.773	−0.768	−0.764	−0.760	−0.753	−0.744	−0.736	−0.729	−0.725	−0.721	−0.716	−0.713
1.0	−0.566	−0.556	−0.546	−0.537	−0.527	−0.511	−0.494	−0.476	−0.460	−0.450	−0.442	−0.430	−0.422
2.0	−0.244	−0.211	−0.174	−0.141	−0.111	−0.064	−0.016	0.034	0.084	0.115	0.147	0.191	0.221
3.0	−0.082	−0.003	0.086	0.151	0.220	0.320	0.416	0.514	0.608	0.680	0.737	0.815	0.857
5.0	0.033	0.200	0.412	0.559	0.703	0.934	1.155	1.362	1.560	1.699	1.807	1.935	2.031

iv. GARCH(1, 1)

0.5	−0.777	−0.774	−0.770	−0.766	−0.762	−0.755	−0.747	−0.740	−0.733	−0.729	−0.725	−0.721	−0.718
1.0	−0.555	−0.548	−0.541	−0.534	−0.525	−0.512	−0.497	−0.482	−0.470	−0.461	−0.454	−0.447	−0.442
2.0	−0.121	−0.110	−0.095	−0.080	−0.063	−0.036	−0.005	0.025	0.053	0.071	0.084	0.101	0.113
3.0	0.281	0.302	0.322	0.347	0.375	0.420	0.470	0.521	0.571	0.601	0.629	0.664	0.685
5.0	0.928	0.978	1.037	1.094	1.150	1.250	1.352	1.461	1.569	1.641	1.709	1.790	1.859

Notes: This table is based on $J = 10,000$ simulated paths for each of the four models. In Panel A, the column τ_0 is the theoretically predicted slope, under the MSM, in the regression of the logarithm of realized power variation on the logarithm Δt (equation 8.2). The column $\bar{\tau}$ shows the average slope over the J paths, and s.d. the standard deviation. Panel B provides the percentage of the simulated paths with slope values less than observed in the daily DM/USD data, and Panel C gives percentiles of the simulated distribution under each model.

TABLE 8.2. Realized Power Variation: Sum of Squared Errors

A. Mean SSE from Simulated Models and DM/USD Data

q	DM/USD Data SSE	i. MSM SSE	i. MSM s.d.	ii. MSM ($H=1/2$) SSE	ii. MSM ($H=1/2$) s.d.	iii. FIGARCH ($1,d,0$) SSE	iii. FIGARCH ($1,d,0$) s.d.	iv. GARCH ($1,1$) SSE	iv. GARCH ($1,1$) s.d.
0.5	0.018	0.020	0.008	0.021	0.008	0.024	0.009	0.021	0.008
1.0	0.0507	0.060	0.027	0.064	0.027	0.083	0.042	0.059	0.023
2.0	0.159	0.330	0.213	0.311	0.167	0.635	0.635	0.210	0.09
3.0	0.42	1.50	1.14	1.29	0.864	2.98	2.95	0.70	0.39
5.0	2.76	10.2	7.19	9.84	6.01	17.3	13.7	4.91	3.54

B. Probabilities that the Simulated Model SSE are Less than in the DM/USD Data

q	i. MSM	ii. MSM	iii. FIGARCH	iv. GARCH
0.5	0.4652	0.3914	0.2541	0.3733
1.0	0.4225	0.3553	0.1648	0.4191
2.0	0.1019	0.1000	0.0204	0.3211
3.0	0.0139	0.0197	0.0026	0.1902
5.0	0.0175	0.0283	0.0034	0.2293

C. Percentiles of the Simulated Model SSE

i. MSM

q	P0.5	P1	P2.5	P5	P10	P25	P50	P75	P90	P95	P97.5	P99	P99.5
0.5	0.0072	0.0079	0.0092	0.010	0.012	0.015	0.019	0.024	0.030	0.034	0.039	0.046	0.050
1.0	0.0204	0.0229	0.0261	0.029	0.034	0.042	0.055	0.072	0.093	0.111	0.129	0.150	0.165

2.0	0.095	0.106	0.121	0.136	0.158	0.206	0.279	0.395	0.561	0.698	0.849	1.05	1.27
3.0	0.352	0.396	0.462	0.530	0.630	0.842	1.18	1.78	2.69	3.44	4.31	5.81	7.12
5.0	2.25	2.52	2.97	3.46	4.16	5.68	8.25	12.5	18.4	23.2	28.9	36.8	42.8

ii. MSM ($H = 1/2$)

0.5	0.008	0.008	0.010	0.011	0.013	0.016	0.020	0.025	0.031	0.036	0.040	0.048	0.053
1.0	0.022	0.024	0.028	0.032	0.036	0.045	0.058	0.076	0.097	0.113	0.131	0.155	0.184
2.0	0.096	0.106	0.122	0.138	0.161	0.204	0.272	0.375	0.511	0.622	0.752	0.92	1.11
3.0	0.333	0.382	0.441	0.507	0.591	0.768	1.07	1.58	2.26	2.87	3.63	4.93	6.11
5.0	2.04	2.34	2.74	3.17	3.76	5.04	7.26	10.9	16.3	20.4	25.5	33.8	38.1

iii. FIGARCH(1, d, 0)

0.5	0.00873	0.00969	0.0112	0.0126	0.0144	0.0179	0.0229	0.0287	0.0355	0.0403	0.0447	0.0507	0.0561
1.0	0.026	0.0291	0.034	0.0386	0.0448	0.0572	0.0745	0.0984	0.129	0.155	0.185	0.228	0.276
2.0	0.126	0.14	0.165	0.192	0.227	0.31	0.461	0.73	1.18	1.62	2.14	3.1	4.18
3.0	0.453	0.527	0.64	0.751	0.931	1.34	2.11	3.6	5.75	7.74	10.3	14.3	19.4
5.0	2.99	3.42	4.13	4.94	6.07	8.73	13.5	21.4	32.1	41.5	52.4	68.9	85.3

iv. GARCH(1, 1)

0.5	0.00804	0.00872	0.00995	0.0111	0.0128	0.0159	0.0202	0.0254	0.0315	0.0357	0.0397	0.0455	0.05
1.0	0.0212	0.0232	0.0265	0.0299	0.0343	0.0427	0.0546	0.0697	0.0874	0.101	0.115	0.135	0.149
2.0	0.0725	0.0793	0.091	0.103	0.116	0.147	0.19	0.249	0.325	0.383	0.449	0.548	0.624
3.0	0.214	0.237	0.27	0.31	0.356	0.456	0.608	0.827	1.13	1.39	1.64	2.07	2.46
5.0	1.25	1.39	1.59	1.83	2.14	2.84	3.95	5.83	8.5	11.1	13.9	18.4	23.2

Notes: This table is based on the same simulated paths as Table 8.1. In Panel A, the column SSE shows the average, over the $J = 10{,}000$ paths for each model, of the sum of squared errors from the regression of the logarithm of realized power variation on the logarithm of Δt. The column s.d. gives the standard deviation of the sum of squared errors over the 10,000 simulations. Panel B gives the percentage of simulated paths with SSE less than in the daily DM/USD data, and Panel C provides percentiles of the simulated SSE under each model.

8.1.5   Global Tests of Fit

We summarize these observations with several tests of global fit, drawing on the literature that suggests specification tests using simulated moments (e.g., Ingram and Lee, 1991; Duffie and Singleton, 1993). For a given model $m \in \{1, \ldots, 4\}$, each path Y_j^m generates a column vector of slope and SSE estimates[10]:

$$h(Y_j^m) = \{[\hat{\tau}(q, Y_j^m), \ln SSE(q, Y_j^m)]_{q \in Q}\}'.$$

Denote the data by $X = \{X_t\}_{t=1}^T$ and arrange the simulated paths in a $J \times T$ matrix $Y^m = [Y_1^m, \ldots, Y_J^m]'$. We then consider

$$H(X, Y^m) = h(X) - \frac{1}{J} \sum_{j=1}^J h(Y_j^m).$$

The function H is useful to test how a particular model fits the moment properties of the data. In particular, we can define a global statistic $G = H'WH$ for any positive-definite matrix W. We use four different weighting matrices W_m, $m \in \{1, \ldots, 4\}$, each of which is obtained by inverting the simulated covariance matrix of moment conditions:

$$W_m = \left[\sum_{j=1}^J H(Y_j^m, Y^m) H(Y_j^m, Y^m)'/J \right]^{-1}.$$

The global statistics

$$G_{m,n}(X) = H(X, Y^m)' W_n H(X, Y^m), \qquad m, n \in \{1, \ldots, 4\}, \qquad (8.3)$$

are indexed by the model m that generates the simulated data Y^m and the model n that generates the weighting matrix W_n. This gives a set of 16 global statistics. Assuming that m is the true model, we can estimate the cumulative distribution function $\mathbb{F}_{m,n}$ of each statistic from the set $\{G_{m,n}(Y_j^m)\}_{1 \le j \le J}$, and then quantify the p-value $1 - \mathbb{F}_{m,n}[G_{m,n}(X)]$.

The global statistics $G_{m,n}(X)$ and their associated p-values are reported in Table 8.3. Each column of the results uses a different weighting matrix, so that within column comparisons provide four separate views of ability to fit the data. Each weighting matrix provides different power against a given model, and asymptotic theory suggests that the most powerful weighting matrix for each model is provided by the inverse of its own covariance

---

[10] We use the logarithm of the SSE in calculating the global statistics because Table 8.2 shows that the SSE are heavily right-skewed.

TABLE 8.3. Global Tests for DM/USD Scaling

| | Weighting | | | |
Model	W_1	W_2	W_3	W_4
	Test Statistics and Simulated p-values			
MSM	**7.70**	10.11	7.50	27.21
	(0.506)	(0.451)	(0.523)	(0.317)
MSM($H = 1/2$)	11.29	**12.81**	11.49	20.15
	(0.199)	**(0.210)**	(0.185)	(0.297)
FIGARCH($1, d, 0$)	24.45	28.94	**25.96**	58.79
	(0.114)	(0.163)	**(0.043)**	(0.259)
GARCH($1, 1$)	20.65	22.81	25.34	**27.04**
	(0.0290)	(0.024)	(0.030)	**(0.032)**

Notes: The weighting matrices $W_1, \ldots, W_4$ correspond to the inverse covariance matrix of the moment conditions under the four models: MSM, MSM($H = 1/2$), FIGARCH, and GARCH. The 10 moment conditions used are the expected slope and sum of squared errors for the 5 moments $q = 0.5, 1, 2, 3, 5$, conditioned on each model, from the regression of the logarithm of realized power variation on the logarithm of Δt (equation 8.2). The expectations and covariances of the moment conditions are obtained by simulating 10,000 paths under each model. The statistics reported are from the daily DM/USD data, and the p-values show the probability of observing a larger statistic conditioning upon the assumed model. Asymptotic theory suggests that the diagonal entries will have most power against each model.

matrix of moment conditions. We expect the diagonal entries of the table to provide the greatest power to reject each model, and this is consistent with the results. Whether evaluated column-wise or by the diagonal elements, the results confirm that the multifractal model best replicates the scaling properties of the data.

8.2   Power Variation in Equity Markets

After observing multifractal properties in DM/USD exchange rates, it is natural to test the model on other financial data. This section presents evidence of moment-scaling in a sample of five major U.S. stocks and one equity index.

The Center for Research in Security Prices (CRSP) provides daily stock returns for 9,190 trading days from July 1962 to December 1998. We present results for the value-weighted NYSE-AMEX-NASDAQ index (CRSP Index) and five stocks: Archer Daniels Midland (ADM), General Motors (GM), Lockheed Martin, Motorola, and United Airlines (UAL). The individual stocks are issued by large, well-known corporations from various economic sectors, and have reported data for the full CRSP sample

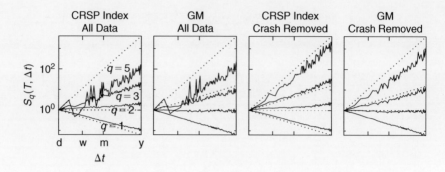

FIGURE 8.8. **Realized Power Variations for CRSP Index and GM.** The data spans from 1962 to 1998, and the time increments labeled "d," "w," "m," and "y" correspond to one day, one week, one month, and one year, respectively. When the full data sets are used, we observe scaling in the first three moments, and for horizons $\Delta t \geq 3$ days in the fifth moments. The drop in the fifth moments between two and three days is caused by sharp rebounds for both series from the 1987 crash. After removing the crash from the data, the second two panels show striking linearity, but change the slopes of the full-sample plots to increase and thus appear more Brownian.

span. For each series, we convert the daily return data into a renormalized log-price series X_t, and then we calculate realized power variations for a range of time intervals Δt.[11]

Figure 8.8 shows results for the CRSP index and General Motors. In the first two panels, the full data sets are used with increments Δt ranging from one day to approximately one year. The partition functions for moments $q = \{1, 2, 3\}$ are approximately linear for both series, with little variation around the apparent slope. The slope for the moment $q = 2$ is noticeably positive for the CRSP index, indicating persistence. This characteristic is atypical of individual securities, although short horizon persistence is a common feature of index returns, often attributed to asynchronous trading (e.g., Boudoukh, Richardson, and Whitelaw, 1994). In contrast to the results for low moments, the realized power variations from both series vary considerably for the moment $q = 5$. This suggests investigation of the tails of the data. The second two panels of Figure 8.8 display striking linearity after simply removing the day of the October 1987 stock market crash from both data sets. Not surprisingly, removing the crash also results in the power variation plots moving toward the Brownian benchmark, thus appearing more "mild."

The other four stocks scale remarkably well despite the crash, as shown in Figure 8.9. Consistent with the martingale hypothesis for returns, three of

---

[11] The CRSP holding period returns $r_t = (P_t - P_{t-1} + D_t)/P_{t-1}$ include cash distributions D_t. We construct the series $\{X_t\}_{t=0}^T$ by $X_0 = 0$, $X_t = X_{t-1} + \ln(1 + r_t)$.

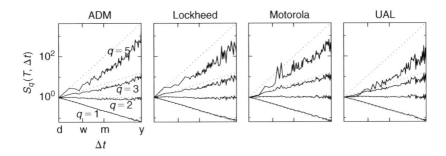

FIGURE 8.9. **Realized Power Variations for ADM, Lockheed, Motorola, and UAL.** The plots, which are based on all daily returns between July 1962 and December 1998, show strong scaling properties.

the four stocks have almost exactly flat realized power variations for $q = 2$, while Archer Daniels Midland has a slight negative slope. The difference between Brownian scaling and multiscaling becomes perceptible for $q = 3$, and for the fifth moment, this difference is pronounced. United Airlines appears to be the most variable, with lower slopes at higher moments and thus a wider multifractal spectrum.

8.3   Additional Moments

Besides power variation scaling, other properties of MSM can be useful to estimate the model, assess its fit, and compare with alternative specifications. For instance, the autocorrelograms of powers of absolute returns, $Cov(|r_t|^q, |r_{t+s}|^q)$, scale as power laws of s on a wide range of lags, as is shown by Proposition 1 in Chapter 3. Arneodo, Muzy, and Sornette (1998) provide visual confirmation of this property in currency data, and Lux (2008) uses the autocorrelations of powers of returns to estimate MSM. We have also shown in Chapter 3 that the tail statistics of simulated MSM data closely approximate the tail statistics of actual currency returns. Thus, MSM parsimoniously captures a variety of economically important features of financial series.

In Calvet and Fisher (2002b), we used the simulated method of moments (Ingram and Lee, 1991; Duffie and Singleton, 1993) in a Monte Carlo study to compare the informativeness of different moment properties of the multifractal model. Implementing the simulated method of moments requires only a small extension of the global test of fit described previously. Given a set of empirical moments $h(X)$, we draw J i.i.d. paths $\{Y_j(\psi)\}_{j=1}^{J}$ of the same lengths as the data under the assumed model with parameter vector ψ. For a fixed weighting matrix W, we estimate the model by computing the vector $\widehat{\psi}$ that minimizes the objective function

$$G(Y(\psi), X, W) = H'WH,$$

where

$$H\left(X, Y\left(\psi\right)\right) = h\left(X\right) - \frac{1}{J} \sum_{j=1}^{J} h\left[Y_j\left(\psi\right)\right],$$

and $Y\left(\psi\right)$ is a matrix containing all of the simulated paths Y_j.[12]

In order to assess the properties of different simulated method of moments estimators, we repeatedly simulated time series from a fixed MSM process, and then applied the simulation estimator to each series using different sets of moment conditions. The moment conditions we used in estimation can be divided into four categories: 1) moments based on the scaling properties of realized power variations (implemented previously in this chapter); 2) moments based on the hyperbolic decline of the covariance of the qth absolute moment of returns $Cov(|r_t|^q, |r_{t+s}|^q)$; 3) higher-frequency autocovariances, as suggested by Andersen and Sørensen (1996) and an early version of Lux (2008); and 4) estimated tail statistics of absolute returns.[13] We focused on comparing the ability of each of these sets of moment conditions to consistently and efficiently estimate the binomial parameter m_0.

Our findings demonstrated that each of the four types of moment conditions are individually informative, giving approximately unbiased estimates of the binomial parameter m_0. Turning to efficiency, moments based on the hyperbolic decline of the covariogram and the tail index produced lower root-mean-square errors than estimators based on either power variation scaling or high-frequency autocovariances. By combining the tail index and estimates of power law decline from the autocovariograms we obtained a root-mean-square-error for m_0 approximately 50% larger than for the maximally efficient ML estimator discussed in Chapter 3.[14]

---

[12] All random draws used to generate the simulations are held constant as ψ varies in order to obtain a smooth objective function.

[13] The power variation moments included the estimated slopes $\hat{\tau}(q)$ and SSE for $q \in \{0.5, 1, 2, 3, 5\}$ from the linear regressions (8.2). For autocovariograms, following Proposition 1 in Chapter 3 we regress the log autocovariance $\ln Cov(|r_t|^q, |r_{t+s}|^q)$ against the lag $\ln(s)$, and obtain the corresponding slopes and the SSE for the set of moments q described previously. We similarly estimated the hyperbolic rate of decline $\hat{d}_q$ in the autocovariograms by implementing the log-periodogram regression of Geweke and Porter-Hudak (1983). Using bias reduction methods such as Andrews and Guggenberger (2003) did not appreciably affect the results, which is not surprising because the simulated method of moments matches estimated parameters against estimated parameters. The high-frequency autocovariances we used focused on lags of 1, 2, 4, and 8 days. The tail index was estimated by linear fit of the empirical cumulative density function, in logarithms, of the 100 largest absolute returns. The Monte Carlo study used a sample size of 5,000 and $\bar{k} = 8$, normalized $\bar{\sigma}$ to 1, and set $b = 2.5$, $m_0 = 1.4$, $\gamma_k = 0.386$.

[14] Given sufficient computing power one can of course match the efficiency of the MLE estimator using the particle filter described in Chapter 4. In the current chapter we focus instead on moments that emphasize some of the important economic properties of MSM.

The availability of multiple types of moments suggests extending the global tests of fit discussed in the previous subsection. Correspondingly, we applied the global test (8.3) using tail index and covariogram moments, with a set of MSM models having $\bar{k}$ varying from 1 to 10 and parameters taken from the ML estimates for each of the four currency datasets described in Chapter 3.[15] Specifications with a low number of components $\bar{k}$ were rejected with high confidence in all datasets, but specifications with $\bar{k}$ large were not rejected in three of the four exchange rate series. Thus, whether evaluated by power variation scaling, declines of autocovariograms, or tail statistics, the properties of MSM appear consistent with financial data.

8.4 Discussion

The empirical analysis in this chapter indicates that multifractal moment-scaling is a prominent feature of many financial series. Over a range of observational frequencies from approximately two hours to 180 days, and over a time series spanning 24 years, realized power variations of DM/USD exchange rate returns grow approximately like a power law in the time step. We obtain an estimate of the multifractal spectrum by a Legendre transform of the moments' growth rates. We simulate the implied process and confirm that the multifractal model replicates the moment behavior found in the data. We also demonstrate scaling behavior in an equity index and five major U.S. stocks.

Beyond our research on moment-scaling in 1997, numerous complementary studies confirm that multiscaling is exhibited by many financial time series, focusing on a variety of aspects of the data including power variations, autocovariograms, and tail distributions (e.g., Pasquini and Serva, 1999, 2000; Richards, 2000; Vandewalle and Ausloos, 1998). In addition, the literature on power variation, while often having a slightly different emphasis, has independently confirmed some of these characteristics of financial data (e.g., Andersen, Bollerslev, Diebold, and Labys, 2001; Barndorff-Nielsen and Shephard, 2003). MSM is thus consistent with numerous important properties of financial returns.

In addition to the method of moments (this chapter) and particle filter (Chapter 4), MSM also may be estimated using its closed form likelihood (Chapters 3 and 4). In Part III, we show how MSM can be productively incorporated into asset pricing frameworks in both discrete and continuous time.

---

[15] The specific moments used were the slopes and SSE from log covariogram regressions with $q = 1, 2, 4$ and two tail statistics, estimated from the largest 100 and 2400 absolute returns.

Part III

Equilibrium Pricing

9

Multifrequency News and Stock Returns

In the final part of this book, encompassing Chapters 9 and 10, we explore the implications of multifrequency risk for the valuation of financial assets. We assume that fundamentals are subject to multifrequency risk, and derive the resulting price dynamics in a consumption-based asset equilibrium framework, as developed in Lucas (1978) and surveyed in Campbell (2003). The multifrequency approach allows us to apply consumption-based modeling to high-frequency data, and can be viewed as a first step toward bridging the gap between the macro finance and financial econometrics literatures. For readers who are not familiar with consumption-based asset pricing, the models presented in this section provide examples of martingale pricing, in which dividend news and the stochastic discount factor are driven by components of multiple frequencies. Other pricing kernels can of course be considered in applications. The present chapter focuses on the valuation of equity claims in discrete-time economies, while Chapter 10 examines endogenous jumps in stock prices in continuous time.

The assumption that fundamentals are subjected to multifrequency risk seems reasonable given the heterogeneity of the news that drive financial returns. At short horizons, corporate and macroeconomic announcements (e.g., MacKinlay, 1997; Andersen, Bollerslev, Diebold, and Vega, 2003), weather news (Roll, 1984a), and analyst reports (e.g., Womack, 1996) affect investor forecasts of future cash flows and discount rates, and in turn the dynamics of daily returns. Equity markets also price lower-frequency fundamentals such as demographics (Abel, 2003), technological innovation (Pastor and Veronesi, 2008), and variations in consumption, dividends, and macroeconomic uncertainty (Bansal and Yaron, 2004; Lettau, Ludvigson, and Wachter, 2004).[1] As has been discussed in Chapter 5, there is also

---

[1] Other examples of financial news operating at different frequencies include the relatively high-frequency impact of liquidity uncertainty (Gennotte and Leland, 1990), intermediate contributions from political cycles (Santa-Clara and Valkanov, 2003), and low-frequency uncertainty regarding exhaustible energy resources.

This chapter is based on an earlier paper: "Multifrequency News and Stock Returns" (with A. Fisher), *Journal of Financial Economics*, 86: 178–212, October 2007.

pervasive evidence of multifractality in weather patterns and other natural phenomena affecting the economy.

We develop a parsimonious asset pricing equilibrium model with exogenous shocks of heterogeneous durations. A consumer receives an exogenous consumption stream and prices a flow of dividends with MSM volatility dynamics.[2] The model generates volatility feedback, the property that upward revisions to anticipated future volatility tend to decrease current returns. Consistent with a multifrequency perspective, previous research investigates volatility feedback at a range of different horizons. For example, French, Schwert, and Stambaugh (1987), Campbell and Hentschel (1992, hereafter CH), and Wu (2001) assess feedback effects in daily, weekly, and monthly data, while Pindyck (1984), Poterba and Summers (1986), Bansal and Yaron (2004), and Lettau, Ludvigson, and Wachter (2004) emphasize volatility movements at the business cycle range and beyond.[3] Intuition suggests that a multifrequency approach can be useful in this context since high-frequency volatility shocks can help to capture the dynamics of typical day-to-day variations, while lower-frequency movements can generate the strong feedback required to fit the most extreme daily returns.

We estimate the model by maximum likelihood on an index of U.S. equities over the period 1926 to 2003, and find that using six to eight volatility frequencies provides significant improvements relative to lower-dimensional settings. The model improves in-sample on earlier specifications of single-frequency news arrivals (CH), even though it uses fewer parameters. The multifrequency equilibrium also generates substantially larger feedback than previous research. For instance, CH find that feedback amplifies the volatility of dividend news by only about 1 to 2%, depending on the sample. With our MSM specification, feedback rises with the number of components and the likelihood function, increasing to between 20 and 40% for the preferred specifications. Hence, the multifrequency equilibrium model generates an unconditional feedback that is 10 to 40 times larger than in previous literature.

---

[2] Following Hamilton (1989), researchers have used regime-switching to help explain financial phenomena, including stock market volatility, return predictability, the relation between conditional risk and return, the term structure of interest rates, and the recent growth of the stock market. Contributions include Abel (1999), Bansal and Zhou (2002), Cecchetti, Lam, and Mark (1990), David (1997), Hung (1994), Kandel and Stambaugh (1990), Lettau, Ludvigson, and Wachter (2004), Turner, Startz, and Nelson (1989), Veronesi (1999, 2000, 2004), Wachter (2006), and Whitelaw (2000).

[3] General equilibrium investigation of volatility feedback was pioneered by Barsky (1989) in a two-period setting and Abel (1988) in the dynamic case. French, Schwert, and Stambaugh (1987) and CH use GARCH-type processes to show that ex post returns are negatively affected by positive innovations in volatility. Bekaert and Wu (2000) provide further support for this hypothesis.

We next investigate the pricing implications of investor learning about volatility. We observe that investors may learn quickly about volatility increases, because a single extreme fluctuation is highly improbable with low volatility. By contrast, learning about reduced risk takes time because observations near the mean are a relatively likely outcome regardless of the true state. Thus, bad news about volatility is incorporated into prices quickly, while good news is assimilated slowly. As a consequence, information quality controls a novel trade-off between endogenous skewness and kurtosis, and economies with intermediate signal precisions best capture the higher moments of daily stock returns. These results complement earlier research by Veronesi (2000) on how information quality affects stock returns. Whereas Veronesi considers learning about the drift in a two-state Lucas economy, our investors receive signals about an arbitrary number of dividend volatility components. By incorporating multiple shocks of heterogeneous durations, we obtain a structural learning model that is empirically relevant for higher-frequency daily stock returns.[4]

We finally extend the multifrequency equilibrium to include long-run consumption risk, as in Bansal and Yaron (2004) and Lettau, Ludvigson, and Wachter (2004). With a relative risk aversion as low as $\alpha = 10$, the model generates a sizeable equity premium while maintaining substantial endogenous feedback. This extension offers a pure regime-switching formulation of long-run risks in a multifrequency environment.

9.1 An Asset Pricing Model with Regime-Switching Dividends

This section develops a discrete-time consumption-based equilibrium with regime shifts in the mean and volatility of dividend growth. The demand for financial assets is modeled by a utility-maximizing representative agent who receives and consumes an exogenous income flow, as in Lucas (1978). The model generates a negative relation between volatility and prices for all preference parameters.

---

[4] Empirical implementation of learning models tends to focus on lower frequencies. For example, Veronesi (2004) calibrates to yearly returns and considers horizons ranging from 20 to 200 years. Lettau, Ludvigson, and Wachter (2004) similarly consider highly persistent shocks with durations of about three decades. David (1997) and Brennan and Xia (2001) calibrate to a monthly frequency. Guidolin and Timmermann (2003) develop estimation and forecasting for a model of learning about the drift on a binomial lattice, and apply this to pricing options at a weekly frequency. At a monthly frequency, Turner, Startz, and Nelson (1989) and Kim, Morley, and Nelson (2004) consider learning about volatility in a two-state specification with feedback effects, where the signals that drive investor learning are not specified.

9.1.1   Preferences, Consumption, and Dividends

We consider an exchange economy defined on the regular grid $t = 0, 1,$ $2, \ldots, \infty$. As in Epstein and Zin (1989) and Weil (1989), the representative agent has isoelastic recursive utility

$$U_t = \left\{ (1 - \delta) C_t^{\frac{1-\alpha}{\theta}} + \delta [\mathbb{E}_t (U_{t+1}^{1-\alpha})]^{\frac{1}{\theta}} \right\}^{\frac{\theta}{1-\alpha}},$$

where α is the coefficient of relative risk aversion, ψ is the elasticity of intertemporal substitution (EIS), and $\theta = (1 - \alpha)/(1 - \psi^{-1})$. When $\alpha = \psi^{-1}$, the specification reduces to expected utility.

The agent receives an exogenous consumption stream $\{C_t\}$. The log-consumption $c_t = \ln C_t$ follows a random walk with constant drift and volatility,

$$c_t - c_{t-1} = g_c + \sigma_c \varepsilon_{c,t}, \tag{9.1}$$

where the shocks $\varepsilon_{c,t}$ are i.i.d. standard normal. This standard specification is consistent with the empirical evidence that consumption growth is approximately i.i.d. in postwar U.S. consumption data (e.g., Campbell, 2003). In Section 9.5, we extend the model to allow for small but highly persistent components in consumption, as in Bansal and Yaron (2004).[5]

The volatility feedback literature suggests that aggregate stock prices decrease with the volatility of dividend news. When the stock market is a claim on aggregate consumption, a negative relation arises in equilibrium only for specific preferences. For Epstein-Zin-Weil utility, volatility reduces prices only if $\theta < 0$,[6] which necessitates that the EIS and risk aversion are either both strictly larger than unity ($\alpha > 1$ and $\psi > 1$) or both strictly lower than unity ($\alpha < 1$ and $\psi < 1$), as noted by Bansal and Yaron (2004) and Lettau, Ludvigson, and Wachter (2004). While there is abundant evidence that $\alpha > 1$, the empirical validity of the EIS restriction has not been settled.[7]

We resolve this ambiguity by (i) separating dividends from consumption, and (ii) permitting that dividend volatility shocks do not simultaneously

---

[5] Arguments in favor of long-run consumption risks are given by Bansal and Lundblad (2002), Bansal, Khatchatrian, and Yaron (2005), and Lettau, Ludvigson, and Wachter (2004).

[6] As the Appendix shows, the aggregate consumption claim has a constant price-dividend ratio P_c that satisfies

$$\frac{P_c}{1 + P_c} = \delta \exp \left[(1 - \psi^{-1}) g_c + (1 - \alpha)^2 \sigma_c^2 / (2\theta) \right].$$

The equilibrium price decreases with volatility if and only if $\theta < 0$.

[7] Attanasio and Weber (1993), Vissing-Jørgensen (2002), and Bansal and Yaron (2004) report estimates of ψ larger than one, while Campbell and Mankiw (1989), Campbell (2003), and Yogo (2004) find that ψ is small and in many cases statistically indistinguishable from zero.

impact consumption. The log-dividend $d_t = \ln D_t$ follows a random walk with state-dependent drift and volatility,

$$d_t - d_{t-1} = \mu_d(M_t) - \frac{\sigma_d^2(M_t)}{2} + \sigma_d(M_t)\varepsilon_{d,t}, \tag{9.2}$$

where $\varepsilon_{d,t}$ is i.i.d. standard normal and correlated with $\varepsilon_{c,t}$. The state M_t is a first-order Markov vector with $\bar{k} < \infty$ elements. We will later assume that M_t follows an MSM($\bar{k}$), but for now the vector M_t is a general Markov process. The drift μ_d and volatility σ_d are deterministic functions of the state M_t, and the Itô term $\sigma_d^2(M_t)/2$ guarantees that expected dividend growth $\mathbb{E}[D_t/D_{t-1}|M_t] = e^{\mu_d(M_t)}$ is controlled only by $\mu_d(M_t)$. We leave the exact specification of drift and volatility fully general in the rest of this section.

The model separates stock returns from aggregate consumption growth and the stochastic discount factor. This common assumption (e.g., Campbell, 1996; Campbell and Cochrane, 1999) is consistent with the imperfect correlation between real consumption growth and real dividend growth. For instance, Campbell (2003) reports correlation estimates less than 0.5 in U.S. data, while Bansal and Yaron (2004) report and use in calibration a value of approximately 0.55. The disconnect between d_t and c_t is reasonable because corporate profits account for a small portion of national income. In U.S. data, corporate profits and personal consumption, respectively, account for approximately 10% and 70% of national income over the period 1929 to 2002. Consumption and dividend shocks should thus be correlated but not identical.

9.1.2 Asset Pricing under Complete Information

We begin by assuming that the agent directly observes the true state of the economy and has the *full information* set $I_t = \{(C_s, D_s, M_s); s \leq t\}$. This assumption holds if agents observe the macroeconomic quantities determining the state or obtain M_t by engaging in fundamental research.

The stochastic discount factor satisfies

$$SDF_{t+1} = \delta'\left(\frac{C_{t+1}}{C_t}\right)^{-\alpha}, \tag{9.3}$$

where $\delta' = \delta\{\mathbb{E}[(C_{t+1}/C_t)^{1-\alpha}]\}^{\frac{1}{\theta}-1}$, as shown in the Appendix. This expression is proportional to the stochastic discount factor obtained under expected utility ($\theta = 1$), suggesting that the elasticity of intertemporal substitution affects the interest rate but not the price of risk.

The interest rate $r_f = -\ln \mathbb{E}_t(SDF_{t+1})$ is constant:

$$r_f = -\ln \delta + g_c/\psi - [\alpha + (\alpha - 1)/\psi]\sigma_c^2/2. \tag{9.4}$$

Consistent with earlier research (e.g., Hung, 1994), the equilibrium price-dividend ratio is controlled by the Markov state: $P_t/D_t = Q(M_t)$. The gross return on the stock,

$$\frac{D_{t+1} + P_{t+1}}{P_t} = \frac{D_{t+1}}{D_t} \frac{1 + Q(M_{t+1})}{Q(M_t)}, \tag{9.5}$$

satisfies the Euler equation

$$\delta' \mathbb{E}\left[\left(\frac{C_{t+1}}{C_t}\right)^{-\alpha} \frac{D_{t+1}}{D_t} \frac{1 + Q(M_{t+1})}{Q(M_t)} \middle| I_t \right] = 1.$$

The price-dividend ratio therefore solves the fixed-point equation

$$Q(M_t) = \mathbb{E}_t \left\{ [1 + Q(M_{t+1})] e^{\mu_d(M_{t+1}) - r_f - \alpha \rho_{c,d} \sigma_c \sigma_d(M_{t+1})} \right\}, \tag{9.6}$$

where $\rho_{c,d} \equiv Corr(\varepsilon_{c,t}, \varepsilon_{d,t}) > 0$ denotes the constant correlation between the Gaussian noises in consumption and dividends. When the volatility $\{\sigma_d(M_t)\}$ is persistent, a large standard deviation of dividend growth at a given date t implies a low contemporaneous price-dividend ratio.[8] High volatility therefore feeds into low asset prices for any choices of the relative risk aversion α and the EIS ψ.

When the Markov vector M_t takes a finite number of values $m^1, \ldots, m^d$, the equilibrium price-dividend ratio can be computed numerically for every state $Q(m^1), \ldots, Q(m^d)$ by solving the fixed-point equation (9.6). Econometric inference is straightforward. While the investor observes the true state M_t, we assume as in Campbell and Hentschel (1992) that the econometrician observes only excess returns and thus has the smaller information set $\mathcal{R}_t = \{r_s\}_{s=1}^{t}$. By (9.5), the log excess return $r_{t+1} \equiv \ln((D_{t+1} + P_{t+1})/P_t) - r_f$ is determined by the price-dividend ratio and the realization of dividend growth:

$$r_{t+1} = \ln \frac{1 + Q(M_{t+1})}{Q(M_t)} + \mu_d(M_{t+1}) - r_f - \frac{\sigma_d^2(M_{t+1})}{2} + \sigma_d(M_{t+1}) \varepsilon_{d,t+1}. \tag{9.7}$$

The likelihood function $L(r_1, \ldots, r_T)$ has the closed-form expression given in the Appendix.

---

[8] Forward iteration implies $Q(M_t) = \mathbb{E}_t \sum_{n=1}^{+\infty} [\Pi_{h=1}^{n} e^{\mu_d(M_{t+h}) - r_f - \alpha \rho_{c,d} \sigma_c \sigma_d(M_{t+h})}]$.

9.2 Volatility Feedback with Multifrequency Shocks

We now apply the above equilibrium to the case of multifrequency dividend news.

9.2.1 Multifrequency Dividend News

We assume that the volatility of dividend news follows a binomial MSM process $(m_0, \bar{\sigma}_d, b, \gamma_{\bar{k}})$, as in Chapter 3. That is, given a state vector $M_t = (M_{1,t}; M_{2,t}; \ldots; M_{\bar{k},t}) \in \mathbb{R}_+^{\bar{k}}$, volatility is specified by

$$\sigma_d(M_t) \equiv \bar{\sigma}_d \left(\prod_{k=1}^{\bar{k}} M_{k,t} \right)^{1/2}, \tag{9.8}$$

where $\bar{\sigma}_d > 0$ is constant. The components $M_{k,t}$ take two possible values, $m_0 \in [1, 2]$ and $2 - m_0 \in [0, 1]$, with equal probability, and the transition probabilities γ_k are parameterized by $\gamma_k = 1 - (1 - \gamma_{\bar{k}})^{(b^{k-\bar{k}})}$. Consistent with empirical evidence, the first component may have transitions measured in years or even decades, corresponding to low-frequency shocks to technology or demographics. Medium-run components might represent business cycle fluctuations, and high-frequency components may capture liquidity or other transient effects. We need not specify the source of these fluctuations in advance. As in earlier chapters, the number of components and their frequencies will be inferred directly from returns.

Following earlier research (e.g., CH), we initially restrict the dividend growth rate to be constant:

$$\mu_d(M_t) \equiv \bar{\mu}_d.$$

We later extend the empirical implementation to include a state-dependent drift in dividend news.

The MSM volatility specification has a number of appealing properties in the context of equity modeling. Low-frequency multipliers deliver persistent and discrete switches, consistent with evidence of apparent nonstationarity in stock returns (e.g., Schwert, 1989; Pagan and Schwert, 1990). High-frequency multipliers give additional outliers through their direct effect on the tails of the dividend news process. Furthermore, multiplicative interaction implies that total volatility can quickly switch from an extreme to a normal level, as has been observed in equity data (e.g., Schwert, 1990a). We expect that these features of MSM will help to fit U.S. stock returns over a long time span as well as to generate substantial volatility feedback.

9.2.2   Equilibrium Stock Returns

We combine the general regime-switching economy in Section 9.1 with the MSM specification for dividend news. Equilibrium excess returns on the stock satisfy

$$r_{t+1} = \ln \frac{1 + Q(M_{t+1})}{Q(M_t)} + \bar{\mu}_d - r_f - \frac{\sigma_d^2(M_{t+1})}{2} + \sigma_d(M_{t+1})\varepsilon_{d,t+1}. \quad (9.9)$$

Volatility feedback appears through the term $\ln([1 + Q(M_{t+1})]/Q(M_t))$. Intuitively, an increase in a volatility component causes a decrease in the price-dividend ratio, which leads to a low realized return. In the Appendix, we use a loglinearized return equation to confirm this logic and show that (i) the magnitude of the feedback due to a shift in an individual component is approximately proportional to the inverse of the persistence level γ_k; (ii) the conditional return increases with the magnitude of the volatility components. Thus, lower-frequency components drive the conditional mean and can induce large feedback effects.

The structural model implies tight specifications for consumption, dividends, the riskless interest rate (9.4), the price-dividend ratio (9.6), and excess stock returns (9.9). The economy is specified by preferences (α, δ, ψ), consumption (g_c, σ_c), dividends $(m_0, \gamma_{\bar{k}}, b, \bar{\mu}_d, \bar{\sigma}_d)$, and the correlation $\rho_{c,d}$.

The variables g_c, ψ, and δ appear only in the interest rate equation. For any desired values of g_c, ψ, and the other parameters (α and σ_c), we can choose δ to match an arbitrary fixed interest rate. Without loss of generality, we therefore calibrate the interest rate to its long-run value $\bar{r}_f$. In this chapter, the implied δ always takes annualized values in the 0.96 to 0.995 range, which seems reasonable.

Following the literature, we calibrate the mean price-dividend ratio to a plausible long-run value

$$\mathbb{E}\left[Q(M_t)\right] = \bar{Q}, \quad (9.10)$$

where $\bar{Q}$ is obtained from aggregate dividend data. Since $\mathbb{E}\left[Q(M_t)\right]$ monotonically decreases in $\alpha\sigma_c\rho_{c,d}$, the restriction on the average price-dividend ratio identifies $\alpha\sigma_c\rho_{c,d}$, conditional on the values of the five dividend parameters. By taking values of σ_c and $\rho_{c,d}$ from consumption and dividend data, we can then infer an implied value for the risk aversion coefficient α. Given our standard setup, we anticipate that matching the equity premium in long-run data will require relatively large risk aversion, as suggested by Hansen and Jagannathan (1991). To demonstrate that our base results are robust to lower values of α, we conclude this chapter with an extension that adds long-run consumption risk.

Given calibrated values of the risk-free rate and the average price-dividend ratio, excess stock returns are specified by

$$(m_0, \gamma_{\bar{k}}, b, \bar{\mu}_d, \bar{\sigma}_d) \in \mathbb{R}^5.$$

The parameters $\bar{\mu}_d$ and $\bar{\sigma}_d$ are important variables in any consumption-based asset pricing model, while $m_0, \gamma_{\bar{k}}$, and b are specific to the MSM specification. We calibrate $\bar{\mu}_d$ and $\bar{\sigma}_d$ to commonly used values derived from aggregate dividend data, and we estimate the MSM parameters by maximizing the likelihood of daily excess returns.

This approach is motivated by the relative advantages of dividends versus stock returns in estimating parameters of the news process. We want the estimated model to be consistent with reasonable values for the long-run mean and standard deviation of dividend growth, and this is easily accomplished by directly calibrating the parameters $\bar{\mu}_d$ and $\bar{\sigma}_d$ to observed dividends. On the other hand, the dynamics of news volatility may be better reflected in stock prices than in dividends themselves. We therefore infer $m_0, \gamma_{\bar{k}}$, and b from stock return data.

Unlike the existing literature, the MSM setup can accommodate an arbitrarily large number of volatility frequencies while retaining a small and constant number of parameters. This allows us to estimate a fully specified structural model of volatility feedback at a daily observation frequency.

9.3 Empirical Results with Fully Informed Investors

9.3.1 Excess Return Data

We estimate the multifrequency equilibrium model on the daily excess returns of a U.S. equity index from January 1926 to December 2003. As in CH, we combine the Schwert (1990b) daily index from 1926 to 1963 with CRSP value-weighted returns from 1963 onward, and we subtract a daily risk-free rate imputed from 30-day Treasury bills. The entire period contains 20,765 observations ("full sample"). We also report results for the period beginning in 1952, which corresponds to a change in interest rate regime with the Fed-Treasury Accord. This latter sample contains 13,109 observations ("postwar sample").

Figure 9.1 depicts the data, demonstrating the thick tails, low-frequency cycles, and negative skewness that are widely recognized characteristics of aggregate stock returns. To further indicate how conditions change across different periods over the long span of the data, Table 9.1 reports moments of the excess return series for four evenly spaced subperiods of each sample. These vary substantially, consistent with Schwert (1989) and Pagan and

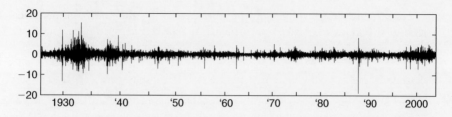

FIGURE 9.1. **Daily Excess Returns on U.S. Aggregate Equity.** This figure shows daily excess returns on U.S. aggregate equity from 1926 to 2003. The market return series splices the Schwert (1990a) data from 1926–1963 with the CRSP value-weighted index from 1963–2003. The risk-free rate is proxied by the return on 30-day U.S. Treasury bills.

TABLE 9.1. Excess Return Moments

	Sample Moment	By Subperiod			
		1	2	3	4
	A. Full Sample: 1926–2003				
Mean	0.022	0.010	0.043	0.013	0.024
Standard deviation	1.10	1.64	0.76	0.77	1.00
Skewness	−0.30	0.09	0.96	0.07	−1.55
Kurtosis	20.5	11.5	11.4	5.79	32.2
	B. Postwar: 1952–2003				
Mean	0.023	0.044	−0.004	0.021	0.030
Standard deviation	0.86	0.67	0.77	0.93	1.02
Skewness	−1.05	−0.70	0.13	−2.83	−0.21
Kurtosis	26.5	13.3	5.76	59.8	7.18

Notes: This table reports statistics of the first four moments of daily excess returns on U.S. aggregate equity for the full sample (1926–2003, Panel A) and the postwar sample (1952–2003, Panel B). Each panel also shows the value of the statistics in four evenly spaced subsamples. All four moments show considerable variability across subsamples.

Schwert (1990). The data therefore contain high-frequency variations as well as substantial movements at low frequencies.

9.3.2   Maximum Likelihood Estimation and Volatility Feedback

We begin by investigating the model under a single set of calibrated values. We choose the average price-dividend ratio $\bar{Q} = 25$, similar to the long-run estimates reported by Campbell (2003) and Fama and French (2002). For the standard deviation of real dividend growth, we initially set $\bar{\sigma}_d = 0.70\%$

per day (about 11% per year), in the middle of the range of U.S. historical estimates[9] and also close to values used in earlier literature (e.g., Campbell and Cochrane, 1999; Bansal and Yaron, 2004). To acknowledge the uncertainty surrounding $\bar{\sigma}_d$ and the importance of this parameter, we examine $\bar{\sigma}_d$ closely in subsequent sensitivity analysis, using values ranging from 7.75 to 12.4% annually. Finally, we choose $\bar{\mu}_d$ to approximate the long-run average dividend growth rate and give a reasonable equity premium. The initial calibration sets $\bar{\mu}_d - r_f$ to 0.5 basis points (bp) per day, or about 1.2% per year. Given an annual risk-free rate of 1%, this implies $\bar{\mu}_d = 2.2\%$ per year, implying an average equity premium of about 4.6% annually. The base calibration thus ensures reasonable values for the real dividend growth mean and variance, price-dividend ratio, and equity premium.

Table 9.2 reports maximum likelihood (ML) estimation results for the MSM volatility parameters $(m_0, \gamma_{\bar{k}}, b)$, conditional on the calibrated parameters. For the full sample in Panel A, and the postwar sample in Panel B, we consider a range of volatility components $\bar{k}$ varying from one to eight. The first row ($\bar{k} = 1$) of each panel corresponds to a standard regime-switching model with only two possible volatility states. Examining the likelihood as $\bar{k}$ increases, we see the benefits of a multifrequency specification. Moving from one to two volatility components, the log-likelihood increases by over 3,000 points in the full sample and over 700 points in the postwar sample. Since this requires adding only one more parameter (from two to three), the increase in likelihood is large by any standard model selection criterion.[10] Increasing the number of frequencies from two to three raises the log-likelihood by an additional 1,360 points in the full sample and 260 points in the postwar sample, but does not increase the number of parameters. Substantial increases in the likelihood continue, without adding more parameters, throughout the set of $\bar{k}$ that we examine. The likelihood function appears monotonically increasing and concave in $\bar{k}$, and flattens markedly by the time we reach the maximum value of $\bar{k} = 8$.

We assess significance in the log-likelihood differences using the Vuong (1989) test and the heteroskedasticity and autocorrelation consistent (HAC) version proposed in Chapter 3. For each sample and each value of $\bar{k} \in \{1, \ldots, 7\}$, we test the hypothesis that the specification has a higher likelihood than the model with $\bar{k} = 8$ components. The statistical

---

[9]Earlier research gives a relatively wide range of estimates for the standard deviation of U.S. real dividend growth. Campbell (2003) reports a standard deviation of 14.02% over the 1891 to 1998 period and of 16.80% between 1970 and 1998. Fama and French (2002) estimate a standard deviation of real dividend growth equal to 5.09% between 1951 and 2000, and 12.37% between 1872 and 2000. Bansal and Yaron (2004) report a value of 11.49% for the annual 1929 to 1998 series.

[10]For example, using the Akaike Information Criterion (AIC) or Bayesian Information Criterion (BIC), the necessary increase in likelihood to justify one additional parameter would be less than five points for either sample size.

TABLE 9.2. Combined Calibration/Estimation

	Calibrated Parameters						Estimated Parameters				Return Moments					
$\bar{k}$	$\bar{\sigma}_d$	$\bar{\mu}_d - r_f$	P/D	AEP	$\alpha\sigma_{c,d}$	m_0	$\gamma_{\bar{k}}$	b	ln L	mean	s.d.	skew	kurt	FB	LDY
	(%/d)	(%/d)	(a)	(a)	(%/d)	(d)	(d)	(d)	(d)	(%d)	(%d)	(d)	(d)	(%)	(a)

A. Full Sample: 1926–2003

$\bar{k}$	$\bar{\sigma}_d$	$\bar{\mu}_d - r_f$	P/D	AEP	$\alpha\sigma_{c,d}$	m_0	$\gamma_{\bar{k}}$	b	ln L	mean	s.d.	skew	kurt	FB	LDY
1	0.70	0.005	25.0	4.61	0.024	1.774 (0.005)	0.057 (0.005)	—	64820.3	0.019	0.702	−0.038	4.8	0.7	0.1
2	0.70	0.005	25.0	4.61	0.026	1.724 (0.004)	0.056 (0.005)	21.30 (2.10)	67860.9	0.019	0.742	−0.063	14.4	12.5	1.6
3	0.70	0.005	25.0	4.61	0.028	1.703 (0.005)	0.054 (0.005)	4.92 (0.31)	69224.9	0.019	0.755	−0.099	18.7	16.3	1.8
4	0.70	0.005	25.0	4.61	0.029	1.637 (0.006)	0.087 (0.004)	5.95 (0.23)	69752.3	0.019	0.838	−0.078	233.1	43.3	9.6
5	0.70	0.005	25.0	4.61	0.028	1.558 (0.008)	0.047 (0.004)	2.54 (0.08)	70066.9	0.019	0.774	−0.099	29.5	22.4	3.7
6	0.70	0.005	25.0	4.61	0.029	1.523 (0.007)	0.059 (0.007)	2.84 (0.17)	70214.6	0.019	0.837	−0.080	164.8	43.1	12.7
7	0.70	0.005	25.0	4.61	0.029	1.477 (0.007)	0.058 (0.006)	2.73 (0.11)	70318.1	0.019	0.863	−0.065	298.9	51.8	29.0
8	0.70	0.005	25.0	4.61	0.028	1.435 (0.008)	0.058 (0.009)	2.19 (0.11)	70355.7	0.019	0.830	−0.072	131.7	40.5	16.9

B. Postwar: 1952–2003

$\bar{k}$															
1	0.70	0.005	25.0	4.61	0.023	1.645 (0.008)	0.038 (0.005)	—	45028.6	0.019	0.702	−0.025	4.2	0.6	0.1
2	0.70	0.005	25.0	4.61	0.024	1.599 (0.008)	0.036 (0.006)	3.91 (0.55)	45730.4	0.019	0.710	−0.046	5.5	2.7	0.4
3	0.70	0.005	25.0	4.61	0.025	1.527 (0.010)	0.051 (0.008)	5.31 (0.45)	45990.9	0.019	0.731	−0.049	10.4	9.0	2.2
4	0.70	0.005	25.0	4.61	0.025	1.479 (0.009)	0.037 (0.006)	3.06 (0.20)	46116.0	0.019	0.741	−0.054	13.7	12.0	3.2
5	0.70	0.005	25.0	4.61	0.025	1.444 (0.007)	0.042 (0.006)	2.45 (0.12)	46183.3	0.019	0.743	−0.058	14.0	12.8	3.6
6	0.70	0.005	25.0	4.61	0.025	1.390 (0.010)	0.037 (0.006)	2.00 (0.10)	46206.4	0.019	0.739	−0.054	11.2	11.5	3.6
7	0.70	0.005	25.0	4.61	0.025	1.371 (0.012)	0.053 (0.009)	2.28 (0.10)	46227.0	0.019	0.770	−0.048	43.2	21.0	10.9
8	0.70	0.005	25.0	4.61	0.026	1.369 (0.010)	0.047 (0.010)	2.15 (0.13)	46241.6	0.019	0.796	−0.049	84.8	29.4	18.2

Notes: This table shows parameter estimates for the full-information regime-switching model for a number of volatility components $\bar{k}$ ranging from one to eight. The table holds constant the calibrated dividend volatility $\bar{\sigma}_d = 0.7\%$ per day (about 11% per year), excess dividend growth $\bar{\mu}_d - r_f = 0.5$ bp per day (about 1.2% per year), and an annual price dividend ratio of 25. For each value of $\bar{k}$, the MSM volatility parameters m_0, $\gamma_{\bar{k}}$, and b are then estimated on daily data by maximum likelihood. The optimized value of the likelihood function is given by ln L. Excess dividend growth and average P/D determine the annual equity premium (AEP), and the constraint on average P/D identifies the product $\alpha\sigma_{c,d} \equiv \alpha\bar{\sigma}_d\sigma_c\rho_{c,d}$. The table reports implied statistics for the first four moments of daily returns, the feedback (FB), and the duration of the lowest-frequency shock in years (LDY). Where a variable depends on time scale or units, it is noted in parentheses under the variable description using the notation "d" for day and "a" for annual. Asymptotic standard errors for the estimated parameters are reported in parentheses beneath each reported value, conditional on the values of the calibrated parameters.

significance of the preference for the model with $\bar{k} = 8$ components is moderate in the postwar sample and strong in the full sample.

The parameter estimates in Table 9.2 follow reasonable patterns as $\bar{k}$ varies. In both samples, the multiplier m_0 decreases monotonically as components are added, as in Chapters 3 and 4. The switching probability $\gamma_{\bar{k}}$ of the highest-frequency component is fairly stable across specifications, while the spacing parameter b tends to fall with $\bar{k}$. These results imply that the highest-frequency volatility shocks have durations of approximately 15 to 30 days. Adding volatility components tends to tighten the intrafrequency spacing b as well as to extend the low-frequency range of volatility variations.

We report the largest duration in yearly units (LDY) in the next-to-last column of Table 9.2. For low $\bar{k}$, LDY tends to be under one year. Under the preferred specifications with six to eight components, the lowest-frequency shocks are in the range of 10 to 20 years, a potentially reasonable value for technology or demographic changes. Since the frequency parameters driving the LDY statistics are estimated directly through the equilibrium likelihood function, this finding provides additional support for earlier specifications emphasizing low-frequency shocks. The estimated durations of LDY are roughly consistent with the durations assumed by Lettau, Ludvigson, and Wachter (2004) and suggest that the approximately 2.5-year half-life of shocks in Bansal and Yaron (2004) may even be somewhat conservative.

Table 9.2 also reports statistics of the first four moments for each specification. The mean return of approximately 1.9 bp per day is close to the values of 2.2 in the full sample and 2.3 in the postwar sample, and does not vary substantially across specifications with different $\bar{k}$. The volatility of excess returns tends to increase with $\bar{k}$. In the postwar sample, the specifications with large $\bar{k}$ have standard deviations of 0.8% per day, which is similar to the empirical value of 0.85%. In the full sample, the unconditional standard deviation is larger for $\bar{k} = 8$ at 0.83% per day, but is still substantially smaller than the approximately 1.1% in the data. The model produces moderate negative skewness, but not as much as in the data, and specifications with large $\bar{k}$ seem to have high kurtosis relative to the data. We later use investor learning to endogenously attenuate kurtosis and enhance negative skewness.

The unconditional volatility feedback

$$FB = \frac{Var(r_{t+1})}{Var(d_{t+1} - d_t)} - 1$$

is presented in the last column of Table 9.2. Feedback increases as components are added: for the best performing models with $\bar{k} \geq 6$, equilibrium pricing amplifies the variance of dividends by about 40 to 50% in the full sample and 11 to 30% in the postwar data. These numbers are substantially higher than the 1 to 2% reported by Campbell and Hentschel (1992).

9.3.3   Comparison with Campbell and Hentschel (1992)

The CH specification, described in the Appendix, provides a good comparison for our approach. Table 9.3 reports ML estimation results for the CH model on both samples. Panel A provides parameter estimates that are comparable to those found in the original CH study. The implied half-life of a volatility shock is about six months for both samples, which is again consistent with CH (1992). As in the original study, feedback contributes between 1 and 2% of unconditional variance and is thus small relative to the MSM equilibrium.

Panel B compares the in-sample fit of the CH model to the multi-frequency specification with $\bar{k} = 8$ volatility components. Although the MSM equilibrium has four fewer free parameters, its likelihood is over 400 points larger in the full sample and almost 200 points larger in the postwar sample. We adjust for the number of parameters by calculating the Bayesian Information Criterion statistic for each specification, and we assess significance using the Vuong (1989) test and the HAC-adjusted version defined

TABLE 9.3. Comparison with Campbell and Hentschel (1992)

A. CH Parameter Estimates							
	$\omega \times 10^7$	α_1	α_2	β	$b \times 10^3$	$\mu \times 10^4$	γ
Full Sample	1.87	0.140	−0.073	0.925	3.05	3.60	0.14
	(0.78)	(0.01)	(0.01)	(0.004)	(0.18)	(0.53)	(0.03)
Postwar	0.53	0.145	−0.088	0.934	3.04	3.47	0.47
	(0.74)	(0.01)	(0.01)	(0.005)	(0.20)	(0.57)	(0.09)

B. Likelihood Comparison						
					BIC p-value vs. MSM	
		Free Parameters	$\ln L$	BIC	Vuong (1989)	HAC Adj
Full Sample	MSM	3	70355.7	−6.7749		
	QGARCH	7	69920.7	−6.7311	< 0.001	< 0.001
Postwar	MSM	3	46241.6	−7.0527		
	QGARCH	7	46057.3	−7.0218	< 0.001	< 0.001

Notes: Panel A shows parameter estimates from the CH volatility feedback model. Panel B gives a comparison of the in-sample fit versus the multifrequency regime-switching economy. The Bayesian Information Criterion is given by $BIC = T^{-1}(-2\ln L + NP\ln T)$. The last two columns in Panel B give p-values from a test that the QGARCH dividend specification dominates the MSM equilibrium by the BIC criterion. The first value uses the Vuong (1989) methodology, and the second value adjusts the test for heteroskedasticity and autocorrelation. A low p-value indicates that the CH specification would be rejected in favor of the MSM equilibrium.

in Chapter 3. The difference is significant in both samples. MSM equilibria with $\bar{k} > 4$ volatility components have a higher likelihood than CH in the full sample, and in the postwar sample MSM specifications with $\bar{k} > 3$ have a higher likelihood, confirming that the multifrequency equilibrium generates large feedback effects and performs well in-sample relative to an important benchmark.

9.3.4   Conditional Inference

In the full-information framework, investors directly observe the volatility state M_t, but the empiricist makes inferences based only on excess returns $\mathcal{R}_t \equiv \{r_s; s \leq t\}$. The Appendix explains how to calculate the *filtered* probabilities $\hat{\Pi}_t^j \equiv \mathbb{P}\left(M_t = m^j \,|\, \mathcal{R}_t\right)$ as well as the *smoothed* probabilities $\hat{\Psi}_t^j \equiv \mathbb{P}\left(M_t = m^j \,|\, \mathcal{R}_T\right)$ for $j \in \{1, \ldots, 2^{\bar{k}}\}$. The filtered probabilities are useful for forecasting, while their smoothed versions allow for the most informative ex post analysis of the data.

Figure 9.2 displays the corresponding marginals of each component when $\bar{k} = 8$. Let

$$\hat{\Pi}_t^{M(k)} \equiv \mathbb{P}\left(M_{k,t} = m_0 \,|\, \mathcal{R}_t\right) \quad \text{and} \quad \hat{\Psi}_t^{M(k)} \equiv \mathbb{P}\left(M_{k,t} = m_0 \,|\, \mathcal{R}_T\right),$$

respectively, denote the filtered and smoothed probabilities that volatility component $k \in \{1, \ldots, \bar{k}\}$ is in a high state. Filtered probabilities on the left side of the figure show sensible patterns. For the lowest frequency $k = 1$, the probability rises over time from 0.5 to around 0.75 until the 1987 crash, at which point it jumps immediately to almost 1.0. The model therefore attributes a portion of the very large price drop to an increase in low-frequency volatility. By contrast, when a smaller but still substantial price decline of about -8% occurs just after 1955, probabilities about the first $k = 1$ and second $k = 2$ components move little, but the third component $k = 3$ jumps upward substantially. For low values of k, the conditional distribution of the volatility state spends considerable time at the extreme values of zero and one. By contrast, at high frequencies, probabilities move up and down rapidly, but rarely reach their boundaries. The smoothed marginals move less frequently but in larger increments, and spend more time near the boundaries of zero and one.

In Figure 9.3, we use the filtered probabilities to compute the one-step-ahead conditional mean and variance of returns. As implied by equilibrium conditions, these are positively correlated, showing small peaks in the early 1970s and high levels in 1987 and around 2000. Recent literature (Ghysels, Santa-Clara, and Valkanov, 2005; Lundblad, 2007) finds empirical support for this type of relation.

The asset pricing literature emphasizes that the market discount rate exhibits small and persistent variations over time, as reviewed in Campbell

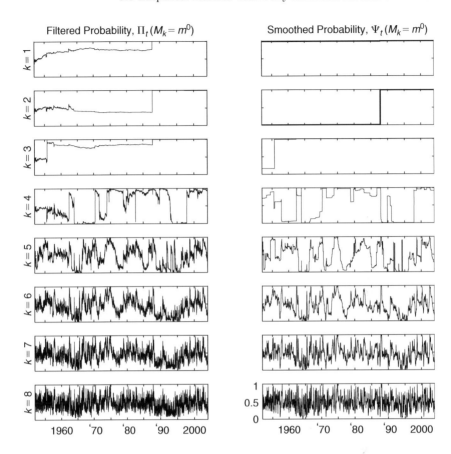

FIGURE 9.2. **Conditional Probabilities of Volatility Components.** This figure illustrates the filtered and smoothed probabilities that each volatility component $k, 1 \leq k \leq 8$ is in the high state on a given day. Inference is based on the full-information MSM equilibrium with $\bar{k} = 8$ components, and parameters estimated from the postwar data. The filtered probabilities Π_t are in the left-hand column, and the smoothed probabilites Ψ_t are in the right-hand column. Volatility components progress from low ($k = 1$) to high ($k = 8$) frequency from top to bottom of the figure.

(2003). Feedback models focus on cyclical variations in dividend news volatility as a possible source of these fluctuations. While our multi-frequency volatility specification permits multiple sources of volatility fluctuations in accord with economic intuition, one might worry that this would lead to a conditional mean that is "too variable" or "too jumpy." Figure 9.3 shows that this is not in fact the case. The conditional discount rate moves slowly because it is dominated by the most persistent volatility components.

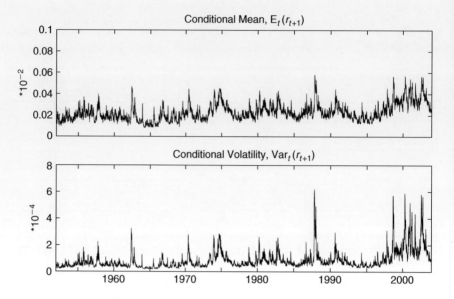

FIGURE 9.3. **Ex Ante Conditional Mean and Volatility.** This figure shows the conditional mean and variance of excess returns under the full-information MSM equilibrium with $\bar{k} = 8$ volatility components, and parameters estimated from postwar data. Conditioning information is the ex ante information set of returns up to and including date t.

9.3.5 Return Decomposition

We now develop an ex post decomposition of U.S. equity returns. At time $t + 1$ or later, the fully informed investor observes the excess return r_{t+1} and can implement

$$r_{t+1} = \mathbb{E}\left(r_{t+1}|M_t\right) + \left[\mathbb{E}\left(r_{t+1}|M_t, M_{t+1}\right) - \mathbb{E}\left(r_{t+1}|M_t\right)\right] + \sigma_d(M_{t+1})\varepsilon_{d,t+1}.$$

This separates the realized return into its expected value at time t, the innovation due to the volatility feedback, and the multifrequency dividend news.

The empiricist with the smaller information set $\mathcal{R}_T$ can derive an analogous but less precise decomposition derived in the Appendix. The relation $r_{t+1} = \mathbb{E}\left(r_{t+1}|\mathcal{R}_T\right)$ implies

$$r_{t+1} = \mathbb{E}_{\hat{\Psi}_t} r_{t+1} + \left(\mathbb{E}_{\hat{\Psi}_{t+1}} - \mathbb{E}_{\hat{\Psi}_t}\right) r_{t+1} + \hat{e}_{d,t+1}, \qquad (9.11)$$

where

$$\hat{e}_{d,t+1} \equiv \mathbb{E}[\sigma_d(M_{t+1})\varepsilon_{d,t+1}|\mathcal{R}_T] \qquad (9.12)$$

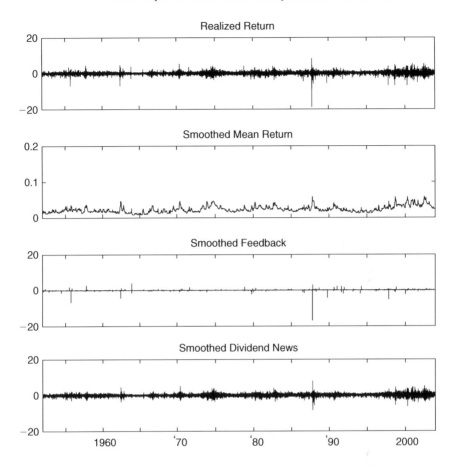

FIGURE 9.4. **Ex Post Return Decomposition.** This figure shows an ex post decomposition of realized returns using the full-information MSM equilibrium with $\bar{k} = 8$ components and parameters estimated on postwar data. The decomposition uses the smoothed beliefs Ψ_t obtained by using the conditioning information set of all returns. The first panel shows actual returns. The second panel shows the mean return at time $t + 1$ conditional on the beliefs Ψ_t. The third panel shows the estimated amount of returns due to volatility feedback at time $t + 1$ conditional on all of the data. The final panel is the smoothed estimate of dividend news, equal to the realized return less the second and third panels.

is the ex post estimate of realized dividend news. By the law of iterated expectations, $\hat{e}_{d,t+1}$ has mean zero.

We implement the ex post decomposition in Figure 9.4. The top panel illustrates the excess return series $\{r_t\}$, and the remaining panels show the three smoothed terms of (9.11), that is the conditional return, volatility feedback, and dividend news. The smoothed conditional return in the second panel of Figure 9.4 shows small persistent variations, very much like the ex ante conditional return in Figure 9.3. By contrast, the smoothed feedback in the third panel appears in intermittent bursts. On most days it is small, but its occurrences coincide with the most substantial variations in the series, and on these days it contributes a large portion of realized returns. These features are consistent with the intuition that low-frequency volatility changes are infrequent but have a large price impact. This ex post analysis attributes over half of the 1987 crash to volatility feedback.

In the bottom panel of Figure 9.4, the residual $\hat{e}_{d,t+1}$ is the filtered version of a symmetric MSM process. We calculate its sample moments and find variance of 0.635, skewness of -0.123, and kurtosis of 8.00. Relative to the actual return data, the residual variance is approximately 16% smaller, skewness is 88% smaller, and kurtosis is 79% smaller. These findings suggest that endogenous volatility feedback plays an important role in explaining the higher moments of returns in our sample.

9.3.6 Alternative Calibrations

We now examine the robustness of the results to alternative calibrations of the main economic parameters. Specifically, we explore different values of the calibrated mean $\bar{\mu}_d$ and standard deviation $\bar{\sigma}_d$ of dividend growth and of the average price-dividend ratio $\bar{Q}$. For each alternative calibration, we reestimate the volatility parameters $(m_0, \gamma_{\bar{k}}, b)$ of the MSM equilibrium with $\bar{k} = 8$ components using the constrained likelihood function.

We also assess how likely each model is to generate return moments similar to the data. For each specification, we simulate 1,000 paths of the same length as the data and calculate the fraction of paths for which a given statistic (mean, variance, skewness, kurtosis) exceeds the corresponding empirical moment.

The results of the estimations and simulated p-values are reported in Table 9.4. The first four rows in each panel hold $\bar{\sigma}_d$ constant at 0.7% per day, but allow for varying combinations of $\bar{Q} \in \{25, 30\}$ and $\bar{\mu}_d - r_f \in \{0.5, 1.0\}$ bp per day, or 1.2% and 2.4% on an annual basis. Increasing the price-dividend ratio $\bar{Q}$ leads to a lower equity premium (through the Gordon growth formula), which decreases feedback. To partially compensate, the estimates of m_0 and b increase slightly, implying somewhat larger and more persistent volatility shocks. Overall, the effect of the lower equity premium dominates, and the feedback measure FB declines as the average price-dividend ratio increases. Similarly, raising the dividend growth rate $\bar{\mu}_d$ augments the equity premium and the magnitude of price shocks. The parameters m_0 and b decrease to partially compensate, and the net effect on feedback is positive. The likelihood tends to increase with $\bar{\mu}_d$ and decrease with $\bar{Q}$, and thus favors specifications with a larger feedback.

The final three rows in each panel hold $\bar{\mu}_d$ and $\bar{Q}$ constant at their original values and allow dividend volatility $\bar{\sigma}_d$ to increase to 0.8% per day (approximately 12.4% annually) or to decrease to 0.6 or 0.5% per day (9.3 and 7.7% annually). These changes in dividend volatility have a considerable impact. When $\bar{\sigma}_d$ is low, the model needs to generate large feedback in order to better approximate the volatility of excess stock returns. Generally, this tends to favor larger and more persistent volatility shocks. In the full sample, the model with $\bar{\sigma}_d = 0.5$ generates extremely large kurtosis (1,481) and very persistent shocks (LDY = 160 years); the estimated feedback is over 150%. Larger values of $\bar{\sigma}_d$ generate more moderate feedback in the range of 30 to 50%, and have substantially higher likelihood. In the postwar period, for which average return volatility is not as high, the model better accommodates low values of $\bar{\sigma}_d$. The highest likelihood in the postwar data occurs in the base case in which $\bar{\sigma}_d = 0.7$.

The simulated p-values show that the model captures well the mean return. The empirical skewness is more negative than expected under the model, but typically within the range of values that can be generated with our sample sizes. In the postwar period, the return volatility is lower than implied by the model, but the p-values are not significant. In the full sample, the p-values for the second moment are significant at the 5% level. All of the full-sample specifications and some of the postwar specifications have significant p-values for a kurtosis that is too large. In summary, large feedback effects are robust across different calibrations, but kurtosis can become excessive when dividend volatility is very low. In the next section, we maintain the symmetric MSM dividend process and show that learning about stochastic volatility can be a powerful method to endogenously amplify negative skewness and reduce kurtosis.

9.4   Learning about Volatility and Endogenous Skewness

Financial economists have long considered that investors observe only noisy signals about fundamentals, and a large literature has investigated how Bayesian learning about future cash flows and discount rates can affect asset prices and other equilibrium outcomes (e.g., Brennan, 1998; Brennan and Xia, 2001; David, 1997; Guidolin and Timmermann, 2003; Pastor and Veronesi, 2008; Timmermann, 1993, 1996; Veronesi, 1999, 2000, 2004). Following this tradition, we assume in this section that investors receive only imperfect signals about the volatility state vector M_t. Signal quality controls a trade-off between endogenous skewness and kurtosis: as information quality deteriorates, returns exhibit less kurtosis and more negative skewness. We show that (i) the size of the volatility feedback effect is not highly sensitive to the learning environment, and (ii) intermediate information levels best capture the higher moments of stock returns.

TABLE 9.4. Alternative Calibrations

Calibrated Parameters					Estimated Parameters				Return Moments				FB	LDY
$\bar{\sigma}_d$	$\bar{\mu}_d - r_f$	P/D	AEP	$\alpha\sigma_{c,d}$	m_0	γ_k	b	$\ln L$	mean	s.d.	skew	kurt		
(%/d)	(%/d)	(a)	(a)	(%/d)	(d)	(d)	(d)	(d)	(%/d)	(%/d)	(d)	(d)	(%)	(a)

A. Full Sample: 1926–2003

$\bar{\sigma}_d$	$\bar{\mu}_d - r_f$	P/D	AEP	$\alpha\sigma_{c,d}$	m_0	γ_k	b	$\ln L$	mean	s.d.	skew	kurt	FB	LDY
0.70	0.005	25.0	4.61	0.028	1.435 (0.008)	0.058 (0.009)	2.19 (0.11)	70355.7	0.019 (0.755)	0.830 (0.991)	−0.072 (0.368)	131.7 (0.003)	40.5	16.9
0.70	0.005	30.0	3.95	0.024	1.438 (0.008)	0.057 (0.008)	2.24 (0.09)	70347.0	0.016 (0.893)	0.818 (0.991)	−0.070 (0.386)	138.3 (0.005)	36.5	20.0
0.70	0.010	25.0	5.81	0.034	1.430 (0.008)	0.061 (0.003)	2.12 (0.04)	70365.3	0.024 (0.349)	0.866 (0.992)	−0.073 (0.368)	150.9 (0.000)	53.0	12.7
0.70	0.010	30.0	5.15	0.031	1.432 (0.007)	0.059 (0.007)	2.14 (0.08)	70359.5	0.021 (0.578)	0.855 (0.985)	−0.072 (0.387)	158.0 (0.000)	49.1	14.2
0.80	0.005	25.0	4.43	0.027	1.422 (0.008)	0.059 (0.009)	2.24 (0.10)	70378.6	0.018 (0.765)	0.913 (0.907)	−0.069 (0.355)	96.4 (0.010)	30.2	19.2
0.60	0.005	25.0	4.77	0.030	1.475 (0.006)	0.066 (0.008)	2.73 (0.13)	70339.6	0.020 (0.718)	0.822 (0.927)	−0.055 (0.441)	695.2 (0.000)	87.6	68.9
0.50	0.005	25.0	4.90	0.032	1.514 (0.006)	0.085 (0.009)	3.23 (0.16)	70261.8	0.020 (0.642)	0.786 (0.920)	−0.042 (0.483)	1481.0 (0.000)	247.2	170.8

B. Postwar: 1952–2003

0.70	0.005	25.0	4.61	0.026	1.369 (0.010)	0.047 (0.010)	2.15 (0.13)	46241.6	0.019 (0.754)	0.796 (0.717)	-0.049 (0.185)	84.8 (0.071)	29.4	18.2
0.70	0.005	30.0	3.95	0.023	1.371 (0.010)	0.045 (0.008)	2.19 (0.10)	46235.6	0.016 (0.881)	0.787 (0.742)	-0.047 (0.236)	87.9 (0.132)	26.5	21.6
0.70	0.010	25.0	5.81	0.032	1.365 (0.010)	0.049 (0.010)	2.07 (0.12)	46249.0	0.024 (0.420)	0.824 (0.602)	-0.052 (0.195)	99.5 (0.043)	38.5	13.4
0.70	0.010	30.0	5.15	0.029	1.367 (0.010)	0.047 (0.012)	2.10 (0.16)	46245.1	0.021 (0.591)	0.816 (0.647)	-0.051 (0.200)	104.8 (0.045)	35.8	15.2
0.80	0.005	25.0	4.43	0.025	1.337 (0.012)	0.064 (0.014)	2.07 (0.10)	46237.3	0.018 (0.739)	0.854 (0.558)	-0.047 (0.001)	21.5 (0.719)	13.9	10.3
0.60	0.005	25.0	4.77	0.026	1.372 (0.012)	0.057 (0.006)	2.25 (0.07)	46231.4	0.020 (0.743)	0.713 (0.885)	-0.047 (0.266)	154.0 (0.039)	41.4	20.8
0.50	0.005	25.0	4.90	0.027	1.405 (0.010)	0.048 (0.008)	2.49 (0.14)	46217.0	0.020 (0.722)	0.686 (0.889)	-0.037 (0.377)	593.9 (0.007)	88.1	49.8

Notes: This table shows parameter estimates conditional on alternative calibrations of the structural parameters in the MSM equilibrium. All estimated economies use $\bar{k} = 8$ components. The first group of four rows in each panel holds constant average dividend volatility $\bar{\sigma}_d = 0.7\%$ per day (about 11% per year) and considers combinations of excess dividend growth $\bar{\mu}_d - r_f \in \{0.5, 1.0\}$ bp per day (about 1.2% or 2.4% per year) and annual average P/D ratio $\bar{Q} \in \{25, 30\}$. For each combination of calibrated values, the MSM volatility parameters m_0, $\gamma_{\bar{k}}$, and b are reestimated on daily data by maximum likelihood. The optimized value of the likelihood function is given by $\ln L$. Excess dividend growth and average P/D determine the annual equity premium (AEP), and the constraint on average P/D identifies the product $\alpha\sigma_{c,d} \equiv \alpha\bar{\sigma}_d\sigma_c\rho_{c,d}$. The table reports implied statistics for the first four moments of daily returns, the feedback (FB), and the duration of the lowest-frequency shock in years (LDY). When a variable depends on time scale or units, it is noted in parentheses under the variable description using the notation "d" for day and "a" for annual. Asymptotic standard errors for the estimated parameters are reported in parentheses beneath each reported value, conditional on the values of the calibrated parameters. The second grouping of three rows in each panel holds $\bar{\mu}_d - r_f$ and average P/D constant at their original values, and considers alternative values of dividend growth volatility $\bar{\sigma}_d \in \{0.5, 0.6, 0.8\}\%$ per day, or approximately 7.7, 9.3, and 12.4% annually.

9.4.1   Investor Information and Stock Returns

Each period investors observe consumption, dividends, and noisy observations of the volatility components

$$\delta_t = M_t + \sigma_\delta z_t, \tag{9.13}$$

where σ_δ is a nonnegative scalar and $z_t \in \mathbb{R}^{\bar{k}}$ is an i.i.d. vector of independent standard normals. This specification nests the full information case $(\sigma_\delta = 0)$. The information set $I_t = \{(C_{t'}, D_{t'}, \delta_{t'}); t' \leq t\}$ generates a conditional probability distribution Π_t over the volatility states $\{m^1, \ldots, m^d\}$, which can be computed recursively.

The stochastic discount factor depends only on consumption and is thus the same as in the full information economy. The price-dividend ratio

$$Q(\Pi_t) = \mathbb{E}\left[\sum_{i=1}^{\infty} \delta'^i \left(\frac{C_{t+i}}{C_t}\right)^{-\alpha} \frac{D_{t+i}}{D_t} \,\middle|\, I_t\right] \tag{9.14}$$

is the conditional expectation of exogenous variables driven by the first-order Markov state M_t. We infer that it is linear in the current belief[11]

$$Q(\Pi_t) = \mathbb{E}\left[Q(M_t)\,|\, I_t\right] = \sum_{j=1}^{d} Q(m^j)\Pi_t^j, \tag{9.15}$$

where $Q(m^j)$ is the price-dividend ratio computed under full information. The setup is highly tractable because prices are a belief-weighted average of state prices from the full information model.

The excess return is determined by the volatility state and investor belief:

$$r_{t+1} = \ln \frac{1 + Q(\Pi_{t+1})}{Q(\Pi_t)} + \bar{\mu}_d - r_f - \frac{\sigma_d^2(M_{t+1})}{2} + \sigma_d(M_{t+1})\varepsilon_{d,t+1}. \tag{9.16}$$

When a new state occurs, investors may learn of it gradually and generate less extreme returns than in the full-information economy. Simulating the return process with learning is straightforward, as discussed in the Appendix.

The equilibrium impact of signal variability σ_δ is conveniently analyzed from (9.15) for fixed values of the other structural parameters. The price-dividend ratio is the filtered version of its full-information counterpart, which implies equality of the means: $\mathbb{E}[Q(\Pi_t)] = \mathbb{E}[Q(M_t)]$. Information

---

[11] In a representative agent economy with Epstein-Zin-Weil utility, the price-dividend ratio is linear in beliefs if dividend growth is driven by a Markov state, and consumption growth is a separate i.i.d. process.

quality therefore has essentially no effect on the equity premium. The variance satisfies the orthogonality condition $Var[Q(M_t)] = Var[Q(\Pi_t)] + \mathbb{E}\{[Q(\Pi_t) - Q(M_t)]^2\}$. This equation is the analog of the variance bounds considered by LeRoy and Porter (1981) and Shiller (1981). In our framework, we expect the difference in variances to be small: the variance of the price-dividend ratio is dominated by changes in the most persistent components. Since learning about these changes is rare and transitory, the difference $Q(\Pi_t) - Q(M_t)$ is likely to be modest most of the time. This suggests that the variances of the price-dividend ratio and returns should be relatively insensitive to information quality.

The linearity property (9.15) implies that this model does not contain the "uncertainty channel" previously considered in the learning literature (e.g., Veronesi, 1999; Lettau, Ludvigson, and Wachter, 2004). In these models, signals are informative about both future dividend news and future marginal rates of substitution, which generates a higher sensitivity of returns about bad news in good times than about good news in bad times. Our model illustrates that even in the absence of such effects, learning about stochastic volatility can be a powerful source of endogenous skewness.

9.4.2   Learning Model Results

Despite the simplicity of the pricing and updating rules, econometric inference is computationally expensive in the imperfect information equilibrium. The state consists of the volatility vector M_{t+1} and the investor belief Π_{t+1}. Since the econometrician observes only excess returns, evaluating the likelihood of the data would require integrating over the conditional distribution of the state (Π_t, M_t). When $\bar{k} = 8$, this would entail estimating a distribution defined on $\mathbb{R}^{256} \times \{m^1, \ldots, m^{256}\}$.

Instead we use a simulation-based approach and focus on the two base specifications with $\bar{k} = 8$ frequencies considered previously. Specifically, we assign the daily values $\bar{\mu}_d - r_f = 0.5$ bp and $\bar{\sigma}_d = 0.70\%$, and we set the parameters $(m_0, \gamma_{\bar{k}}, b)$ to the full-information ML estimates reported in Table 9.2. Consistent with the empirical estimates and calibration in Bansal and Yaron (2004), we choose $\rho_{c,d} = 0.6$. Unreported robustness checks show that the learning results are not highly sensitive to the choice of $\rho_{c,d}$ over a wide range.

To evaluate the impact of information quality, we consider signal volatilities $\sigma_\delta \in \{0, .1, \ldots, 1, 1.25, \ldots 2, 3, 4, 5, 10, 15, 20\}$. For each value, we simulate a single long sample of excess returns and calculate the first four moments of returns as well as the feedback using the same set of random draws. We report a subset of the results in Table 9.5. For simplicity, we focus our discussion on the postwar period. In Panel B, the average mean return is equal to 1.93 bp per day for all values of the signal precision. The simulated means and standard deviations are nearly invariant to

TABLE 9.5. Moments of the Learning Model

	Signal Standard Deviation σ_δ					
	0	0.2	0.5	1	1.5	2
	A. Full Sample: 1926–2003					
$E[r_t]$	0.0195	0.0195	0.0195	0.0195	0.0195	0.0195
$Var[r_t]^{1/2}$	0.825	0.825	0.824	0.825	0.825	0.824
$Skew[r_t]$	−0.069	−0.127	−0.509	−0.926	−1.076	−1.181
$Kurt[r_t]$	133.2	99.2	42.6	22.9	17.5	15.5
Feedback	38.9	38.9	38.7	38.8	38.8	38.6
	B. Postwar: 1952–2003					
$E[r_t]$	0.0193	0.0193	0.0193	0.0193	0.0193	0.0193
$Var[r_t]^{1/2}$	0.796	0.796	0.796	0.796	0.796	0.796
$Skew[r_t]$	−0.054	−0.097	−0.441	−0.804	−0.958	−1.06
$Kurt[r_t]$	83.4	54.1	23.5	13.8	11.5	10.7
Feedback	29.4	29.4	29.4	29.1	29.2	29.2

Notes: This table shows the effect of learning on different moments of the data. For each panel, the base parameters $m_0, \bar{\sigma}_d, \bar{\mu}_d - r, \gamma_{\bar{k}}$, are taken from the estimates in Table 9.2 for the specification with $\bar{k} = 8$ components. These values, as well as the calibrated value $\rho_{c,d} = 0.6$, are held constant across all simulations. Columns vary only by the value of the reported signal standard deviation σ_δ. Investors have full information when $\sigma_\delta = 0$, and as σ_δ increases the signal precision weakens. For each specification, we simulate a single long series of $T = 10^7$ returns using the same set of random draws, and report moments of the simulated data. Mean, variance, and feedback are nearly constant across simulations. Skewness becomes more negative, and kurtosis declines as information quality deteriorates.

information quality, as previously anticipated. Hence, volatility feedback is robust across different learning environments.

We do, however, find large and systematic differences in skewness and kurtosis as signal precision varies. Skewness is close to zero at about −0.05 when $\sigma_\delta = 0$, falling to −0.44 when $\sigma_\delta = 0.5$ and to −1.06 when $\sigma_\delta = 2$. Returns become more negatively skewed as investor information becomes less precise. Kurtosis takes its highest value of about 83 when investor information is perfect. With a value of $\sigma_\delta = 0.5$, kurtosis drops to 24, and when $\sigma_\delta = 2$, it falls to 11. The numerical simulations therefore confirm the trade-off between skewness and kurtosis. With full information, kurtosis is large but skewness is close to zero. As the quality of investor information deteriorates, returns become more negatively skewed and kurtosis falls as well. Figure 9.5 depicts the trade-off between skewness and kurtosis. Intermediate information qualities approximately in the range $\sigma_\delta \in [0.5, 1.0]$ seem most consistent with the data.

To understand these results, consider the role played by dividend growth in investor updating. When information is perfect, dividend growth is

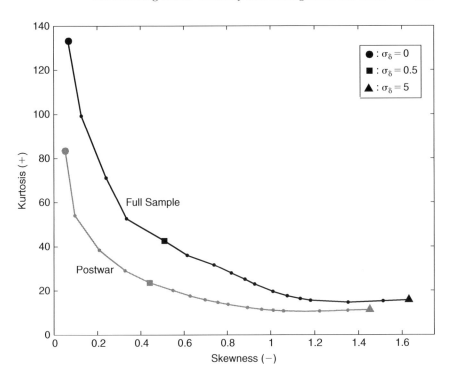

FIGURE 9.5. **Skewness and Kurtosis of Daily Returns in the Learning Model.** This figure shows skewness and kurtosis for different information environments in the simulated learning model. For each curve, the base parameters $m_0, \bar{\sigma}_d, \bar{\mu}_d - r, \gamma_{\bar{k}}$, are taken from the estimates in Table 9.2 for the specification with $\bar{k} = 8$ components. These values, as well as $\rho_{c,d} = 0.6$, are held constant across all simulations. Each simulation is then based on a different value of the signal standard deviation $\sigma_\delta \in \{0, 0.1, \ldots, 1, 1.25, \ldots, 2, 3, 4, 5\}$. Investors have full information when $\sigma_\delta = 0$, and as σ_δ increases the signal precision weakens. For each economy, we simulate a single long series of $T = 10^7$ returns using the same set of random draws. Each marked point on the plot represents a different simulation, progressing from $\sigma_\delta = 0$ in the top left to $\sigma_\delta = 5$ in the bottom right.

irrelevant to investor beliefs. Investors find out immediately and fully incorporate the impact of any changes into prices. The speed of learning is independent of the direction of the volatility change, and returns are approximately symmetric. Kurtosis is high and skewness is close to zero.

At the other extreme, when σ_δ is arbitrarily large, the corresponding signals are not useful. Investors then rely on dividend news to infer the latent state. If volatility increases, investors may observe a single extreme realization of the signal that is implausible under their existing beliefs. In this case beliefs quickly revise upward. On the other hand, a volatility decrease (good news) can only be revealed slowly. This is because investors learn about low volatility by observing dividend growth close to its mean, but this is a relatively likely outcome regardless of the volatility level. Thus, bad news about increased volatility can be incorporated into price quickly, while good news about low volatility trickles out slowly. This asymmetry explains why skewness increases and kurtosis falls as information quality deteriorates.

To further illustrate the effect of information quality, Figure 9.6 displays four simulations with length $T = 20,000$ of the learning economy with different signal precisions. From top to bottom, $\sigma_\delta = 0$ corresponds to full information, $\sigma_\delta = 0.5$ and $\sigma_\delta = 1.0$ to two intermediate values, and $\sigma_\delta = 20$ to nearly uninformative signals. All simulations use identical sets of random draws to facilitate comparison. With perfect information, large and symmetric feedback generates substantial outliers of both signs. As information quality decreases, gradual learning causes feedback to be spread out across multiple days, and fewer extreme returns occur. The attenuation is stronger for positive returns, and skewness becomes more pronounced with σ_δ. When $\sigma_\delta = 20$, this effect is so extreme that no large positive returns occur in the simulation. The intermediate cases in which $\sigma_\delta = 0.5$ and $\sigma_\delta = 1.0$ appear most consistent with daily stock returns.

9.5   Preference Implications and Extension to Multifrequency Consumption Risk

In this section we discuss the role of the preference parameters in the previous empirical results. We also examine the robustness of volatility feedback to alternative specifications of consumption and dividend drift.

As discussed in Section 9.2, the preference parameters of our model can be chosen to match the average return on the bond and the stock. Calibrating to the long-run price-dividend ratio $\bar{Q}$ implies a unique value for $\alpha\sigma_{c,d} \equiv \alpha\sigma_c\bar{\sigma}_d\rho_{c,d}$, which is equal to 2.8 bp per day in the base postwar example reported in Table 9.2. As in the learning section, we additionally specify $\rho_{c,d} = 0.6$. We calibrate aggregate consumption to U.S. values and use $g_c = 1.8\%$ and $\sigma_c = 2.93\%$ per year. Given these specifications, we can infer that our base examples imply risk aversion of about $\alpha \approx 35$. If the elasticity of intertemporal substitution (EIS) is set equal to $\psi = 1$, the discount rate $\delta = 97.8\%$ per year then matches the interest rate $r_f = 1\%$.

The results in Section 9.3 therefore imply reasonable levels of the EIS and subjective discount rate, but large relative risk aversion. Previous calibrations in the literature use α in this range (e.g., Lettau, Ludvigson, and Wachter use a value of 40). Nonetheless, we would like to better understand the importance of risk aversion for volatility feedback in our framework. The loglinear approximation derived in the Appendix shows that α controls both the magnitude of the equity premium and the price impact of volatility changes. In order to achieve a reasonable equity

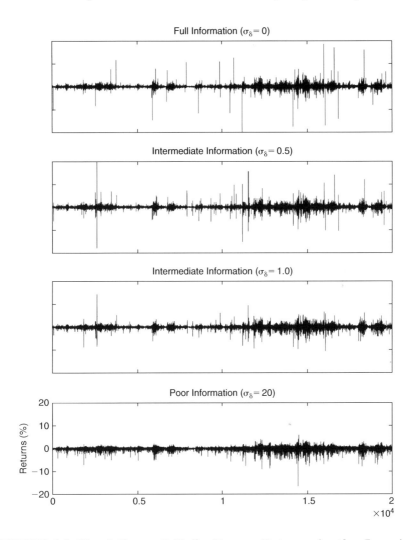

FIGURE 9.6. **Simulations of Daily Excess Returns in the Learning Model.** This figure shows learning economy simulations with length $T = 20,000$. All simulations are based on the base parameters estimated from the full sample with $\bar{k} = 8$ components: $m_0 = 1.435$, $\bar{\sigma}_d = 0.70\%$ per day, $\bar{\mu} - r_f = 0.5$ bp per day, $\gamma_{\bar{k}} = 0.058$, and $b = 2.19$. All simulations also use the identical set of random draws for dividends, signal noises, and multipliers. The only value that changes across the panels is the signal variability parameter, σ_δ. The top panel where $\sigma_\delta = 0$ corresponds to full investor information; the middle two panels show intermediate signal precision; and in the final panel information quality is poor. Noise in the investor signals attenuates extreme feedback realizations, but attenuation is stronger for positive than negative realizations. This generates increasingly negative skewness and reduces kurtosis as information quality deteriorates.

premium using a lower risk aversion, we need an additional source of risk in stock returns.

Small but persistent variations in the drift and volatility of consumption have been empirically documented by Bansal and Lundblad (2002), Bansal, Khatchatrian, and Yaron (2005), and Lettau, Ludvigson, and Wachter (2004). Bansal and Yaron (2004) demonstrate that these variations help to solve the equity premium puzzle. They calibrate a model in which an autoregressive state with a half-life of about 2.5 years drives the drift and volatility of consumption. Lettau, Ludvigson, and Wachter estimate a four-state regime-switching model in which the good state has a duration of over 30 years.

This earlier research motivates the following extension of our asset pricing model. Consumption growth exhibits regime shifts in drift and volatility:

$$c_t - c_{t-1} = g_c(M'_t) + \sigma_c(M'_t)\varepsilon_{c,t},$$

where $\{\varepsilon_{c,t}\}$ is i.i.d. $\mathcal{N}(0,1)$ and $M'_t \in \mathbb{R}^{\bar{\ell}}_+$ is a multifrequency state vector with $\bar{\ell}$ components. Each component of the state M'_t takes the values $m_{c0} > 1$ and $2 - m_{c0}$ with equal probability. Drift and volatility are specified by

$$g_c(M'_t) \equiv \bar{g}_c - \lambda_c \sum_{k=1}^{\bar{\ell}}(M'_{k,t} - 1)$$

$$\sigma_c(M'_t) \equiv \sigma_c(M'_{1,t}...M'_{\bar{\ell},t})^{1/2}.$$

Consumption volatility is the product of the components $M'_{k,t}$, as in the dividend news process. We define the drift, on the other hand, as the sum of the state components, which permits a symmetric distribution around $\bar{g}_c$. Similarly, the dividend growth process (9.2) exhibits regime switches in drift

$$\mu_d(M_t) = \bar{\mu}_d - \lambda_d \sum_{k=1}^{\bar{k}}(M_{k,t} - 1),$$

as well as the usual MSM volatility (9.8).

The extended specification allows us to capture the variations in macro-economic risk that have been documented at various frequencies in the literature. When $\lambda_c > 0$, a high $M'_{k,t}$ implies both a low drift and a higher volatility, consistent with empirical evidence on business cycles. We assume $\bar{\ell} \leq \bar{k}$, consistent with the idea of consumption smoothing at short horizons. For instance, consumption may be affected by business cycles, technology, and demographic shocks, but not by shorter-lived shocks that can affect dividend news. For simplicity, we assume that the consumption and volatility components are perfectly correlated; that is, $M'_{k,t} = m_{c0}$ if and only if $M_{k,t} = m_0$ for every k. Asset prices are easily derived as shown in the Appendix.

We calibrate the model using statistics reported by Bansal and Yaron (2004). We set aggregate consumption to $g_c = 1.80\%$ per year and $\sigma_c = 2.89\%$ per year, and dividends satisfy $\bar{\mu}_d = g_c$ and $\bar{\sigma}_d = 0.80\%$ per day. There are $\ell = 4$ consumption components and $k = 5$ dividend components. We choose the dividend volatility parameter $m_0 = 1.50$, which is close to the values estimated in Table 9.2, and set $m_{c0} = 1.40$. The drift parameter λ_c satisfies $\lambda_c(m_{c0} - 1) = 0.30\%$ on an annualized basis, implying that the state-dependent consumption drift varies between 0.6 and 3% per year. Similarly, the dividend drift switches are specified by $\lambda_d(m_0 - 1) = 0.5\%$, implying state-dependent drifts varying between -0.7 and 4.3% per year. We set the correlation $\rho_{c,d}$ to 0.64, and frequencies are specified by $b = 2.4$ and $1/\gamma_1 = 20$ years. The duration of the consumption components therefore ranges between 1.44 and 20 years, while the shortest dividend duration is 0.6 years. The coefficient of relative risk aversion is $\alpha = 10$, and the other preference parameters are $\psi = 1.5$ and $\delta = 0.993$.

The dynamics of consumption are consistent with the existing literature and evidence. The standard deviation of consumption growth is almost identical to the value used by Bansal and Yaron, and consumption growth autocorrelations are 0.032 at a one-year horizon, 0.015 over five years, and 0.009 over ten years. These values would be hard to distinguish from white noise and are in fact much lower than the autocorrelations in Bansal and Yaron. Similarly, the variance ratios do not exceed 1.21 over a 10-year horizon, again lower than the values in Bansal and Yaron. Hence, the consumption specification appears to be consistent with earlier empirical evidence.

We first shut down the stochastic volatility of dividends by forcing $m_0 = 1.0$ and consequently $\sigma_d(M_t) = \bar{\sigma}_d$. This yields a risk premium of 2.16%, an average price-dividend ratio equal to 46.7, and an average risk-free rate equal to 1.02% per year. The variance of the stock return is 4.2% higher than the dividend variance; that is, $FB = 4.2\%$.

We then reintroduce stochastic volatility in dividends by specifying $m_0 = 1.50$. The consumption process, stochastic discount factor, and interest rate regimes are unchanged. The equity premium on the stock increases to 3.29%, and the price-dividend ratio falls to 31.1. The price-dividend regimes vary between 22.9 and 37.7. The feedback increases to 25.9%, which is more than six times larger than when dividend volatility is constant. The marginal contribution of multifrequency dividend volatility to return volatility is thus $25.9\% - 4.2\% = 21.7\%$, which is comparable to the feedback estimates obtained with i.i.d. consumption and high risk aversion.

In sum, by incorporating long-run risks in consumption, we can use a lower risk aversion ($\alpha = 10$) to match the equity premium and still generate a substantial contribution of dividend volatility feedback. The extension also offers a pure regime-switching formulation of long-run risks in a multifrequency environment, opening new directions for future research.

9.6   Discussion

In this chapter, we develop a tractable asset pricing framework with multifrequency shocks to fundamentals and discount rates, focusing on a dividend news specification with constant mean, multifrequency stochastic volatility, and conditionally Gaussian noise. The structural equilibrium with three free parameters accounts for endogenous skewness, thick tails, time-varying volatility, and sizeable feedback in over 80 years of daily stock returns.

Two economic mechanisms play important roles. First, endogenous volatility feedback amplifies dividend variance by 20 to 40% in favored specifications, or 10 to 40 times the feedback obtained in the previous literature (e.g., Campbell and Hentschel, 1992). Feedback from persistent components helps to capture extreme returns, while higher-frequency variations match day-to-day volatility movements. Second, investor learning generates substantial endogenous skewness. Building on Veronesi (2000), we consider investor signals about the volatility state and show that information quality creates a trade-off between skewness and kurtosis. Intermediate information environments best match the data.

The chapter illustrates that a multifrequency approach helps connect the low-frequency macro-finance and learning literatures with higher-frequency financial econometrics. Convergence of these areas follows from bringing multifrequency shocks into pure regime-switching economies, which traditionally offer three major benefits: (i) asset pricing is straightforward in a Markov chain setup; (ii) the econometrics of regime-switching, based on simple filtering theory, is well understood; and (iii) learning is easily incorporated by using similar filtering techniques. The multifrequency approach expands the practical range of equilibrium regime-switching economies from a few states to several hundred and from lower frequencies to daily returns.

We develop an extension based on joint modeling of multifrequency regime switches in consumption and dividends. This generates large feedback and a reasonable equity premium with moderate values of relative risk aversion. This framework offers potential for further development, particularly in modeling the impact of long-run risks on high-frequency financial data.

10
Multifrequency Jump-Diffusions

The multifractal diffusions considered in Part II are exogenously specified and have continuous sample paths. We now endogenize the price process by considering a continuous-time version of the exchange economy developed in Chapter 9. Dividends and consumption follow continuous diffusions, but their drift rates and volatilities can undergo discrete Markov switches. These regime changes in fundamentals trigger endogenous jumps in asset prices, consistent with the well-known property that discrete arrivals of information about cash flows and discount rates can cause price discontinuities in equilibrium.

When dividends follow a continuous-time MSM, the construction generates a new class of stochastic processes, which we call multifrequency jump-diffusions. The stock price displays endogenous jumps of heterogeneous frequencies, and the largest discontinuities are triggered by the most persistent volatility shocks. The model thus produces many small jumps and fewer large jumps, as in Madan, Carr, and Chang (1998), Carr, Geman, Madan, and Yor (2002), and others. Our equilibrium model contributes to the literature on jump and Lévy processes by endogenizing the heterogeneity of jump sizes, and the association between jump-size and frequency.

We investigate the limiting behavior of the economy when the number of volatility components goes to infinity. As in Chapter 7, the dividend process weakly converges to a multifractal diffusion with continuous sample paths. We also show that the equilibrium price-dividend ratio converges to an infinite intensity pure jump process with heterogeneous frequencies. Prices are then the sum of a continuous multifractal diffusion and an infinite intensity, pure jump process, yielding a new stochastic process that we accordingly call a *multifractal jump-diffusion*. A jump in the stock price occurs in the neighborhood of any instant, but the process is continuous almost everywhere.

For simplicity, the chapter focuses mainly on time-separable preferences. The stochastic discount factor is then continuous, and endogenous jumps in stock valuations are "unpriced" in the sense that they do not affect expected excess stock returns (e.g., Merton, 1976). In the final section, we obtain priced jumps and endogenous discontinuities in the stochastic discount factor by assuming nonseparable preferences, as in Epstein and Zin (1989), Weil (1989), and Duffie and Epstein (1992). This extension provides additional flexibility in structural modeling of jump-diffusions.

This chapter is based on an earlier paper: "Multifrequency Jump-Diffusions: An Equilibrium Approach" (with A. Fisher), *Journal of Mathematical Economics*, 44: 207–261, January 2008.

10.1   An Equilibrium Model with Endogenous Price Jumps

This section develops a continuous-time equilibrium model with regime-shifts in the drift and volatility of fundamentals. We do not require that the state follows an MSM process, and the setup developed in this section can therefore be used directly in other contexts.

10.1.1   Preferences, Information, and Income

We consider an exchange economy with a single consumption good defined on the set of instants $t \in [0, \infty)$. The information structure is represented by a filtration $\{\mathcal{F}_t\}$ on the probability space $(\Omega, \mathcal{F}, \mathbb{P})$.

The economy is specified by two independent stochastic processes: a bivariate Brownian motion $Z_t = (Z_Y(t), Z_D(t)) \in \mathbb{R}^2$ and a random state vector $M_t \in \mathbb{R}_+^{\bar{k}}$, where $\bar{k}$ is a finite integer. The processes Z and M are mutually independent and adapted to the filtration $\{\mathcal{F}_t\}$. The bivariate Brownian Z has zero mean and covariance matrix

$$\begin{pmatrix} 1 & \rho_{Y,D} \\ \rho_{Y,D} & 1 \end{pmatrix},$$

where the correlation coefficient $\rho_{Y,D} = Cov(dZ_Y, dZ_D)/dt$ is strictly positive. The vector M_t is a stationary Markov process with right-continuous sample paths.

The economy is populated by a finite set of identical investors $h \in \{1, \ldots, H\}$, who have homogeneous information, preferences, and endowments. Investors observe the realization of the processes Z and M, and have information set $I_t = \{(Z_s, M_s); s \leq t\}$. The common utility is given by

$$U_t = \mathbb{E}\left[\int_0^{+\infty} e^{-\delta s} u(c_{t+s}) ds \,\middle|\, I_t \right],$$

where the discount rate is a positive constant: $\delta \in (0, \infty)$. The Bernoulli utility $u(\cdot)$ is twice continuously differentiable and satisfies the usual monotonicity and concavity conditions: $u' > 0$ and $u'' < 0$. Furthermore, the Inada conditions hold: $\lim_{c \to 0} u'(c) = +\infty$ and $\lim_{c \to +\infty} u'(c) = 0$.

Every agent continuously receives the exogenous endowment stream $Y_t \in (0, \infty)$. The process Y_t is identical across the population and follows a geometric Brownian motion with stochastic drift and volatility. Specifically, let $g_Y(\cdot)$ and $\sigma_Y(\cdot)$ denote deterministic measurable functions defined on $\mathbb{R}_+^{\bar{k}}$ and taking values on the real line.

Condition 7 (Income) *The moments* $\mathbb{E}\left[\int_0^t |g_Y(M_s)|\, ds\right]$ *and* $\mathbb{E}\left[\int_0^t \sigma_Y^2\right.$
$\left.(M_s) ds\right]$ *are finite, and the exogenous income stream is given by*

$$\ln(Y_t) \equiv \ln(Y_0) + \int_0^t \left[g_Y(M_s) - \frac{\sigma_Y^2(M_s)}{2}\right] ds + \int_0^t \sigma_Y(M_s)dZ_Y(s)$$

at every instant $t \in [0, \infty)$.

The moment conditions guarantee that the stochastic integrals are well defined. By Itô's lemma, the income flow satisfies the stochastic differential equation

$$\frac{dY_t}{Y_t} = g_Y(M_t)dt + \sigma_Y(M_t)dZ_Y(t). \tag{10.1}$$

10.1.2 Financial Markets and Equilibrium

Agents can trade two financial assets: a bond and a stock. The bond has an instantaneous rate of return $r_f(t)$, which is endogenously determined in equilibrium. Its net supply is equal to zero.

The stock is a claim on the stochastic dividend stream $\{D_t\}_{t \geq 0}$.

Condition 8 (Dividend process) *The dividend stream is given by:*

$$\ln(D_t) \equiv \ln(D_0) + \int_0^t \left[g_D(M_s) - \frac{\sigma_D^2(M_s)}{2}\right] ds + \int_0^t \sigma_D(M_s)dZ_D(s),$$

where $g_D(\cdot)$ *and* $\sigma_D(\cdot)$ *are measurable functions defined on* $\mathbb{R}_+^{\bar{k}}$ *and valued in* $\mathbb{R}$ *such that* $\mathbb{E}\left[\int_0^t |g_D(M_s)|\, ds\right] < \infty$ *and* $\mathbb{E}\left[\int_0^t \sigma_D^2(M_s)ds\right] < \infty$ *for all* t.

We infer from Itô's lemma:

$$\frac{dD_t}{D_t} = g_D(M_t)dt + \sigma_D(M_t)dZ_D(t). \tag{10.2}$$

The dividend process D_t has continuous sample paths, but its drift and volatility can exhibit discontinuities. Every agent is initially endowed with $N_s \in \mathbb{R}_+$ units of stock, where one unit represents one claim on the flow D_t. We treat the difference $Y_t - N_s D_t$ as the nontradable component of the endowment flow.[1]

---

[1] Distinguishing between aggregate endowment flow and dividends on public equity is common in asset pricing settings. For example, Brennan and Xia (2001) invoke nontraded labor income as a wedge between the aggregate endowment flow and dividends. In our

Each agent selects a consumption-portfolio strategy (c^h, N^h, B^h) defined on $\Omega \times [0, \infty)$ and taking values on $\mathbb{R}_+ \times \mathbb{R} \times \mathbb{R}$, where $c^h(\omega, t)$, $N^h(\omega, t)$ and $B^h(\omega, t)$ respectively denote consumption, stockholdings and bondholdings in every date-event (ω, t). A strategy is called *admissible* if it is adapted, self-financing, and implies nonnegative wealth at all times.[2] We assume that there are no transaction costs.

Definition 7 (General equilibrium) *A general equilibrium consists of a stock price process P, an interest rate process r_f, and a collection of individual admissible consumption-portfolio plans $(c^h, N^h, B^h)_{1 \leq h \leq H}$, such that (i) for every h, (c^h, N^h, B^h) maximizes utility over all admissible plans; (ii) goods markets and securities markets clear:*

$$\frac{1}{H} \sum_h c^h(t, \omega) = Y(t, \omega), \quad \frac{1}{H} \sum_{h=1}^{H} N^h(t, \omega) = N_s, \text{ and } \frac{1}{H} \sum_{h=1}^{H} B^h(t, \omega) = 0$$

for almost all (t, ω).

In our setting, agents are fully symmetric, and autarky is the unique equilibrium. Individual consumption coincides with individual income: $c^h(t, \omega) = Y(t, \omega)$ for every h, t, ω, and it is convenient to denote $C_t \equiv Y_t$, $Z_C \equiv Z_Y$, $g_C(.) \equiv g_Y(.)$, $\sigma_C(.) \equiv \sigma_Y(.)$, and $\rho_{C,D} \equiv \rho_{Y,D}$.

The stochastic discount factor (SDF) is equal to instantaneous marginal utility:

$$\Lambda_t = e^{-\delta t} u'(C_t). \tag{10.3}$$

It satisfies the stochastic differential equation:

$$\frac{d\Lambda_t}{\Lambda_t} = -r_f(M_t)dt - \alpha(C_t)\sigma_C(M_t)dZ_C(t),$$

where $\alpha(c) \equiv -cu''(c)/u'(c)$ denotes the coefficient of relative risk aversion and $\pi(c) \equiv -cu'''(c)/u''(c)$ is the coefficient of relative risk prudence. The instantaneous interest rate

$$r_f(M_t) = \delta + \alpha(C_t)g_C(M_t) - \alpha(C_t)\pi(C_t)\sigma_C^2(M_t)/2 \tag{10.4}$$

---

economy, the difference $Y_t - N_s D_t$ can be either positive or negative since Y_t and D_t are imperfectly correlated diffusions: hence we prefer the more general interpretation of an unmodeled endowment flow shock. Recent literature (e.g., Cochrane, Longstaff, and Santa-Clara, 2008; Santos and Veronesi, 2005) proposes methods to ensure positivity of the nontraded portion of the endowment while maintaining tractable asset prices.

[2]The wealth nonnegativity constraint prevents agents from using doubling strategies to create arbitrage profits (Dybvig and Huang, 1988).

increases with investor impatience and the growth rate of the economy, and is reduced by the precautionary motive.

In equilibrium, the stock price P_t is given by

$$\frac{P_t}{D_t} = \mathbb{E}\left[\left.\int_0^{+\infty} e^{-\delta s}\frac{u'(C_{t+s})}{u'(C_t)}\frac{D_{t+s}}{D_t}ds\right| I_t\right].$$

The joint distribution of $(C_{t+s}; D_{t+s}/D_t)$ depends on the state M_t and the consumption level C_t, but not on the initial dividend D_t. The P/D ratio is therefore a deterministic function of M_t and C_t, which will henceforth be denoted by $Q(M_t, C_t)$.

Shifts in the state M_t induce discontinuous changes in the P/D ratio and the stock price. We use lower cases for the logarithms of all variables.

Proposition 12 (Equilibrium stock price) *The stock price follows a jump-diffusion, which can be written in logs as the sum of the continuous dividend process and the price-dividend ratio:*

$$p_t = d_t + q(M_t, C_t).$$

A price jump occurs when there is a discontinuous change in the Markov state M_t driving the continuous dividend and consumption processes.

The endogenous price jumps contrast with the continuity of the fundamentals and the SDF.

10.1.3 Equilibrium Dynamics under Isoelastic Utility

We assume that every investor has the same constant relative risk aversion $\alpha \in (0, \infty)$, that is,

$$u(c) \equiv \begin{cases} c^{1-\alpha}/(1-\alpha) & \text{if } \alpha \neq 1, \\ \ln(c) & \text{if } \alpha = 1. \end{cases}$$

The P/D ratio then simplifies as follows.

Proposition 13 (Equilibrium with isoelastic utility) *The P/D ratio is a deterministic function of the Markov state:*

$$q(M_t) = \ln \mathbb{E}_t\left(\int_0^{+\infty} e^{-\int_0^s [r_f(M_{t+h}) - g_D(M_{t+h}) + \alpha\sigma_C(M_{t+h})\sigma_D(M_{t+h})\rho_{C,D}]dh} ds\right),$$

$$(10.5)$$

where $\mathbb{E}_t$ denotes the conditional expectation given M_t.

When dividends and consumption are uncorrelated ($\rho_{C,D} = 0$) and regime-swiches affect only dividend volatility, the price-dividend ratio is constant, and the equilibrium value of the equity claim follows a continuous-time MSM (with continuous sample paths). Outside this special case, equity prices exhibit jumps. Over an infinitesimal time interval, the stock price changes by

$$d(p_t) = d(d_t) + \Delta(q_t),$$

where $\Delta(q_t) \equiv q_t - q_{t-}$ denotes the finite variation of the price-dividend ratio in case of a discontinuous regime change.[3] Consider the effect of a Markov switch that increases the volatility of current and future dividends (without impacting consumption). The P/D ratio falls and induces a negative realization of $\Delta(q_t)$. Market pricing can thus generate an endogenous negative correlation between volatility changes and price jumps. This contrasts with earlier jump models in which the relation between discontinuities and volatility is exogenously postulated (e.g., Duffie, Pan, and Singleton, 2000; Carr and Wu, 2004).

Under isoelastic utility, our results can be made robust to some degree of investor heterogeneity. Assume that in addition to the stock and bond, a complete set of traded financial assets exists, and investors can hedge the risks implicit in the state vector M_t. If agents have heterogeneous coefficients of relative risk aversion α_h and homogeneous discount rates $\delta > 0$, Huang (1987) and Duffie and Zame (1989) show that equilibrium asset prices are supported by an isoelastic representative investor. Thus, when markets are complete, the SDF (10.3) is consistent with heterogeneity in risk aversion. Extensions to investor heterogeneity under incomplete markets are likely to lead to more novel implications (e.g., Constantinides and Duffie, 1996; Calvet, 2001) and are well-deserving of further research.[4]

---

[3] We denote by q_{t-} the left limit of q at t.

[4] A large literature in economics also considers the pricing implications of bounded rationality and heterogeneous beliefs (e.g., Arthur et al., 1997; Brock and Hommes, 1998; Brock, Lakonishok, and LeBaron, 1992; Brock and LeBaron, 1996; Buraschi and Jiltsov, 2006; Chan, LeBaron, Lo, and Poggio, 1998; DeLong, Shleifer, Summers, and Waldman, 1990; Froot, Scharfstein, and Stein, 1992; Grandmont, 1998; Hong and Stein, 2003, 2007; Kirman, 1991; LeBaron, 2000; LeBaron, Arthur, and Palmer, 1999; Lettau, 1997; Lux 1997, 1998; Lux and Marchesi, 1999; Scharfstein and Stein, 1990). A related line of research, often associated with econophysics and the Santa Fe Institute, is surveyed by Bouchaud and Potters (2003), Challet, Marsili, and Zhang (2005), LeBaron (2006), and Mantegna and Stanley (2000). See also Farmer and Geanakoplos (2008) for a recent discussion of the interplay between equilibrium modeling and finance.

10.2   A Multifrequency Jump-Diffusion for Equilibrium Stock Prices

We now incorporate multifrequency shocks into dividends and consumption and investigate the resulting price jump-diffusion.

10.2.1   Dividends with Multifrequency Volatility

We introduce shocks of multiple frequencies by assuming that dividends follow a continuous-time MSM, as defined in Chapter 7. That is, given the Markov state vector $M_t = (M_{1,t}; M_{2,t}; \ldots; M_{\bar{k},t}) \in \mathbb{R}_+^{\bar{k}}$ at date t,

$M_{k,t+dt}$ is drawn from distribution M with probability $\gamma_k dt$,

$M_{k,t+dt} = M_{k,t}$ with probability $1 - \gamma_k dt$.

For parsimony, we assume that M is specified by a single parameter $m_0 \in \mathbb{R}$. The arrival intensities satisfy $\gamma_k = \gamma_1 b^{k-1}$ for all k, and the growth rate b is strictly larger than unity. Stochastic volatility is the renormalized product

$$\sigma_D(M_t) \equiv \bar{\sigma}_D \left(\prod_{k=1}^{\bar{k}} M_{k,t} \right)^{1/2}.$$

The parameter $\bar{\sigma}_D$ is the unconditional standard deviation of the dividend growth process: $Var(dD_t/D_t) = \bar{\sigma}_D^2 dt$.

We assume that dividends have the constant growth rate

$$g_D(M_t) \equiv \bar{g}_D,$$

which focuses attention on the rich volatility dynamics. MSM generates both short and long swings in volatility and thick tails in the dividend growth series, while by design there are no jumps in the dividends themselves.

10.2.2   Multifrequency Economies

We now turn to the specification of aggregate consumption, which will close the description of the exchange economy.

Specification C1: Lucas tree economy. The stock is a claim on aggregate consumption: $D_t = C_t$. By Proposition 13, the P/D ratio is given by

$$\mathbb{E}_t \left(\int_0^{+\infty} e^{-[\delta - (1-\alpha)\bar{g}_D]s - \frac{\alpha(1-\alpha)}{2} \int_0^s \sigma_D^2(M_{t+h})dh} ds \right). \quad (10.6)$$

An increase in volatility reduces the price-dividend ratio only if $\alpha < 1$, which is consistent with earlier research in discrete time (e.g., Barsky, 1989; Abel, 1988).[5]

Specification C2: i.i.d. consumption. We can alternatively assume that consumption has a constant drift and volatility. The interest rate (10.4) is then constant, and the price-dividend ratio is equal to

$$\mathbb{E}_t \left(\int_0^{+\infty} e^{-(r_f - \bar{g}_D)s - \alpha \rho_{C,D} \bar{\sigma}_C \int_0^s \sigma_D (M_{t+h}) dh} ds \right).$$

High volatility feeds into low asset prices for any choices of relative risk aversion α. This approach fits well with the discrete-time volatility feedback literature reviewed in the previous chapter.

Specification C3: multivariate MSM. In the Appendix we develop a multivariate extension of MSM that permits more flexible specifications of consumption. This approach helps to construct SDF models with a stochastic volatility that is only partially correlated to the stochastic volatility of dividends. We focus for expositional simplicity on the tree and i.i.d. specifications in the remainder of the chapter.

10.2.3   The Equilibrium Stock Price

Jumps in equilibrium prices are triggered by regime changes in the volatility state vector. Since the components have heterogeneous persistence levels, the model avoids the difficult choice of a unique frequency and size for "rare events", which is a common issue in specifying traditional jump-diffusions.[6]

The relation between the frequency and size of a jump is easily quantified by loglinearizing the price-dividend ratio. Consider the parametric family of state processes $M_t(\varepsilon) = 1 + \varepsilon(\nu_t - 1)$, $t \in \mathbb{R}_+$, $\varepsilon \in [0, 1)$, where ν is itself a fixed MSM state vector.

---

[5]When future consumption becomes riskier, two opposite economic effects impact the P/D ratio, as can be seen in (10.5). First, investors perceive an increase in the covariance $\sigma_C(M_{t+h})\sigma_D(M_{t+h})\rho_{C,D}$ between future consumption and dividends (systematic risk), which *reduces* the price-dividend ratio. Second, the precautionary motive increases the expected marginal utility of future consumption, which lowers future interest rates $r_f(M_{t+h})$ and *increases* P/D. The negative impact of systematic risk dominates when $\alpha < 1$.

[6]In the simplest exogenously specified jump-diffusions, it is often possible that discontinuities of heterogeneous but fixed sizes and different frequencies can be aggregated into a single collective jump process with an intensity equal to the sum of all the individual jumps and a random distribution of sizes. A comparable analogy can be made for the state vector M_t in our model, but due to the equilibrium linkages between jump size and the duration of volatility shocks, and the state dependence of price jumps, no such reduction to a single aggregated frequency is possible for the equilibrium stock price.

Proposition 14 (First-order expansion of P/D) *The log of the P/D ratio is approximated around $\varepsilon = 0$ by the first-order Taylor expansion:*

$$q[M_t(\varepsilon)] = \bar{q} - q_1 \sum_{k=1}^{\bar{k}} \frac{M_{k,t}(\varepsilon) - 1}{\delta' + \gamma_k} + o(\varepsilon). \qquad (10.7)$$

The Lucas tree economy implies $\delta' = \delta - (1 - \alpha)\bar{g}_D + \alpha(1 - \alpha)\bar{\sigma}_D^2/2$, $\bar{q} = -\ln(\delta')$ and $q_1 = \alpha(1 - \alpha)\bar{\sigma}_D^2/2$. When consumption is i.i.d., the parameters instead are $\delta' = r_f - \bar{g}_D + \alpha\rho_{C,D}\bar{\sigma}_C\bar{\sigma}_D$, $\bar{q} = -\ln(\delta')$ and $q_1 = \alpha\rho_{C,D}\bar{\sigma}_C\bar{\sigma}_D/2$.

When the distribution M is close to unity, the P/D ratio is approximated by a persistence-weighted sum of the volatility components. Low-frequency multipliers deliver persistent and discrete switches, which have a large impact on the P/D ratio. By contrast, higher-frequency components have no noticeable effect on prices, but give additional outliers in returns through their direct effect on the tails of the dividend process. The price process is thus characterized by a large number of small jumps (high-frequency $M_{k,t}$), a moderate number of moderate jumps (intermediate frequency $M_{k,t}$), and a small number of very large jumps. Earlier empirical research suggests that this is a good characterization of the dynamics of stock returns.

In Figure 10.1 we illustrate the endogenous multifrequency pricing dynamics of the model, in the case where consumption is i.i.d.. The top two panels present a simulated dividend process, in growth rates and in logarithms of the level, respectively. The middle two panels then display the corresponding stock returns and log prices. The price series exhibits much larger movements than dividends, due to the presence of endogenous jumps in the P/D ratio. To see this clearly, the bottom two panels show consecutively: (1) the "feedback" effects, defined as the difference between log stock returns and log dividend growth, and (2) the price-dividend ratio. We observe a few infrequent but large jumps in prices, with more numerous small discontinuities. The simulation demonstrates that the difference between stock returns and dividend growth can be large even when the P/D ratio varies in a plausible and relatively modest range (between 26 and 33 in the figure). The pricing model thus captures multifrequency stochastic volatility, endogenous multifrequency jumps in prices, and endogenous correlation between volatility and price innovations.

10.3 Price Dynamics with an Infinity of Frequencies

We now investigate how the price diffusion evolves as $\bar{k} \to \infty$, that is, as components of increasingly high frequency are added into the state vector.

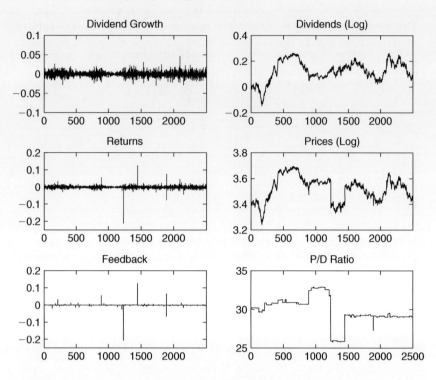

FIGURE 10.1. **Equilibrium Price and Return Dynamics.** This figure illustrates the relation between exogenous dividends and equilibrium prices when consumption is i.i.d. The top two panels display simulated dividend growth rates and dividend levels. The parameters used in the specification are $m_0 = 1.35, \bar{\sigma}_D = 0.7, b = 2.2$, and $\bar{g}_D = 0.0001$. The middle two panels demonstrate the result of equilibrium pricing. In these panels we use the preference and consumption parameters $\alpha = 25, \delta = 0.00005, \bar{g}_C = 0.00005, \rho_{C,D}\bar{\sigma}_C = 0.0012$. The left-hand side displays returns, and the right side shows the log-price realization. Both show more variability, and in particular jumps, relative to the dividend processes. To isolate the endogenous pricing effects in returns and prices, the bottom left panel shows the volatility "feedback" effect, defined as the difference between log-returns and log-dividend growth, that is, $\Delta p_t - \Delta d_t$, or the difference between the middle left and top left panels. To show the same endogenous pricing effects in levels, the bottom right-hand panel shows the price-dividend ratio.

Specifically, the parameters $(\bar{g}_D, \bar{\sigma}_D, \gamma_1, b)$ and the distribution M are fixed, and $M_t = (M_{k,t})_{k=1}^{\infty} \in \mathbb{R}_+^{\infty}$ is an MSM Markov state with countably many frequencies. Each component $M_{k,t}$ is characterized by the arrival intensity $\gamma_k = \gamma_1 b^{k-1}$.

As in Chapter 7, we characterize dividend dynamics by the time deformation

$$\theta_{\bar{k}}(t) = \int_0^t \sigma_{D,\bar{k}}^2(M_s)ds. \tag{10.8}$$

The dividend process $d_{\bar{k}}(t)$ is then represented by $d_0 + \bar{g}_D t - \theta_{\bar{k}}(t)/2 + B[\theta_{\bar{k}}(t)]$, where B is a standard Brownian. When $\mathbb{E}(M^2) < b$, the trading time sequence $\theta_{\bar{k}}$ has a limit θ_∞ with continuous sample paths. The dividend process therefore converges to

$$d_\infty(t) \equiv d_0 + \bar{g}_D t - \theta_\infty(t)/2 + B[\theta_\infty(t)].$$

The local Hölder exponent of $d_\infty(t)$ takes a *continuum* of values in any time interval.

We now examine the equilibrium impact of increasingly permitting many frequencies in the volatility of dividends. A particularly striking example is provided by Lucas tree economies. We consider

Condition 9 $\alpha \leq 1$ *and* $\rho = \delta - (1 - \alpha)\bar{g}_D > 0$.

For finite $\bar{k}$, the equilibrium price-dividend ratio is given by (10.6), or equivalently,

$$q_{\bar{k}}(t) = \ln \mathbb{E}\left[\left. \int_0^{+\infty} e^{-\rho s - \frac{\alpha(1-\alpha)}{2}[\theta_{\bar{k}}(t+s)-\theta_{\bar{k}}(t)]} ds \right| (M_{k,t})_{k=1}^{\bar{k}} \right]. \qquad (10.9)$$

The price process has therefore the same distribution as

$$p_{\bar{k}}(t) \equiv d_{\bar{k}}(t) + q_{\bar{k}}(t).$$

When the number of frequencies goes to infinity, the dividend process has a well-defined limit. As we show in the Appendix, the P/D ratio (10.9) is a positive submartingale, which also converges to a limit as $\bar{k} \to \infty$.

Proposition 15 (Jump-diffusion with countably many frequencies)
When the number of frequencies goes to infinity, the log-price process weakly converges to

$$p_\infty(t) \equiv d_\infty(t) + q_\infty(t),$$

where

$$q_\infty(t) = \ln \mathbb{E}\left[\left. \int_0^{+\infty} e^{-\rho s - \frac{\alpha(1-\alpha)}{2}[\theta_\infty(t+s)-\theta_\infty(t)]} ds \right| (M_{k,t})_{k=1}^{\infty} \right]$$

is a pure jump process. The limiting price is thus a jump-diffusion with countably many frequencies.

In an economy with countably many frequencies, the log-price process is the sum of (1) the continuous multifractal diffusion $d_\infty(t)$; and (2) the pure jump process $q_\infty(t)$. We correspondingly call $p_\infty(t)$ a *multifractal jump-diffusion*.

When $\bar{k} = \infty$, the state space is a continuum, while the Lucas tree econ-
omy is still specified by the seven parameters $(\bar{g}_D, \bar{\sigma}_D, m_0, \gamma_1, b, \alpha, \delta)$. The
equilibrium P/D ratio $q_\infty(t)$ exhibits rich dynamic properties. Within any
bounded time interval, there exists almost surely (a.s.) at least one multiplier $M_{k,t}$ that switches and triggers a jump in the stock price. This
property implies that a jump in price occurs a.s. in the neighborhood
of any instant. The number of switches is also countable a.s. within any
bounded time interval, implying that the process has infinite activity and

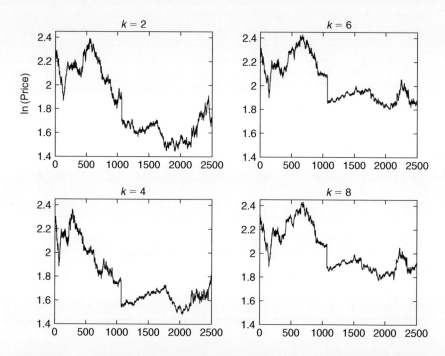

FIGURE 10.2. **Convergence to Multifractal Jump-Diffusion.** This figure
illustrates convergence of the equilibrium price process as the number of high-
frequency volatility components becomes large. The panels show, consecutively,
simulations of the log-price process $p_{\bar{k}}(t) = d_0 + \bar{g}_D t - \theta_{\bar{k}}(t)/2 + B[\theta_{\bar{k}}(t)] + q_{\bar{k}}(t)$ for
$\bar{k} = 2, 4, 6, 8$. All panels hold constant the Brownian $B(t)$. The multipliers $M_{k,t}$
are also drawn only once and then held constant as higher level multipliers are
added. The construction is thus recursive in $\bar{k}$, with each increment requiring the
previously drawn nondeformed dividends and multipliers from the preceding level,
plus new random draws for the next set of (higher-frequency) multipliers being
incorporated. We observe large differences between the panels corresponding to
$\bar{k} = 2$ and $\bar{k} = 4$, more moderate changes between $\bar{k} = 4$ and $\bar{k} = 6$, and only
modest differences between $\bar{k} = 6$ and $\bar{k} = 8$. In this set of simulations, we use
the Lucas economy specification with $T = 2,500$, $m_0 = 1.4, b = 3.25$, $\gamma_1 = 0.25 b^7 \approx$
0.0001, $\bar{\sigma}_C = 0.0125$, $\bar{g}_D = 0.00008$, $\delta = 0.00003$, and $\alpha = 0.5$.

is continuous almost everywhere. Equilibrium valuation therefore generates a limit P/D ratio that follows an infinite intensity pure jump process.

In Figure 10.2 we illustrate the convergence of the equilibrium price processes as $\bar{k}$ becomes large. The first panel shows a simulation with $\bar{k} = 2$ volatility components, and the following panels consecutively add higher-frequency components to obtain paths with $\bar{k} = 4$, $\bar{k} = 6$, and $\bar{k} = 8$ components. Consistent with the theoretical construction, the figure is obtained by randomly drawing a trajectory of the Brownian motion B in stage $\bar{k} = 0$, which is thereafter taken as fixed. Similarly, each multiplier $M_{k,t}$ is drawn only once, so that $(M_{k,t})_{k=1}^{\bar{k}}$ does not vary when we move from stage $\bar{k}$ to stage $\bar{k} + 1$. The figure suggests that the price process becomes progressively insensitive to the addition of new high-frequency components, and the sample path of the price process stabilizes. For low $\bar{k}$, adding components has a significant impact, and as $\bar{k}$ increases the process converges.

10.4   Recursive Utility and Priced Jumps

We showed in Chapter 9 that the equity premium can be matched with reasonable levels of risk aversion when investors have Epstein-Zin-Weil utility and consumption undergoes regime switches. The recursive preference equilibrium easily generalizes to continuous time, permitting discontinuities in the SDF and priced jumps, as we now show.

Agents have a stochastic differential utility V_t (Duffie and Epstein, 1992), which is specified by a normalized aggregator $f(c, v)$ and satisfies the fixed-point equation

$$V_t = \mathbb{E}_t \left[\int_t^T f(C_s, V_s)ds + V_T \right] \tag{10.10}$$

for any instants $T \geq t \geq 0$. The aggregator is given by

$$f(c, v) \equiv \frac{\delta}{1 - \psi^{-1}} \frac{c^{1-\psi^{-1}} - [(1 - \alpha)v]^\theta}{[(1 - \alpha)v]^{\theta - 1}},$$

where α is the coefficient of relative risk aversion, ψ is the elasticity of intertemporal substitution, and $\theta = (1 - \psi^{-1})/(1 - \alpha)$. The case where $\theta = 1$ corresponds to isoelastic utility as considered previously.

Under the consumption process in Condition 7, the recursive utility has functional form $V(c, M_t) = \varphi(M_t)c^{1-\alpha}/(1 - \alpha)$. [7] The stochastic discount

---

[7] The fixed-point equation (10.10) can be written as $f(C_t, V_t)dt + \mathbb{E}_t(dV_t) = 0$. Let $\varphi_1, \ldots, \varphi_d$ denote the value of φ in all possible states $m^1, \ldots, m^d$. The fixed-point

factor is then $\Lambda_t = \delta^{-1} \exp\left[\int_0^t f_v(C_s, V_s)ds\right] f_c(C_t, V_t)$ (Duffie and Epstein, 1992; Duffie and Skiadas, 1994), or equivalently

$$\Lambda_t = [\varphi(M_t)]^{1-\theta} C_t^{-\alpha} e^{-\frac{\delta}{\theta}t + \delta\left(1-\frac{1}{\theta}\right)\int_0^t [\varphi(M_s)]^{-\theta} ds}.$$

Consumption and the exponential expression are continuous. On the other hand, the first factor in the equation is a function of $\varphi(M_t)$, which depends on the Markov state and can therefore vary discontinuously through time. In the simplifying case where $\theta = 1$ (power utility), the factor $[\varphi(M_t)]^{1-\theta}$ drops out, and the SDF has continuous sample paths, reducing to $\Lambda_t = e^{-\delta t} C_t^{-\alpha}$. On the other hand, if $\theta \neq 1$, the term $[\varphi(M_t)]^{1-\theta}$ is discontinuous, and the marginal utility of consumption depends on the current state. Discrete changes in the state vector M_t thus cause jumps in the SDF.

Since switches in M_t trigger simultaneous jumps in the stochastic discount factor and the P/D ratio, they impact expected returns, and hence are "priced" in equilibrium. To see this, we denote by $\gamma = \sum_{k=1}^{\bar{k}} \gamma_k$ the intensity that at least one arrival occurs. Furthermore, let $\mathbb{E}_{t,A}$ denote the expectation operator conditional on (1) the investor information set I_t; and (2) the occurrence of at least one arrival between t and $t + dt$. The conditional equity premium is then:

$$-\frac{1}{dt}\mathbb{E}_t\left(\frac{d\Lambda_t}{\Lambda_t}\frac{dP_t}{P_t}\right) = \alpha\sigma_C(M_t)\sigma_D(M_t)\rho_{C,D} + \gamma\mathbb{E}_{t,A}\left(-\frac{\Delta\Lambda_t}{\Lambda_t}\frac{\Delta P_t}{P_t}\right).$$

When $\theta \neq 1$, the final term is generally nonzero, confirming that the possibility of a discontinuity modifies the expected return required by investors on the stock. Jumps represent a priced risk in equilibrium.

The ability of our framework to accommodate priced jumps is potentially useful for empirical applications. For example, we have used nonseparable preferences in Chapter 9 to obtain priced switches in a calibration that simultaneously fits, with reasonable levels of risk aversion, the equity premium, equity volatility, and the drifts and volatilities of consumption and dividends. In a recent contribution, Bhamra, Kuehn, and Strebulaev (2006) extend this framework by considering levered claims on the priced asset. They find that the ability to capture priced jumps is empirically important

---

equation is then

$$\frac{\delta}{\theta}(\varphi_i^{1-\theta} - \varphi_i) + \varphi_i\left[(1-\alpha)g_C(m^i) + \frac{\alpha(\alpha-1)}{2}\sigma_C^2(m^i)\right] + \sum_{j\neq i} a_{i,j}(\varphi_j - \varphi_i) = 0,$$

where $a_{i,j} = \mathbb{P}\left(M_{t+dt} = m^j | M_t = m^i\right)/dt$. Existence and uniqueness can then be analyzed using standard methods.

in simultaneously reconciling the equity premium, default spreads, and empirically observed default rates. We anticipate that future work will use our structural approach to modeling priced jumps in other applications, including, for example, pricing options and other derivatives.

10.5   Discussion

In this chapter, we develop a continuous-time asset pricing economy with endogenous multifrequency jumps in stock prices. Equilibrium valuation gives a number of appealing features that are often assumed exogenously in previous literature, including: (1) heterogeneous jump sizes with many and frequent small jumps and few large jumps; and (2) endogenous correlation between jumps in prices and volatility. Furthermore, jumps are priced in equilibrium under nonseparable preferences.

We consider the weak limit of our economic equilibrium as the number of components driving fundamentals becomes large. Under appropriate conditions, the stock price converges to a new mathematical object called a multifractal jump-diffusion. The equity value can be decomposed into the continuous multifractal diffusion followed by the exogenous dividend process, and an infinite-intensity pure jump process corresponding to endogenous variations in the price-dividend ratio.

The chapter can be viewed as bridging a gap between exogenously specified jump-diffusions and discrete-time equilibrium models of volatility feedback, such as in Chapter 9. More generally, the model illustrates that equilibrium is a powerful method to generate endogenous price discontinuities in financial economics.

11
Conclusion

The Markov-switching approach to multifractal modeling offers a parsimonious and accurate statistical description of financial time series based on the concept of scale-invariant multifrequency risk. In the most basic construction, MSM is driven by a Markov state vector with multiple components, whose rescaled product defines total volatility. Each of the components, or multipliers, can switch to a new level with a different probability per unit time, generating volatility shocks of multiple frequencies. When an arrival does occur in a given multiplier, a new value is drawn from a fixed distribution independently of all other variables in the model. The marginal distributions of all volatility components are hence identical, which provides parsimony to MSM and finds empirical support at standard confidence levels. The construction works equally well in discrete and continuous time, and easily extends to multivariate settings.

From a statistical point of view, elaborated in Parts I and II of the book, MSM captures thick tails, long-memory features, and intertwined volatility cycles of heterogeneous durations. When volatility components have a discrete distribution, MSM is a latent Markov chain, and its parameters can be estimated by maximizing the closed-form likelihood of the return series. Alternatively, return moments can be used to quickly calibrate or estimate MSM. Once the parameters have been imputed, the applied researcher can readily compute the conditional distribution of the volatility state and returns at any instant. Bayesian updating permits filtering of volatility components, and the Markov construction implies tractable multistep prediction. The research presented in this book and subsequent studies have shown that MSM performs well in-sample, produces good forecasts of volatility, and generates reliable estimates of the value-at-risk in a position or portfolio of assets.

MSM also captures the unconditional moments of returns, and in particular the "power variations" of many financial series, which have been studied extensively (e.g., Andersen et al., 2001; Barndorff-Nielsen and Shephard, 2003; Calvet and Fisher, 2002a; Calvet, Fisher, and Mandelbrot, 1997; Galluccio et al., 1997; Ghashghaie et al., 1996; Pasquini and Serva, 1999, 2000; Richards, 2000; Vandewalle and Ausloos, 1998; Vassilicos, Demos, and Tata, 1993). The multifractal model implies that the qth moment of absolute returns scales as a power function of the frequency of observation, provided that the qth moment exists. Furthermore, across q the scaling exponents used in the power functions form a nonlinear strictly convex function of q. Extensive research, including results presented in this book, shows that these scaling properties hold in a variety of currency and equity series.

The transition between discrete- and continuous-time versions of MSM is remarkably straightforward, which is a substantial operational advantage of our approach. Additional insights can be gained from continuous-time MSM by considering the limit time deformation when the number of high-frequency components goes to infinity. Because local volatility exhibits increasingly extreme fluctuations, the Lebesgue dominated convergence theorem does not apply and in fact gives the misleading intuition that the limit trading time converges to zero. By contrast, a correct analysis using the martingale convergence theorem and appropriate tightness conditions implies that the trading-time sequence converges to a nondegenerate time deformation process. The limiting multifractal diffusion is driven by countably many components, and its sample paths contain a continuum of local Hölder exponents in any time interval.

In Part III we show that MSM integrates easily into equilibrium models, providing a tractable framework within which to analyze the impact of multifrequency shocks on endogenous asset prices. We consider a consumption-based economy as in Lucas (1978) with MSM shocks to dividend news, and in some cases, consumption growth. The presence of volatility shocks of heterogeneous durations generates endogenous variations in the price-dividend ratio, and the volatility of returns can be substantially higher than the volatility of dividends. Investor learning endogenously generates negative skewness in stock returns because increases in volatility (bad news) tend to be revealed abruptly while decreases in volatility (good news) are likely to be inferred gradually. Long-run risk is naturally present in MSM, and helps to generate equilibrium stock returns consistent with the equity premium. In continuous time, volatility shocks of heterogeneous durations lead to endogenous jumps in prices, with many small discontinuities, frequent moderate jumps, and rare extreme events. As the number of volatility components diverges to infinity, the continuous-time equilibrium approach generates a new mathematical object, which is the sum of a continuous multifractal diffusion and an infinite intensity pure jump process. We call this new process a multifractal jump-diffusion.

Numerous applications, extensions, and research questions emerge naturally from the research developed in this book. For example, practitioners interested in the implementation of MSM on real-time data can impute the parameters of MSM by either maximizing the closed-form likelihood or using a moment-based calibration, as illustrated in Chapter 8. The inferred data generating process can be used to forecast volatility or produce estimates of value-at-risk. Lux (2008) provides additional discussion of simplified estimation and forecasting methods. Practitioners may also seek to use MSM to price options, for instance by considering multifrequency variants of the Hull and White (1987) model. In ongoing research, we have found evidence that MSM can be very helpful in pricing options and other derivatives. We anticipate that applications of multifractals to derivatives valuation will be a growth area in coming years.

Econometricians may be interested in further expanding and developing applications of fractal-type methods. MSM illustrates that pure regime-switching models can match and in some cases outperform smoothly autoregressive volatility processes. As suggested by Hamilton (2006), the general approach of investigating high-dimensional but parsimonious and structured regime-switching offers considerable promise and will likely receive further attention.

Theoretical researchers can use the models in this book to reexamine the common view that wild fluctuations in financial markets are inconsistent with the concept of economic equilibrium (e.g., Mandelbrot and Hudson, 2004). As pointed out by Bansal and Yaron (2004), risk premia can be high and returns volatile in a world where fundamentals are very persistent. MSM equilibrium models accommodate these low-frequency features, while simultaneously providing sufficient realism at high frequencies that the model can be estimated using maximum likelihood on daily data. Through this approach, we are able to bring together aspects of both the high-frequency financial econometrics and lower-frequency macro-finance literatures.

Recent literature in financial economics and asset management has generated renewed interest in the modeling and pricing implications of rare events (e.g., Barro, 2006; Taleb, 2007). MSM provides new insights on how these risks can be specified and are likely to affect asset prices. To develop intuition, one can begin by considering a single-frequency MSM specification with a very low value of γ_1. Changes in the drift or volatility of fundamentals are very rare, but produce extreme asset returns in equilibrium when they do occur. Estimation is course difficult in such an environment, as it is effectively based on very few observations or perhaps none at all.

The multifractal setting implies that rare events need not be studied in isolation. In particular, the structure imposed by MSM, which appears to be consistent with empirical evidence, suggests that variations at high and medium frequencies may help to build a reasonable framework for lower-frequency events. From an intuitive point of view, gradations in size and frequency exist even in the context of disaster, depression, and war, and models assuming a dichotomy between normal and catastrophic states can miss such regularities. Furthermore given an existing MSM specification, one can easily contemplate adding in additional possibilities for rare events by either lowering the intensity of arrival γ_1 of the most persistent component, or equivalently by assuming that some component of arrival intensity $\gamma_0 = \gamma_1/b$ has not switched during recorded history. The structure of MSM allows the applied researcher to infer the likely size and price impact of such shocks, and thus stress-test pricing and risk management models. The recent turbulence in the financial markets highlights the usefulness of considering shocks larger than those that have been hitherto observed.

MSM offers the finance profession an opportunity to tie together various phenomena that have been previously modeled in isolation. The interaction of shocks with heterogeneous frequencies is a potent source of price dynamics that can explain financial data at all horizons with a very limited number of parameters. We anticipate that future research will further demonstrate the validity of this approach.

Appendices

A.1 Appendix to Chapter 3

A.1.1 Proof of Proposition 1

Consider a sequence of processes with fixed parameter vector $\psi = (m_0, \bar{\sigma}, b, \gamma^*)$. Note in particular that $\gamma_{\bar{k}} = \gamma^*$ for all $\bar{k}$. For any integer $n \geq 0$ and real $q \in [0, \infty)$, it is convenient to define $K_q(n) = \mathbb{E}(|r_t|^q |r_{t+n}|^q)/[\mathbb{E}(|r_t|^{2q})]$ and $c_q = [\mathbb{E}(|\varepsilon_t|^q)]^2/[\mathbb{E}(|\varepsilon_t|^{2q})]$. Multipliers in different stages of the cascade are statistically independent. The definition of returns, $r_t = \bar{\sigma}(M_{1,t} M_{2,t} \ldots M_{\bar{k},t})^{1/2}\varepsilon_t$ and $r_{t+n} = \bar{\sigma}(M_{1,t+n}M_{2,t+n} \ldots M_{\bar{k},t+n})^{1/2}\varepsilon_{t+n}$, implies

$$K_q(n) = c_q[\mathbb{E}(M^q)]^{-\bar{k}} \prod_{k=1}^{\bar{k}} \mathbb{E}(M_{k,t}^{q/2} M_{k,t+n}^{q/2}).$$

Note that $\mathbb{E}(M_{k,t}^{q/2} M_{k,t+n}^{q/2}) = \mathbb{E}(M^q)(1 - \gamma_k)^n + [\mathbb{E}(M^{q/2})]^2[1 - (1 - \gamma_k)^n]$ or equivalently

$$\mathbb{E}(M_{k,t}^{q/2} M_{k,t+n}^{q/2}) = [\mathbb{E}(M^{q/2})]^2 \quad [1 + a_q(1 - \gamma_k)^n],$$

where $a_q = \mathbb{E}(M^q)/[\mathbb{E}(M^{q/2})]^2 - 1$. Since $1 - \gamma_k = (1 - \gamma_{\bar{k}})^{b^{k-\bar{k}}}$ and $\gamma_{\bar{k}} = \gamma^*$, we obtain

$$\ln \frac{K_q(n)}{c_q} = \sum_{k=1}^{\bar{k}} \ln \frac{1 + a_q(1 - \gamma^*)^{nb^{k-\bar{k}}}}{1 + a_q}. \tag{A.1}$$

As k increases from 1 to $\bar{k}$, the expression $(1 - \gamma^*)^{nb^{k-\bar{k}}}$ declines from $(1 - \gamma^*)^{nb^{1-\bar{k}}}$ to $(1 - \gamma^*)^n$. The maximum $(1 - \gamma^*)^{nb^{1-\bar{k}}}$ is close to 1 and the minimum $(1 - \gamma^*)^n$ is close to 0 when $b^{\bar{k}}/n$ and n are large. Intermediate values are observed when $(1 - \gamma^*)^{nb^{k-\bar{k}}} \approx 1 - \gamma^*$, or equivalently $k \approx \log_b(b^{\bar{k}}/n)$. Let $i(n)$ denote the unique integer such that $i(n) \leq \log_b(b^{\bar{k}}/n) < i(n) + 1$. We surmise that

$$\ln \frac{K_q(n)}{c_q} \approx \sum_{k=i(n)+1}^{\bar{k}} \ln \frac{1}{1 + a_q} = -[\bar{k} - i(n)] \ln(1 + a_q),$$

and thus $\ln[K_q(n)] \approx -(\log_b n)\ln(1 + a_q) = -\delta(q) \ln n$.

To formalize this intuition, consider the interval $I_{\bar{k}} = \{n : \alpha_1 \log_b(b^{\bar{k}}) \leq \log_b n \leq \alpha_2 \log_b(b^k)\}$. Note that $\log_b(b^k/n) \geq (1 - \alpha_2) \log_b(b^k)$ for all $n \in I_{\bar{k}}$. We henceforth assume that $\bar{k}$ is sufficiently large so that $i(n) \geq b$ $\forall\, n \in I_{\bar{k}}$. Consider an arbitrary sequence of strictly positive integers $j(n)$ monotonically diverging to $+\infty$. The precise definition of $j(n)$ is temporarily postponed. Let

$$u_n = j(n) \ln(1 + a_q) + \sum_{k=i(n)-j(n)+1}^{i(n)+j(n)} \ln \frac{1 + a_q(1 - \gamma^*)^{nb^{k-\bar{k}}}}{1 + a_q}.$$

By (A.1), $\ln[K_q(n)/c_q]$ can be decomposed into four components:

$$\ln \frac{K_q(n)}{c_q} = -[\bar{k} - i(n)] \ln(1 + a_q) + \sum_{k=1}^{i(n)-j(n)} \ln \frac{1 + a_q(1 - \gamma^*)^{nb^{k-\bar{k}}}}{1 + a_q} \qquad (A.2)$$

$$+ u_n + \sum_{k=i(n)+j(n)+1}^{\bar{k}} \ln[1 + a_q(1 - \gamma^*)^{nb^{k-\bar{k}}}].$$

We successively examine each component on the right-hand side.

- The first component is between $-\delta(q)\,(\ln n + \ln b)$ and $-\delta(q) \ln n$.

- The second component contains terms $(1 - \gamma^*)^{nb^{k-\bar{k}}}$ that are bounded below by $(1 - \gamma^*)^{nb^{i(n)-j(n)-\bar{k}}}$. The definition of $i(n)$ implies $nb^{i(n)-\bar{k}} \leq 1$ and thus

$$\left| \sum_{k=1}^{i(n)-j(n)} \ln \frac{1 + a_q(1 - \gamma^*)^{nb^{k-\bar{k}}}}{1 + a_q} \right| \leq i(n) \ln \frac{1 + a_q}{1 + a_q(1 - \gamma^*)^{b^{-j(n)}}}.$$

By standard concavity arguments, we infer $\ln \frac{1+a_q}{1+a_q(1-\gamma^*)^{b^{-j(n)}}} \leq a_q$ $[1 - (1 - \gamma^*)^{b^{-j(n)}}]$ and $1 - e^{b^{-j(n)} \ln(1-\gamma^*)} \leq b^{-j(n)} |\ln(1 - \gamma^*)|$. The second component of (A.2) is therefore bounded by $i(n) b^{-j(n)} a_q |\ln(1 - \gamma^*)|$.

- The third component, u_n, contains terms $1 + a_q(1 - \gamma^*)^{nb^{k-\bar{k}}}$ that are between 1 and $1 + a_q$. Hence $|u_n| \leq j(n) \ln(1 + a_q) \leq a_q j(n)$.

- The fourth component is positive and bounded above by

$$a_q \sum_{k=i(n)+j(n)+1}^{\bar{k}} (1 - \gamma^*)^{nb^{k-\bar{k}}} \leq a_q \sum_{k=0}^{\infty} (1 - \gamma^*)^{b^k nb^{i(n)+j(n)+1-\bar{k}}}.$$

We check that $nb^{i(n)+j(n)+1-\bar{k}} \geq 1$ and $b^k \geq k(b-1)$. The fourth component is therefore bounded above by $a_q \sum_{k=0}^{\infty}(1-\gamma^*)^{k(b-1)} = \frac{a_q}{1-(1-\gamma^*)^{b-1}}$.

This establishes that

$$\left| \frac{\ln K_q(n)}{\ln n^{-\delta(q)}} - 1 \right| \leq \frac{c_q^* + a_q j(n) + a_q i(n) b^{-j(n)} |\ln(1-\gamma^*)|}{\delta(q)\ln n},$$

where $c_q^* = \delta(q)\ln b + |\ln c_q| + a_q/[1 - (1-\gamma^*)^{(b-1)}]$. We now choose a sequence $j(n)$ such that the right-hand side of the inequality converges to 0. More specifically, consider the unique integer such that[1] $j(n) \leq 2\log_b i(n) < j(n)+1$. It is easy to check that $i(n)b^{-j(n)} = b^{\log_b i(n)-j(n)} \leq 1$ and $j(n) \leq 2\log_b \bar{k}$. For all $n \in I_{\bar{k}}$, the quantity $\left| \frac{\ln K_q(n)}{\ln n^{-\delta(q)}} - 1 \right|$ is therefore bounded above by

$$\eta_{\bar{k}} = \frac{1}{\bar{k}\,\delta(q)\alpha_1 \ln b} \left[2a_q \log_b \bar{k} + c_q^* + a_q |\ln(1-\gamma^*)| \right], \qquad \text{(A.3)}$$

which is independent of n. We infer that $\sup_{n \in I_{\bar{k}}} \left| \frac{\ln K_q(n)}{\ln n^{-\delta(q)}} - 1 \right| \to 0$ as $\bar{k} \to +\infty$.

Finally, we observe that

$$\left| \frac{\ln \rho_q(n)}{\ln n^{-\delta(q)}} - 1 \right| \leq \left| \frac{\log_b [\rho_q(n)/K_q(n)]}{\ln n^{-\delta(q)}} \right| + \left| \frac{\ln K_q(n)}{\ln n^{-\delta(q)}} - 1 \right|.$$

The autocorrelation $\rho_q(n)$ satisfies

$$1 \leq \frac{K_q(n)}{\rho_q(n)} = \frac{1 - c_q(1+a_q)^{-\bar{k}}}{1 - c_q(1+a_q)^{-\bar{k}}/K_q(n)} \leq \frac{1}{1 - c_q(1+a_q)^{-\bar{k}}/K_q(n)}. \qquad \text{(A.4)}$$

Equation (A.3) implies that for all $n \in I_{\bar{k}}$, $\log_b K_q(n) \geq -\delta(q)(1+\eta_{\bar{k}})\alpha_2 \bar{k}$, and thus

$$\log_b[K_q(n)/(1+a_q)^{-\bar{k}}] \geq \bar{k}\delta(q)(1 - \alpha_2 - \alpha_2\eta_{\bar{k}}). \qquad \text{(A.5)}$$

Combining (A.4) and (A.5), we conclude that $\sup_{n \in I_{\bar{k}}} \left| \ln \frac{K_q(n)}{\rho_q(n)} \right| \to 0$ and that the Proposition holds.

---

[1] We check that when $\bar{k}$ is large enough, $1 \leq j(n) \leq i(n)$ and $j(n) + i(n) \leq \bar{k}$ for all $n \in I_{\bar{k}}$.

A.1.2   HAC-Adjusted Vuong Test

We consider the probability space $(\Omega, \mathcal{F}, \mathbb{P}^0)$ and a stochastic process $\{r_t\}_{t=1}^{+\infty}$. Each r_t is a random variable taking values on the real line. For every t, it is convenient to consider the vector of past values $\mathcal{R}_{t-1} = \{r_s\}_{s=1}^{t-1}$. The econometrician directly observes a finite number of realizations of r_t but does not know the true data-generating process. She instead considers two competing families of models specified by their conditional densities $\mathcal{M}_f = \{f(r_t|\mathcal{R}_{t-1}, \theta); \theta \in \Theta\}$ and $\mathcal{M}_g = \{g(r_t|\mathcal{R}_{t-1}, \gamma); \gamma \in \Gamma\}$. These families may or may not contain the true data-generating process. The pseudo true value θ^* specifies the model in $\mathcal{M}_f$ with the optimal Kullback-Leibler Information Criterion:

$$\theta^* = \arg\max_{\theta \in \Theta} \quad \mathbb{E}^0[\ln f(r_t|\mathcal{R}_{t-1}, \theta)].$$

The pseudo true value γ^* is similarly defined.

Consider the log-likelihood functions:

$$L_T^f(\theta) \equiv \sum_{t=1}^{T} \ln f(r_t|\mathcal{R}_{t-1}, \theta), \qquad L_T^g(\gamma) \equiv \sum_{t=1}^{T} \ln g(r_t|\mathcal{R}_{t-1}, \gamma).$$

By definition, the ML estimators $\hat{\theta}_T$ and $\hat{\gamma}_T$ maximize the functions $L_T^f(\theta)$ and $L_T^g(\gamma)$. The corresponding first-order conditions are

$$\frac{\partial L_T^f}{\partial \theta}(\hat{\theta}_T) = 0, \quad \frac{\partial L_T^g}{\partial \theta}(\hat{\gamma}_T) = 0. \tag{A.6}$$

We now examine the likelihood ratio

$$LR_T(\hat{\theta}_T, \hat{\gamma}_T) = L_T^f(\hat{\theta}_T) - L_T^g(\hat{\gamma}_T) = \sum_{t=1}^{T} \ln \frac{f(r_t|\mathcal{R}_{t-1}, \hat{\theta}_T)}{g(r_t|\mathcal{R}_{t-1}, \hat{\gamma}_T)}.$$

By Equation (A.6), a second-order expansion of LR_T implies that $\frac{1}{\sqrt{T}} LR_T(\hat{\theta}_T, \hat{\gamma}_T) = \frac{1}{\sqrt{T}} LR_T(\theta^*, \gamma^*) + o_p(1)$, and thus

$$\frac{1}{\sqrt{T}} LR_T(\hat{\theta}_T, \hat{\gamma}_T) = \frac{1}{\sqrt{T}} \sum_{t=1}^{T} \ln \frac{f(r_t|\mathcal{R}_{t-1}, \theta^*)}{g(r_t|\mathcal{R}_{t-1}, \gamma^*)} + o_p(1).$$

Let $a_t = \ln[f(r_t|\mathcal{R}_{t-1}, \theta^*)/g(r_t|\mathcal{R}_{t-1}, \gamma^*)]$ and $\hat{a}_t = \ln[f(r_t|\mathcal{R}_{t-1}, \hat{\theta}_T)/g(r_t|\mathcal{R}_{t-1}, \hat{\gamma}_T)]$.

When the observations r_t are i.i.d., the addends a_t are also i.i.d.. If the models f and g have equal Kullback-Leibler Information criterion, the central limit theorem implies $T^{-1/2} LR_T(\hat{\theta}_T, \hat{\gamma}_T) \xrightarrow{d} \mathcal{N}(0, \sigma_*^2)$, where $\sigma_*^2 = Var(a_t)$. The variance is consistently estimated by the sample variance of $\{\hat{a}_t\}$.

In the non-i.i.d. case, we need to adjust for the correlation in the addends a_t. Let $\sigma_T^2 = T^{-1} \sum_{s=1}^{T} \sum_{t=1}^{T} \mathbb{E}(a_s a_t)$. We know that $T^{-1/2} LR_T(\hat{\theta}_T, \hat{\gamma}_T) = \sigma_T Z + o_p(1)$, where Z is a standard Gaussian. Following Newey-West (1987), we estimate σ_T by

$$\hat{\sigma}_T^2 = \hat{\Omega}_0 + 2 \sum_{j=1}^{m} w(j, m) \hat{\Omega}_j,$$

where $\hat{\Omega}_j = \sum_{t=j+1}^{T} \hat{a}_t \hat{a}_{t-j} / T$ denotes the sample covariance of $\{\hat{a}_t\}$, and $w(j, m) = 1 - j/(m+1)$ is the Bartlett weight. We choose m using the automatic lag selection method of Newey and West (1994).

A.2   Appendix to Chapter 4

A.2.1   Distribution of the Arrival Vector

The probability of a simultaneous switch is $\mathbb{P}(1_{k,t}^{\alpha} = 1_{k,t}^{\beta} = 1) = \mathbb{P}(1_{k,t}^{\alpha} = 1)$ $\mathbb{P}(1_{k,t}^{\beta} = 1 | 1_{k,t}^{\alpha} = 1)$. The vector $1_{k,t}$ therefore has unconditional distribution:

	Arrival on β	No arrival on β
Arrival on α	$\gamma_k[(1-\lambda)\gamma_k + \lambda]$	$\gamma_k(1-\lambda)(1-\gamma_k)$
No arrival on α	$\gamma_k(1-\gamma_k)(1-\lambda)$	$(1-\gamma_k)[1-\gamma_k(1-\lambda)].$

A.2.2   Ergodic Distribution of Volatility Components

The bivariate process $(M_{k,t}^{\alpha}, M_{k,t}^{\beta})$ can take values $s^1 = s^{H,H} = (m_0^{\alpha}, m_0^{\beta})$, $s^2 = s^{H,L} = (m_0^{\alpha}, m_1^{\beta})$, $s^3 = s^{L,H} = (m_1^{\alpha}, m_0^{\beta})$ and $s^4 = s^{L,L} = (m_1^{\alpha}, m_1^{\beta})$. The transition matrix is $T = (t_{ij})$, where $t_{ij} = \mathbb{P}(s_{t+1} = s^j | s_t = s^i)$. It satisfies

$$T = \begin{bmatrix} p_k & 1 - \frac{\gamma_k}{2} - p_k & 1 - \frac{\gamma_k}{2} - p_k & \gamma_k - 1 + p_k \\ 1 - \frac{\gamma_k}{2} - q_k & q_k & \gamma_k - 1 + q_k & 1 - \frac{\gamma_k}{2} - q_k \\ 1 - \frac{\gamma_k}{2} - q_k & \gamma_k - 1 + q_k & q_k & 1 - \frac{\gamma_k}{2} - q_k \\ \gamma_k - 1 + p_k & 1 - \frac{\gamma_k}{2} - p_k & 1 - \frac{\gamma_k}{2} - p_k & p_k \end{bmatrix},$$

where

$$p_k = 1 - \gamma_k + \gamma_k[(1-\lambda)\gamma_k + \lambda] \frac{1 + \rho_m^*}{4},$$

$$q_k = 1 - \gamma_k + \gamma_k[(1-\lambda)\gamma_k + \lambda] \frac{1 - \rho_m^*}{4}.$$

Simple manipulation implies that the characteristic polynomial of T is

$$P_T(x) = (1-x)(1-\gamma_k-x)^2[2(p_k+q_k+\gamma_k)-3-x].$$

We easily check that $|2(p_k+q_k+\gamma_k)-3| < 1$, and we infer that T has a unique ergodic distribution $\bar{\Pi}_k = (\bar{\Pi}_k^{HH}, \bar{\Pi}_k^{HL}, \bar{\Pi}_k^{LH}, \bar{\Pi}_k^{LL})$. The symmetry of the transition matrix implies that $\bar{\Pi}_k^{HH} = \bar{\Pi}_k^{LL}$ and $\bar{\Pi}_k^{HL} = \bar{\Pi}_k^{LH}$. We easily check that $\bar{\Pi}_k^{HH} = \frac{1}{4}\frac{2-2q_k-\gamma_k}{2-(p_k+q_k)-\gamma_k}$, or equivalently

$$\bar{\Pi}_k^{HH} = \frac{1}{4}\frac{1-(1-\rho_m^*)[(1-\lambda)\gamma_k+\lambda]/2}{1-[(1-\lambda)\gamma_k+\lambda]/2},$$

and finally note that $\bar{\Pi}_k^{HL} = 1/2 - \bar{\Pi}_k^{HH}$. When $\rho_m^* > 0$, the multipliers are more likely to be either both high or both low: $\bar{\Pi}_k^{HH} = \bar{\Pi}_k^{LL} > 1/4 > \bar{\Pi}_k^{HL} = \bar{\Pi}_k^{LH}$.

A.2.3   Particle Filter

As discussed in the main text, the vectors $\hat{M}_{t+1}^{(1)}, \dots, \hat{M}_{t+1}^{(B)}$ are independent draws from the probability distribution $h(m) \equiv \mathbb{P}(M_{t+1} = m|\mathcal{R}_t)$. Consider a continuous function Y defined on $\mathbb{R}_+^{\bar{k}}$ and taking values on the real line. The conditional expectation $\mathbb{E}[Y(M_{t+1})|\mathcal{R}_{t+1}] = \sum_{j=1}^d \mathbb{P}(M_{t+1} = m^j|\mathcal{R}_{t+1})Y(m^j)$ is conveniently rewritten as

$$\mathbb{E}[Y(M_{t+1})|\mathcal{R}_{t+1}] = \sum_{j=1}^d h(m^j)\frac{\mathbb{P}(M_{t+1} = m^j|\mathcal{R}_{t+1})}{h(m^j)}Y(m^j).$$

The Monte Carlo approximation to this integral is

$$\mathbb{E}[Y(M_{t+1})|\mathcal{R}_{t+1}] \approx \frac{1}{B}\sum_{b=1}^B \frac{\mathbb{P}(M_{t+1} = \hat{M}_{t+1}^{(b)}|\mathcal{R}_{t+1})}{h(\hat{M}_{t+1}^{(b)})}Y(\hat{M}_{t+1}^{(b)}).$$

Bayes' rule implies

$$\frac{\mathbb{P}(M_{t+1} = \hat{M}_{t+1}^{(b)}|\mathcal{R}_{t+1})}{B\,h(\hat{M}_{t+1}^{(b)})} = \frac{f_{r_{t+1}}(r_{t+1}|M_{t+1} = \hat{M}_{t+1}^{(b)})}{B\,f_{r_{t+1}}(r_{t+1}|\mathcal{R}_t)}.$$

Since $f_{r_{t+1}}(r_{t+1}|\mathcal{R}_t) \approx \frac{1}{B}\sum_{b'=1}^B f_{r_{t+1}}(r_{t+1}|\hat{M}_{t+1}^{(b')})$, we infer that

$$\frac{\mathbb{P}(M_{t+1} = \hat{M}_{t+1}^{(b)}|\mathcal{R}_{t+1})}{B\,h(\hat{M}_{t|1}^{(b)})} \approx \frac{f_{r_{t+1}}(r_{t+1}|M_{t+1} = \hat{M}_{t+1}^{(b)})}{\sum_{b'-1}^B f_{r_{t+1}}(r_{t+1}|M_{t+1} = \hat{M}_{t+1}^{(b')})}.$$

The right-hand side defines a probability μ_b for every $b \in \{1, \ldots, B\}$. We infer that the random variable $Y(M_{t+1})$ has conditional expectation $\mathbb{E}[Y(M_{t+1})|\mathcal{R}_{t+1}] \approx \sum_{b=1}^{B} \mu_b Y(\hat{M}_{t+1}^{(b)})$. Since this result is valid for any function Y, we conclude that Π_{t+1} can be approximated with a discrete distribution taking on the value $\hat{M}_{t+1}^{(b)}$ with probability μ_b.

A.2.4   Two-Step Estimation

We partition the parameter vector into $\psi \equiv (\psi_1', \psi_2')'$, with $\psi_1 = (m_0^\alpha, m_0^\beta, \bar{\sigma}_\alpha, \bar{\sigma}_\beta, b, \gamma_{\bar{k}})'$ and $\psi_2 = (\rho_\varepsilon, \rho_m^*, \lambda)'$. In the first step, we compute the vector $\hat{\psi}_1$ that maximizes the combined univariate likelihood $L(r_t^\alpha; m_0^\alpha, \bar{\sigma}_\alpha, b, \gamma_{\bar{k}}) + L(r_t^\beta; m_0^\beta, \bar{\sigma}_\beta, b, \gamma_{\bar{k}})$. Note that $\hat{\psi}_1$ is a generalized method of moments (GMM) estimator based on the score $\partial L(r_t^\alpha)/\partial \psi_1 + \partial L(r_t^\beta)/\partial \psi_1$. Under correct specification, the expectation of each derivative is zero, which implies consistency and asymptotic normality of $\hat{\psi}_1$. In the second step, we estimate ψ_2 by maximizing the simulated bivariate likelihood $L(r_t^\alpha, r_t^\beta; \hat{\psi}_1, \psi_2)$ given the first stage estimate $\hat{\psi}_1$. The simulated likelihood is computed using the particle filter with $B = 10,000$ draws.

Standard errors for the two-step estimates are obtained by restating the algorithm as a GMM estimator based on the moment conditions $T^{-1}\sum_{t=1}^{T} g_t(\hat{\psi}) = 0$, where $g_t(\psi)$ is the column vector with components $\partial[\ln f(r_t^\alpha|\mathcal{R}_{t-1}^\alpha) + \ln f(r_t^\beta|\mathcal{R}_{t-1}^\beta)]/\partial \psi_1$ and $\partial \ln f(r_t^\alpha, r_t^\beta|\mathcal{R}_{t-1}^\alpha, \mathcal{R}_{t-1}^\beta)/\partial \psi_2$. Standard GMM arguments imply asymptotic normality

$$\sqrt{T}(\hat{\psi} - \psi_0) \xrightarrow{d} \mathcal{N}[0, H^{-1}V(H')^{-1}]$$

with $H = -\mathbb{E}\partial g_t(\psi_0)/\partial \psi'$ and $V = \text{Var}[T^{-1/2}\sum g_t(\psi_0)]$. To estimate V, we approximate g_t by taking finite difference derivatives of the objective function. Then we estimate V using the formula of Newey and West (1987) with 10 lags. When calculating finite difference derivatives using the particle filter, we use $15,000$ simulations. We estimate H by calculating the sample variance of the first derivatives:

$$\hat{H} = \begin{pmatrix} \hat{H}_{1,1} + \hat{H}_{1,2} & 0 \\ \hat{H}_{2,1} & \hat{H}_{2,2} \end{pmatrix},$$

where $\hat{H}_{1,1}$ and $\hat{H}_{1,2}$ are the 6×6 matrices

$$\hat{H}_{1,1} = T^{-1}\sum \frac{\partial \ln f(r_t^\alpha|\mathcal{R}_{t-1}^\alpha)}{\partial \psi_1} \frac{\partial \ln f(r_t^\alpha|\mathcal{R}_{t-1}^\alpha)}{\partial \psi_1'} \approx -\mathbb{E}\left[\frac{\partial^2 \ln f(r_t^\alpha|\mathcal{R}_{t-1}^\alpha)}{\partial \psi_1 \partial \psi_1'}\right]$$

$$\hat{H}_{1,2} = T^{-1}\sum \frac{\partial \ln f(r_t^\beta|\mathcal{R}_{t-1}^\beta)}{\partial \psi_1} \frac{\partial \ln f(r_t^\beta|\mathcal{R}_{t-1}^\beta)}{\partial \psi_1'} \approx -\mathbb{E}\left[\frac{\partial^2 \ln f(r_t^\beta|\mathcal{R}_{t-1}^\beta)}{\partial \psi_1 \partial \psi_1'}\right].$$

Similarly, $(\widehat{H}_{21}, \widehat{H}_{22})$ are the bottom three rows of the 9×9 matrix

$$T^{-1} \sum \frac{\partial \ln f(r_t^\alpha, r_t^\beta | \mathcal{R}_{t-1}^\alpha, \mathcal{R}_{t-1}^\beta)}{\partial \psi} \frac{\partial \ln f(r_t^\alpha, r_t^\beta | \mathcal{R}_{t-1}^\alpha, \mathcal{R}_{t-1}^\beta)}{\partial \psi'}.$$

The matrix $\widehat{H}$ is consistent since its elements are second derivatives of the univariate or bivariate likelihoods.

A.2.5   Value-at-Risk Forecasts

We use the particle filter to calculate the value-at-risk implied by MSM. The algorithm in Section 4.3 is used to generate volatility draws $M_t^{(1)}, \ldots, M_t^{(B)}$ from the distribution Π_t. For each draw $M_t^{(b)}$, we simulate the bivariate series forward n days to obtain B draws from the cumulative return on the portfolio. We then estimate $VaR_{t,n}(p)$ as the $1 - p^{th}$ empirical quantile.

CC-GARCH provides a closed form expression for one-day value-at-risk forecasts, namely $VaR_{t,1}(p) = -Q_{1-p}\sigma_{t|t-1}$, where Q_{1-p} is the $(1-p)^{th}$ quantile of a standard normal variable and $\sigma_{t|t-1}$ is the standard deviation implied by CC-GARCH. The five-day CC-GARCH forecasts are calculated by simulation. In all cases we use $B = 10,000$ simulated draws.

A.2.6   Extension to Many Assets

In this appendix we introduce two alternative classes of models, multivariate MSM and factor MSM, and then explain how they can be estimated.

Multivariate MSM

Bivariate MSM can be readily extended to economies with an arbitrary number N of financial prices. The construction assumes in every period a volatility component $M_{k,t}^n \in \mathbb{R}_+$ for each frequency $k \in \{1, \ldots, \bar{k}\}$ and asset $n \in \{1, \ldots, N\}$. As in the bivariate case, components $M_{k,t}^n$ and $M_{k',t}^{n'}$ can be correlated across assets $(n \neq n')$, but are statistically independent across frequencies $(k \neq k')$. Specifically, the volatility dynamics are determined by a fixed multivariate distribution M on $\mathbb{R}_+^N$, and an arrival vector $1_{k,t} \in \{0,1\}^N$ for each frequency. The kth component of every asset switches with unconditional probability γ_k ($\mathbb{E}1_{k,t} = \gamma_k 1$), and arrivals across assets are characterized by the correlation matrix:

$$Corr(1_{k,t}) = (\lambda_{n,n'})_{1 \leq n, n' \leq N}.$$

The state vector is defined recursively. At time t, we draw the independent arrival vector $(1_{k,t})_{k=1,\ldots,\bar{k}}$, and sample the new components $M_{k,t}$ from the corresponding marginal distribution of M.

The volatility state is fully specified by the $N \times \bar{k}$ matrix $M_t = (M^n_{k,t})_{n,k}$. Analogous to bivariate MSM, we define returns as $r_t = (M_{1,t}*\ldots*M_{\bar{k},t})^{1/2}*$ ε_t, where ε_t is a centered multivariate Gaussian noise: $\varepsilon_t \sim \mathcal{N}(0, \Sigma)$. When the distribution of M is discrete, the likelihood function is available in closed-form. For large state spaces, estimation can be carried out using a particle filter as is discussed below.

Though natural, this approach requires the specification and estimation of the multivariate distribution M and the arrival correlation matrix $(\lambda_{n,n'})_{1 \le n,n' \le N}$. In a general formulation, the number of parameters therefore grows at least as fast as a quadratic function of N. Like other specifications such as multivariate GARCH, the model is computationally expensive for a large number of assets. The next subsection develops an overlapping class of models, which is based on the same principles as multivariate MSM and yet remains tractable with many assets.

Factor MSM

We consider L volatility factors $F^\ell_t = (F^\ell_{k,t})_{1 \le k \le \bar{k}} \in \mathbb{R}^{\bar{k}}_+$ that can jointly affect all assets. For instance, the vector F^ℓ_t may contain the frequency-specific components determining the volatility of a global risk factor or a specific industry. Each vector F^ℓ_t contains $\bar{k}$ frequency-specific components and follows a specific univariate MSM process with parameters $(b, \gamma_{\bar{k}}, m^\ell_0)$. The volatility of each asset n is also affected by an idiosyncratic shock E^n_t, which is specified by parameters $(b, \gamma_{\bar{k}}, m^{L+n}_0)$. Draws of the factors $F^\ell_{k,t}$ and idiosyncratic shocks $E^n_{k,t}$ are independent, but the timing of arrivals may be correlated. Factors and idiosyncratic components thus follow univariate MSM with identical frequencies.

For every asset n and frequency k, the volatility component $M^n_{k,t}$ is the weighted product of the factors and idiosyncratic shock of same frequency:

$$M^n_{k,t} = C_n \left(F^1_{k,t}\right)^{w^n_1} \ldots \left(F^L_{k,t}\right)^{w^n_L} \left(E^n_{k,t}\right)^{w^n_{L+1}}.$$

The weights are nonnegative and add up to one. The constant C_n is chosen to guarantee that $\mathbb{E}(M^n_{k,t}) = 1$ and is thus not a free parameter.[2] In logarithms, we obtain the familiar additive formulation:

$$\ln M^n_{k,t} = \ln C_n + \sum_{\ell=1}^{L} w^n_\ell \ln F^\ell_{k,t} + w^n_{L+1} \ln E^n_{k,t}.$$

---

[2] We have $C_n = 1/\mathbb{E}[\left(F^1_{k,t}\right)^{w^n_1}] \ldots \mathbb{E}[(F^L_{k,t})^{w^n_L}] \; \mathbb{E}[(E^n_{k,t})^{w^n_{L+1}}]$. This computation is straightforward when the marginal distribution of the shocks are multinomial or lognormal.

Returns are again defined as $r_t = (M_{1,t} * \ldots * M_{\bar{k},t})^{1/2} * \varepsilon_t$, where ε_t is a centered multivariate Gaussian noise: $\varepsilon_t \sim N(0, \Sigma)$.

Two special cases of this setup are of particular interest. First, when arrivals for all factors and idiosyncratic components are simultaneous, factor MSM is a special case of the multivariate MSM in the previous subsection. New draws of $M_{\bar{k},t}^n$ are then independent of all past multipliers, and the factor model generates univariate series that are consistent with univariate MSM. Furthermore, when the distribution of factors and idiosyncratic shocks is lognormal, the resulting multipliers $M_{\bar{k},t}^n$ are lognormal as well. Stochastic volatility is now fully specified by (1) the frequency parameters b and $\gamma_{\bar{k}}$; (2) the distribution parameters of factors and idiosyncratic shocks $(m_0^1, \ldots, m_0^{L+N})$; and (3) the factor loadings $w^n = (w_1^n, \ldots, w_L^n)$ of each asset. The model is thus defined by $N(L+1) + L + 2$ volatility parameters.

The second interesting special case is when arrivals of factors and idiosyncratic shocks are independent. It is easy to verify that this specification has the same number of parameters as when arrivals are simultaneous. Furthermore, this choice permits that at time t some but not all factors and idiosyncratic components may change. The univariate volatility components $M_{\bar{k},t}^n$ then take new values without requiring a completely independent draw from M. Thus, the implied univariate volatility dynamics are smoother than standard MSM, but can still generate thick tails and long-memory volatility persistence.

Inference in Multivariate MSM and Factor MSM

For either multivariate MSM or factor MSM, we seek to estimate the covariance matrix $\Sigma = Var(\varepsilon_t)$ and the vector of volatility parameters ψ. One possibility is to choose a tight specification for Σ and use the particle filter to optimize the simulated likelihood over all parameters.

In the general case, estimation can be conducted in two steps: (1) Estimate the covariance matrix of the Gaussian noises; and (2) use the particle filter to estimate the volatility parameters ψ by simulated maximum likelihood. Step (2) is straightforward, and step (1) can be conducted as follows. For any two assets α and β, we know that

$$\mathbb{E}[r_t^{(\alpha)} r_t^{(\beta)}] = \Gamma_{\alpha,\beta} \mathbb{E}[\varepsilon_t^{(\alpha)} \varepsilon_t^{(\beta)}] \text{ and } \mathbb{E}|r_t^{(\alpha)} r_t^{(\beta)}| = \Gamma_{\alpha,\beta} \mathbb{E}|\varepsilon_t^{(\alpha)} \varepsilon_t^{(\beta)}|,$$

where $\Gamma_{\alpha,\beta} = \prod_{k=1}^{\bar{k}} \mathbb{E}\{[M_{k,t}^\alpha M_{k,t}^\beta]^{1/2}\}$. We infer

$$\frac{\sum_t r_t^{(\alpha)} r_t^{(\beta)}}{\sum_t |r_t^{(\alpha)} r_t^{(\beta)}|} \xrightarrow{a.s.} \frac{\mathbb{E}[\varepsilon_t^{(\alpha)} \varepsilon_t^{(\beta)}]}{\mathbb{E}|\varepsilon_t^{(\alpha)} \varepsilon_t^{(\beta)}|} = \varphi(\rho_{\alpha,\beta}),$$

where $\rho_{\alpha,\beta} = Corr[\varepsilon_t^{(\alpha)}; \varepsilon_t^{(\beta)}]$ and $\varphi(\rho) \equiv \frac{\pi}{2} \frac{\rho}{\sqrt{1-\rho^2} + \rho \arcsin \rho}$. The function φ is strictly increasing and maps $[-1,1]$ onto $[-1,1]$. A consistent estimator of the correlation coefficient is therefore

$$\hat{\rho}_{\alpha,\beta} = \varphi^{-1}\left(\frac{\sum_t r_t^{(\alpha)} r_t^{(\beta)}}{\sum_t |r_t^{(\alpha)} r_t^{(\beta)}|} \right).$$

The variance of the Gaussians is consistently estimated by $\hat{\sigma}_\alpha^2 = \frac{1}{T} \sum_t [r_t^{(\alpha)}]^2$. Since the covariance matrix defined by the above estimates may not be positive definite, we then apply the methodology of Ledoit, Santa-Clara, and Wolf (2003) to obtain a positive semidefinite matrix $\hat{\Sigma}$.

A.3   Appendix to Chapter 5

A.3.1   Properties of $\mathcal{D}$

Consider a fixed instant $t \in [0,1]$. For all $\varepsilon > 0$, there exists a dyadic number t_n such that $|t_n - t| < \varepsilon$. We can then find a number $\Delta_n = b^{-k_n} < \varepsilon$ for which $(t_n, \Delta_n) \in \mathcal{D}$. In the plane $\mathbb{R}^2$, the point $(t,0)$ is thus the limit of the sequence $(t_n, \Delta_n) \in \mathcal{D}$. This establishes that the closure of $\mathcal{D}$ contains the set $[0,1] \times \{0\}$. The scaling relation (5.4) thus holds "in the neighborhood of any instant."

A.3.2   Interpretation of $f(\alpha)$ as a Fractal Dimension

Fractal geometry considers irregular and winding structures that are not well described by their Euclidean length. For instance, a geographer measuring the length of a coastline will find very different results as she increases the precision of her measurement. In fact, the structure of the coastline is usually so intricate that the measured length diverges to infinity as the geographer's measurement scale goes to zero. For this reason, it is natural to introduce a new concept of dimension (Mandelbrot 1982). Given a precision level $\varepsilon > 0$, we consider coverings of the coastline with balls of diameter ε. Let $N(\varepsilon)$ denote the smallest number of balls required for such a covering. The approximate length of the coastline is defined by $L(\varepsilon) = \varepsilon N(\varepsilon)$. In many cases, $N(\varepsilon)$ satisfies a power law as ε goes to zero:

$$N(\varepsilon) \sim \varepsilon^{-D},$$

where D is a constant called the *fractal dimension*.

Fractal dimension helps to analyze the structure of a fixed multifractal. For any $\alpha \geq 0$, we can define the set $T(\alpha)$ of instants with Hölder exponent α. As any subset of the real line, $T(\alpha)$ has a fractal dimension $D(\alpha)$, which satisfies $0 \leq D(\alpha) \leq 1$. For a large class of multifractals, the dimension $D(\alpha)$

coincides with the multifractal spectrum $f(\alpha)$ (Frisch and Parisi, 1985; Halsey *et al.*, 1986; Peyrière 1991).

In the case of measures, we can provide a heuristic interpretation of this result based on coarse Hölder exponents. Denoting by $N(\alpha, \Delta t)$ the number of intervals $[t, t + \Delta t]$ required to cover $T(\alpha)$, we infer from Equation (5.5) that $N(\alpha, \Delta t) \sim (\Delta t)^{-f(\alpha)}$. We then rewrite the total mass $\mu[0, T] = \sum \mu(\Delta t) \sim \sum (\Delta t)^{\alpha(t)}$ and rearrange it as a sum over Hölder exponents:

$$\mu[0, T] \sim \int (\Delta t)^{\alpha - f(\alpha)} \, d\alpha.$$

The integral is dominated by the contribution of the Hölder exponent α_1 that minimizes $\alpha - f(\alpha)$, and therefore

$$\mu[0, T] \sim (\Delta t)^{\alpha_1 - f(\alpha_1)}.$$

Since the total mass $\mu[0, T]$ is positive, we infer that $f(\alpha_1) = \alpha_1$, and $f(\alpha) \leq \alpha$ for all α. When f is differentiable, the coefficient α_1 also satisfies $f'(\alpha_1) = 1$. The spectrum $f(\alpha)$ then lies under the 45° line, with tangential contact at $\alpha = \alpha_1$.

A.3.3   Heuristic Proof of Proposition 3

Consider a *conservative* multiplicative measure μ. We subdivide the range of α's into intervals of length $\Delta \alpha$ and denote by $N_k(\alpha)$ the number of coarse Hölder exponents in between α and $\alpha + \Delta \alpha$. For large values of k, we write

$$\frac{1}{k} \log_b \left[\frac{N_k(\alpha)}{b^k} \right] \sim \frac{1}{k} \log_b \mathbb{P} \left\{ \alpha < \alpha_k \leq \alpha + \Delta \alpha \right\}. \tag{A.7}$$

We infer from (5.6) and Cramér's theorem that for any $\alpha > \alpha_0$

$$\frac{1}{k} \log_b \mathbb{P} \left\{ \alpha_k > \alpha \right\} \to \inf_Q \log_b \left[\mathbb{E} \, e^{(\alpha - V_1)Q} \right]. \tag{A.8}$$

We consider the change of variables $q = Q / \ln(b)$, and obtain:

$$\frac{1}{k} \log_b \mathbb{P} \left\{ \alpha_k > \alpha \right\} \to \inf_q \log_b \left[\mathbb{E} \, e^{(\alpha - V_1)q \ln b} \right]$$

$$= \inf_q \left[\alpha q + \log_b \left(\mathbb{E} \, e^{-V_1 q \ln b} \right) \right]. \tag{A.9}$$

Since the scaling function satisfies (5.2), the limit simplifies to $\inf_q [\alpha q - \tau(q)] - 1$. Combining this with (5.5) and (A.7), it follows that the Proposition holds.

These arguments easily extend to a *canonical* measure μ. Given a b-adic instant t, the coarse exponent $\alpha_k(t) = \ln \mu[t, t + \Delta t]/\ln \Delta t$ is the sum of a high-frequency component, $-k^{-1} \log_b \Omega_{\eta_1,\ldots,\eta_k}$, and of the familiar low-frequency average $\alpha_{k,L}(t) = -[\log_b M_{\eta_1} + \cdots + \log_b M_{\eta_1,\ldots,\eta_k}]/k$. The exponent $\alpha_k(t)$ converges almost surely to $\alpha_0 = -\mathbb{E}(\log_b M)$, and the multifractal spectrum is again the Legendre transform of the scaling function $\tau(q)$.

A.4   Appendix to Chapter 6

A.4.1   Concavity of the Scaling Function $\tau(q)$

Consider two exponents q_1, q_2, two positive weights w_1, w_2 adding up to one, and the corresponding weighted average $q = w_1 q_1 + w_2 q_2$. Hölder's inequality implies

$$\mathbb{E}\left(|X(t)|^q\right) \le \left[\mathbb{E}\left(|X(t)|^{q_1}\right)\right]^{w_1} \left[\mathbb{E}\left(|X(t)|^{q_2}\right)\right]^{w_2}. \tag{A.10}$$

Since $\mathbb{E}\left(|X(t)|^q\right) \sim c_X(q) t^{\tau_X(q)}$ and $\left[\mathbb{E}\left(|X(t)|^{q_1}\right)\right]^{w_1} \left[\mathbb{E}\left(|X(t)|^{q_2}\right)\right]^{w_2} \sim [c_X(q_1)]^{w_1} [c_X(q_2)]^{w_2} t^{w_1 \tau_X(q_1)+w_2 \tau_X(q_2)}$, we obtain

$$\tau_X(q) \ge w_1 \tau_X(q_1) + w_2 \tau_X(q_2), \tag{A.11}$$

which establishes the concavity of τ_X.

This proof also contains additional information on multifractal processes. Assume that the moment-scaling relation (6.1) holds exactly for $t \in [0, \infty)$. Inequality (A.10) also holds as t goes to infinity, which implies the reverse of inequality (A.11). The function $\tau_X(q)$ is therefore linear. This establishes that exact multiscaling with a nonlinear $\tau_X(q)$ can hold only on bounded time intervals.

A.4.2   Proof of Proposition 5

Let $\mathcal{F}_t$ and $\mathcal{F}'_t$ denote the natural filtrations of $\{X(t)\}$ and $\{X(t), \theta(t)\}$. For any t, T, u, the independence of B and θ implies

$$\mathbb{E}\left\{X(t+T)\,|\,\mathcal{F}'_t, \theta(t+T) = u\right\} = \mathbb{E}\left\{B(u)\,|\,\mathcal{F}'_t\right\}$$

$$= B[\theta(t)],$$

since $\{B(t)\}$ is a martingale. Hence $\mathbb{E}\left[X(t+T)\,|\,\mathcal{F}_t\right] = X(t)$. This establishes that $X(t)$ is a martingale and has uncorrelated increments. The price $P(t)$ is a smooth function of $X(t)$ and is therefore a semimartingale.

A.4.3   Proof of Proposition 7

Trading Time

Consider a canonical cascade after $k \geq 1$ stages. Consistent with the notation of Chapter 5, the interval $[0, T]$ is partitioned into cells of length $\Delta t = b^{-k}T$, and $I_1 = [t_1, t_1 + \Delta t]$ and $I_2 = [t_2, t_2 + \Delta t]$ denote two distinct b−adic cells with lower endpoints of the form $t_1/T = \overline{0.\eta_1 \ldots \eta_k}$ and $t_2/T = \overline{0.\zeta_1 \ldots \zeta_k}$. Assume that the first $l \geq 1$ terms are equal in the b-adic expansions of t_1/T and t_2/T, so that $\zeta_1 = \eta_1, \ldots, \zeta_l = \eta_l$, and $\zeta_{l+1} \neq \eta_{l+1}$. The distance $t = |t_2 - t_1|$ satisfies $b^{-l-1} \leq t/T < b^{-l}$, and the product $\mu(I_1)^q \mu(I_2)^q$, which is equal to

$$\Omega_{\eta_1,..,\eta_k}^q \, \Omega_{\zeta_1,..,\zeta_k}^q \, (M_{\eta_1}^{2q}..M_{\eta_1,..,\eta_l}^{2q})$$

$$(M_{\eta_1,..,\eta_{l+1}}^q..M_{\eta_1,..,\eta_k}^q)(M_{\zeta_1,..,\zeta_{l+1}}^q..M_{\zeta_1,..,\zeta_k}^q),$$

has mean $[\mathbb{E}(\Omega^q)]^2 \, [\mathbb{E}(M^{2q})]^l [\mathbb{E}(M^q)]^{2(k-l)}$. We conclude that

$$Cov[\mu(I_1)^q; \mu(I_2)^q] = [\mathbb{E}(\Omega^q)]^2 \, [\mathbb{E}(M^q)]^{2k} \left\{ [(\mathbb{E}M^{2q})/(\mathbb{E}M^q)^2]^l - 1 \right\}$$

$$= C_1(\Delta t)^{2\tau_\theta(q)+2} \left[b^{-l[\tau_\theta(2q)-2\tau_\theta(q)-1]} - 1 \right]$$

is bounded by two hyperbolic functions of t.

Log-Price

Since $B(t)$ and $\theta(t)$ are independent processes, the conditional expectation

$$\mathbb{E}\left\{ |X(0, \Delta t)X(t, \Delta t)|^q \,|\, \theta(\Delta t) = u_1, \theta(t) = u_2, \theta(t + \Delta t) = u_3 \right\}, \quad \text{(A.12)}$$

simplifies to $|u_1|^{q/2} \, |u_3 - u_2|^{q/2} \, [\mathbb{E}|B(1)|^q]^2$. Taking expectations, we infer that

$$\mathbb{E}\left[|X(0, \Delta t)X(t, \Delta t)|^q \right] = \mathbb{E}\left[\theta(0, \Delta t)^{q/2}\theta(t, \Delta t)^{q/2} \right] \, [\mathbb{E}|B(1)|^q]^2$$

declines hyperbolically.

A.4.4   Proof of Proposition 8

Given a process Z, denote $\alpha_Z(t)$ as its local scale at date t, and $T_Z(\alpha)$ as the set of instants with scale α. At any date, the infinitesimal variation of the log-price $X(t + \triangle t) - X(t) = B[\theta(t + \triangle t)] - B[\theta(t)]$ satisfies

$$|X(t + \triangle t) - X(t)| \sim |\theta(t + \triangle t) - \theta(t)|^{1/2} \sim |\triangle t|^{\alpha_\theta(t)/2},$$

implying $\alpha_X(t) \equiv \alpha_\theta(t)/2$. The sets $T_X(\alpha)$ and $T_\theta(2\alpha)$ coincide and in particular have identical fractal dimensions: $f_X(\alpha) \equiv f_\theta(2\alpha)$. Moreover, since the price $P(t)$ is a differentiable function of $X(t)$, the two processes have identical local Hölder exponents and spectra.

A.5   Appendix to Chapter 7

A.5.1   Multivariate Version of Continuous-Time MSM

The bivariate specification of MSM presented in Chapter 4 easily extends to continuous time. Consider two economic processes α and β. For every frequency k, the processes have volatility components

$$M_{k,t} = \begin{bmatrix} M_{k,t}^\alpha \\ M_{k,t}^\beta \end{bmatrix} \in \mathbb{R}_+^2.$$

The period-t volatility column vectors $M_{k,t}$ are stacked into the $2 \times \bar{k}$ matrix

$$M_t = (M_{1,t}; M_{2,t}; \ldots; M_{\bar{k},t}).$$

As in univariate MSM, we assume that $M_{1,t}, M_{2,t} \ldots M_{\bar{k},t}$ at a given time t are statistically independent. The main task is to choose appropriate dynamics for each vector $M_{k,t}$.

Economic intuition suggests that volatility arrivals are correlated but not necessarily simultaneous across economic series. For this reason, we allow arrivals across series to be characterized by a correlation coefficient $\rho^* \in [0, 1]$. Assume that the volatility vector $M_{k,s}$ has been constructed up to date t. Over the following interval of infinitesimal length dt, each series $c \in \{\alpha, \beta\}$ is hit by an arrival with probability $\gamma_k dt$. If $\rho^* = 0$, the arrivals are assumed to be independent. On the other hand, if $\rho^* \in (0, 1]$, the probability of an arrival on β conditional on an arrival on α is ρ^*, and the intensity of a β arrival conditional on no α arrival is $(1 - \rho^*)\gamma_k$.

The construction of the volatility components $M_{k,t}$ is then based on a bivariate distribution $M = (M^\alpha, M^\beta) \in \mathbb{R}_+^2$. If arrivals hit both series, the state vector $M_{k,t+dt}$ is drawn from M. If only series $c \in \{\alpha, \beta\}$ receives an arrival, the new component $M_{k,t+dt}^c$ is sampled from the marginal M^c of the bivariate distribution M. Finally, $M_{k,t+dt} = M_{k,t}$ if there is no arrival.

As in the univariate case, the transition probabilities $(\gamma_1, \gamma_2, \ldots, \gamma_{\bar{k}})$ are defined as $\gamma_k = \gamma_1 b^{k-1}$, where $\gamma_1 > 0$ and $b \in (1, \infty)$. This completes the specification of bivariate MSM in continuous time. We can extend the construction to a larger number of assets by rewriting in continuous time the multivariate MSM and factor MSM processes described in the Appendix to Chapter 4.

A.5.2   Proof of Proposition 9

We assume without loss of generality that $T = 1$ and $\bar{\sigma} = 1$. Let $\mathcal{C}$ denote the space of continuous functions defined on $[0, 1]$. For any instants $t_1, .., t_p$, the vector sequence $\{\theta_k(t_1), , \ldots, \theta_k(t_p)\}_k$ is a positive martingale and therefore has a limit distribution. The sequence $\{\theta_k\}$ thus has at most one cluster point.

A cluster point exists if the sequence $\{\theta^k\}$ is tight. For any continuous function $x \in \mathcal{C}$ and $\delta \in (0, 1]$, it is convenient to consider the *modulus of continuity*

$$w(x, \delta) = \sup_{|t-s| \leq \delta} |x(t) - x(s)|.$$

Our discussion is based on the following result, proved in Billingsley (1999).

Theorem 1 *The sequence $\{\theta_k\}$ is tight if and only if these two conditions hold:*

(i) *For every $\eta > 0$, there exist a and K such that $\mathbb{P}\{|\theta^k(0)| \geq a\} \leq \eta$ for all $k \geq K$.*

(ii) *For every $\varepsilon > 0$, $\lim_{\delta \to 0} \limsup_{k \to \infty} \mathbb{P}\{w(\theta^k, \delta) \geq \varepsilon\} = 0$.*

The first condition is trivially satisfied in our setup since $\theta_k(0) \equiv 0$. We now turn to the second condition. Since the function $\limsup_k \mathbb{P}\{w(\theta^k, \delta) \geq \varepsilon\}$ is increasing in δ, we can restrict our attention to step sizes of the form $\delta_n = 1/n$, $n = 1, 2, .., \infty$. For a given n, consider the regularly spaced grid $t_0 = 0 < t_1 = \delta_n < \ldots < t_n = 1$. Since the function θ_k is increasing, Theorem 7.4 in Billingsley (1999) implies

$$\mathbb{P}\{w(\theta^k, \delta_n) \geq \varepsilon\} \leq \sum_{i=0}^{n-1} \mathbb{P}\left\{\theta^k(t_{i+1}) - \theta^k(t_i) \geq \frac{\varepsilon}{3}\right\}.$$

Each increment $\theta^k(t_{i+1}) - \theta^k(t_i)$ is distributed like $\theta^k(\delta_n)$, implying

$$\mathbb{P}\{w(\theta^k, \delta_n) \geq \varepsilon\} \leq \left(\frac{3}{\varepsilon}\right)^q n \, \mathbb{E}\left[\theta_k(\delta_n)^q\right] \qquad (A.13)$$

for any $q > 0$.

The right-hand side does not converge to 0 when $q = 1$. We focus instead on the second moment ($q = 2$), and observe that for any t,

$$\mathbb{E}\left[\theta_{k+1}(t)^2\right] = \int_0^t \int_0^t \mathbb{E}(M_{1,u} M_{1,v}) \ldots \mathbb{E}(M_{k,u} M_{k,v}) \mathbb{E}(M_{k+1,u} M_{k+1,v}) du dv.$$

Since $\mathbb{E}(M_{k+1,u}M_{k+1,v}) = 1 + Var(M)e^{-\gamma_{k+1}|u-v|}$, we infer that the sequence $\mathbb{E}\left[\theta_{k+1}(t)^2\right]$ increases in k and that

$$\mathbb{E}\left[\theta_{k+1}(t)^2\right] \le \mathbb{E}\left[\theta_k(t)^2\right] + Var(M)\left[\mathbb{E}(M^2)\right]^k \int_0^t\int_0^t e^{-\gamma_{k+1}|u-v|}dudv.$$

Lemma 1 *The following inequality holds:*

$$\int_0^t\int_0^t e^{-\gamma_{k+1}|u-v|}dudv \le 2\frac{t^{1+\varphi}}{\gamma_{k+1}^{1-\varphi}}$$

for any $t \ge 0$ and $\varphi \in [0,1]$.

Proof   The integral is available in closed form:

$$\int_0^t\int_0^t e^{-\gamma_{k+1}|u-v|}dudv = \int_0^t \frac{2 - e^{-\gamma_{k+1}v} - e^{-\gamma_{k+1}(t-v)}}{\gamma_{k+1}}dv$$

$$= \frac{2}{\gamma_{k+1}}t - 2\frac{1 - e^{-\gamma_{k+1}t}}{\gamma_{k+1}^2}$$

$$= \frac{2}{\gamma_{k+1}^2}\left(e^{-\gamma_{k+1}t} - 1 + \gamma_{k+1}t\right).$$

We note that $e^{-x} - 1 + x \le x^2/2 \le x^{1+\varphi}/2$ if $x \in [0,1]$, and $e^{-x} - 1 + x \le x \le x^{1+\varphi}$ if $x \in [1,+\infty)$. Hence $e^{-x} - 1 + x \le x^{1+\varphi}$ for all $x \ge 0$. We conclude that

$$\int_0^t\int_0^t e^{-\gamma_{k+1}|u-v|}dudv \le \frac{2}{\gamma_{k+1}^2}(\gamma_{k+1}t)^{1+\varphi} = 2\frac{t^{1+\varphi}}{\gamma_{k+1}^{1-\varphi}}.$$

holds for all $t \ge 0$ and $\varphi \in [0,1]$.   ∎

Since $\mathbb{E}(M^2) < b$, there exists by continuity a real number $\varphi \in (0,1)$ such that $\mathbb{E}(M^2) < b^{1-\varphi}$. We infer from the lemma that

$$\mathbb{E}\left[\theta_{k+1}(t)^2\right] \le \mathbb{E}\left[\theta_k(t)^2\right] + \frac{2Var(M)t^{1+\varphi}}{\gamma_1^{1-\varphi}}\left[\frac{\mathbb{E}(M^2)}{b^{1-\varphi}}\right]^k.$$

Hence $\mathbb{E}\left[\theta_k(t)^2\right]$ has a finite limit and

$$\lim_{k\to\infty} \mathbb{E}\left[\theta_k(t)^2\right] \le t^2 + \frac{2Var(M)t^{1+\varphi}}{\gamma_1^{1-\varphi}}\sum_{k=0}^{+\infty}\left[\frac{\mathbb{E}(M^2)}{b^{1-\varphi}}\right]^k.$$

We infer immediately that $\lim_{t \to 0} \limsup_{k \to \infty} t^{-1} \mathbb{E}[\theta^k(t)^2] = 0$. By (A.13), $\limsup_k \mathbb{P}\{w(\theta^k, \delta_n) \geq \varepsilon\}$ converges to zero as $n \to \infty$.

A.5.3   Proof of Proposition 10

We begin by showing:

Lemma 2 *If* $\mathbb{E}[\theta_\infty(t)^q]$ *is finite for some instant* $t > 0$, *then* $\mathbb{E}[\theta_\infty(t')^q]$ *is also finite for every* $t' \in (0, \infty)$.

Proof   If $t' \leq t$, we know that $\theta_\infty(t') \leq \theta_\infty(t)$, and we infer that $\mathbb{E}[\theta_\infty(t')^q]$ is also finite. The next step is to show that $\mathbb{E}[\theta_\infty(nt)^q]$ is also finite for every $n > 2$. We note that

$$\theta_\infty(nt)^q = \left\{ \sum_{i=1}^{n} [\theta_\infty((i+1)t) - \theta_\infty(it)] \right\}^q$$

is bounded above by[3] $\max(n^{q-1}, 1) \sum_{i=0}^{n-1} \{[\theta_\infty((i+1)t) - \theta_\infty(it)]^q$. This implies

$$\mathbb{E}\left[\theta_\infty(nt)^q\right] \leq \max(n^{q-1}, 1)\mathbb{E}[\theta_\infty(t)^q] \tag{A.14}$$

is finite. ∎

The critical moment $q_{crit} = \sup\{q : \mathbb{E}[\theta_\infty(t)^q] < \infty\}$ does not depend on t. Inequality (A.14) also suggests the concavity of $\mathbb{E}[\theta_\infty(t)^q]$ as t varies. We easily show:

Lemma 3   (Moment concavity/convexity) *The function* $t \longmapsto \mathbb{E}[\theta_\infty(t)^q]$ *is concave in* t *if* $q \in (0, 1)$, *linear if* $q = 1$, *and convex if* $q \in (1, q_{crit})$.

Proof   Let $\lambda_{\bar{k}}(t) = \mathbb{E}[\theta_{\bar{k}}(t)^q]$. If $q \geq 1$, we observe that

$$\lambda_{\bar{k}}'(t + h) = \mathbb{E}\left[q\sigma_{\bar{k}}^2(M_{t+h}) \left(\int_0^{t+h} \theta_{\bar{k}}(s)ds \right)^{q-1} \right]$$

$$\geq \mathbb{E}\left[q\sigma_{\bar{k}}^2(M_{t+h}) \left(\int_h^{t+h} \theta_{\bar{k}}(s)ds \right)^{q-1} \right] = \lambda_{\bar{k}}'(t).$$

The function $\lambda_{\bar{k}}(t)$ is therefore convex for all $\bar{k}$, and we conclude that $\mathbb{E}[\theta_\infty(t)^q]$ is convex. A similar argument holds if $q \leq 1$. ∎

---

[3] Recall that $(\sum_{i=1}^{n} x_i)^q \leq \max(n^{q-1}, 1) \sum_{i=1}^{n} x_i^q$ for any $n \geq 1$, $(x_1, .., x_n) \in \mathbb{R}_+^n$, $q \geq 0$.

For any $\bar{k} \in \{1, \dots \infty\}$, let $\Theta_{\bar{k}}(\gamma_1)$ denote the trading time $\theta_{\bar{k}}(1)$ at $t = 1$ in continuous-time MSM with frequency parameters γ_1 and b.

Lemma 4 (Invariance property) *Trading time satisfies*

$$\theta_\infty(t) \stackrel{d}{=} t\Theta_\infty(t\gamma_1) \tag{A.15}$$

for all $t \in [0, \infty)$ and $\gamma_1 > 0$.

Proof   For any finite $\bar{k}$, trading time is given by $\theta_{\bar{k}}(t) \equiv \int_0^t \sigma_{\bar{k}}^2(M_s)ds$. Consider the change of variables $u = s/t$. We infer that

$$\theta_{\bar{k}}(t) \equiv t \int_0^1 \sigma_{\bar{k}}^2(M_{ut})du.$$

The state vector $M_u' = M_{ut}$ is driven by arrivals of intensity $t\gamma_1, \dots,$ $t\gamma_1 b^{\bar{k}-1}$. We conclude that $\theta_{\bar{k}}(t) \stackrel{d}{=} t\Theta_{\bar{k}}(t\gamma_1)$ for all $\bar{k}$, implying $\theta_\infty(t) \stackrel{d}{=} t\Theta_\infty(t\gamma_1)$. ∎

When the frequency γ is close to zero, the first-stage multiplier is constant on the unit interval with high probability, which suggests that $\Theta_\infty(\gamma) \approx M \Theta_\infty(b\gamma)$ and thus $\mathbb{E}[\Theta_\infty(\gamma)^q] \approx \mathbb{E}(M^q) \mathbb{E}[\Theta_\infty(b\gamma)^q]$. This intuition can be used to show:

Lemma 5 (Scaling) $\mathbb{E}[\Theta_\infty(\gamma)^q] \sim \mathbb{E}(M^q) \mathbb{E}[\Theta_\infty(b\gamma)^q]$ *as $\gamma \to 0$.*

Proof   We consider $g(\gamma) = \mathbb{E}[\Theta_\infty(\gamma)^q]$. Let $t_1 < \dots < t_N$ denote the dates in the unit interval when a first-stage multiplier is drawn. We also define $t_0 = 0$ and $t_{N+1} = 1$. Simple conditioning implies

$$g(\gamma) = \mathbb{E}(M^q) g(b\gamma) e^{-\gamma} + \sum_{n=1}^\infty \frac{e^{-\gamma}\gamma^n}{n!} \mathbb{E}[\Theta_\infty(\gamma)^q | N = n].$$

As in the proof of lemma 2, the relation $\Theta_\infty(\gamma) = \sum_{j=0}^N [\theta_\infty(t_{j+1}) - \theta_\infty(t_j)]$ implies

$$\Theta_\infty(\gamma)^q \le \max \left[(N+1)^{q-1}, 1\right] \sum_{j=0}^N [\theta_\infty(t_{j+1}) - \theta_\infty(t_j)]^q.$$

The conditional expectation $\mathbb{E}[\Theta_\infty(\gamma)^q | N = n]$ is therefore bounded above by

$$\max \left[(n+1)^{q-1}, 1\right] (n+1)\mathbb{E}(M^q)g(b\gamma).$$

and thus

$$1 \le \frac{e^\gamma g(\gamma)}{\mathbb{E}(M^q)\,g(b\gamma)} \le 1 + \sum_{n=1}^{\infty} \frac{\gamma^n}{n!}(n+1)^{\max(q,1)}.$$

This implies $g(\gamma) \sim \mathbb{E}(M^q)\,g(b\gamma)$ when $\gamma \to 0$. ∎

The qth moment of trading time satisfies $\mathbb{E}\{[\theta_\infty(t)]^q\} \sim [\mathbb{E}(M^q)/b^q]$ $\mathbb{E}\{[\theta_\infty(bt)]^q\}$. Combined with Lemma 3, this property implies that $\mathbb{E}\{[\theta_\infty(t)]^q\} \sim c_q t^{\tau_\theta(q)+1}$ as $t \to 0$. We also infer from Lemma 3 that $\tau_\theta(q) > 0$ for all admissible moments greater than unity, implying that $\tau_\theta(q_{crit}) \ge 0$.

A.5.4   Proof of Corollary 1

We know that the restriction of $(\theta_{\bar{k}})$ on any bounded subinterval $[0,T]$ is uniformly equicontinuous and has a continuous limiting process. Theorem 16.8 in Billingsley (1999) implies that the sequence $\theta_{\bar{k}}$ is also tight on $D[0,\infty)$. We conclude that the sequence $\theta_{\bar{k}}$ converges in $D[0,\infty)$ to a limit process θ_∞ with continuous sample paths.

A.5.5   Proof of Proposition 11

Our proof is based on the following result, proved in Billingsley (1999).

Theorem 2 *If*

$$[\theta_k^*(t_1), .., \theta_k^*(t_p)] \xrightarrow{d} [\theta(t_1), .., \theta(t_p)] \tag{A.16}$$

holds for all $t_1, .., t_p$, and if

$$\lim_{\delta \to 0} \limsup_{k \to \infty} \mathbb{P}\{w(\theta_k^*, \delta) \ge \varepsilon\} = 0 \tag{A.17}$$

for each positive ε, then θ_k^* weakly converges to θ.

We successively establish the convergence of the marginals (A.16) and the tightness condition (A.17).

Convergence of the Marginals

The proof is based on coupled trading times. We assume without loss of generality that $T = 1$ and $\bar{\sigma} = 1$. Consider the sequence $\{\theta_{\bar{k}}\}_{k=1}^\infty$ used in the construction of the continuous time trading time θ_∞, and assume for simplicity that $\{\theta_{\bar{k}}\}_{k=1}^\infty$ is defined on $[0,\infty)$. Stage k relies on the starting time $t_{k,0} = 0$, and arrival times $t_{k,n}$ $(n \ge 1)$. The difference between two consecutive arrivals, $E_{k,n+1} = t_{k,n+1} - t_{k,n}$, has an exponential distribution with density $\gamma_k \exp(-\gamma_k t)$. By a slight abuse of notation, we denote by $M_{k,n}$ the value of the multiplier over the interval $[t_{k,n}; t_{k,n+1})$.

We can similarly construct a coupled trading time $\theta_{\bar{k}}^*$ with discretized arrival times. Let $[x]$ denote for all $x \in \mathbb{R}$ the unique integer such that $[x] \leq x < [x] + 1$. For a given integer $c > 1$, consider the uniform grid 0, $1/c^{\bar{k}}, .., 1$. We discretize the sequence $\{t_{k,n}\}$ on the grid by letting $s_{k,0} = 0$, and

$$s_{k,n} = \sum_{i=1}^{n} \frac{[c^{\bar{k}} E_{k,i}] + 1}{c^{\bar{k}}} \text{ for every } n \geq 1.$$

We observe that the random variable $c^{\bar{k}}(s_{k,n+1} - s_{k,n})$ has a geometric distribution with parameter $\gamma_{k,\bar{k}} = 1 - \exp(-\gamma_1 b^{k-1}/c^{\bar{k}})$ since

$$\mathbb{P}\left\{ s_{k,n+1} - s_{k,n} = \frac{m}{c^{\bar{k}}} \right\} = \mathbb{P}\left\{ \frac{m-1}{c^{\bar{k}}} \leq E_{k,n+1} < \frac{m}{c^{\bar{k}}} \right\} = (1-\gamma_{k,\bar{k}})^{m-1}\gamma_{k,\bar{k}}.$$

The multiplier over $[s_{k,n}, s_{k,n+1})$ is set equal to the value $M_{k,n}$ of the multiplier on the fixed interval $[t_{k,n}; t_{k,n+1})$ in the continuous construction.

Let N_k^* denote the highest integer n such that $s_{k,n} < 1$ in the kth stage of the discrete-time construction. For any $n_1, .., n_{\bar{k}}$, let $\Delta^*(n_1, .., n_{\bar{k}})$ be the length of the largest subinterval of $[0, 1]$ over which multipliers are given by $M_{1,n_1}, \ldots, M_{\bar{k},n_{\bar{k}}}$.[4] We know that

$$\theta_{\bar{k}}^*(1) = \sum_{n_1=0}^{N_1^*} \cdots \sum_{n_{\bar{k}}=0}^{N_{\bar{k}}^*} M_{1,n_1} \ldots M_{\bar{k},n_{\bar{k}}} \Delta^*(n_1, .., n_{\bar{k}}).$$

For the continuous-time construction, we can similarly define $N_{\bar{k}}$ and $\Delta(n_1, .., n_{\bar{k}})$, and write

$$\theta_{\bar{k}}(1) = \sum_{n_1=0}^{N_1} \cdots \sum_{n_{\bar{k}}=0}^{N_{\bar{k}}} M_{1,n_1} \ldots M_{\bar{k},n_{\bar{k}}} \Delta(n_1, .., n_{\bar{k}}).$$

Let $H_k = \max(N_k^*, N_k)$. The intervals attached to a given set of multipliers in the paired constructions differ in length by:

$$\delta_{n_1,..,n_k} = \Delta^*(n_1, .., n_k) - \Delta(n_1, .., n_k).$$

With this notation, the discretized and continuous versions of trading time differ by

$$\theta_{\bar{k}}^*(1) - \theta_{\bar{k}}(1) = \sum_{n_1=0}^{H_1} \cdots \sum_{n_{\bar{k}}=0}^{H_{\bar{k}}} M_{1,n_1} \ldots M_{\bar{k},n_{\bar{k}}} \delta_{n_1,..,n_{\bar{k}}}. \qquad (A.18)$$

---

[4] That is, $\Delta^*(n_1, .., n_{\bar{k}})$ is the length of the intersection of $[s_{k,n_k}; \min(1, s_{k,n_k+1}))$, $k \in \{1, .., \bar{k}\}$.

As is shown below, the first or second moment of $\left|\theta_{\bar{k}}^*(1) - \theta_{\bar{k}}(1)\right|$ converges to zero as $\bar{k} \to \infty$. Since this argument applies equally well to all time intervals, we conclude that $\theta_{\bar{k}}^*(t) \xrightarrow{d} \theta_\infty(t)$ for all t.

First Moment. We note that

$$\mathbb{E} \left|\theta_{\bar{k}}^*(1) - \theta_{\bar{k}}(1)\right| \leq \mathbb{E} \left(\sum_{n_1,\dots,n_{\bar{k}}} \left|\delta_{n_1,\dots,n_{\bar{k}}}\right| \right).$$

The average number of nonzero mismatches $\delta_{n_1,\dots,n_{\bar{k}}}$ in the unit interval is of order $b^{\bar{k}}$, and their size is of order $1/c^{\bar{k}}$. As in Calvet and Fisher (2001), we can therefore verify that the first moment $\mathbb{E}\left|\theta_{\bar{k}}^*(1) - \theta_{\bar{k}}(1)\right|$ is bounded above by a multiple of $(b/c)^{\bar{k}}$. Hence $\mathbb{E}\left|\theta_{\bar{k}}^*(1) - \theta_{\bar{k}}(1)\right| \to 0$ under Condition 5.

Second Moment. We note that

$$\mathbb{E} \left\{ \left[\theta_{\bar{k}}^*(1) - \theta_{\bar{k}}(1)\right]^2 \right\} \leq \left[\mathbb{E}(M^2)\right]^{\bar{k}} \mathbb{E} \left(\sum_{m_1,\dots,m_{\bar{k}},n_1,\dots,n_{\bar{k}}} \delta_{m_1,\dots,m_{\bar{k}}} \delta_{n_1,\dots,n_{\bar{k}}} \right). \tag{A.19}$$

The number of nonzero $\delta_{m_1,\dots,m_{\bar{k}}} \delta_{n_1,\dots,n_{\bar{k}}}$ is of order $b^{\bar{k}}$, while their size is of order $c^{-2\bar{k}}$. We can verify that the second moment $\mathbb{E} \left\{ \left[\theta_{\bar{k}}^*(1) - \theta_{\bar{k}}(1)\right]^2 \right\}$ is bounded above by a multiple of $\left[\mathbb{E}(M^2)b/c^2\right]^{\bar{k}}$ and therefore converges to zero under Condition 6.

Tightness

Let $\delta = c^{-l}$. As in the proof of Proposition 9, we infer from Theorem 7.4 in Billingsley (1999) that for any $k \geq 1$,

$$\mathbb{P}\{w(\theta_{\bar{k}}^*, \delta) \geq \varepsilon\} \leq \delta^{-1}\mathbb{P}\left\{\theta_{\bar{k}}^*(\delta) \geq \varepsilon/3\right\}.$$

Since $\theta_{\bar{k}}^*(\delta) \xrightarrow{d} \theta_\infty(\delta)$, the function $\limsup_k \mathbb{P}\{w(\theta_{\bar{k}}^*, \delta) \geq \varepsilon\}$ is bounded above by $\delta^{-1}\mathbb{P}\{\theta_\infty(\delta) \geq \varepsilon/3\}$. Given a number $q > 0$ satisfying $\tau_\theta(q) > 0$, Chebyshev's inequality implies that $\limsup_{\bar{k}} \mathbb{P}\{w(\theta_{\bar{k}}^*, \delta) \geq \varepsilon\}$ is bounded above by $(3/\varepsilon)^q \delta^{-1}\mathbb{E}\left[\theta_\infty(\delta)^q\right]$. Letting $\delta \to 0$, we infer that $\delta^{-1}\mathbb{E}\left[\theta_\infty(\delta)^q\right] \sim c_q\delta^{\tau_\theta(q)} \to 0$ and conclude that condition (A.17) is satisfied. We have thus established that $\theta_{\bar{k}}^*$ weakly converges to θ_∞ as $\bar{k} \to \infty$.

A.5.6   MSM with Dependent Arrivals

To aid the discussion, let A_t denote the set of arrival instants for component k. In Calvet and Fisher (1999, 2001), we specify that if an arrival occurs in component k at instant t, then arrivals are triggered in all higher-frequency components $k' > k$. Hence $A_k \subseteq A_{k'}$ for all $k' > k$. In addition, we assume that arrivals that are specific to stage-k can occur with intensity $\gamma_1 b^{k-1}$. Weak convergence of the "dependent" construction then holds under Condition 5 or Condition 6.

We note that for any $k > 1$, the average number of stage-k arrivals is larger in the "dependent" construction than in the "independent" MSM construction. Specifically, the cumulative intensity of level-k arrivals, including arrivals triggered by lower frequencies, is

$$\gamma_1 \sum_{j=1}^{k} b^{j-1} = \gamma_1 \frac{b^k - 1}{b - 1} > \gamma_1 b^{k-1}.$$

For large values of b, the average number of arrivals is approximately the same in the "dependent" and "independent" constructions. For b close to one, on the other hand, the cumulative arrival intensities is substantially larger than under independence.

This suggests that a dependent arrivals construction more directly comparable to the "independent" construction would specify the *total* Poisson intensity at level k to be given by (7.1). To achieve this, we can specify that for $k > 1$ the intensity of stage-k arrivals (that are not triggered by lower-frequency events) be equal to $\gamma_1 \left(b^{k-1} - b^{k-2} \right)$. An interesting feature of this construction is that it allows a dependent arrivals construction where b can approach one without causing the cumulative arrival intensity to diverge.

A.5.7 Autocovariogram of Log Volatility in MSM

Since multipliers are independent, the autocovariogram is:

$$Cov\left[\omega_\Delta(t), \omega_\Delta(t + \tau)\right] = \frac{1}{4} \sum_{k=1}^{\bar{k}} Cov\left[\ln(M_{k,t}); \ln(M_{k,t+\tau})\right].$$

Assume that t is on the grid and that $\tau = n\Delta$. The probability of no-arrival on the kth multiplier is $(1 - \gamma_{k,\Delta})^n$ and therefore $Cov\left[\ln(M_{k,t}); \ln(M_{k,t+\tau})\right] = 4\lambda^2(1 - \gamma_{k,\Delta})^n$. This implies the exact formula:

$$Cov\left[\omega_\Delta(t), \omega_\Delta(t + \tau)\right] = \lambda^2 \sum_{k=1}^{\bar{k}} e^{-b^{k-1}\tau/T_1}.$$

A.5.8 Limiting MRW Process

In the MRW continuous lognormal cascade, the magnitude process $\omega_\Delta(u)$ is defined as the integral of a Gaussian process $dW(t, s)$ over a cone $C(t)$ in the plane of time and scales:

$$\omega_\Delta(u) = \int_\Delta^T \int_{u-s}^{u+s} dW(v, s).$$

The integral is truncated at Δ and T to guarantee convergence. The Gaussian process has mean $\mathbb{E}\left[dW(v,s)\right] = -(\lambda^2/s^2)dvds$, and covariance

$$Cov\left[dW(v,s); dW(v',s')\right] = (\lambda^2/s^2)\delta(v-v')\delta(s-s')dvds,$$

where δ denotes the Dirac function. The limiting trading time

$$\theta(t) = \lim_{\Delta \to 0} \int_0^t e^{2\omega_\Delta(u)} du.$$

satisfies the exact moment-scaling relation $\mathbb{E}[\theta(t)^q] = c_\theta(q)t^{\tau_\theta(q)+1}$ at all instants $t \leq T$. We refer the reader to Bacry, Kozhemyak and Muzy (2008) for an excellent review of these developments.

The fact that exact scaling holds only on a bounded interval in MRW stems from a fundamental limitation of multiscaling. As shown in the Appendix to Chapter 6, Hölder's inequality implies that moment-scaling, whether exact or asymptotic, cannot be maintained as t goes to infinity for a nonlinear $\tau_\theta(q)$. For MSM, the asymptotic scaling relation (7.5) holds remarkably accurately for practical ranges of frequencies (see Chapter 8), and hence in typical empirical applications the difference in scaling between the two models is probably quite difficult to distinguish.

A.6   Appendix to Chapter 9

A.6.1   Full-Information Economies

Stochastic Discount Factor

As Epstein and Zin (1989) show, a utility-maximizing agent with budget constraint $W_{t+1} = (W_t - C_t)(1 + R_{t+1})$ has stochastic discount factor

$$SDF_{t+1} = \left[\delta\left(\frac{C_{t+1}}{C_t}\right)^{-\frac{1}{\psi}}\right]^\theta \left[\frac{1}{1+R_{t+1}}\right]^{1-\theta},$$

where R_{t+1} is the simple net return on the optimal portfolio.

In our setup, the representative agent can be viewed as holding a long-lived claim on the aggregate consumption stream $\{C_t\}_{t=0}^\infty$. The tree has price $P_c C_t$ and yields the return $1 + R_{c,t+1} = (1 + 1/P_c)C_{t+1}/C_t$. The stochastic discount factor is thus

$$SDF_{t+1} = \delta^\theta (1 + 1/P_c)^{\theta-1} \left(\frac{C_{t+1}}{C_t}\right)^{-\alpha}.$$

The condition $\mathbb{E}_t[SDF_{t+1}(1+R_{c,t+1})] = 1$ implies that $\delta^\theta (1+1/P_c)^\theta$ $\mathbb{E}[(C_{t+1}/C_t)^{1-\alpha}] = 1$, or equivalently,

$$1 + 1/P_c = \delta^{-1}\{\mathbb{E}[(C_{t+1}/C_t)^{1-\alpha}]\}^{-\frac{1}{\theta}}.$$

We conclude that Equation (9.3) holds.

Bayesian Updating and Closed-Form Likelihood

At any instant t, the econometrician has probabilities $\hat{\Pi}_t = (\hat{\Pi}_t^1, \ldots, \hat{\Pi}_t^d)$ over the state space conditional on the set of past returns $\mathcal{R}_t = \{r_1, \ldots, r_t\}$. Bayes' rule implies that these probabilities can be computed recursively:

$$\hat{\Pi}_{t+1} \propto \hat{\Pi}_t [A * F(r_{t+1})], \tag{A.20}$$

where $*$ denotes element-by-element multiplication, $A = (a_{i,j})_{1 \leq i,j \leq d}$ is the matrix of transition probabilities $a_{i,j} = P(M_{t+1} = m^j | M_t = m^i)$, and $F(r)$ is the matrix with elements $F_{i,j}(r) \equiv f_{r_{t+1}}(r | M_t = m^i, M_{t+1} = m^j)$. The log-likelihood of the return process is therefore

$$\ln L(r_1, \ldots, r_T) = \sum_{t=1}^{T} \ln \left\{ \hat{\Pi}_{t-1} [A * F(r_t)] \mathbf{1}' \right\}. \tag{A.21}$$

Loglinearized Economy

We now develop intuition for the multifrequency equilibrium by loglinearizing the pricing equation. Specifically, assume that the price-dividend ratio is loglinear in the volatility components:

$$\ln Q(M_t) \approx \bar{q} - \sum_{k=1}^{\bar{k}} q_k (M_{k,t} - 1). \tag{A.22}$$

Equilibrium fixed-point condition (9.6) implies:

Proposition 16 *The coefficients of the loglinear solution satisfy*

$$q_k = \frac{\alpha \sigma_{c,d}}{2} \frac{1 - \gamma_k}{1 - (1 - \gamma_k)\rho}, \tag{A.23}$$

$$\ln\left(\frac{e^{\bar{q}}}{1 + e^{\bar{q}}}\right) \equiv \bar{\mu}_d - r_f - \alpha \sigma_{c,d}, \tag{A.24}$$

where $\rho = e^{\bar{q}}/(1 + e^{\bar{q}})$ and $\sigma_{c,d} = \sigma_c \bar{\sigma}_d \rho_{c,d}$.

Proof By (9.6), the price-dividend ratio satisfies the loglinearized Euler equation:

$$\ln Q(M_t) = \bar{\mu}_d - r_f - \alpha \sigma_{c,d} + \ln \mathbb{E}_t \left\{ [1 + Q(M_{t+1})] e^{-\alpha \sigma_c \rho_{c,d} [\sigma_d (M_{t+1}) - \bar{\sigma}_d]} \right\}. \tag{A.25}$$

We assume that the distribution M is concentrated around 1, and we look for a linear approximate solution to this fixed-point equation. The conditional expectation

$$\mathbb{E}_t \left\{ [1 + e^{\bar{q} - \sum_{k=1}^{\bar{k}} q_k (M_{k,t+1} - 1)}] e^{-\alpha \sigma_c \rho_{c,d} [\sigma_d (M_{t+1}) - \bar{\sigma}_d]} \right\} \qquad (A.26)$$

is approximately

$$(1 + e^{\bar{q}}) \mathbb{E}_t \left[1 - \sum \left(\rho q_k + \frac{\alpha \sigma_{c,d}}{2} \right) (M_{k,t+1} - 1) \right].$$

Since $\mathbb{E}_t (M_{k,t+1} - 1) = (1 - \gamma_k)(M_{k,t} - 1)$, we infer that (A.26) is approximately equal to $(1 + e^{\bar{q}}) \left[1 - \sum_{k=1}^{\bar{k}} (1 - \gamma_k) \left(\rho q_k + \frac{\alpha \sigma_{c,d}}{2} \right) (M_{k,t} - 1) \right]$. The loglinearized Euler equation (A.25) can thus be rewritten as:

$$\bar{q} - \sum_{k=1}^{\bar{k}} q_k (M_{k,t} - 1) \approx \bar{\mu}_d - r_f - \alpha \sigma_{c,d} + \ln(1 + e^{\bar{q}})$$

$$- \sum_{k=1}^{\bar{k}} (1 - \gamma_k) \left(\rho q_k + \frac{\alpha \sigma_{c,d}}{2} \right) (M_{k,t} - 1).$$

We infer that Equations (A.23)–(A.24) hold. ∎

The price-dividend ratio (A.22) is therefore a persistence-weighted sum of the volatility components. High-frequency components have negligible effects on the P/D ratio: $q_k \to 0$ when $\gamma_k \to 1$. On the other hand, for very persistent components, the coefficient q_k is large since ρ is empirically close to one at the usual frequencies.

Smooth Probabilities

The econometrician's smoothed probabilities satisfy the backward recursion

$$\hat{\Psi}_t^i = \hat{\Pi}_t^i \sum_{j=1}^{d} a_{ij} \frac{\hat{\Psi}_{t+1}^j}{\hat{\Pi}_{t+1}^j} \left[\frac{F_{i,j}(r_{t+1})}{f_{r_{t+1}}(r_{t+1} | \mathcal{R}_t)} \right], \qquad (A.27)$$

$i \in \{1, \dots, d\}$, and the final condition $\hat{\Psi}_T = \hat{\Pi}_T$.

Ex post Decomposition

We condition the return Equation (9.9) with respect to the econometrician's information set $\mathcal{R}_T$:

$$r_{t+1} = \bar{\mu}_d - r_f + \mathbb{E} \left[\ln \frac{1 + Q(M_{t+1})}{Q(M_t)} - \frac{\sigma_d (M_{t+1})^2}{2} \middle| \mathcal{R}_T \right] + \hat{e}_{d,t+1}.$$

The definition of smoothed probabilities implies

$$r_{t+1} = \bar{\mu}_d - r_f + \mathbb{E}_{\hat{\Psi}_{t+1}} \left(\ln[1 + Q(M_{t+1})] - \sigma_d(M_{t+1})^2/2 \right)$$

$$- \mathbb{E}_{\hat{\Psi}_t} \ln Q(M_t) + \hat{e}_{d,t+1}.$$

Since $\mathbb{E}_{\hat{\Psi}_t} r_{t+1} = \bar{\mu}_d - r_f + \mathbb{E}_{\hat{\Psi}_t} (\ln[1 + Q(M_{t+1})] - \sigma_d(M_{t+1})^2/2 - \ln Q(M_t))$, we conclude that (9.11) holds.

The Campbell-Hentschel Model

The CH specification is based on a QGARCH$(1, 2)$ process for dividend news (Engle, 1990; Sentana, 1995). Excess returns satisfy

$$r_{t+1} = \mu + \gamma \sigma_t^2 + (1 + 2\lambda b)\eta_{d,t+1} - \lambda \left(\eta_{d,t+1}^2 - \sigma_t^2 \right), \qquad (A.28)$$

where the dividend news $\eta_{d,t+1}$ is $\mathcal{N} \left(0, \sigma_t^2 \right)$, with

$$\sigma_t^2 = \varpi + \alpha_1 \left(\eta_{d,t} - b \right)^2 + \alpha_2 \left(\eta_{d,t-1} - b \right)^2 + \beta \sigma_{t-1}^2,$$

$$\lambda = \frac{\gamma \rho \left(\alpha_1 + \rho \alpha_2 \right)}{1 - \rho \left(\alpha_1 + \rho \alpha_2 + \beta \right)}.$$

The parameter ρ is calibrated to the empirical price-dividend ratio, and the seven parameters $(\mu, \gamma, \varpi, \alpha_1, \alpha_2, b, \beta)$ are estimated by maximum likelihood.

The conditional return $\mathbb{E}_t r_{t+1} = \mu + \gamma \sigma_t^2$ increases in conditional volatility and γ, which is related to risk aversion. Feedback appears in (A.28) through a quadratic term in dividend news, $\lambda(2b\eta_{d,t+1} + \sigma_t^2 - \eta_{d,t+1}^2)$. After an extreme innovation $\eta_{d,t+1}$, the investor knows that volatility will increase, and price drops. The location parameter b differentiates QGARCH from traditional GARCH. When $b > 0$, negative dividend news $\eta_{d,t}$ has a higher impact on volatility than positive news of the same size.

A.6.2   Learning Economies

Consider the volatility state and investor probability distribution (M_t, Π_t) at the end of period t. The state of the economy in the following period is computed in three steps.

First, we compute the latent state of nature at date $t+1$. That is, we draw the volatility state M_{t+1} given M_t, and sample $\bar{k} + 2$ independent standard normals $(z_{1,t+1}; \ldots; z_{\bar{k},t+1}; \varepsilon_{d,t+1}; \eta_{c,t+1})$. The Gaussian consumption noise is $\varepsilon_{c,t+1} = \rho_{c,d}\varepsilon_{d,t+1} + \sqrt{1 - \rho_{c,d}^2} \eta_{c,t+1}$. We then compute the consumption, dividend, and signal in period $t + 1$.

Second, we compute the corresponding investor belief. The investor observes $(\delta_{t+1}, c_{t+1} - c_t, d_{t+1} - d_t)$ and uses Bayes' rule to derive her new probability distribution over volatility states: $\Pi^j_{t+1} \propto f(\delta_{t+1}, c_{t+1} - c_t, d_{t+1} - d_t | M_{t+1} = m^j) \sum_{i=1}^d a_{i,j} \Pi^i_t$.

Third, we compute the corresponding excess return using (9.16).

A.6.3   Multifrequency Consumption Risk

In the presence of consumption switches, the tree has price $P_c(M'_t)C_t$, and the stochastic discount factor is given by

$$SDF_{t+1} = \delta^\theta \left[\frac{1 + P_c(M'_{t+1})}{P_c(M'_t)} \right]^{\theta-1} \left(\frac{C_{t+1}}{C_t} \right)^{-\alpha}.$$

We index the consumption states by $i = 1, \ldots, N = 2^\ell$. Let $\pi_{i,j}$ denote the transition probability from state i to state j. The price-consumption ratio satisfies the fixed-point equation

$$P_c(i) = \delta \left(\sum_{j=1}^N \pi_{i,j} \left[1 + P_c(j)\right]^\theta e^{(1-\alpha)g_c(j) + \sigma_c^2(j)(1-\alpha)^2/2} \right)^{1/\theta}. \quad \text{(A.29)}$$

The interest rate $r_f = -\ln \mathbb{E}_t(SDF_{t+1})$ is then

$$r_f(i) = -\theta \ln \delta - \ln \left\{ \sum_j \pi_{i,j} \left[\frac{1 + P_c(j)}{P_c(i)} \right]^{\theta-1} e^{-\alpha g_c(j) + \alpha^2 \sigma_c^2(j)/2} \right\}.$$

Finally, the price-dividend ratio of the stock satisfies the fixed-point equation

$$Q(M_t) = \delta^\theta \mathbb{E}_t \left\{ \left[\frac{1 + P_c(M'_{t+1})}{P_c(M'_t)} \right]^{\theta-1} e^{\phi(M_{t+1}, M'_{t+1})} [1 + Q(M_{t+1})] \right\}, \quad \text{(A.30)}$$

where $\phi(M_{t+1}, M'_{t+1}) = \mu_d(M_{t+1}) - \alpha g_c(M'_{t+1}) + \alpha^2 \sigma_c^2(M'_{t+1})/2 - \alpha \sigma_c (M'_{t+1}) \sigma_d(M_{t+1}) \rho_{c,d}$.

A.7   Appendix to Chapter 10

A.7.1   Proof of Proposition 13

The price-dividend ratio satisfies

$$Q(M_t) = \mathbb{E} \left(\int_0^{+\infty} \frac{\Lambda_{t+s}}{\Lambda_t} \frac{D_{t+s}}{D_t} ds \,\middle|\, M_t \right).$$

Since

$$d \ln \Lambda_t = \left[-r_f(M_t) - \alpha^2 \sigma_C^2(M_t)/2 \right] dt - \alpha \sigma_C(M_t) dZ_C(t),$$

$$d \ln D_t = \left[g_D(M_t) - \sigma_D^2(M_t)/2 \right] dt + \sigma_D(M_t) dZ_D(t),$$

we infer that

$$\ln \frac{\Lambda_{t+s}}{\Lambda_t} + \ln \frac{D_{t+s}}{D_t} = \int_0^s \left[g_D(M_{t+h}) - r_f(M_{t+h}) \right.$$

$$\left. - \frac{\sigma_D^2(M_{t+h}) + \alpha^2 \sigma_C^2(M_{t+h})}{2} \right] dh$$

$$+ \int_0^s [\sigma_D(M_{t+h}) dZ_D(t+h) - \alpha \sigma_C(M_{t+h}) dZ_C(t+h)]$$

is conditionally Gaussian with mean $\int_0^s \left[g_D(M_{t+h}) - r_f(M_{t+h}) - \frac{\sigma_D^2(M_{t+h}) + \alpha^2 \sigma_C^2(M_{t+h})}{2} \right] dh$ and variance $\int_0^s [\alpha^2 \sigma_C^2(M_{t+h}) + \sigma_D^2(M_{t+h}) - 2\alpha \rho_{C,D} \sigma_C(M_{t+h}) \sigma_D(M_{t+h})] dh$. We then easily check that

$$\mathbb{E}\left(\frac{\Lambda_{t+s}}{\Lambda_t} \frac{D_{t+s}}{D_t} \Big| M_t \right) = \mathbb{E}_t e^{\int_0^s [g_D(M_{t+h}) - r_f(M_{t+h}) - \alpha \rho_{C,D} \sigma_C(M_{t+h}) \sigma_D(M_{t+h})] dh}.$$

A.7.2 Multivariate Extensions

The asset pricing models in the main text are based on univariate MSM and assume either i.i.d. consumption or Lucas tree economies. We now introduce an extension of MSM that permits intermediate comovements of consumption and dividends. As in multivariate MSM (see Chapter 4 and Appendix to Chapter 7), we assume that the consumption and dividend processes have constant drifts but stochastic volatilities

$$\sigma_C(M_t) = \bar{\sigma}_C (M_{1,t}^\alpha M_{2,t}^\alpha \ldots M_{\bar{\ell},t}^\alpha)^{1/2},$$

$$\sigma_D(M_t) = \bar{\sigma}_D (M_{1,t}^\beta M_{2,t}^\beta \ldots M_{\bar{k},t}^\beta)^{1/2},$$

where $\bar{\ell} \leq \bar{k}$. The specification permits correlation in volatility across series through the bivariate distribution M and correlation in returns through the Brownian motions Z_C and Z_D. This flexible setup permits us to construct a more general class of jump-diffusions for stock prices. We note that the model reduces to i.i.d. consumption if $\bar{\ell} = 0$, and to a Lucas tree economy if $\bar{\ell} = \bar{k}$ and multipliers are perfectly correlated.

The generalized model might also be useful for option pricing. In our environment, the price of a European option $f(P_T)$ is therefore given by[5]

$$f_0 = \mathbb{E}_0 \left[\frac{\Lambda_T}{\Lambda_0} f(P_T) \right].$$

As in Hull and White (1987), let $f[(M_t)_{t \in [0,T]}] = \mathbb{E}_0 \left[\Lambda_T f(P_T)/\Lambda_0 \right| (M_t)_{t \in [0,T]}]$ denote the option price conditional on the state history. The law of iterated expectations implies $f_0 = \mathbb{E}_0 f\left((M_t)_{t \in [0,T]}\right)$, which can be useful in empirical settings.

A.7.3   Proof of Proposition 14

Given an initial state ν_t, the P/D ratio of the Lucas tree economy can be written as

$$Q(\varepsilon) = \mathbb{E} \left(\int_0^{+\infty} e^{-\delta' s - \frac{\alpha(1-\alpha)}{2} \int_0^s \left(\sigma_D^2 [M_{t+h}(\varepsilon)] - \bar{\sigma}_D^2 \right) dh} ds \, \middle| \, \nu_t \right).$$

We note that $Q(0) = 1/\delta'$. By the dominated convergence theorem, the function Q is differentiable and

$$Q'(0) = -q_1 \mathbb{E} \left\{ \int_0^{+\infty} e^{-\delta' s} \left[\int_0^s \sum_{k=1}^{\bar{k}} (\nu_{k,t+h} - 1) dh \right] ds \, \middle| \, \nu_t \right\}.$$

Since $\mathbb{E}_t(\nu_{k,t+h} - 1) = e^{-\gamma_k h}(\nu_{k,t} - 1)$, we infer that

$$Q'(0) = -q_1 \sum_{k=1}^{\bar{k}} (\nu_{k,t} - 1) \left(\int_0^{+\infty} e^{-\delta' s} \int_0^s e^{-\gamma_k h} dh \, ds \right)$$

$$= -q_1 \sum_{k=1}^{\bar{k}} \frac{\nu_{k,t} - 1}{\delta'(\delta' + \gamma_k)}.$$

Hence

$$Q(\varepsilon) = Q(0) \left(1 - q_1 \sum_{k=1}^{\bar{k}} \frac{\nu_{k,t} - 1}{\delta' + \gamma_k} \varepsilon \right) + o(\varepsilon).$$

We take the log and conclude that (10.7) holds. A similar argument holds in the i.i.d. consumption case.

---

[5] See Anderson and Raimondo (2005), David and Veronesi (2002), Garcia, Luger, and Renault (2003) and Garleanu, Pedersen, and Poteshman (2006) for recent work on consumption-based option pricing.

A.7.4   Proof of Proposition 15

Consider

$$Q_{\bar{k}}(t) \equiv \mathbb{E}\left[\int_0^{+\infty} e^{-\rho s} e^{-\lambda[\theta_{\bar{k}}(t+s)-\theta_{\bar{k}}(t)]} ds \,\middle|\, M_t\right],$$

where $\lambda = \alpha(1-\alpha)/2 > 0$. We easily check that $Q_{\bar{k}}(t)$ is a positive and bounded submartingale:

$$Q_{\bar{k}}(t) \le \mathbb{E}_{\bar{k}}\left[Q_{\bar{k}+1}(t)\right] \le 1/\rho.$$

The P/D ratio $Q_{\bar{k}}(t)$ therefore converges to a limit distribution, which we now easily characterize.

Consider the function $\Phi : D[0,\infty) \to D[0,\infty)$ defined for every cadlag function f by the integral transform

$$(\Phi f)(t) = \int_0^{+\infty} \exp\left\{-\rho s - \lambda[f(t+s) - f(t)]\right\} ds.$$

The function Φ is bounded with respect to the Skorohod distance since $(\Phi f)(t) \in [0, 1/\rho]$ for all t. We also check that it is continuous. Since $\theta_k \to \theta_\infty$, we infer that $\Phi\theta_k$ weakly converges to $\Phi\theta_\infty$. Hence, $Q_{\bar{k}}(t) \to Q_\infty(t)$, and the proposition holds.

References

Abadir, K. M., W. Distaso, and L. Giraitis. 2008. Two estimators of the long-run variance: beyond short memory. Working paper. Imperial College London.

Abel, A. 1988. Stock prices under time-varying dividend risk: an exact solution in an infinite horizon general equilibrium model. *Journal of Monetary Economics* 22: 375–95.

Abel, A. 1999. Risk premia and term premia in general equilibrium. *Journal of Monetary Economics* 43: 3–33.

Abel, A. 2003. The effects of a baby boom on stock prices and capital accumulation in the presence of social security. *Econometrica* 71: 551–78.

Adelman, I. 1965. Long cycles: fact or artefact? *American Economic Review* 55: 444–63.

Adrian, T. and J. Rosenberg. 2008. Stock returns and volatility: pricing the long-run and short-run components of market risk. *Journal of Finance*, forthcoming.

Agterberg, F. 2007. New applications of the model of de Wijs in regional geochemistry. *Mathematical Geology* 39: 1–25.

Ait-Sahalia, Y. 2002. Telling from discrete data whether the underlying continuous-time model is a diffusion. *Journal of Finance* 57: 2075–112.

Ait-Sahalia, Y. and J. Jacod. 2008. Testing for jumps in a discretely observed process. *Annals of Statistics*, forthcoming.

Akgiray, V. 1989. Conditional heteroskedasticity in time series of stock returns: evidence and forecasts. *Journal of Business* 62: 55–80.

Albert, J. and S. Chib. 1993. Bayes inference via Gibbs sampling of autoregressive time series subject to Markov means and variance shifts. *Journal of Business and Economic Statistics* 11: 1–15.

Alizadeh, S., M. Brandt, and F. X. Diebold. 2002. Range-based estimation of stochastic volatility models. *Journal of Finance* 57: 1047–91.

Andersen, T. 1994. Stochastic autoregressive volatility: a framework for volatility modeling. *Mathematical Finance* 4: 75–102.

Andersen, T. 1996. Return volatility and trading volume: an information flow interpretation of stochastic volatility. *Journal of Finance* 51: 169–204.

Andersen, T. G. and L. Benzoni. 2008. Stochastic volatility. In *Encyclopedia of Complexity and System Science*, ed. B. Mizrach. Springer.

Andersen, T., L. Benzoni, and J. Lund. 2002. An empirical investigation of continuous-time models for equity returns. *Journal of Finance* 57: 1239–84.

Andersen, T. and T. Bollerslev. 1998a. Answering the skeptics: yes, standard volatility models do provide accurate forecasts. *International Economic Review* 39: 885–905.

Andersen, T. and T. Bollerslev. 1998b. Deutsche-mark dollar volatility: intraday activity patterns, macroeconomic announcements, and longer-run dependencies. *Journal of Finance* 53: 219–65.

Andersen, T., T. Bollerslev, and F. X. Diebold. 2007. Roughing it up: including jump components in the measurement, modeling, and forecasting of return volatility. *Review of Economics and Statistics* 89: 701–20.

Andersen, T., T. Bollerslev, F. X. Diebold, and P. Labys. 2001. The distribution of realized exchange rate volatility. *Journal of the American Statistical Association* 96: 42–55.

Andersen, T., T. Bollerslev, F. X. Diebold, and P. Labys. 2003. Modeling and forecasting realized volatility. *Econometrica* 71: 579–625.

Andersen, T., T. Bollerslev, F. X. Diebold, and C. Vega. 2003. Real-time price discovery in foreign exchange. *American Economic Review* 93: 38–62.

Andersen, T., T. Bollerslev, and N. Meddahi. 2005. Correcting the errors: volatility forecast evaluation using high-frequency data and realized volatilities. *Econometrica* 73: 279–96.

Andersen, T. and B. Sørensen. 1996. GMM estimation of a stochastic volatility model: a Monte Carlo study. *Journal of Business and Economic Statistics* 14: 328–52.

Anderson, R. M. and R. C. Raimondo. 2005. Market clearing and derivative pricing. *Economic Theory* 25: 21–34.

Andrews, D. F. and C. L. Mallows. 1974. Scale mixtures of normal distributions. *Journal of the Royal Statistical Society B* 36: 99–102.

Andrews, D. W. K. 1991. Heteroskedasticity and autocorrelation consistent covariance matrix estimation. *Econometrica* 59: 817–54.

Andrews, D. W. K. and P. Guggenberger. 2003. A bias-reduced log-periodogram regression for the long-memory parameter. *Econometrica* 71: 675–712.

Andrews, D. W. K. and C. Monahan. 1992. An improved heteroskedasticity and autocorrelation consistent covariance matrix estimator. *Econometrica* 60: 953–66.

Arneodo, A., J.-P. Bouchaud, R. Cont, J.-F. Muzy, M. Potters, and D. Sornette. 1996. Comment on "Turbulent cascades in foreign exchange markets," arXiv:cond-mat/9607120v1.

Arneodo, A., J.-F. Muzy, and D. Sornette. 1998. Direct causal cascade in the stock market. *European Physical Journal B* 2: 277–82.

Arthur, W. B., J. Holland, B. LeBaron, R. Palmer, and P. Tayler. 1997. Asset pricing under endogenous expectations in an artificial stock market. In *The Economy as an Evolving Complex System II*, eds. W. B. Arthur, S. N. Durlauf, and D. Lane, pp. 15–44. Addison-Wesley.

Attanasio, O. and G. Weber. 1993. Consumption growth, the interest rate, and aggregation. *Review of Economic Studies* 60: 631–49.

Atzori, L., N. Aste, and M. Isola. 2006. Estimation of multifractal parameters in traffic measurement: an accuracy-based real-time approach. *Computer Communications* 29: 1879–88.

Aydemir, A. C., M. Gallmeyer, and B. Hollifield. 2006. Financial leverage does not cause the leverage effect. Working paper. Texas A&M University and Carnegie Mellon University.

Bachelier, L. 1900. Theory of speculation. In *The Random Character of Stock Market Prices*, ed. P. Cootner. MIT Press, 1964, Reprint.

Backus, D. K. and S. E. Zin. 1993. Long memory inflation uncertainty: evidence from the term structure of interest rates. *Journal of Money, Credit and Banking* 25: 681–700.

Bacry, E., J. Delour, and J.-F. Muzy. 2001. Multifractal random walks. *Physical Review E* 64: 026103–06.

Bacry, E., A. Kozhemyak, and J.-F. Muzy. 2008. Continuous cascade models for asset returns. *Journal of Economic Dynamics and Control* 32(1): 156–99.

Bacry, E. and J.-F. Muzy. 2003. Log-infinitely divisible multifractal processes. *Communications in Mathematical Physics* 236: 449–75.

Baillie, R. 1996. Long memory processes and fractional integration in econometrics. *Journal of Econometrics* 73: 5–59.

Baillie, R. and T. Bollerslev. 1989. The message in daily exchange rates: a conditional variance tale. *Journal of Business and Economic Statistics* 7: 297–305.

Baillie, R., T. Bollerslev, and H. O. Mikkelsen. 1996. Fractionally integrated generalized autoregressive conditional heteroscedasticity. *Journal of Econometrics* 74: 3–30.

Baillie, R., C. F. Chung, and M. A. Tieslau. 1996. Analyzing inflation by the fractionally integrated ARFIMA-GARCH model. *Journal of Applied Econometrics* 11: 23–40.

Bakshi, G., H. Cao, and X. Chen. 1997. Empirical performance of alternative option pricing models. *Journal of Finance* 52: 2003–49.

Ball, C. and W. Torous. 1985. On jumps in common stock prices and their impact on call option pricing. *Journal of Finance* 40: 155–73.

Bansal, R., V. Khatchatrian, and A. Yaron. 2005. Interpretable asset markets? *European Economic Review* 49: 531–60.

Bansal, R. and C. Lundblad. 2002. Market efficiency, fundamental values, and the size of the risk premium in global equity markets. *Journal of Econometrics* 109: 195–237.

Bansal, R. and A. Yaron. 2004. Risks for the long run: a potential resolution of asset pricing puzzles. *Journal of Finance* 49: 1481–509.

Bansal, R. and H. Zhou. 2002. Term structure of interest rates with regime shifts. *Journal of Finance* 57: 1997–2043.

Barndorff-Nielsen, O. 1998. Processes of normal-inverse Gaussian type. *Finance and Stochastics* 2: 41–68.

Barndorff-Nielsen, O. and N. Shephard. 2001. Non-Gaussian Ornstein-Uhlenbeck-based models and some of their uses in financial economics. *Journal of the Royal Statistical Society B* 63: 167–241.

Barndorff-Nielsen, O. and N. Shephard. 2003. Realized power variation and stochastic volatility models. *Bernoulli* 9: 243–65.

Barndorff-Nielsen, O. and N. Shephard. 2004. Power and bipower variation with stochastic volatility and jumps. *Journal of Financial Econometrics* 2(1): 1–37.

Barndorff-Nielsen, O. and N. Shephard. 2006. Econometrics of testing for jumps in financial econometrics using bipower variation. *Journal of Financial Econometrics* 4: 1–30.

Barone-Adesi, G., R. F. Engle, and L. Mancini. 2008. A GARCH option pricing model with filtered historical simulation. *Review of Financial Studies*, forthcoming.

Barral, J. and B. B. Mandelbrot. 2002. Multifractal products of cylindrical pulses. *Probability Theory and Related Fields* 124: 409–30.

Barro, R. 2006. Rare disasters and asset markets in the twentieth century. *Quarterly Journal of Economics* 121: 823–66.

Barsky, R. 1989. Why don't the prices of stocks and bonds move together? *American Economic Review* 79: 1132–45.

Bates, D. 1996. Jumps and stochastic volatility: exchange rate process implicit in Deutsche Mark options. *Review of Financial Studies* 9: 69–107.

Bates, D. 2000. Post '87 crash fears in the S&P 500 futures option market. *Journal of Econometrics* 94(1/2): 181–238.

Baum, L., T. Petrie, G. Soules, and N. Weiss. 1980. A maximization technique occurring in the statistical analysis of probabilistic functions of Markov chains. *Annals of Mathematical Statistics* 41: 164–71.

Baxter, M. and A. Rennie. 1996. *Financial Calculus: An Introduction to Derivative Pricing*. Cambridge University Press.

Beaver, W. 1968. The information content of annual earnings announcements. *Journal of Accounting Research* 6: 67–92.

Bekaert, G. and G. Wu. 2000. Asymmetric volatility and risk in equity markets. *Review of Financial Studies* 13: 1–42.

Bera, A. K. and S. Lee. 1992. Information matrix test, parameter heterogeneity and ARCH: a synthesis. *Review of Economic Studies* 60: 229–40.

Beran, J. 1994. *Statistics for Long-Memory Processes.* Chapman and Hall.

Beveridge, W. H. 1925. Weather and harvest cycles. *Economic Journal* 31: 429–52.

Bhamra, H., L. Kuehn, and I. Strebulaev. 2006. The levered equity risk premium and credit spreads: a unified framework. Working paper. University of British Columbia.

Bhattacharya, R., V. Gupta, and E. Waymire. 1983. The Hurst effect under trends. *Journal of Applied Probability* 20: 649–62.

Billingsley, P. 1979. *Probability and Measure.* John Wiley and Sons.

Billingsley, P. 1999. *Convergence of Probability Measures*, 2nd edition. John Wiley and Sons.

Bjork, T. 2004. *Arbitrage Theory in Continuous Time*, 2nd edition. Oxford University Press.

Black, F. 1976. Studies of stock price volatility changes. *Proceedings of the 1976 Meetings of the American Statistical Association, Business and Economical Statistics Section*, pp. 177–81.

Black, F. and M. Scholes. 1972. The valuation of options contracts and a test of market efficiency. *Journal of Finance* 27: 399–418.

Black, F. and M. Scholes. 1973. The pricing of options and corporate liabilities. *Journal of Political Economy* 81: 637–54.

Blattberg, R. and N. Gonedes. 1974. A comparison of stable and Student distributions as statistical models for stock prices. *Journal of Business* 47: 244–80.

Bochner, S. 1949. Diffusion equation and stochastic processes. *Proceedings of the National Academy of Science of the United States of America* 85: 369–70.

Bollen, N., S. Gray, and R. Whaley. 2000. Regime switching in foreign exchange rates: evidence from currency option prices. *Journal of Econometrics* 94: 239–76.

Bollerslev, T. 1986. Generalized autoregressive conditional heteroskedasticity. *Journal of Econometrics* 31: 307–27.

Bollerslev, T. 1987. A conditional heteroskedastic time series model for speculative prices and rates of return. *Review of Economics and Statistics* 69: 542–47.

Bollerslev, T. 1990. Modeling the coherence in short-run nominal exchange rates: a multivariate generalized ARCH approach. *Review of Economics and Statistics* 72: 498–505.

Bollerslev, T., R. Y. Chou, and K. F. Kroner. 1992. ARCH modeling in finance: a review of the theory and empirical evidence. *Journal of Econometrics* 52: 5–59.

Bollerslev, T., R. F. Engle, and D. Nelson. 1994. ARCH Models. In *Handbook of Econometrics*, Vol. 4, eds. R. Engle, and D. McFadden. North-Holland.

Bollerslev, T., R. F. Engle, and J. Wooldridge. 1988. A capital asset pricing model with time varying covariances. *Journal of Political Economy* 96: 116–31.

Bollerslev, T. and H. Zhou. 2002. Estimating stochastic volatility diffusions using conditional moments of integrated volatility. *Journal of Econometrics* 109: 33–65.

Bookstaber, R. M. and S. Pomerantz. 1989. An information-based model for market volatility. *Financial Analysts Journal* 45: 37–46.

Borda de Agua, L., S. Hubbell, and M. MacAllister. 2002. Species-area curves, diversity indices, and species abundance distributions: a multifractal analysis. *The American Naturalist* 159: 138–55.

Borgani, S. 1995. Scaling in the Universe. *Physics Reports* 251: 1–152.

Bouchaud, J.-P. and M. Potters. 2003. *Theory of Financial Risk and Derivative Pricing.* Cambridge University Press.

Boudoukh, J., M. Richardson, and R. Whitelaw. 1994. A tale of three schools: insights on autocorrelations of short-horizon stock returns. *Review of Financial Studies* 7: 539–73.

Boufadel, M., S. Lu, S. Molz, and D. Lavallee. 2000. Multifractal scaling of the intrinsic permeability. *Water Resources Research* 36.

Brandt, M. and C. Jones. 2006. Volatility forecasting with range-based EGARCH models. *Journal of Business and Economic Statistics* 24: 470–86.

Breidt, J., N. Crato, and P. de Lima. 1998. The detection and estimation of long-memory in stochastic volatility. *Journal of Econometrics* 73: 325–48.

Brennan, M. 1998. The role of learning in dynamic portfolio decisions. *European Economic Review* 1: 295–396.

Brennan, M. and Y. Xia. 2001. Stock price volatility and the equity premium. *Journal of Monetary Economics* 47: 249–83.

Brock, W. A. and C. H. Hommes. 1998. Heterogeneous beliefs and routes to chaos in a simple asset pricing model. *Journal of Economic Dynamics and Control* 22: 1235–74.

Brock, W. A., J. Lakonishok, and B. LeBaron. 1992. Simple technical trading rules and the stochastic properties of stock returns. *Journal of Finance* 47: 1731–64.

Brock, W. A. and B. LeBaron. 1996. A dynamic structural model for stock return volatility and trading volume. *Review of Economics and Statistics* 78: 94–110.

Buraschi, A. and A. Jiltsov. 2006. Model uncertainty and option markets with heterogeneous beliefs. *Journal of Finance* 61: 2841–97.

Cai, J. 1994. A Markov model of switching-regime ARCH. *Journal of Business and Economic Statistics* 12: 309–16.

Calvet, L. E. 2001. Incomplete markets and volatility. *Journal of Economic Theory* 98: 295–38.

Calvet, L. E. and A. J. Fisher. 1999. Forecasting multifractal volatility. Harvard University Working paper and NYU Department of Finance Working paper FIN-99–017. Available at http://w4.stern.nyu.edu/faculty/research.

Calvet, L. E. and A. J. Fisher. 2001. Forecasting multifractal volatility. *Journal of Econometrics* 105: 27–58.

Calvet, L. E. and A. J. Fisher. 2002a. Multifractality in asset returns: theory and evidence. *Review of Economics and Statistics* 84: 381–406.

Calvet, L. E. and A. J. Fisher. 2002b. Regime-switching and the estimation of multifractal processes. Available at http://www.cirano.qc.ca/realisations/grandes_conferences/risques_financiers/25-10-02/Calvet-Fisher.pdf.

Calvet, L. E. and A. J. Fisher. 2004. How to forecast long-run volatility: regime-switching and the estimation of multifractal processes. *Journal of Financial Econometrics* 2: 49–83.

Calvet, L. E. and A. J. Fisher. 2007. Multifrequency news and stock returns. *Journal of Financial Economics* 86: 178–212.

Calvet, L. E. and A. J. Fisher. 2008. Multifrequency jump-diffusions: an equilibrium approach. *Journal of Mathematical Economics* 44: 207–26.

Calvet, L. E., A. J. Fisher, and B. B. Mandelbrot. 1997. Cowles Foundation Discussion Papers No. 1164–1166, Yale University. Papers available from http://cowles.econ.yale.edu or http://www.ssrn.com.

Calvet, L. E., A. J. Fisher, and S. B. Thompson. 2006. Volatility comovement: a multifrequency approach. *Journal of Econometrics* 131: 179–215.

Campbell, J. Y. 1996. Understanding risk and return. *Journal of Political Economy* 104: 298–345.

Campbell, J. Y. 2003. Consumption-based asset pricing. In *Handbook of the Economics of Finance*, eds. G. Constantinides, and M. Harris. North-Holland.

Campbell, J. Y. and J. Cochrane. 1999. By force of habit: a consumption-based explanation of aggregate stock market behavior. *Journal of Political Economy* 107: 205–51.

Campbell, J. Y. and L. Hentschel. 1992. No news is good news: an asymmetric model of changing volatility in stock returns. *Journal of Financial Economics* 31: 281–318.

Campbell, J. Y., A. Lo, and A. C. MacKinlay. 1997. *The Econometrics of Financial Markets*. Princeton University Press.

Campbell, J. Y. and N. G. Mankiw. 1987. Are output fluctuations transitory? *Quarterly Journal of Economics* 102: 857–80.

Campbell, J. Y. and N. G. Mankiw. 1989. Consumption, income and interest rates: reinterpreting the time series evidence. In *NBER Macroeconomics Annual*, eds. O. Blanchard, and S. Fischer, pp. 185–216. MIT Press.

Carr, P., H. Geman, D. Madan, and M. Yor. 2002. The fine structure of asset returns: an empirical investigation. *Journal of Business*, pp. 305–32.

Carr, P. and L. Wu. 2003. What type of process underlies options? A simple robust test. *Journal of Finance* 58: 2581–2610.

Carr, P. and L. Wu. 2004. Time-changed Lévy processes and option pricing. *Journal of Financial Economics* 71: 113–41.

Carvalho, L., D. Lavallee, and C. Jones. 2002. Multifractal properties of evolving convective systems over tropical South America. *Geophysical Research Letters* 29(3): 1–4.

Cecchetti, S., P.-S. Lam, and N. Mark. 1990. Mean reversion in equilibrium asset prices. *American Economic Review* 80: 398–418.

Chacko, G. and L. Viceira. 2003. Spectral GMM estimation of continuous time processes. *Journal of Econometrics* 116: 259–92.

Challet, D., M. Marsili, and Y.-C. Zhang. 2005. *Minority Games*. Oxford University Press.

Chan, N. B., B. LeBaron, A. W. Lo, and T. Poggio. 1998. Information dissemination and aggregation in asset markets with simple intelligent traders. MIT Artificial Intelligence Lab Technical Memorandum 1646.

Cheng, Q. 1999. Multifractality and spatial statistics. *Computers and Geosciences* 25: 946–61.

Cheng, Q. and F. Agterberg. 1995. Multifractality modeling and spatial point processes. *Mathematical Geology* 27: 831–45.

Chernov, M., A. R. Gallant, E. Ghysels, and G. Tauchen. 2003. Alternative models of stock price dynamics. *Journal of Econometrics* 116: 225–57.

Chib, S., F. Nardari, and N. Shephard. 2002. Markov chain Monte Carlo methods for stochastic volatility models. *Journal of Econometrics* 108: 281–316.

Chou, R. 1988. Persistent volatility and stock returns – some empirical evidence using GARCH. *Journal of Applied Econometrics* 3: 279–94.

Chou, R., R. F. Engle, and A. Kane. 1992. Measuring risk-aversion from excess returns on a stock index. *Journal of Econometrics* 52: 201–24.

Christoffersen, P., K. Jacobs, and Y. Wang. 2008. Option valuation with long-run and short-run volatility components. *Journal of Financial Economics*, forthcoming.

Clark, P. K. 1973. A subordinated stochastic process model with finite variance for speculative prices. *Econometrica* 41: 135–56.

Cochrane, J. 2005. *Asset Pricing*. Princeton University Press.

Cochrane, J., F. Longstaff, and P. Santa-Clara. 2008. Two trees. *Review of Financial Studies* 21: 347–85.

Comte, F. and E. Renault. 1998. Long memory in continuous time stochastic volatility models. *Mathematical Finance* 8: 291–323.

Constantinides, G. and D. Duffie. 1996. Asset pricing with heterogeneous consumers. *Journal of Political Economy* 104: 219–40.

Cont, R. and P. Tankov. 2003. *Financial Modeling with Jump Processes*. Chapman and Hall/CRC Press.

Cornforth, D. and H. Jelinek. 2008. Automated classification reveals morphological factors associated with dementia. *Applied Soft Computing* 8: 182–90.

Dacorogna, M., U. Müller, R. Nagler, R. Olsen, and O. Pictet. 1993. A geographical model for the daily and weekly seasonal volatility in the foreign exchange market. *Journal of International Money and Finance* 12: 413–38.

Dana, R.-A. and M. Jeanblanc. 2007. *Financial Markets in Continuous Time.* Springer.

Dathe, A., A. Tarquis, and E. Perrier. 2006. Multifractal analysis of the pore- and solid-phases in binary two-dimensional images of natural porous structures. *Geoderma* 134: 318–26.

David, A. 1997. Fluctuating confidence in stock markets: implications for returns and volatility. *Journal of Financial and Quantitative Analysis* 32: 427–62.

David, A. and P. Veronesi. 2002. Option prices with uncertain fundamentals. Working paper. Washington University and University of Chicago.

Davidson, J. 1994. *Stochastic Limit Theory.* Oxford University Press.

Davis, A., A. Marshak, W. Wiscombe, and R. Cahalan. 1994. Multifractal characterizations of nonstationarity and intermittency in geophysical fields: observed, retrieved, or simulated. *Journal of Geophysical Research* 99: 8055–72.

de Haan, L. and S. Resnick. 1980. A simple asymptotic estimate for the index of a stable distribution. *Journal of the Royal Statistical Society* 42: 83–87.

de Wijs, H. 1951. Statistics of ore distribution, Part I. *Geologie en Mijnbouw* 13: 365–75.

Deidda, R. 2000. Rainfall downscaling in a space-time multifractal framework. *Water Resources Research* 36: 1779–94.

DeLong, J. B., A. Shleifer, L. Summers, and R. Waldman. 1990. Positive feedback investment strategies and destabilizing rational speculation. *Journal of Finance* 45: 379–95.

Dembo, A. and O. Zeitouni. 1998. *Large Deviations Techniques and Applications,* 2nd edition. Springer.

den Haan, W. and A. Levin. 1997. A practitioner's guide to robust covariance matrix estimation. In *Handbook of Statistics: Robust Inference,* eds. G. S. Maddala, and C. R. Rao, Vol. 15. North-Holland.

Deo, C. and C. M. Hurvich. 2001. On the log periodogram regression estimator of the memory parameter in long memory stochastic volatility models. *Econometric Theory* 17: 686–710.

Deo, R. S., C. M. Hurvich, and Y. Lu. 2006. Forecasting realized volatility using a long memory stochastic volatility model: estimation, prediction and seasonal adjustment. *Journal of Econometrics* 131: 29–58.

Diebold, F. X. 1988. *Empirical Modeling of Exchange Rate Dynamics.* Springer.

Diebold, F. X. 2004. The Nobel Memorial Prize for Robert F. Engle. *Scandinavian Journal of Economics* 106: 165–85.

Diebold, F. X., T. A. Gunther, and S. A. Tay. 1998. Evaluating density forecasts, with applications to financial risk management. *International Economic Review* 39: 863–83.

Diebold, F. X. and A. Inoue. 2001. Long memory and regime switching. *Journal of Econometrics* 105: 27–58.

Diebold, F. X., J.-H. Lee, and G. Weinbach. 1994. Regime switching with time-varying transition probabilities. In *Nonstationary Time Series Analysis and Cointegration,* ed. C. Hargreaves. Oxford University Press.

Diebold, F. X. and M. Nerlove. 1989. The dynamics of exchange rate volatility: a multivariate latent factor ARCH model. *Journal of Applied Econometrics* 4: 1–21.

Diebold, F. X. and G. D. Rudebusch. 1989. Long memory and persistence in aggregate output. *Journal of Monetary Economics* 24: 189–209.

Ding, Z. and C. W. J. Granger. 1996. Modeling volatility persistence of speculative returns: a new approach. *Journal of Econometrics* 73: 185–215.

Ding, Z., C. W. J. Granger, and R. F. Engle. 1993. A long memory property of stock market returns and a new model. *Journal of Empirical Finance* 1: 83–106.

Dothan, M. 1990. *Prices in Financial Markets*. Oxford University Press.

Drake, J. and J. Weishampel. 2001. Simulating vertical and horizontal multifractal patterns of a longleaf pine savanna. *Ecological Modeling* 145: 129–42.

Drost, F. C. and T. E. Nijman. 1993. Temporal aggregation of GARCH processes. *Econometrica* 61: 909–27.

Duffie, D. 1988. *Security Markets: Stochastic Models*. Academic Press.

Duffie, D. 2001. *Dynamic Asset Pricing Theory*, 3rd edition. Princeton University Press.

Duffie, D. and L. Epstein. 1992. Asset pricing with stochastic differential utility. *Review of Financial Studies* 5: 411–36.

Duffie, D., J. Pan, and K. J. Singleton. 2000. Transform analysis and asset pricing for affine jump-diffusions. *Econometrica* 68: 1343–76.

Duffie, D. and K. J. Singleton. 1993. Simulated moments estimation of Markov models of asset prices. *Econometrica* 61: 929–52.

Duffie, D. and C. Skiadas. 1994. Continuous-time security pricing: a utility gradient approach. *Journal of Mathematical Economics* 23: 107–31.

Duffie, D. and W. Zame. 1989. The consumption-based capital asset pricing model. *Econometrica* 57: 1279–97.

Durland, M. and T. McCurdy. 1994. Duration-dependent transitions in a Markov model of US GNP growth. *Journal of Business and Economic Statistics* 12: 279–88.

Dybvig, P. and C. F. Huang. 1988. Nonnegative wealth, absence of arbitrage, and feasible consumption plans. *Review of Financial Studies* 1: 377–401.

Eberlein, E., U. Keller, and K. Prause. 1998. New insights into smile, mispricing, and value at risk. *Journal of Business* 71: 371–405.

Elerian, O., S. Chib, and N. Shephard. 2001. Likelihood inference for discretely observed nonlinear diffusions. *Econometrica* 69: 959–93.

Embrechts, P. and M. Maejima. 2002. *Selfsimilar Processes*. Princeton University Press.

Engel, C. and K. West. 2005. Exchange rates and fundamentals. *Journal of Political Economy* 113: 485–517.

Engle, R. F. 1982. Autoregressive conditional heteroscedasticity with estimates of the variance of United Kingdom inflation. *Econometrica* 50: 987–1007.

Engle, R. F. 1987. Multivariate GARCH with factor structures—cointegration in variance. Working paper. Department of Economics, University of California, San Diego.

Engle, R. F. 1990. Discussion: stock market volatility and the crash of '87. *Review of Financial Studies* 3: 103–6.

Engle, R. F. 2002a. New frontiers for ARCH models. *Journal of Applied Econometrics* 17: 425–46.

Engle, R. F. 2002b. Dynamic conditional correlation: a simple class of multivariate generalized autoregressive conditional heteroskedasticity models. *Journal of Business and Economic Statistics* 20: 339–50.

Engle, R. F. 2004. Risk and volatility: econometric models and financial practice. *American Economic Review* 94: 405–20.

Engle, R. F. and G. Gonzalez-Rivera. 1991. Semiparametric ARCH models. *Journal of Business and Economic Statistics* 9: 345–59.

Engle, R. F., T. Ito, and W.-L. Lin. 1990. Meteor showers or heat waves? Heteroskedastic intra-daily volatility in the foreign exchange market. *Econometrica* 58: 525–42.

Engle, R. F. and K. Kroner. 1995. Multivariate simultaneous generalized ARCH. *Econometric Theory* 11: 122–50.

Engle, R. F. and G. Lee. 1999. A permanent and transitory component model of stock return volatility. In *Cointegration, Causality, and Forecasting: A Festschrift in Honor of Clive W. Granger*, eds. R. Engle, and H. White. Oxford University Press.

Engle, R. F., D. M. Lilien, and R. P. Robins. 1987. Estimating time varying risk premia in the term structure: the ARCH-M model. *Econometrica* 55: 391–407.

Engle, R. F. and J. Mezrich. 1996. GARCH for groups. *Risk* 9: 36–40.

Engle, R. F. and V. K. Ng. 1993. Measuring and testing the impact of news on volatility. *Journal of Finance* 48: 1749–78.

Engle, R. F., V. Ng, and M. Rothschild. 1990. Asset pricing with a factor ARCH covariance structure: empirical estimates for Treasury bills. *Journal of Econometrics* 45: 213–38.

Engle, R. F. and J. G. Rangel. 2007. The spline-GARCH model for unconditional volatility and its global macroeconomic causes. *Review of Financial Studies*, forthcoming.

Epstein, L. and S. Zin. 1989. Substitution, risk aversion and the temporal behavior of consumption and asset returns: a theoretical framework. *Econometrica* 57: 937–68.

Eraker, B. 2001. MCMC analysis of diffusion models with applications to finance. *Journal of Business and Economic Statistics* 19: 177–91.

Eraker, B. 2004. Do stock prices and volatility jump? Reconciling evidence from spot and option prices. *Journal of Finance* 59: 1367–403.

Eraker, B., M. Johannes, and N. Polson. 2003. The impact of jumps in volatility and returns. *Journal of Finance* 58: 1269–300.

Ethier, S. N. and T. G. Kurtz. 1986. *Markov Processes: Characterization and Convergence*. John Wiley and Sons.

Fama, E. 1963. Mandelbrot and the stable Paretian hypothesis. *Journal of Business* 36: 420–29.

Fama, E. 1965. The behavior of stock market prices. *Journal of Business* 38: 34–105.

Fama, E. 1970. Efficient capital markets: a review of theory and empirical work. *Journal of Finance* 25: 383–417.

Fama, E. and K. French. 2002. The equity premium. *Journal of Finance* 57: 637–59.

Fama, E. and R. Roll. 1971. Parameter estimates for symmetric stable distributions. *Journal of the American Statistical Association* 66: 331–38.

Farmer, J. D. and J. Geanakoplos. 2008. The virtues and vices of equilibrium and the future of financial economics. Cowles Foundation Discussion Paper No. 1647, Yale University.

Faust, J. 1992. When are variance ratio rests for serial dependence optimal? *Econometrica* 60: 1215–26.

Fernandez, E., J. Bolea, G. Ortega, and E. Louis. 1999. Are neurons multifractals? *Journal of Neuroscience Methods* 89: 151–57.

Fielitz, B. 1971. Stationarity of random data: some implications for the distribution of stock price changes. *Journal of Financial and Quantitative Analysis* 6: 1025–34.

Fielitz, B. 1976. Further results on asymmetric stable distributions of stock price changes. *Journal of Financial and Quantitative Analysis* 11: 39–55.

Filardo, A. 1994. Business cycle phases and their transitional dynamics. *Journal of Business and Economic Statistics* 12: 299–308.

Fisher, L. and J. Lorie. 1970. Some studies of variability of returns on investments in common stocks. *Journal of Business* 43: 99–134.

Folorunso, O., C. Puente, D. Rolston, and J. Pinzón. 1994. Statistical and fractal evaluation of the spatial characteristics of soil surface strength. *Soil Science Society of America Journal* 58: 284–94.

French, K., G. W. Schwert, and R. F. Stambaugh. 1987. Expected stock returns and volatility. *Journal of Financial Economics* 19: 3–29.

Frisch, U. and G. Parisi. 1985. Fully developed turbulence and intermittency. In *Turbulence and Predictability in Geophysical Fluid Dynamics and Climate Dynamics*, ed. M. Ghil, pp. 84–88. North-Holland.

Froot, K., D. Scharfstein, and J. Stein. 1992. Herd on the Street: informational inefficiencies in a market with short-term speculation. *Journal of Finance* 47: 1461–84.

Gabaix, X., P. Gopikrishnan, V. Plerou, and H. E. Stanley. 2003. A theory of power law distributions in financial market fluctuations. *Nature* 423: 267–70.

Gabaix, X., P. Gopikrishnan, V. Plerou, and H. E. Stanley. 2006. Institutional investors and stock market volatility. *Quarterly Journal of Economics* 121: 461–504.

Gallant, A. R., D. A. Hsieh, and G. Tauchen. 1991. On fitting a recalcitrant series: the pound/dollar exchange rate 1974–83. In *Nonparametric and Semiparametric Methods in Econometrics and Statistics*, eds. W. A. Barnett, D. J. Powell, and G. Tauchen. Cambridge University Press.

Gallant, A. R., D. A. Hsieh, and G. Tauchen. 1997. Estimation of stochastic volatility models with diagnostics. *Journal of Econometrics* 81: 159–92.

Gallant, A. R., C. T. Hsu, and G. Tauchen. 1999. Using daily range data to calibrate volatility diffusions and extract the forward integrated variance. *Review of Economics and Statistics* 81: 617–31.

Gallant, A. R., P. E. Rossi, and G. Tauchen. 1992. Stock prices and volume. *Review of Financial Studies* 5: 199–242.

Gallant, A. R., P. E. Rossi, and G. Tauchen. 1993. Nonlinear dynamic structures. *Econometrica* 61: 871–907.

Gallant, A. R. and G. Tauchen. 1989. Semi non-parametric estimation of conditionally constrained heterogeneous processes: asset pricing applications. *Econometrica* 57: 1091–120.

Galluccio, S., G. Caldarelli, M. Marsili, and Y. C. Zhang. 1997. Scaling in currency exchange. *Physica A* 245: 423–36.

Garcia, R. 1998. Asymptotic null distribution of the likelihood ratio test in Markov switching models. *International Economic Review* 39: 763–88.

Garcia, R., R. Luger, and E. Renault. 2003. Empirical assessment of an intertemporal option pricing model with latent variables. *Journal of Econometrics* 116: 49–83.

Garcia, R., N. Meddahi, and R. Tédongap. 2008. An analytical framework for assessing asset pricing models and predictability. Working paper. EDHEC, Imperial College London, and Stockholm School of Economics.

Garcia, R. and P. Perron. 1996. An analysis of the real interest rate under regime shifts. *Review of Economics and Statistics* 78: 111–25.

Garleanu, N., L. Pedersen, and A. Poteshman. 2006. Demand-based option pricing. Working paper. NYU, Wharton and UIUC.

Geilikman, M., T. Golubeva, and V. Pisarenko. 1990. Multifractal patterns of seismicity. *Earth and Planetary Science Letters* 99: 127–32.

Gennotte, G. and H. Leland. 1990. Market liquidity, hedging and crashes. *American Economic Review* 80: 999–1021.

Geweke, J. 1989. Exact predictive densities in linear models with ARCH disturbances. *Journal of Econometrics* 44: 307–25.

Geweke, J. and S. Porter-Hudak. 1983. The estimation and application of long-memory time series models. *Journal of Time Series Analysis* 4: 221–37.

Ghashghaie, S., W. Breymann, J. Peinke, P. Talkner, and Y. Dodge. 1996. Turbulent cascades in foreign exchange markets. *Nature* 381: 767–70.

Ghysels, E., A. Harvey, and E. Renault. 1996. Stochastic Volatility. In *Handbook of Statistics*, eds. G. S. Maddala, and C. R. Rao, 14: 119–91. North-Holland.

Ghysels, E., P. Santa-Clara, and R. Valkanov. 2005. There is a risk-return trade-off after all. *Journal of Financial Economics* 76: 509–48.

Gilbert, A., W. Willinger, and A. Feldmann. 1999. Scaling analysis of conservative cascades, with applications to network traffic. *IEEE Transactions on Information Theory* 45: 971–91.

Glosten, L., R. Jagannathan, and D. Runkle. 1993. On the relation between the expected value and the volatility of the nominal excess return on stocks. *Journal of Finance* 48: 1779–801.

Godano, C. and V. Caruso. 1995. Multifractal analysis of earthquake catalogues. *Geophysical Journal International* 121: 385–92.

Goncalves, M. 2001. Characterization of geochemical distributions using multifractal models. *Mathematical Geology* 33: 41–61.

Gonçalves da Silva, A. and P. M. Robinson. 2007. Fractional cointegration in stochastic volatility models. *Econometric Theory*, forthcoming.

Gouriéroux, C. and J. Jasiak. 2002. Nonlinear autocorrelograms: an application to inter-trade durations. *Journal of Time Series Analysis* 23: 127–54.

Gouriéroux, C. and A. Montfort. 1992. Qualitative threshold ARCH models. *Journal of Econometrics* 52: 159–99.

Grandmont, J. M. 1998. Expectations formation and stability of large socioeconomic systems. *Econometrica* 66: 741–81.

Granger, C. W. J. 1980. Long-memory relationships and the aggregation of dynamic models. *Journal of Econometrics* 14: 227–38.

Granger, C. W. J. and N. Hyung. 1999. Occasional structural breaks and long memory. Discussion paper 99–14, University of California, San Diego.

Granger, C. W. J. and R. Joyeux. 1980. An introduction to long memory time series models and fractional differencing. *Journal of Time Series Analysis* 1: 15–29.

Granger, C. W. J. and O. Morgenstern. 1970. *Predictability of Stock Market Prices*. Heath-Lexington, Lexington, MA.

Gray, S. 1996. Modeling the conditional distribution of interest rates as a regime-switching process. *Journal of Financial Economics* 42: 27–62.

Greenspan, A. 2007. *The Age of Turbulence: Adventures in a New World*. Penguin Press.

Greenwood, J. and B. Jovanovic. 1999. The information-technology revolution and the stock market. *American Economic Review* 89: 116–22.

Grout, H., A. Tarquis, and M. Wiesner. 1998. Multifractal analysis of particle size distributions in soil. *Environmental Science and Technology* 32: 1176–82.

Guidolin, M. and A. Timmermann. 2003. Option prices under Bayesian learning: implied volatility dynamics and predictive densities. *Journal of Economic Dynamics and Control* 27: 717–69.

Guivarc'h, Y. 1987. Remarques sur les solutions d'une équation fonctionnelle non linéaire de Benoît Mandelbrot. *Comptes Rendus de l'Académie des Sciences de Paris* 3051: 139.

Gutierrez, J., M. Rodriguez, and G. Abramson. 2001. Multifractal analysis of DNA sequences using a novel chaos-game representation. *Physica A* 300: 271–84.

Hall, P. 1982. On some simple estimates of an exponent of regular variations. *Journal of the Royal Statistical Society Series B* 44: 37–42.

Halsey, T. C., M. H. Jensen, L. P. Kadanoff, I. Procaccia, and B. I. Shraiman. 1986. Fractal measures and their singularities: the characterization of strange sets. *Physical Review Letters A* 33: 1141.

Hamilton, J. D. 1988. Rational expectations econometric analysis of changes in regimes: an investigation of the term structure of interest rates. *Journal of Economic Dynamics and Control* 12: 385–423.

Hamilton, J. D. 1989. A new approach to the economic analysis of nonstationary time series and the business cycle. *Econometrica* 57: 357–84.

Hamilton, J. D. 1990. Analysis of time series subject to change in regime. *Journal of Econometrics* 45: 39–70.

Hamilton, J. D. 1994. *Time Series Analysis*. Princeton University Press.

Hamilton, J. D. 2003. What is an oil shock? *Journal of Econometrics* 113: 363–98.

Hamilton, J. D. 2006. Regime-switching models. In *New Palgrave Dictionary of Economics*, 2nd edition, eds. S. Durlauf, and L. Blume, forthcoming. Palgrave McMillan Ltd.

Hamilton, J. D. and G. Lin. 1996. Stock market volatility and the business cycle. *Journal of Applied Econometrics* 11: 573–93.

Hamilton, J. D. and G. Pérez-Quirós. 1996. What do the leading indicators lead? *Journal of Business* 69: 27–49.

Hamilton, J. D. and B. Raj. 2002. New directions in business cycle research and financial analysis. *Empirical Economics* 27: 149–62.

Hamilton, J. D. and R. Susmel. 1994. Autoregressive conditional heteroskedasticity and changes in regime. *Journal of Econometrics* 64: 307–33.

Hansen, B. 1992. The likelihood ratio test under non-standard conditions: testing the Markov-switching model of GNP. *Journal of Applied Econometrics* 7: 561–82.

Hansen, L. P., L. Heaton, and N. Li. 2005. Consumption strikes back? Measuring long run risk. NBER Working paper No. 11476.

Hansen, L. P. and R. Jagannathan. 1991. Implications of security market data for models of dynamic economies. *Journal of Political Economy* 99: 225–62.

Hansen, P. and A. Lunde. 2005. A forecast comparison of volatility models: Does anything beat a GARCH(1,1)? *Journal of Applied Econometrics* 20: 873–89.

Harrison, J. M. and D. Kreps. 1979. Martingales and arbitrage in multiperiod securities markets. *Journal of Economic Theory* 20: 381–408.

Harvey, A. 1998. Long memory in stochastic volatility. In *Forecasting Volatility in Financial Markets*, eds. J. Knight, and S. Satchell, pp. 307–20. Butterworth-Heinemann.

Harvey, A., E. Ruiz, and N. Shephard. 1994. Multivariate stochastic variance models. *Review of Economic Studies* 61: 247–64.

Heston, S. L. 1993. A closed-form solution for options with stochastic volatility, with applications to bond and currency options. *Review of Financial Studies* 6: 327–43.

Hidalgo, J. and P. M. Robinson. 1996. Testing for structural change in a long-memory environment. *Journal of Econometrics* 70: 159–74.

Hill, B. M. 1975. A simple general approach to inference about the tail of a distribution. *Annals of Statistics* 3: 1163–74.

Hols, M. and C. de Vries. 1991. The limiting distribution of extremal exchange rate returns. *Journal of Applied Econometrics* 6: 287–302.

Hong, H. and J. Stein. 2003. Differences of opinion, short-sales constraints and market crashes. *Review of Financial Studies* 16: 487–525.

Hong, H. and J. Stein. 2007. Disagreement and the stock market. *Journal of Economic Perspectives* 21: 109–28.

Hosking, J. R. M. 1981. Fractional differencing. *Biometrika* 68: 165–76.

Hsu, D., R. Miller, and D. Wichern. 1974. On the stable Paretian behavior of stock-market prices. *Journal of the American Statistical Association* 345: 108–13.

Huang, C. 1987. An intertemporal general equilibrium asset pricing model: the case of diffusion information. *Econometrica* 55: 117–42.

Huang, X. and G. Tauchen. 2005. The relative contribution of jumps to total price variance. *Journal of Financial Econometrics* 4: 456–99.

Hull, J. and A. White. 1987. The pricing of options on assets with stochastic volatility. *Journal of Finance* 42: 281–300.

Hung, M.-W. 1994. The interaction between nonexpected utility and asymmetric market fundamentals. *Journal of Finance* 49: 325–43.

Hunt, P. and J. Kennedy. 2004. *Financial Derivatives in Theory and Practice*. Wiley.

Hurvich, C. M. and W. W. Chen. 2000. An efficient taper for potentially overdifferenced long-memory time series. *Journal of Time Series Analysis* 21: 155–80.

Hurvich, C. M., R. Deo, and J. Brodsky. 1998. The mean square error of Geweke and Porter-Hudak's estimator of the memory parameter of a long-memory time series. *Journal of Time Series Analysis* 19: 19–46.

Hurvich, C. M., E. Moulines, and P. Soulier. 2005. Estimating long memory in volatility. *Econometrica* 73: 1283–328.

Hurvich, C. M. and B. K. Ray. 2003. The local Whittle estimator of long-memory stochastic volatility. *Journal of Financial Econometrics* 1: 445–70.

Ingersoll, J. 1987. *Theory of Financial Decision-Making*. Rowman and Littlefield.

Ingram, B. F. and S. B. Lee. 1991. Simulation estimation of time series models. *Journal of Econometrics* 47: 197–250.

Jacquier, E., N. Polson, and P. Rossi. 1994. Bayesian analysis of stochastic volatility models. *Journal of Business and Economic Statistics* 12: 371–417.

Jacquier, E., N. Polson, and P. Rossi. 2004. Bayesian analysis of stochastic volatility models with fat-tails and correlated errors. *Journal of Econometrics* 122: 185–212.

Jansen, D. and C. de Vries. 1991. On the frequency of large stock returns: putting booms and busts into perspective. *Review of Economics and Statistics* 73: 18–24.

Jarrow, R. and E. Rosenfeld. 1984. Jump risks and the intertemporal capital asset pricing model. *Journal of Business* 57: 337–51.

Johannes, M., N. Polson, and J. Stroud. 2002. Sequential optimal portfolio performance: market and volatility timing. Working paper. University of Chicago Graduate School of Business.

Jones, B., V. Martinez, E. Saar, and J. Einasto. 1988. Multifractal description of the large-scale structure of the Universe. *Astrophysical Journal* 332: L1–L5.

Jones, B., V. Martinez, E. Saar, and V. Trimble. 2004. Scaling laws in the distribution of galaxies. *Reviews of Modern Physics* 76: 1211–66.

Jones, C. 2003. The dynamics of stochastic volatility: evidence from underlying and options markets. *Journal of Econometrics* 116: 181–224.

Jorion, P. 1988. On jump processes in the foreign exchange and stock markets. *Review of Financial Studies* 1: 427–45.

Jorion, P. 1997. *Value At Risk: The New Benchmark for Controlling Market Risk*. Mc-Graw Hill.

Kahane, J. P. 1997. A century of interplay between Taylor series, Fourier series and Brownian motion. *Bulletin of the London Mathematical Society* 29: 257–79.

Kandel, S. and R. F. Stambaugh. 1990. Expectations and volatility of consumption and asset returns. *Review of Financial Studies* 3: 207–32.

Karatzas, I. and S. Shreve. 2001. *Methods of Mathematical Finance*, 3rd edition. Springer.

Kassouf. 1969. An econometric model for option price with implications for investors' expectations and audacity. *Econometrica* 37: 685–94.

Kearns, P. and A. Pagan. 1997. Estimating the density tail index for financial time series. *Review of Economics and Statistics* 79: 171–75.

Kim, C.-J. 1994. Dynamic linear models with Markov-switching. *Journal of Econometrics* 60: 1–22.

Kim, C.-J., J. Morley, and C. Nelson. 2004. Is there a positive relationship between stock market volatility and the equity premium? *Journal of Money, Credit and Banking* 36: 339–60.

Kim, C.-J. and C. Nelson. 1999. *State-Space Models with Regime-Switching.* MIT Press.

Kim, S., N. Shephard, and S. Chib. 1998. Stochastic volatility: likelihood inference and comparison with ARCH models. *Review of Economic Studies* 65: 361–93.

Kirkpatrick, L. A. and J. F. Weishampel. 2005. Quantifying spatial structure of volumetric neutral models. *Ecological Modeling* 186: 312–25.

Kirman, A. 1991. Epidemics of opinion and speculative bubbles in financial markets. In *Money and Financial Markets*, ed. M. Taylor, pp. 354–68. Blackwell.

Klaassen, F. 2002. Improving GARCH volatility forecasts with regime-switching GARCH. *Empirical Economics* 27: 363–94.

Klemeš, V. 1974. The Hurst phenomenon: a puzzle? *Water Resources Research* 10: 675–88.

Koedjik, K. G. and C. J. M. Kool. 1992. Tail estimates of East European exchange rates. *Journal of Business and Economic Statistics* 10: 83–96.

Kolmogorov, A. N. 1940. Wienersche Spiralen und einige andere interessante Kurven im Hilbertschen raum. *Doklady Akademii Nauk USSR* 26: 115–18.

Kolmogorov, A. N. 1962. A refinement of previous hypotheses concerning the local structure of turbulence in a viscous incompressible fluid at high Reynolds number. *Journal of Fluid Mechanics* 13: 82–85.

Kon, S. J. 1984. Models of stock returns – a comparison. *Journal of Finance* 39: 147–65.

Koscielny-Bunde, E., J. Kantelhardt, P. Braun, A. Bunde, and S. Havlin. 2006. Long-term persistence and multifractality of river runoff records: detrended fluctuation studies. *Journal of Hydrology* 322: 120–37.

Kraft, D. and R. F. Engle. 1982. Autoregressive conditional heteroskedasticity in multiple time series. Unpublished manuscript, Department of Economics, University of California, San Diego.

Kravchenko, A., D. Bullock, and C. Boast. 2000. Joint multifractal analyses of crop yield and terrain slope. *Agronomy Journal* 91: 1033–41.

Krishna, M., V. Gadre, and U. Desai. 2003. *Multifractal Based Network Traffic Modeling.* Springer.

Künsch, H. 1986. Discrimination between monotonic trends and long-range dependence. *Journal of Applied Probability* 23: 1025–30.

Künsch, H. 1987. Statistical aspects of self-similar processes. In *Proceedings of the First World Congress of the Bernoulli Society*, eds. Y. Prokhorov, and V. Sasanov. VNU Science Press, Utrecht.

Kupiec, P. 1995. Techniques for verifying the accuracy of risk measurement models. *Journal of Derivatives* 2: 73–84.

Labat, D., A. Mangin, and R. Ababou. 2002. Rainfall-runoff relations for Karstic springs: multifractal analyses. *Journal of Hydrology* 256: 176–95.

Latane, H. and R. Rendleman. 1976. Standard deviations of stock price ratios implied in option prices. *Journal of Finance* 31: 369–81.

LeBaron, B. 2000. Agent-based computational finance: suggested readings and early research. *Journal of Economic Dynamics and Control* 24: 679–702.

LeBaron, B. 2001. Stochastic volatility as a simple generator of apparent financial power laws and long memory. *Quantitative Finance* 1: 621–31.

LeBaron, B. 2006. Agent-based computational finance. In *Handbook of Computational Economics*, Vol. 2, eds. L. Tesfatsion, and K. Judd. North-Holland.

LeBaron, B., W. B. Arthur, and R. Palmer. 1999. Time series properties of an artificial stock market. *Journal of Economic Dynamics and Control* 23: 1487–516.

Ledoit, O., P. Santa-Clara, and M. Wolf. 2003. Flexible multivariate GARCH modeling with an application to international stock markets. *Review of Economics and Statistics* 85: 735–47.

LeRoy, S. and R. Porter. 1981. The present-value relation: tests based on implied variance bounds. *Econometrica* 49: 555–74.

Lettau, M. 1997. Explaining the facts with adaptive agents: the case of mutual fund flows. *Journal of Economic Dynamics and Control* 21: 1117–48.

Lettau, M., S. Ludvigson, and J. Wachter. 2004. The declining equity premium: what role does macroeconomic risk play? Working paper. New York University and Wharton. Forthcoming in *Review of Financial Studies*.

Lévy, P. 1924. Théorie des erreurs: la loi de Gauss et les lois exceptionnelles. *Bulletin de la Société Mathématique de France* 52: 49–85.

Lilley, M., S. Lovejoy, N. Desaulniers-Soucy, and D. Schertzer. 2006. Multifractal large number of drops limit in rain. *Journal of Hydrology* 328: 20–37.

Lindgren, G. 1978. Markov regime models for mixed distributions and switching regressions. *Scandinavian Journal of Statistics* 5: 81–91.

Liu, M. 2000. Modeling long memory in stock market volatility. *Journal of Econometrics* 99: 139–71.

Liu, H. and F. Moltz. 1997. Multifractal analyses of hydraulic conductivity distributions. *Water Resources Research* 33: 2483–88.

Liu, J., J. Pan, and T. Wang. 2005. An equilibrium model of rare-event premia and its implication for option smirks. *Review of Financial Studies* 18: 131–64.

Lo, A. W. 1991. Long memory in stock market prices. *Econometrica* 59: 1279–313.

Lo, A. W. and A. C. MacKinlay. 1988. Stock market prices do not follow random walks: evidence from a simple specification test. *Review of Financial Studies* 1: 41–66.

Lobato, I. N. and N. E. Savin. 1997. Real and spurious long-memory properties of stock market data. *Journal of Business and Economic Statistics* 16: 261–83.

Loretan, M. and P. C. B. Phillips. 1994. Testing the covariance stationarity of heavy-tailed time series: an overview of the theory with applications to several financial data series. *Journal of Empirical Finance* 1: 211–48.

Lovejoy, S. and D. Schertzer. 2006. Multifractals, cloud radiances and rain. *Journal of Hydrology* 322: 59–88.

Lucas, R. 1978. Asset prices in an exchange economy. *Econometrica* 46: 1429–45.

Lundblad, C. 2007. The risk-return trade-off in the long-run: 1836–2003. *Journal of Financial Economics* 85: 123–50.

Lux, T. 1997. Time variation of second moments from a noise trader/infection model. *Journal of Economic Dynamics and Control* 22: 1–38.

Lux, T. 1998. The socio-economic dynamics of speculative markets: interacting agents, chaos, and the fat tails of return distributions. *Journal of Economic Behavior and Organization* 33: 143–65.

Lux, T. 2001. Turbulence in financial markets: the surprising explanatory power of simple cascade models. *Quantitative Finance* 1: 632–40.

Lux, T. 2008. The Markov-switching multifractal model of asset returns: GMM estimation and linear forecasting of volatility. *Journal of Business and Economic Statistics* 26: 194–210.

Lux, T. and M. Marchesi. 1999. Scaling and criticality in a stochastic multi-agent model of a financial market. *Nature* 397: 498–500.

Lyons, R. 2001. *The Microstructure Approach to Exchange Rates*. MIT Press.

MacKinlay, A. C. 1997. Event studies in economics and finance. *Journal of Economic Literature* 35: 13–39.

Madan, D., P. Carr, and E. Chang. 1998. The variance gamma process and option pricing model. *European Finance Review* 2: 79–105.

Maheswaran, S. and C. Sims. 1993. Empirical implications of arbitrage-free asset markets. In *Models, Methods and Applications of Econometrics*, ed. P. C. B. Phillips. Basil Blackwell.

Maheu, J. and T. McCurdy. 2000. Volatility dynamics under duration-dependent mixing. *Journal of Empirical Finance* 7: 345–72.

Maheu, J. and T. McCurdy. 2004. News arrival, jump dynamics, and volatility components for individual stock returns. *Journal of Finance* 59: 755–93.

Mandelbrot, B. B. 1963. The variation of certain speculative prices. *Journal of Business* 36: 394–419.

Mandelbrot, B. B. 1965a. Une classe de processus stochastiques homothétiques à soi. *Comptes Rendus de l'Académie des Sciences de Paris* 260: 3274–77.

Mandelbrot, B. B. 1965b. Time varying channels, $1/f$ noises and the infrared catastrophe, or: why does the low frequency energy sometimes seem infinite. *Conference Record of the 1st IEEE Annual Communications Convention, Boulder, Colorado*.

Mandelbrot, B. B. 1967. The variation of some other speculative prices. *Journal of Business* 40: 393–413.

Mandelbrot, B. B. 1972. Possible refinement of the lognormal hypothesis concerning the distribution of energy dissipation in intermittent turbulence. In *Statistical Models and Turbulence*, Lecture Note in Physics, eds. M. Rosenblatt, and C. Van Atta, 12: 333–51. Springer.

Mandelbrot, B. B. 1974. Intermittent turbulence in self-similar cascades: divergence of high moments and dimension of the carrier. *Journal of Fluid Mechanics* 62: 331–58.

Mandelbrot, B. B. 1982. *The Fractal Geometry of Nature*. Freeman.

Mandelbrot, B. B. 1989. Multifractal measures, especially for the geophysicist. *Pure and Applied Geophysics* 131: 5–42.

Mandelbrot, B. B. 1997. *Fractals and Scaling in Finance*. Springer.

Mandelbrot, B. B. 1999. *Multifractals and $1/f$ Noise: Wild Self-Affinity in Physics*. Springer.

Mandelbrot, B. B. 2001. Stochastic volatility, power laws, and long-memory. *Quantitative Finance* 1: 558–59.

Mandelbrot, B. B. and R. Hudson. 2004. *The (Mis) behavior of Markets*. Basic Books.

Mandelbrot, B. B. and H. W. Taylor. 1967. On the distribution of stock price differences. *Operations Research* 15: 1057–62.

Mandelbrot, B. B. and J. W. van Ness. 1968. Fractional Brownian motion, fractional noises and application. *SIAM Review* 10: 422–37.

Mantegna, R. and H. E. Stanley. 1996. Turbulence and financial markets. *Nature* 383: 587–88.

Mantegna, R. and H. E. Stanley. 2000. *An Introduction to Econophysics: Correlations and Complexity in Finance*. Cambridge University Press.

Martin, M. and E. Montero. 2002. Laser diffraction and multifractal analysis for the characterization of dry soil volume-size distributions. *Soil & Tillage Research* 64: 113–23.

Martinez, V. 1999. Is the universe fractal? *Science* 284: 445–46.

McCurdy, T. and I. Morgan. 1987. Tests of the martingale hypothesis for foreign currency futures with time varying volatility. *International Journal of Forecasting* 3: 131–48.

Meese, R. and K. Rogoff. 1983. Empirical exchange rate models of the seventies: do they fit out of sample? *Journal of International Economics* 14: 3–24.

Mehra, R. and E. C. Prescott. 1985. The equity premium: a puzzle. *Journal of Monetary Economics* 15: 145–61.

Melino, A. and S. M. Turnbull. 1990. Pricing foreign currency options with stochastic volatility. *Journal of Econometrics* 45: 239–65.

Meneveau, C. and K. Sreenivasan. 1987. Simple multifractal cascade model for fully developed turbulence. *Physical Review Letters* 59: 1424–27.

Meneveau, C. and K. Sreenivasan. 1991. The multifractal nature of turbulent energy dissipation. *Journal of Fluid Mechanics* 224: 429–84.

Merton, R. 1973. Rational theory of option pricing. *Bell Journal of Economics and Management Science* 4: 141–83.

Merton, R. C. 1976. Option pricing when underlying stock returns are discontinuous. *Journal of Financial Economics* 3: 125–44.

Merton, R. C. 1990. *Continuous-Time Finance*. Cambridge, Massachusetts, Blackwell.

Milhoj, A. 1987. A conditional variance model for daily deviations of an exchange rate. *Journal of Business and Economic Statistics* 5: 99–103.

Mincer, J. and V. Zarnowitz. 1969. The evaluation of economic forecasts. In *Economic Forecasts and Expectations*, ed. J. Mincer. National Bureau of Economic Research, New York.

Molchan, G. and T. Kronrod. 2007. Seismic interevent time: a spatial scaling and multifractality. *Pure and Applied Geophysics* 164: 75–96.

Müller, U., M. Dacorogna, R. Davé, O. Pictet, R. Olsen, and J. Ward. 1995. Fractals and intrinsic time: a challenge to econometricians. Discussion Paper Presented at the 1993 International Conference of the Applied Econometrics Association held in Luxembourg.

Müller, U., M. Dacorogna, R. Olsen, O. Pictet, M. Schwarz, and C. Morgenegg. 1990. Statistical study of foreign exchange rates, empirical evidence of a price change scaling law, and intraday analysis. *Journal of Banking and Finance* 14: 1189–1208.

Musiela, M. and M. Rutkowski. 2007. *Martingale Methods in Financial Modeling*. 2nd edition. Springer.

Muzy, J.-F. and E. Bacry. 2002. Multifractal stationary random measures and multifractal random walks with log infinitely divisible scaling laws. *Physical Review E* 66: 056121.

Muzy, J.-F., E. Bacry, and A. Arneodo. 1991. Wavelets and multifractal formalism for singular signals: application to turbulence data. *Physical Review Letters* 67: 3515–18.

Muzy, J.-F., J. Delour, and E. Bacry. 2000. Modeling fluctuations of financial time series: from cascade process to stochastic volatility model. *European Physical Journal* B 17: 537–48.

Naik, V. and M. Lee. 1990. General equilibrium pricing of options on the market portfolio with discontinuous returns. *Review of Financial Studies* 3: 493–521.

Nakaya, S. and T. Hashimoto. 2002. Temporal variation of multifractal properties of seismicity in the region affected by the mainshock of the October 6, 2000 Western Tottori Prefecture, Japan, earthquake ($M = 7.3$). *Geophysical Research Letters* 29(10): 1–4.

Neftci, S. 2000. *Introduction to the Mathematics of Financial Derivatives*, 2nd edition. Academic Press.

Nelson, D. 1989. Modeling stock market volatility changes. *Proceedings from the American Statistical Association, Business and Economics Statistics Section*, 93–98.

Nelson, D. 1990. ARCH models as diffusion aproximations. *Journal of Econometrics* 45: 7–38.

Nelson, D. 1991. Conditional heteroskedasticity in asset returns: a new approach. *Econometrica* 45: 7–38.

Newey, W. and K. West. 1987. A simple, positive semi-definite, heteroskedasticity and autocorrelation consistent covariance matrix. *Econometrica* 55: 703–8.

Newey, W. and K. West. 1994. Automatic lag selection in covariance matrix estimation. *Review of Economic Studies* 61: 631–54.

Nicolato, E. and E. Venardos. 2003. Option pricing in stochastic volatility models of the Ornstein-Uhlenbeck type. *Mathematical Finance* 13: 445–66.

Nielsen, L. T. 1999. *Pricing and Hedging of Derivative Securities*. Oxford University Press.

Nijman, T. and F. Palm. 1993. GARCH modeling of volatility: an introduction to theory and applications. In *Advanced Lectures in Quantitative Economics*, ed. A. J. de Zeeuw. Academic Press.

Officer, R. 1972. The distribution of stock returns. *Journal of the American Statistical Association* 67: 807–12.

Officer, R. 1973. The variability of the market factor of the New York Stock Exchange. *Journal of Business* 46: 434–53.

Olsson, J. and J. Niemczynowicz. 1996. Multifractal analysis of daily spatial rainfall distributions. *Journal of Hydrology* 187: 29–43.

Oprisan, S., A. Ardelean, and P. Frangopol. 2000. Self-organization and competition in the immune response to cancer invasion: a phase-oriented computational model of oncogenesis. *Bioinformatics* 16: 96–100.

Osborne, M. 1962. Periodic structure in the Brownian motion of stock prices. *Operations Research* 10: 345–79.

Pagan, A. and Y. Hong. 1991. Nonparametric estimation and the risk premium. In *Nonparametric and Semiparametric Methods in Econometrics and Statistics*, eds. W. A., Barnett, D. J. Powell, and G. Tauchen. Cambridge University Press.

Pagan, A. and W. Schwert. 1990. Alternative models for conditional stock volatility. *Journal of Econometrics* 45: 267–90.

Pan, J. 2002. The jump-risk premia implicit in options: evidence from an integrated time-series study. *Journal of Financial Economics* 63: 3–50.

Pandey, G., S. Lovejoy, and D. Schertzer. 1998. Multifractal analysis of daily river flows including extremes for basins of five to two million square kilometers, one day to seventy-five years. *Journal of Hydrology* 208: 62–81.

Paredes, C. and F. Elorza. 1999. Fractal and multifractal analysis of fractured geological media: surface-subsurface correlation. *Computers and Geosciences* 25: 1081–96.

Pasquini, M. and M. Serva. 1999. Multiscale behavior of volatility autocorrelations in a financial market. *Economics Letters* 65: 275–79.

Pasquini, M. and M. Serva. 2000. Clustering of volatility as a multiscale phenomenon. *European Physical Journal B* 16: 195–201.

Pastor, L. and P. Veronesi. 2008. Technological revolutions and stock prices. Working paper. University of Chicago.

Pérez-Quirós, G. and A. Timmermann. 2000. Firm size and cyclical variations in stock returns. *Journal of Finance* 55: 1229–62.

Peyrière, J. 1991. Multifractal measures. In *Proceedings of the NATO ASI "Probabilistic Stochastic Methods in Analysis, with Applications."*

Phillips, P. C. B. 1999. Discrete Fourier transforms of fractional processes. Cowles Foundation Discussion Paper no. 1243, Yale University.

Phillips, P. C. B., J. W. McFarland, and P. C. McMahon. 1996. Robust tests of forward exchange market efficiency with empirical evidence from the 1920's. *Journal of Applied Econometrics* 11: 1–22.

Phillips, P. C. B. and K. Shimotsu. 2004. Local Whittle estimation in nonstationary and unit root cases. *Annals of Statistics* 32: 656–92.

Pickands, J. 1975. Statistical inference using extreme order statistics. *Annals of Statistics* 3: 119–31.

Pietronero, L. 1987. The fractal structure of the universe: correlations of galaxies and clusters and the average mass density. *Physica A* 144: 257–84.

Pindyck, R. 1984. Risk, inflation, and the stock market. *American Economic Review* 74: 334–51.

Pitt, M. and N. Shephard. 1999. Filtering via simulation: auxiliary particle filter. *Journal of the American Statistical Association* 94: 590–99.

Pollard, D. 1984. *Convergence of Stochastic Processes.* Springer.

Posadas, A., D. Gimenez, R. Quiroz, and R. Protz. 2003. Multifractal characterization of soil pore systems. *Soil Science Society of America Journal* 67: 1351–69.

Poterba, J. and L. Summers. 1986. The persistence of volatility and stock market fluctuations. *American Economic Review* 76: 1142–51.

Praetz, P. 1969. Australian share prices and the random walk hypothesis. *Australian Journal of Statistics* 11: 123–39.

Praetz, P. 1972. The distribution of share price changes. *Journal of Business* 45: 49–55.

Press, S. J. 1967. A compound events model for security prices. *Journal of Business* 40: 317–35.

Quintos, C., Z. Fan, and P. C. B. Phillips. 2001. Structural change tests in tail behavior and the Asian crisis. *Review of Economic Studies* 68: 633–63.

Raimondo, R. C. 2005. Market clearing, utility functions and securities prices. *Economic Theory* 25: 265–85.

Renault, E. and N. Touzi. 1996. Option hedging and implied volatilities in a stochastic volatility model. *Mathematical Finance* 6: 279–302.

Richards, G. 2000. The fractal structure of exchange rates: measurement and forecasting. *Journal of International Financial Markets, Institutions and Money* 10: 163–80.

Richardson, M. and J. Stock. 1989. Drawing inferences from statistics based on multi-year asset returns. *Journal of Financial Economics* 25: 323–48.

Riedi, R., M. Crouse, V. Ribeiro, and R. Baraniuk. 1999. A multifractal wavelet model with application to network traffic. *IEEE Transactions on Information Theory* 45: 992–1018.

Rivers, D. and Q. Vuong. 2002. Model selection tests for nonlinear dynamic models. *Econometrics Journal* 5(1): 1–39.

Robinson, P. M. 1978. Statistical inference for a random coefficient autoregressive model. *Scandinavian Journal of Statistics* 5: 163–68.

Robinson, P. M. 1991. Testing for strong serial correlation and dynamic conditional heteroskedasticity in multiple regression. *Journal of Econometrics* 47: 67–84.

Robinson, P. M. 1995a. Log-periodogram regression of time series with long range dependence. *Annals of Statistics* 23: 1048–72.

Robinson, P. M. 1995b. Gaussian semiparametric estimation of long range dependence. *Annals of Statistics* 23: 1630–61.

Robinson, P. M. 2001. The memory of stochastic volatility models. *Journal of Econometrics* 101: 195–218.

Robinson, P. M. 2003. *Time Series with Long Memory.* Oxford University Press.

Robinson, P. M. 2005. Robust covariance matrix estimation: HAC estimates with long memory/antipersistence correction. *Econometric Theory* 21: 171–80.

Robinson, P. M. and P. Zaffaroni. 1998. Nonlinear time series with long memory: a model for stochastic volatility. *Journal of Statistical Planning and Inference* 68: 359–71.

Rogers, L. C. G. and D. Williams. 2000. *Diffusions, Markov Processes and Martingales.* Cambridge University Press.

Rogoff, K. 1999. Perspectives on exchange rate volatility. In *International Capital Flows*, ed. M. Feldstein, pp. 441–53. University of Chicago Press.

Roll, R. 1984a. Orange juice and the weather. *American Economic Review* 74: 861–80.

Roll, R. 1984b. A simple implicit measure of the effective bid-ask spread in an efficient market. *Journal of Finance* 39: 1127–40.

Rosenberg, B. 1972. The behavior of random variables with nonstationary variance and the distribution of security prices. Working paper. UC Berkeley. Reprinted in Shephard (2005).

Rosenblatt, M. 1952. Remarks on a multivariate transformation. *Annals of Mathematical Statistics* 23: 470–72.

Rossi, P. 1996. *Modeling Stock Market Volatility: Bridging the Gap to Continuous Time*. Academic Press.

Samorodnitsky, G. and M. S. Taqqu. 1994. *Stable Non-Gaussian Random Processes*. Chapman and Hall.

Samuelson, P. 1967. Efficient portfolio selection for Pareto-Lévy investments. *Journal of Financial and Quantitative Analysis* 2: 107–22.

Samuelson, P. 1976. Limited liability, short selling, bounded utility, and infinite-variance stable distributions. *Journal of Financial and Quantitative Analysis* 3: 485–503.

Santa-Clara, P. and R. Valkanov. 2003. The presidential puzzle: political cycles and the stock market. *Journal of Finance* 58: 1841–72.

Santos, T. and P. Veronesi. 2005. Labor income and predictable stock returns. *Review of Financial Studies* 19: 1–44.

Sarno, L. and M. Taylor. 2002. *The Economics of Exchange Rates*. Cambridge University Press.

Scharfstein, D. and J. Stein. 1990. Herd behavior and investment. *American Economic Review* 80: 465–79.

Schertzer, D. and S. Lovejoy. 1987. Physical modeling and analysis of rain and clouds by anisotropic scaling of multiplicative processes. *Journal of Geophysical Research* 92: 9693–714.

Schmalensee, R. and R. Trippi. 1978. Common stock volatility expectations implied by option premia. *Journal of Finance* 33: 129–47.

Schwert, G. W. 1989. Why does stock market volatility change over time? *Journal of Finance* 44: 1115–53.

Schwert, G. W. 1990a. Stock volatility and the crash of '87. *Review of Financial Studies* 3: 77–102.

Schwert, G. W. 1990b. Indexes of United States stock prices from 1802 to 1987. *Journal of Business* 63: 399–426.

Sentana, E. 1995. Quadratic ARCH models. *Review of Economic Studies* 62: 639–61.

Shephard, N. 1994. Partial non-Gaussian state space. *Biometrika* 81: 115–31.

Shephard, N. 2005. *Stochastic Volatility: Selected Readings*, edited volume. Oxford University Press.

Shiller, R. 1981. Do stock prices move too much to be justified by subsequent changes in dividends? *American Economic Review* 71: 421–36.

Shimotsu, K. and P. C. B. Phillips. 2005. Exact local Whittle estimation of fractional integration. *Annals of Statistics* 33: 1890–933.

Shimotsu, K. and P. C. B. Phillips. 2006. Local Whittle estimation of fractional integration and some of its variants. *Journal of Econometrics* 130: 209–33.

Shorack, G. and J. Wellner. 1986. *Empirical Processes with Applications to Statistics*. John Wiley and Sons.

Shreve, S. 2005. *Stochastic Calculus for Finance*. Springer.

Smith, T., G. Lange, and W. Marks. 1996. Fractal methods and results in cellular morphology – dimensions, lacunarity, and multifractals. *Journal of Neuroscience Methods* 69: 123–36.

Sornette, D. 2004. *Critical Phenomena in Natural Sciences.* Springer.

Sornette, D. and G. Ouillon. 2005. Multifractal scaling of thermally activated rupture processes. *Physical Review Letters* 94: 038501, 1–4.

Sowell, F. B. 1992. Modeling long run behavior with the fractional ARIMA model. *Journal of Monetary Economics* 29: 277–302.

Stanley, H. E. and P. Meakin. 1988. Multifractal phenomena in physics and chemistry. *Nature* 335: 405–09.

Stanley, H. E. and V. Plerou. 2001. Scaling and universality in economics: empirical results and theoretical interpretation. *Quantitative Finance* 1: 563–67.

Stein, E. M. and J. Stein. 1991. Stock price distributions with stochastic volatility: an analytic approach. *Review of Financial Studies* 4: 727–52.

Stock, J. H. 1987. Measuring business cycle time. *Journal of Political Economy* 95: 1240–61.

Stock, J. H. 1988. Estimating continuous time processes subject to time deformation. *Journal of the American Statistical Association* 83: 77–85.

Stock, J. and M. Watson. 2003. Has the business cycle changed? Evidence and explanations. In *Monetary Policy and Uncertainty*, Federal Reserve Bank of Kansas City, 9–56.

Stojic, T., I. Reljin, and B. Reljin. 2006. Adaptation of multifractal analysis to segmentation of microcalcifications in digital mammograms. *Physica A* 367: 494–508.

Takahashi, T., T. Murata, K. Narita, T. Hamada, H. Kosaka, M. Omori, K. Takahashi, H. Kimura, H. Yoshida, and Y. Wada. 2004. Quantitative evaluation of age-related white matter microstructural changes on MRI by multifractal analysis. *Journal of Neurological Science* 225: 33–37.

Taleb, N. 2007. *The Black Swan: The Impact of the Highly Improbable.* Random House.

Taylor, S. J. 1982. Financial returns modelled by the product of two stochastic processes – a study of daily sugar prices 1961–79. In *Time Series Analysis: Theory and Practice*, ed. O. D. Andesron, 1: 203–26. North-Holland.

Taylor, S. J. 1986. *Modeling Financial Time Series.* John Wiley and Sons.

Tessier, Y., S. Lovejoy, and D. Schertzer. 1994. The multifractal global raingage network: analysis and simulation. *Journal of Applied Meteorology* 32: 223–350.

Teverovsky, V. and M. S. Taqqu. 1997. Testing for long-range dependence in the presence of shifting means or a slowly-varying declining trend using a variance-type estimator. *Journal of Time Series Analysis* 18: 279–304.

Thompson, S. B. 2000. Specification tests for continuous time models. University of California at Berkeley, Ph.D. Dissertation (Chapter 3).

Timmermann, A. G. 1993. How learning in financial markets generates excess volatility and predictability in stock prices. *Quarterly Journal of Economics* 108: 1135–45.

Timmermann, A. G. 1996. Excess volatility and predictability of stock prices in autoregressive dividend models with learning. *Review of Economic Studies* 63: 523–57.

Tino, P. 2002. Multifractal properties of Hao's geometric representations of DNA sequences. *Physica A* 304: 480–94.

Turner, C., R. Startz, and C. Nelson. 1989. A Markov model of heteroskedasticity, risk and learning in the stock market. *Journal of Financial Economics* 25: 3–22.

Valdarnini, R., S. Borgani, and A. Provenzale. 1992. Multifractal properties of cosmological N-body simulations. *Astrophysical Journal* 394: 422–41.

van der Vaart, A. W. 1998. *Asymptotic Statistics.* Cambridge University Press.

Vandewalle, N. and M. Ausloos. 1998. Multi-affine analysis of typical currency exchange rates. *European Physical Journal B* 4: 257–61.

Vassilicos, J. C., A. Demos, and F. Tata. 1993. No evidence of chaos but some evidence of multifractals in the foreign exchange and the stock market. In *Applications of Fractals and Chaos*, eds. A. J. Crilly, R. A. Earnshaw, and H. Jones, pp. 249–65. Springer.

Velasco, C. 1999. Gaussian semiparametric estimation of non-stationary time series. *Journal of Time Series Analysis* 20: 87–127.

Veronesi, P. 1999. Stock market overreaction to bad news in good times: a rational expectations equilibrium model. *Review of Financial Studies* 12: 975–1007.

Veronesi, P. 2000. How does information quality affect stock returns? *Journal of Finance* 55: 807–37.

Veronesi, P. 2004. The peso problem hypothesis and stock market returns. *Journal of Economic Dynamics and Control* 28: 707–25.

Vissing-Jørgensen, A. 2002. Limited asset market participation and the elasticity of intertemporal substitution. *Journal of Political Economy* 110: 825–53.

Vuong, Q. 1989. Likelihood ratio tests for model selection and non-nested hypotheses. *Econometrica* 57: 307–33.

Wachter, J. 2006. A consumption-based model of the term–structure of interest rates. *Journal of Financial Economics* 79: 365–99.

Wagner, N. and T. Marsh. 2005. Measuring tail thickness under GARCH and an application to extreme exchange rate changes. *Journal of Empirical Finance* 12: 165–85.

Weil, P. 1989. The equity premium puzzle and the risk-free rate puzzle. *Journal of Monetary Economics* 24: 401–21.

West, K. and D. Cho. 1995. The predictive ability of several models of exchange rate volatility. *Journal of Econometrics* 69: 367–91.

West, K. and M. McCracken. 1998. Regression-based tests of predictive ability. *International Economic Review* 39: 817–40.

Whitelaw, R. 2000. Stock market risk and return: an equilibrium approach. *Review of Financial Studies* 13: 521–47.

Wiggins, J. B. 1987. Option values under stochastic volatility: theory and empirical estimates. *Journal of Financial Economics* 19: 351–72.

Wilmott, P. 2006. *Paul Wilmott on Quantitative Finance*, 2nd edition. John Wiley and Sons.

Womack, K. 1996. Do brokerage analysts' recommendations have investment value? *Journal of Finance* 51: 137–67.

Wu, G. 2001. The determinants of asymmetric volatility. *Review of Financial Studies* 14: 837–59.

Xie, S. and Z. Bao. 2004. Fractal and multifractal properties of geochemical fields. *Mathematical Geology* 36: 847–64.

Xu, X. and S. J. Taylor. 1994. The term structure of volatility implied by foreign exchange options. *Journal of Financial and Quantitative Analysis* 29: 57–74.

Yaglom, A. M. 1966. On the influence of fluctuations in energy dissipation on the form of turbulence characteristics in the inertial range. *Doklady Akademii Nauk USSR* 166: 49.

Yogo, M. 2004. Estimating the elasticity of intertemporal substitution when instruments are weak. *Review of Economics and Statistics* 86: 797–810.

Yu, Z.-G., V. Anh, and K.-S. Lao. 2003. Multifractal and correlation analyses of protein sequences from complete genomes. *Physical Review E* 68: 021913, 1–10.

Zaffaroni, P. 2007. Memory and aggregation for models of changing volatility. *Journal of Econometrics* 136: 237–49.

Zakoian, J.-M. 1994. Threshold heteroskedastic models. *Journal of Economic Dynamics and Control* 18: 931–55.

Zeleke, T. and B. Si. 2004. Scaling properties of topographic indices and crop yield: multifractal and joint multifractal approaches. *Agronomy Journal* 96: 1082–90.

Index

Printed and bound by CPI Group (UK) Ltd, Croydon, CR0 4YY

13/05/2025

01870665-0001